DRAWDOWN

Drawdown

The American Way of Postwar

Edited by Jason W. Warren

NEW YORK UNIVERSITY PRESS
New York

NEW YORK UNIVERSITY PRESS
New York
www.nyupress.org

The views herein reflect those of the authors and not the Department of Defense or U.S. Army War College.

References to Internet websites (URLs) were accurate at the time of writing. Neither the author nor New York University Press is responsible for URLs that may have expired or changed since the manuscript was prepared.

Library of Congress Cataloging-in-Publication Data
Names: Warren, Jason W., 1977– editor.
Title: Drawdown : the American way of postwar / edited by Jason W. Warren.
Other titles: American way of postwar
Description: New York : New York University Press, [2016] | Includes bibliographical references and index.
Identifiers: LCCN 2016020572| ISBN 978-1-4798-2840-1 (hbk. : alk. paper) | ISBN 978-1-4798-7557-3 (pbk. : alk. paper)
Subjects: LCSH: United States. Army—Demobilization. | United States. Army—Reorganization—History. | United States—Armed Forces—Demobilization. | United States—History, Military—Case studies.
Classification: LCC UA917.U5 D73 2016 | DDC 355.2/90973—dc23
LC record available at https://lccn.loc.gov/2016020572

New York University Press books are printed on acid-free paper, and their binding materials are chosen for strength and durability. We strive to use environmentally responsible suppliers and materials to the greatest extent possible in publishing our books.

Manufactured in the United States of America

10 9 8 7 6 5 4 3 2 1

Also available as an ebook

For the men and women of the U.S. military who served their country during the wars in Afghanistan and Iraq.

CONTENTS

FOREWORD

PETER MANSOOR

The United States is currently undergoing a drawdown of its military establishment after nearly a decade and a half of war. The shrinking of the armed forces is not just an economic necessity but a historical inevitability. The essays in this volume explore the past experiences of the American military establishment during periods of contraction from the colonial period to the present. They detail the considerations that policy makers confront in determining how much capability and what types of it are required to keep America safe from harm against immediate threats, while providing the latent capacity to expand the military when national security demands such action. The trade-offs involved in "right-sizing" the defense establishment, underlain by an uncertain security environment and beset by inter-service rivalries, are not always easily reconciled. The need to get these decisions right makes the study of previous drawdowns imperative.

Americans have historically felt ambivalent about their military institutions. They view them as a necessary burden on society, but one that should be kept as light as possible both for reasons of economy and to prevent the standing military establishment from endangering civil liberties. Americans for the most part embrace the tradition of the citizen soldier as embodied by the militia and the National Guard. For much of the nation's history, the Regular Army was relegated to remote frontier posts and coastal fortifications, its structure massively supplemented by volunteers to fight the War of 1812, the war with Mexico, the U.S. Civil War, and the Spanish-American War. The Navy, which was not nearly as much of a danger to civil liberties and which had a functional role in protecting commerce, traditionally enjoyed more support during times of peace.

The three great world wars waged by the United States in the twentieth century and the technological changes wrought to fight them changed this dynamic. The Atlantic and Pacific oceans that once served as moats to protect the nation could in the modern era act as highways in the service of great powers possessing modern navies. The advent of the airpower age left the United States potentially vulnerable to attack by intercontinental bombers and ballistic missiles. America's acquisition of an empire also left its overseas possessions vulnerable, a point emphatically made by the Japanese attack on Pearl Harbor on December 7, 1941. These realities confirmed in the minds of many policy makers and military officers the need to maintain robust military capabilities even in times of peace. Although the large military establishments created to fight World War I and World War II were quickly dismantled upon victory, the Cold War with the Soviet Union and the strategy of containment crafted to hem in Communist power meant for the first time in the nation's history the maintenance of a large peacetime military establishment. There were drawdowns following the Korean and Vietnam wars, but they were limited in comparison with the wholesale gutting of the military establishment after previous conflicts.

The advent of the all-volunteer force following the end of American participation in the Vietnam War reduced the societal burden of military service, but concomitantly made military forces more expensive. Thus the nation could afford fewer active-duty forces for a given expenditure, which in the post-Vietnam era has hovered between 4 and 6 percent of gross domestic product. Military leaders opted for the retention of combat capabilities at the expense of combat-service and combat-service-support organizations and robust headquarters, with significant damaging impact on the ability of the military to conduct the numerous contingency operations of the 1990s and beyond.

The end of the Cold War augured a reversion to the small military establishments that existed for much of the nation's history. However, American policy makers had by then embraced America's role as the global hegemon, the unipolar hyperpower that could keep the peace, protect the global commons, and make the world safe for the liberal capitalist order. A peaceful world bolstered by American power appeared to be good for the spread of democracy and the growth of American business. To be sure, the Clinton administration exacted a peace dividend, with defense budgets dipping below 4 percent of GDP in the latter half of the 1990s, but the defense establishment (and defense spending) remained much more robust than in previous eras following the end of major conflicts.

In any case, the peace dividend came to an end with the terrorist attacks on the United States on September 11, 2001. The Bush administration ramped up military spending to fight the global war on terror, with the U.S. Army and Marine Corps enjoying the largest increases. But after a decade of war, Americans grew weary of continued overseas commitments, leading the Obama administration to end American participation in the Iraq War and to reduce sharply its commitment to support the Afghan government. The withdrawal of U.S. forces from the wars in Iraq and Afghanistan has brought this latest period of defense largesse to a close. Absent a defined enemy, but with a world in turmoil, the future of the American defense establishment looks cloudy at best.

History can help provide the needed context to guide the decisions of policy makers in this world of uncertainty. For much of the nation's history, policy makers could shortchange the defense establishment in the knowledge that they could arrange for the creation of sufficient military forces after the outbreak of war. Planning for industrial mobilization and expansion of cadre organizations during the interwar era of the 1920s and 1930s thus was a key part of American military strategy prior to World War II. It is not so clear at the dawn of the twenty-first century whether the United States can afford a defense strategy that relies on the latent capabilities of the nation to prevail in a major conflict, particularly against a near-peer competitor. Although a short conflict is not guaranteed, the reality of nuclear weapons seems to limit the scale and scope of future major wars. In this regard, achieving military objectives quickly with forces on hand may be the key to victory. This possibility cuts against the grain of American military tradition, with its strong emphasis on the militia tradition, as embodied in the National Guard and reserve forces, and the building of combat forces after the outbreak of war. Policy makers and military leaders must reconcile these factors when allocating scarce resources among the various components of the armed forces, keeping enough combat capability on hand, while creating the organizations and systems required to expand the force when necessary.

Strong alliances can help to cushion the cuts that inevitably occur when the U.S. military draws down after major periods of conflict. From Connecticut's alliance with the Mohegans and Pequots in the seventeenth century to the North Atlantic Treaty Alliance in the twentieth century, Americans have at times enjoyed the shared strength that alliances bring to national defense policy. Although Americans in the last twenty-five years have too often overlooked alliances as mere policy window dressing on largely American ventures abroad, in the end they do matter. U.S. civilian and military policy makers would do well, therefore, to pay close attention to America's foreign allies during the upcoming interwar era.

The most important requirement during drawdown periods, however, is the maintenance of the human intellectual capital of the military. Relatively small expenditures on professional military education and broadening experiences have an outsized impact on the growth of military leaders—the component of combat effectiveness being by far the most difficult to expand quickly when needed. The physical structure of the military, after all, can be reconstituted much more quickly than its intellectual capacity. The War Department created combat-effective divisions in two to three years during World War II following two decades of neglect during the interwar era, but the major generals who commanded those formations had already spent upwards of two decades in the military service, including schooling at their basic branch course, at the Command and General Staff School, and often at the Army War College. The worst option during drawdowns is to "salami slice" fiscal reductions, reducing the budget for professional military education at the same rate as for general-purpose forces and other components. Such action ensures mediocrity across the force and risks a dearth of strategic leadership years down the road.

The mantra for the U.S. Army in the 1980s was "no more Task Force Smiths," the ill-fated unit that faced the North Korean armored juggernaut in the summer of 1950 with too little training, too few soldiers, and inadequate equipment. Soldiers deserve more of their nation than to be committed to battle with little hope of victory. But military leaders must realize that the American people will rarely write them a blank check in interwar eras absent a clear and present danger to the nation. Policy makers and military leaders must therefore think clearly about the demands of the moment and weigh them against the potential demands of the future, making trade-offs as required to keep conventional forces, headquarters, logistics, enabling forces, and professional military educational institutions in balance. Anyone can design a military force in times of plenty; it is in times of scarcity that strategic leaders with foresight are most needed. There is no doubt that drawdowns reduce military capacity. The important issue for policy makers and military leaders is to ensure that enough capability remains to enable the regeneration of overwhelming military force—along with the headquarters to control them and the logistical organizations to sustain them—when the war trumpets sound once again.

ACKNOWLEDGMENTS

I am indebted to Wayne Lee, University of North Carolina at Chapel Hill, for his guidance in bringing this project to a successful conclusion. It was a sincere pleasure to collaborate with the volume's contributors. I owe a special acknowledgment of deep gratitude to Edward A. Gutiérrez, who has been a most steadfast friend and counsel, and who painstakingly formatted the entire volume in record time. I greatly appreciate this opportunity from New York University Press. I am most grateful for my loving children, William and Alice.

Introduction: The American Way of Postwar

The Liberty Dilemma

MICHAEL E. LYNCH

It wasn't a demobilization, it was a rout.
—George C. Marshall[1]

Army Chief of Staff General George C. Marshall presided over the largest mobilization in U.S. history, followed by the largest demobilization in U.S. history. His thoughts convey his despair at the speed of the post–World War II drawdown and its effects on military preparedness. Historian Russell F. Weigley's landmark 1973 work, *The American Way of War*, examined how the United States has prosecuted its wars. He determined that the American way of war used overwhelming force, tactically and logistically, to crush its enemies. That seminal work has spawned countless similar works examining other methods of warfare. This essay, and those that follow, examine the effect of postwar drawdowns on U.S. Army readiness.[2] The "liberty dilemma" that forms the basis for this volume describes a paradox: the need for a strong military often conflicts with other notions, such as a fear of the military and the desire to reduce government expenses. That dilemma has shifted in form and tone over the nation's history, forcing ever-changing adaptations. This clash often affects readiness, and the essays that follow explores the U.S. Army's attempts to maintain that readiness in the context of a "liberty dilemma." The examination of these adaptations reveals the American Way of Postwar.

As the U.S. military enters a postwar period after the conclusion of major combat operations in Iraq and Afghanistan, military leaders begin to prepare for the inevitable drawdown of forces that traditionally follows each conflict. The military leader traditionally abhors the drawdown, fearing any loss of capability that may be difficult to regenerate. The issue is not just the drawdown of forces but the effects of that reduction on readiness or preparedness. The definition of preparedness has changed over the last three centuries. Linked originally to the size of forces available, readiness has come to be defined more recently as a function of the Army's capabilities.[3] Each of the military services is affected by these drawdowns in similar ways, differing only in scale and details of execution. The U.S. Army, the largest of the services, is a traditional and highly visible target for reductions. The essays in this volume examine the history of previous military drawdowns from an Army perspective.

This drawdown is driven by a Congress dedicated to reducing expenses and supported by a populace wearied by over a decade of war. Years of war have brought enhanced technological capabilities, development of new and revised doctrines and tactics, and a highly trained, combat-experienced Army. The conflicts in Afghanistan and Iraq, and in less well-known areas such as the Philippines, have also driven the national budget from an overall surplus of $128.2 billion in January 2001 to a $1.412.7 trillion deficit by January 1, 2009. Though the budget appeared to begin recovery after 2009, the deficit remained at $679.5 billion as of January 1, 2013.[4] These very real financial pressures affect the normal postwar drawdown. The Budget Control Act of 2011 (BCA) has added additional pressures, with reduced budgets and the danger of sequestration should the government fail to balance the budget. This is no empty threat, as sequestration first occurred under BCA in 2012.

The issue at hand is not just the size of the military but rather its capabilities set against its projected requirements. The earliest notions of "preparedness," which we may broadly term "readiness" today, implied capabilities to address current and future requirements. The nature of those capabilities, however, has long caused discord between those who saw the need for standing armies and those who feared them.[5]

The belief in "no large standing armies" is enshrined in American tradition dating back to the Founding Fathers, rooted in the Constitution. The full measure of that belief may be seen in the wording of the so-called Army clause, which specifically limited the funding for such forces: "the Congress shall have the power to raise and support armies, but no appropriation of money to that use shall be for a longer term than two years."[6] The issue was a matter of some discussion at the time. Contemporary observers such as Adam Smith argued that "men of republican principles have been jealous of a standing Army as dangerous to liberty." Alexander Hamilton, on the other hand, argued that certain circumstances call for standing armies, citing the deterrent effect these forces have on aggressive neighbors:

> The jealousy of military establishment, would postpone them as long as possible. The want of fortifications leaving the frontiers of one State open to another, would facilitate inroads. The popular states would with little difficulty overrun less popular neighbours. Conquests would be as easy to be made, as difficult

to be retained. War therefore would be desultory and predatory. Plunder and devastation ever march in the training of irregulars. The calamities of individuals would make the principal figure in the events, which would characterise our military exploits.[7]

This, coupled with a concept of "no entangling alliances" from George Washington's Farewell Address, gave citizens of the Early Republic the illusion of safety and security. Modern notions of these traditions hold these to be basic American ideals, but Kevin McBride, Ashley Bissonette, and Jason Warren argue that these concepts find roots in English traditions. The first two essays in this volume explore colonial conflicts in the seventeenth century and find the earliest indications of a dichotomy between standing professional armies and relatively untrained militias. Each uses a case study to illustrate colonial successes and failures and relate them to contemporary notions of preparedness.

McBride and Bissonette present "The Art of War: Early Anglo-American Translation, 1607–1643," which examines the English and Dutch colonists' experiences in the Pequot War (1636–1637). They illustrate the Connecticut colony's reliance on veteran officers, noncommissioned officers, and soldiers to form its defense. These officers had received European military training and had served in the Thirty Years' War, and then immigrated to the colony. McBride estimates that 30 percent of the soldiers serving in this conflict had such training, and he traces their successes directly to that training. The Connecticut colony, unlike other New England colonies, relied on the "train band" concept, which provided trained and ready forces somewhat parallel to a modern National Guard. The train bands consisted of men from the "better" parts of society, and were thus respectable. While the colonists drew comfort from the lack of a standing Army and its implicit threat of oppression, they also drew comfort from the corps of leaders who brought military experience to the colony.

The earliest colonists arriving in the New World had fled oppressive tyrannies that maintained conformity by force. At best, standing armies symbolized the power of the government to coerce, and at worst, they became the tool of that oppression. Jason Warren examines this defense system in "Liberty Paradox: The Failure of the Military System in Mid-Seventeenth-Century New England." Even that seemingly most republican of actions, the overthrow of the English monarchy and establishment of a commonwealth, did nothing to allay the colonists' fears of oppressive government. Indeed, revolutionary leader Oliver Cromwell was a well-respected British Army officer. Though King Charles I was tried and sentenced to death in the House of Commons in 1649, it was Cromwell and his army that carried out the task, as Parliament was then subject to the Army Committee. Ironically, the formation of the New Model Army during Cromwell's reign signaled the move toward standing professional armies. When the commonwealth was established, however, the fear was that oppression would come from a republican military rather than a royal monarchy. This republican tradition of army submission to Parliament rather than to Crown made it also subject to the financial whims of that body. Though some early colonists rejected the notion of royal rule from across the ocean, a concept that gained support in the eighteenth century and eventually led to revolution, the idea of a standing Army still seemed dangerous. This "liberty dilemma" that forms the basis for this volume describes the paradox: a populace that fears the very military construct that forms the population's defense.

Warren argues that the Great Narragansett War of 1675–1676 turned out much differently for the colonists than had the Pequot War some forty years before. In this case, Connecticut used a very different system than did the other colonies, and emerged from that conflict relatively unscathed compared to them. Connecticut relied upon a small corps of "regulars," aided by militia and experienced Native American allies. Far removed from the conflict in Europe, seventeenth-century colonists in North America often found themselves at war with each other as a result of ongoing wars between their parent nations, such as the series of Anglo-Dutch wars. The colonists of all nations faced a greater threat, however, in the form of the Native American tribes that contested the presence of the colonists. The distance from their parent governments, the relative isolation of the New World, and the short duration of both intercolonial and Indian conflicts bred ambivalence toward defense requirements.

Colonists built forts to give some measure of comfort, and often only the illusion of security, while the militia functioned as the instrument of defense. Modern observers have lamented the "boom and bust" approach to defense spending and the short-sightedness of twentieth-century politicians, but Warren contends that this, too, is a long-standing tradition rooted in early colonial attitudes. The relief that colonists felt at the end of each early conflict often manifested itself as hubris: the conflict just completed would not be replicated because the victory (however defined) ended the danger to the colony. Both McBride and Warren determine that the Indians thus showed a greater adaptability than did the colonists. With the hubris of their European forebears, the colonists often saw the Native Americans as an existentialist threat but often badly underestimated them. The liberty dilemma would continue until the next such threat appeared.

The French and Indian War (1754–1763), the North American theater of the Seven Years' War between Great Britain and France, provided a training ground for future military leaders. Many of the colonists who fought in the British Army in North America against France would also serve some twenty years later as Continental Army (and later U.S. Army) officers during the American Revolution. Most notable among these was George Washington, who after stunning defeats on the Braddock Expedition and at Fort Necessity during that conflict would become the senior American commander in the Revolution. This corps of experienced officers and men provided the backbone for the Continental Army, but it proved to be a thin reed on which to lean.

The idea that the colony or nation need concern itself only with maintaining a corps of experienced officers carried over into the post-Revolutionary period. Samuel Watson explores the U.S. Army's experiences with expansions and contractions during the eighteenth and nineteenth centuries in "Surprisingly Professional: Trajectories in Army Officer Corps Drawdowns, 1783–1848." He determines that political leaders concerned themselves primarily with the officer corps rather than the enlisted men. The officer drawdowns of the Early Republic often reflected the differing political views of the nation's leaders. The difficulties that Jason Warren identified in the early colonial period thus carried over to the years of the Early Republic. With an overweening faith in militias, regular officers came to be viewed as near-mercenaries. This perpetuated the liberty dilemma and gave it a facet that was to grow familiar: the reliance on reserve forces instead of active forces. The fears of an "officer class" and the potential for authoritarian rule on the part of the Jeffersonian republicans militated against Federalist notions of public service. In addition, most citizens (but especially republicans) rejected the idea of taxes to support a standing army—a notion that continues to resonate and affect military appropriations.

Watson argues, however, that closer inspection of officer commissions, reductions, and retentions shows that they were not always as politically motivated as they may seem to have been at first glance. Despite some partisan politics, however, Watson also sees the nascence of a merit-based officer evaluation and promotion system. Watson's critical examination of the system exposes its flaws, but it also shows the Army's careful, and sometimes blundering, steps toward professionalization. These evaluations became important during drawdowns, and in fact the U.S. Army keyed its officer reductions to that critical appraisal. The evaluations focused on the officer's character, valor in combat, and, increasingly, education. The somewhat subjective criteria for character and valor were balanced by a growing objective evaluation of education. Despite its critics, West Point grew to become the standard educational criterion for U.S. Army officers. Fiscal considerations are not new, and Watson identifies some of the same pitfalls in later years that Warren had seen during the colonial period. An unwieldy bureau system, lack of adequate controls over contracting, and the scattered nature of the U.S. Army during the period made logistics costly and inefficient during its early days. The constant clarion call to reduce the size of the U.S. Army, meaning in reality to reduce the number of trained and qualified officers, made the system difficult to sustain over time. During this period we see the first glimpses of the notion of the "cadre" units designed to form the backbone of an expandable army. This concept would be used to a greater extent during the twentieth century, but with results not nearly as good as anticipated.

The U.S. Army has always been long on short-sightedness, and John A. Bonin's "Challenged Competency: U.S. Cavalry before, during, and after the U.S. Civil War" provides a case study. Army mythology allows us to believe that the cavalry gave up its horses unwillingly and against the wishes of the cavalry community, but Bonin reveals more of the story. Rather than being viewed as an arm of decision in the pre–Civil War days, the cavalry was an expensive organization and logistically difficult to maintain. Bonin argues that U.S. Army leaders believed the technological advancements of the mid-nineteenth century had supplanted the cavalry, and therefore the Army need not invest time, energy, and funds into fully developing it—this, despite the recommendations of the Delafield Commission, based on its observations during the Crimean War. The makeup of that commission perhaps indicates the Army's attitude toward cavalry at the time. Headed by Major Richard Delafield, the commission included Major Alfred Mordecai and Captain George B. McClellan. Despite being an engineer and never having served in the cavalry, McClellan served as the commission's cavalry expert. The Army also adopted the cavalry manual that McClellan wrote and the saddle he designed, both based on his observations with the commission.[8]

The Army's use, or rather misuse, of the cavalry was cause for greater concern. Even after prewar belief in a "short war" proved unfounded, Army leaders chose not to invest in this greater capability. Commanders saw utility for cavalry units in the West, covering the vast territories and matching the speed of mounted Indian tribes. In fact, in the U.S. Army at the beginning of the Civil War, the cavalry was seen as being useful only in the West, with regular units in the eastern armies being relegated to picket duty. The militia cavalry was almost uniformly poorly equipped, undertrained, and provided with old, broken-down horses inappropriate for the cavalry. The regular units had better mounts but lacked adequate troop training in horsemanship, causing cavalry units to lose many of the horses they did have. Cavalry horses were considered specialized equipment and were less plentiful than horses for wagons or caissons.

Senior U.S. Army commanders tended to use the cavalry in ways that failed to develop or take full advantage of its potential capabilities. Despite McClellan's supposed prewar expertise, he proved to be deficient in his own use of cavalry in the Army of the Potomac. The Confederate Army, however, did take full advantage of the cavalry's potential, and therefore completely out-fought the federal cavalry for the first two years of the war. Bonin argues that the Confederate Army of Northern Virginia's early advantage in infantry as well stemmed from the better training of Virginia militia compared to dragoon duty on the western frontier or picket duty in the East. He concludes that U.S. Army short-sightedness prevented the cavalry from becoming the decisive arm it could be. The "liberty dilemma" had evolved somewhat from its seventeenth-century predecessor, and formed a pattern more familiar to the modern observer. In this case, the dilemma concerned whether or not to develop and maintain expensive technologies for use in what was sure to be only a brief encounter.

In "The Elusive Lesson: U.S. Army Unpreparedness from 1898 to 1938," Edward A. Gutiérrez and Michael S. Neiberg explore the U.S. Army's experiences beginning in the Spanish-American War, a watershed event in American diplomatic and military history. The United States entered the world stage for the first time as a major power, a position it has never relinquished. The conflict also serves as a model of military unpreparedness, a pattern that the Army has maintained throughout much of the twentieth century. The unpreparedness began with a lack of strategic direction from a government not ready to perform, and not fully cognizant of, the tasks on which it was about to embark. The U.S. Army, reduced to a constabulary force with garrisons scattered across the country, primarily in the West, was then suddenly required to become an expeditionary force. The Army as a whole was completely ill equipped and untrained for the tasks required. Despite the hard lessons learned in Cuba and the Philippines, and the burgeoning unconventional war against *insurrectos* in the Philippines, the U.S. Army remained small. Successive government administrations, Congress, and a majority of the American people failed to understand the growing American role in world affairs, and they failed to see and acknowledge the increasing international dangers. The best defense at the time seemed to be the two oceans, whose size and positions implied safety. Those oceans did provide a certain amount of security, but the development of the airplane, and further naval innovations such as the submarine, reduced the effectiveness of those barriers. Nevertheless, the nation's powerful isolationist lobby argued to keep the United States out of international involvement, citing Washington's Farewell Address and the warning against "no entangling alliances." The oceans also strengthened the U.S. Navy's hand in budget negotiations, as the growing international threats required a naval component for deterrence.

The Army at this time, however, found what appeared to be a legitimate continental threat in Mexico. The Punitive Expedition, mounted in 1916 in response to a cross-border raid by Mexican insurrectionists, allayed the fears of many who were alarmed by just such a foreign invasion. While this relatively small mission proved the Army's inadequate logistical capabilities for expeditionary operations, the crucible of the Great War showed the American Army just how ill prepared it was for twentieth-century warfare on the European scale. Despite the War Department's small movements toward professionalization, with the creation of a General Staff and War College, the U.S. Army remained woefully undermanned, poorly resourced, and inefficiently organized.

World War I also proved to be an unfortunate precedent for Army preparedness. The nation raised and fielded the largest Army in its history in a very short time, then deployed it to fight overseas in a short and, relative to the other nations, bloodless campaign. Shifting to World War I, Gutiérrez and Neiberg outline the American Army's attitude toward the enemy as "inept brutes who would be easy to defeat." Most believed the mere "élan" of the American soldier would be enough to defeat this unworthy enemy. This élan would compensate for the fact that in some units soldiers did not even have weapons, or have the opportunity to fire them prior to deployment. For instance, terrible winter weather and multiple moves during mobilization prevented the 39th Infantry Regiment of the 4th Division from doing any marksmanship training until they arrived in France.[9] Four years of war had wearied the German enemy the Americans encountered, but it remained a formidable force. American casualties could not equal all the horrendous numbers of the other combatants', but they were significant nonetheless.

Political leaders worked to limit American involvement in the postwar occupation, and the U.S. Army came home and quickly demobilized. This pattern of activities set unrealistic expectations for future military operations, apparently confirming the utility of small permanent forces. Large forces could be quickly formed around a small nucleus and be just as quickly trained, equipped, and deployed into battle, where the soldiers' élan would guarantee a rapid and decisive victory. Americans had no interest in, nor stomach for, long postwar involvement, so the force could then be demobilized with alacrity. Such assumptions not only bred lack of preparedness for the immediate future but also generated other systematic decision-making processes that relied upon a short-sighted approach.

Gutiérrez and Neiberg point to the nation's desire for a postwar "Return to Normalcy" as the culprit for such myopia. Taken from President Warren G. Harding's successful slogan in the 1920 election, the phrase lent comfort to a people suddenly terrified by war beyond the scope of their imaginations, only a generation or so removed from the Civil War. Return to normalcy meant *status quo antebellum*: peace, isolation, and a small military. Gutiérrez and Neiberg argue that the return to normalcy has been a constant postwar refrain, with the populace never accepting the idea of *status quo post bellum*. This focus on a prewar environment fails to acknowledge the realities engendered by the conflict itself and the terms of the peace or war termination, and therefore fuels a drive to reduce forces quickly, regardless of the damage this causes. Gutiérrez and Neiberg cite the World War I example and the national desire to return to 1914 rather than acknowledge the changes in the world of 1919. Ironically, the return to antebellum normalcy prevented the military from becoming involved in any large way in any more overseas adventures. This allowed the opportunity for thought and intellectual development.

The lack of overseas engagement and reduced U.S. Army missions launched the first internecine squabble between the Army and the Navy with respect to funding. The U.S. Navy successfully argued for large recapitalization budgets to support its strategic mission, contending specifically that the Army was not a "strategic" force. This competition for funds, and associated roles and missions, has continued to the present. The liberty dilemma thus became a battle for relevancy, as political leaders saw less value in a large land force that required huge resources to muster, train, deploy, and sustain, and that seemed only useful in wartime. The Navy seemed to be a better value, as a relatively self-sustaining, self-mobile instrument of both diplomacy and war.

The bright spot in the post–World War I lean years is the Army's internal focus on preserving intellectual capital and development of officers. Michael Matheny argues in "When the Smoke Clears: The Interwar Years as an Unlikely Success Story" that the focus on scholarly investment saved the Army. The years between World War I and World War II were some of the leanest in the Army's history. The post–World War I drawdown, followed by the deepest and largest financial depression in the nation's history, reduced the Army's fighting strength to almost nothing. Those who remained in the Army endured years of reduced budgets, pay reductions, and almost comical unit manning.

In a military emasculated by financial misfortune, the saving grace of the U.S. Army's future was the development and maintenance of the intellectual environment of the 1920s and 1930s. With any real, meaningful training rendered impossible by budget cuts, the Army chose to address preparedness problems with education. General John J. Pershing had identified the glaring need for properly trained staff officers during World War I, going so far as to create a school in France to mirror Fort Leavenworth to fill that need. After the war, reestablishing the Command and General Staff School and the Army War College became top priority. These schools filled the requirements for education but also created the intellectual milieu that allowed specialized discourse to flower through professional journals.[10]

This effort was not happenstance but rather a deliberate attempt to identify and discuss the lessons learned from the Great War, and inculcate those lessons in training and doctrine for the future. The professional journals of the period were replete with articles on new technology, tactics, planning, and other insights from the war. Notably, Lieutenant Colonel George C. Marshall, future Army chief of staff, published "Profiting by War Experience," which examined how to learn the lessons of the Great War.[11] Many of the future senior offices of World War II also penned articles, including such luminaries as George S. Patton.[12] The topics ranged from tactics to technology, with special attention on the newest weapons. For instance, the machine gun had proven to be a devastating weapon during the war, and the *Infantry Journal* featured articles on the weapon nearly every other month beginning in 1920, with at least a couple published annually after that.[13]

The Army War College had originally been created as a think tank for the War Department General Staff, and this became especially true during the years between the World Wars. Students from the mid-1930s on worked on projects under the direction of the War Department General Staff or one of the senior branch chiefs, such as the chief of infantry. The studies examined issues of critical interest to an Army that foresaw requirements to expand to create a much larger expeditionary force.[14] This professional discourse was only part of the story, however. The U.S. Army accepted its role as an expeditionary force and began planning in its service schools, especially the Army War College, for numerous possible contingencies. The War Department developed a series of war plans addressing potential conflicts with a variety of countries and coalitions. Planners assigned each of the plans a color and worked closely with War College students to develop and refine them. These planning efforts gave the Army's future senior leaders valuable experience in planning, and the planners themselves identified challenges the Army would face in the next war.[15]

The U.S. Army officer corps' small size at the time worked to the Army's advantage in one important way. This small community facilitated the sharing of ideas and knowledge, ensuring that "lessons learned" and new tactics, techniques, and procedures were disseminated across the force, allowing some degree of uniformity.[16] This reduced size, however, did not allow enough opportunities for command, even for the critically small officer corps of the time. Most officers waited for years to command, and some never got this critical professional experience.[17] The sole advantage, however, was the additional time available for schooling. Virtually all officers attended one or more professional schools, and many remained as instructors. This experience benefited both the officers and the Army, as the instructors remained on the cutting edge of combat developments. These schools also served as incubators for growing future senior leaders. Lieutenant Colonel George C. Marshall, assistant commandant of the Infantry School from 1927 to 1932, identified many officers, such as Omar N. Bradley, Matthew B. Ridgway, Maxwell Taylor, Mark Clark, Lucian Truscott, Jonathan M. Wainwright, and Edward M. Almond, who later became senior commanders in World War II.[18]

As Sam Watson had discovered about a previous era, Matheny determines that focusing on training, educating, and molding the officer corps enabled the Army to posture itself for the next war. He concedes that the years between World War I and World War II were financially lean but intellectually robust, and the Army used the time and circumstances to great advantage. The lean budgets forced leaders to think institutionally and strategically, rather than tactically. That environment fostered innovative thinking and detailed planning. The pressure of war would demonstrate the value of the work during these prewar years.

When war began in Europe in the fall of 1939, most Americans were eager to avoid involvement. The need to prepare for a potential war already engulfing Europe, in the face of strong isolationist public sentiment, typified the liberty dilemma for War Department officials. Army Chief of Staff General George C. Marshall anticipated possible future requirements, however, and recommended increases for both the Regular Army and the National Guard. The advantages of the prewar intellectual milieu aside, the Army remained frightfully small. Forces in being on June 30, 1939, included nine understrength active divisions, totaling fewer than 50,000 soldiers. These divisions would require another 180,000 soldiers to bring them to wartime strength. The eighteen existing National Guard divisions, not yet mobilized, would require another 360,000 soldiers to bring them to full strength. As daunting as these numbers were, Marshall and other Army planners knew from Great War experience that war on a European scale would require much more.[19]

The prewar planning period had also fostered the creation of detailed mobilization plans, both military and industrial, building on the lessons of 1917.

When the fall of France in 1940 made Americans feel more vulnerable, FDR began federalizing National Guard units and Congress authorized the nation's first peacetime draft.[20] The liberty dilemma resurfaced as the war in Europe seemed to slow in the winter of 1940–1941. FDR won an unprecedented third term in office against significant isolationist opposition, largely on the basis of his vow to keep the United States out of the European war. By the fall of 1941, Roosevelt had ordered Marshall to begin again drawing down the Army; only Pearl Harbor prevented that planned reduction.[21]

The War Department's "Victory Plan," developed prewar to meet potential global war requirements, called for 213 divisions. As the mobilization progressed, however, this became unworkable. The military competed with civilian industry for manpower. Roosevelt had ordered that men involved in critical war production for Lend Lease should not be drafted, so the pool of available draft-age men dropped from twenty-five million to fifteen million.[22] The semi-autonomous Army Air Corps also pulled away potential draftees from the ground Army. Moreover, this highly technical service, and the growing need for officers, reduced the pool of educated soldiers for the ranks. With these challenges, Marshall decided to limit the mobilization to ninety divisions, to be activated over a three-year period.[23]

In the midst of mobilization, another liberty dilemma presented itself. The growing African American population needed to be included in the calculus for draft-eligible males, but white Army leadership, and a largely white society, were uncomfortable with arming large numbers of black men. This concept harkened back to the Army's experience in the last years of the Civil War. Segregated American society demanded a segregated Army. The War Department had raised two black divisions during World War I, but afterward reduced them to only four permanent regiments: two infantry, and two cavalry. Many African Americans believed that the black soldiers' service in World War I conveyed full citizenship; their liberty dilemma existed in the failure of white society to grant that status. As another war drew closer, many African Americans became wary. Their fathers' service and sacrifice had not been rewarded—black veterans did not enjoy the same respect and dignity as did white veterans. Historian Chad L. Williams studied the plight of these veterans and concluded that they "transferred their war and post war experiences into sustained commitments to fighting for freedom, civil rights, and the broader historical dignity" of African American people.[24] Black soldiers vowed that they would battle to end this liberty dilemma—they would force the nation for which they fought to treat them as equals.[25]

As the mobilization continued, the disadvantages of the small prewar Army became apparent. The very small core of trained, educated officers quickly dissipated to fill out the cadre of mobilizing divisions. The division activation plan called for one year of training, but training failures, equipment shortages, personnel levies for the Army Air Corps, and loss of soldiers to OCS interrupted preparation. Moreover, each of the divisions activated in 1941 and 1942 provided officers and NCO cadre for a division activating the following year. All of these distractions made the mobilization much more difficult and delayed almost all units. The 89th Infantry Division provides an extreme example: despite activating in July 1942, the division did not deploy overseas until January 1945.[26]

The Army had used its time and limited resources after World War I to best advantage, creating an intellectual environment that allowed ideas and innovations to flourish. The strategic plans for military and industrial mobilization proved to be invaluable when war did come, and the operational plans for war on multiple continents also became useful. While these plans helped produce order from chaos, they could not overcome the significant personnel and equipment shortages the Army experienced, nor could they reduce the time required for, and the difficulties in, training.

The quotation from General George C. Marshall that opened this essay gives some indication of the challenges the U.S. Army faced at the end of World War II. Scott Bertinetti and John Bonin explore the Army's mass demobilization after that war in "Searching for the Greatest Generation's Army in 1950." The end of the largest war in the nation's history reintroduced the age-old liberty dilemma: the loss of the existential threat seemed to remove the need for a large military. Bertinetti and Bonin's essay reveals an added economic component to the dilemma, as the large wartime Army had required tremendous resources. Moreover, the burgeoning postwar economy needed the manpower of returning GIs to help convert war industries back to civilian uses. The occupations of Germany and Japan required many more troops than had the post–World War I occupations, but the Army reduced by over 77 percent in the first year after the war. Bertinetti and Bonin contend that the U.S. monopoly on the atomic bomb seemed to obviate the need for a large standing military. President Harry S. Truman favored Universal Military Training (UMT) to mitigate the problems incurred in mass mobilization, but Congress disagreed.

Bertinetti and Bonin trace the evolution of the liberty dilemma from the end of World War II through the beginning of the Cold War. The United States seemed, yet again, unready for the world leadership role thrust upon it, but the growing menace from its erstwhile Soviet ally forced it to accept that role. The overseas occupation forces, especially those in Germany, became bulwarks against the spread of communism.

President Harry S. Truman extended the liberty dilemma in a speech announcing military support of Greece and Turkey in 1947. In a strategy to be termed the "Truman Doctrine," Truman averred that it "must be the policy of the United States to support free peoples who are resisting attempts at subjugation by armed minorities or by outside pressures. . . . [W]e must assist free peoples to work out their own destinies in their own way."[27] This committed the United States to a pattern of international engagement that extends to the present.

Bertinetti and Bonin determine that this engagement became all the more important after the Soviet Union developed its own atomic bomb. The State Department's National Security Council Memorandum–68 identified the failure of the U.S. atomic bomb to deter Soviet expansionism. Despite this, the Army suffered in comparison to the other services. The Army appeared less technologically advanced than the Navy and the new Air Force in a world that seemed to require such attributes. Moreover, the Army had lost both end strength and infrastructure to the Air Force under the National Security Act of 1947, which created the Department of Defense and the Air Force.[28] Bertinetti identifies Korea as a flashpoint in the Cold War to contain worldwide communism. The events there in June 1950 demonstrated just how damaging the post–World War II drawdown and concomitant development of the nuclear deterrent had been. The U.S. Army had withdrawn from Korea in 1949, so when the North Korean Army attacked South Korea, only a small group of 485 advisors remained. The Army's end strength stood at 593,000, some 37,000 short of its authorization. Most of the 87,000 soldiers in Japan belonged to badly understrength divisions, but they were scattered throughout the country on occupation duty.[29]

Moreover, the Far East did not enjoy priority for good soldiers. Far East Command reported to the Pentagon in 1949 that 43 percent of the enlisted men in the command had tested in the two lowest categories on the Army General Classification Test (AGCT), and all had received incomplete training.[30] The U.S. Army began a training plan in 1949 to get the few troops available trained in combat tasks, but the Korean War began before the plan was able to show any progress.

Bertinetti and Bonin conclude that the Korean attack exposed the main flaw in Truman's nuclear strategy: The supposed deterrent failed to prevent the attack, as it also failed to deter the widening of the war with China. Bertinetti and Bonin note that technology is better suited to capability enhancement than it is to doctrine dictation, yet national strategy moved even more toward nuclear containment.

Ray Millen's "Post–Korean War Drawdown under the Eisenhower Administration" examines an Army drawdown in the context of a change in national strategy, and finds it less painful than it first appears. President Dwight D. Eisenhower took quite a different approach from that of General Eisenhower, who had commanded the largest U.S. Army formation ever assembled. In a newly nuclear world, Eisenhower saw nuclear weapons as the ultimate deterrent from nuclear war, and believed the nation's enemies would see such a conflict as unthinkable. That said, he left a nuclear option clearly on the table.

Eisenhower's "New Look" strategy envisioned the deterrent effects of massive retaliatory strikes, eliminating the need for large numbers of ground troops to prosecute a long general war. Eisenhower needed to balance a Congress and a populace frightened by an implacable and seemingly invincible Soviet foe with his pledge to balance the budget, which was also a popular notion with the public. The most cost-effective method of deterring the threat while reducing expenditures seemed to be investment in high-tech weapons rather than a large standing army. The focus on nuclear deterrent assumed away the need for ground troops, and Eisenhower avoided committing ground troops to the extent possible. As a military man, he suspected that senior military leaders would look at all problems as requiring military solutions if they had a large force with which to work. He would have understood the modern-day tongue-in-cheek military maxim, "If all you have is a hammer, everything looks like a nail."

The drawdown of forces, however rationalized at the strategic level, had ill effects at the tactical level. The age-old tension between regular and reserve components surfaced again, as strong Army Reserve and National Guard political lobbies defeated Army leadership attempts to cut reserve component forces. The political arguments related to the reserve constituencies rather than Army readiness. With the Soviet Union now clearly an existential threat with nuclear weapons, the liberty dilemma returned. Large ground forces appeared not only unsuitable but unsurvivable. The key seemed to be building a nuclear capability so large that war was mutually deterred. The active Army also reorganized to meet the presumed threat, and attempted to adapt to a nuclear battlefield, including a mission for tactical nuclear weapons. The new structure, the Pentomic division, ultimately proved unwieldy and was abandoned after a few years. Despite the problems, Millen argues that the drawdown of the Eisenhower era did not degrade the effectiveness of the U.S. Army over the long term, nor did it contribute to the policy failures and organizational malaise of the Vietnam era.

Martin Clemis picks up Millen's argument and further explores the buildup of the Kennedy-Johnson years, which saw a complete repudiation of New Look, as well as the U.S. involvement in Vietnam. "Once Again with the High and Mighty: 'New Look' Austerity, 'Flexible Response' Buildup, and the U.S.

Army in Vietnam, 1954–1970" reminds us that several scholars have pointed out that the U.S. Army that went to Vietnam was the best trained, equipped, and led army the United States had ever fielded up to that time. Reflecting on the nation's history of unpreparedness, this statement says less about the Vietnam-era U.S. Army than it does about those that preceded it, but it is nonetheless true, especially for the first years of the war. The Army declined steeply in quality and leadership as the U.S. involvement in the war grew, and the Army of 1973 was a mere shadow of the force that began taking the field in 1965. The problems the Army experienced were not linked to either budgets or end strength, most of which grew over the period.

Conrad Crane's examination in "Post-Vietnam Drawdown: The Myth of the Abrams Doctrine" debunks one of the Army's great legends, but more importantly provides a cautionary tale for military planners charged with executing the drawdowns. Budgets and end strengths may be externally imposed by congressional mandate, but the mission of deciding what stays, what goes, and why falls to Army leaders. Crane's essay describes General Creighton W. Abrams's creative attempts to address the Army's future combat requirements and projected modernization needs, given the limitations imposed by Congress and the mandate to end the draft. Crane argues that, while these efforts largely succeeded for the combat divisions in the active component, the results were far-reaching and not always positive.

The nature of the small-scale contingencies that have provided most of the Army's deployment experiences in the last forty years has required large numbers of these combat-support and combat-service-support units. Repetitive deployment of these units, especially, has strained relations between the active and reserve components. They also strain relations between the reserve soldiers themselves and their employers. Despite the patriotic fervor in the nation since 9/11, civilian employers have difficulty supporting continual deployments. As the Army now looks to ensure that critical capabilities are maintained either in the active or in the reserve components, the reserve component units normally take the brunt of such redesignation.

Headquarters were always seemingly an easy target. Frank J. Siltman, in a study at the U.S. Army War College, determined that the Army habitually cuts headquarters elements to gain efficiency but does not staff or equip them appropriately. Siltman agrees with Martin Van Creveld that the complexity of modern war requires large staffs to be effective.[31] Cutting these quickly merely passes the requirement to subordinate units, which are then levied to fill the staff requirements.

As the Army worked to remake itself after the Vietnam War, it also looked to other armies and other conflicts to learn lessons. Antulio Echevarria points out in "The 'Good' Drawdown: The Post-Vietnam Alignment of Resources" that this external focus influenced the development of the deterrence doctrine. Echevarria argues that the long period spent in Europe during the Cold War generated an ongoing professional debate over "maneuverist" versus "attritionist" schools.

The drawdown after Vietnam and subsequent "rebalancing" back to Europe strengthened the deterrent force there, but the United States still executed the containment strategy with much smaller forces than its Soviet adversaries had. In order to "Fight Outnumbered and Win," the military adage of the day, the Army again turned to improved training for soldiers and more technologically advanced weapons systems to improve its chances. The idea of "doing more with less" has long been a military aphorism, and the Army of the 1980s realigned doctrines to take advantage of technological advances in order to do just that.

The end of the draft in 1973 and the creation of the All-Volunteer Force (AVF) was a watershed event for the Army. For the first time, the Army intended to create a professional, highly trained, and well-educated fighting force to execute all of its requirements. As it had after World War II, the Army used the post-Vietnam years for theoretical development, and the changes in the world drove a refocusing of Army efforts.

The U.S. Army did receive some significant help in the post-Vietnam era. President Ronald Reagan ushered in the largest peacetime military buildup in U.S. history in 1980, and the increased budgets allowed the full fielding of the "Big 5" weapons systems that had been under development since the 1970s. This period of the 1980s was a counterweight to previous drawdowns, but the success of this buildup lay not just in the additional dollars but in the solid theoretical framework the Army had laid in the leaner years. The many previous drawdowns had shown the Army the need for maintaining its intellectual capital. Part of the change to the fully professional AVF involved the development of new doctrine, and included the inculcation of the lessons-learned process. One of the major benefits of the buildup was the development of the combat training centers (CTC), an idea still rooted in the lean years. The CTCs provided a training opportunity for units to get near-combat experience before deployment. Echevarria argues that the buildup of these conventional forces had a negative effect, however. The exclusive focus on the deterrent provided by large, heavy formations, and a firm commitment to armored warfare on the north German plain, reduced the Army's overall flexibility. The very real deterrent that these forces provided did prevent the large war, but not the many small conflicts in Central and South America, Africa, the Middle East, and the Balkans in which the Army found itself in the 1980s and 1990s. In most cases, the Army found itself wholly unprepared to deal with such contingencies, and needed to retrain and reorient itself. The small number of "light" forces available proved adequate for extended missions, and required support beyond their capabilities.

Three centuries after the colonial forts provided a deterrent to Indian raiders, the U.S. military's forward-deployed forces provided "forts" that represented U.S. power and served as the basis for reinforcement by larger forces. This, too, led to another liberty dilemma in an increasingly complex world, one its seventeenth-century ancestors would recognize. The bases in Europe designed to support the potential large conventional war did nothing to support the small-scale contingencies elsewhere, and the lack of those bases removed any possible deterrent effect.

Richard Lacquement reminds us that the military must be prepared for success in "Preaching after the Devil's Death: U.S. Post–Cold War Drawdown." The fall of the Berlin Wall in November 1989 has become an enduring symbol of the end of the Cold War, and the United States and its allies rightly claimed victory. But the fruits of that military victory carried with them the seeds of discord, as the formerly bipolar world took on a much more anarchic environment as nonstate actors replaced monolithic enemies. That victory resulted from the deterrent effect of America's long-held policy of containment of communism, and the large standing military forces that provided the bulwarks of that policy. Lacquement's title suggests the liberty dilemma for military leaders: U.S. policy changed significantly for the first time since the end of World War II, and large military forces appeared not to be needed. Indeed, planning for force reduction began even before the Berlin Wall fell, as improving relations with the Soviet Union indicated that the Cold War was nearing its end. The difficulty the military faced was convincing its political leadership that the end of the Cold War did not end the need for a strong military.

The sheer length of the Cold War presented difficulties for postwar planning. None of the military or civilian leadership at the time had ever known anything but the Cold War. To some, the end of the Cold War may have recalled V-E Day and V-J Day at the end of World War II—a final victory after a long struggle—and the images of ecstatic joy at the Berlin Wall underscored that notion. Just as the end of that war had brought the clarion call to "bring the boys home," so too did the end of the Cold War. Lacquement argues that General Colin Powell as Chairman, Joint Chiefs of Staff, built on the notion of the "peace dividend" by proposing a 25 percent reduction, but preserved strength by tying that cut to a "base force" considered necessary to execute the new national military strategy of responding to two major regional contingencies. The administration of President George H. W. Bush was able to use the base force concept to forestall other larger and more damaging cuts. Even as the United States began to respond to its first post–Cold War major regional contingencies (MRCs), Operation Desert Shield and Storm, plans were in motion to begin force reductions. At the end of that short conflict, the reductions accelerated as units began deactivating upon redeployment.

As the military reduced its forces, and concurrently began closing bases in the United States and abroad in pursuit of the so-called peace dividend, the "New World Order" envisioned by President George H. W. Bush never materialized, and the world became increasingly disordered. The military that had worked its way to seeming obsolescence at the end of the Cold War became busier than ever, responding to numerous crises that eventually required more time and resources than ever imagined. The terrorist attacks of 9/11 presented the United States with a paradox: a poorly defined enemy, terrorism, that took many different forms and involved both state and nonstate actors.

Lacquement's essay leads to the conclusion that the real peace dividend is not a more peaceful world requiring less military but a more dangerous and fragmented one. That dangerous environment demands even more resources to keep and maintain the peace, and those resources are generally military.

Conclusion

This collection of essays provides a clear-eyed view of previous drawdowns, set in the context of their eras, but with the perspective of time that allows more complete evaluation. The drawdown experience of the past three centuries shows that the U.S. Army has been here before, in some form. In each case, the Army has proven to be resilient and resourceful, and emerged from the drawdown prepared to rebuild itself to meet the next challenge. The service successfully negotiated drawdowns by focusing time, energy, and resources into the critical areas of education, doctrine development, and technological advancement.

There is an optimistic tone to these essays, as the authors describe the ways in which the Army has sought to mitigate the damage drawdown causes. Education, training, doctrine development, and technological advancement have saved the Army's readiness many times when drawdown forces threatened to destroy it. Yet even that optimism cannot hide the irony inherent in the Army's development. The Army has worked to continually reduce forces and restructure remaining units to meet a continued need; developed or leveraged new technology; and enhanced doctrinal development and training opportunities, all in the name of doing more with less. These successful developments have enabled the Army to "do more with less," but they have also made the soldier seem less relevant. The military's successful use of "smart weapons" over the past several years has caused some leaders to question the necessity of a large standing army. The multiple successful deployments of reserve component units has stimulated discussion about why a large active component is necessary, with a capable reserve component available.

These views ignore some important truths, however. First, while technological advances have enabled the Army to do more with less, the scale and complexity of warfare has also changed. The base force that General Colin Powell envisioned to be able to fight two MRCs must now be reviewed as the Army conducts combat, peacekeeping, humanitarian, and engagement missions around the world.[32] Second, any drawdown calculus that includes rapid mobilization and deployment of reserve components is flawed from the outset. This volume also serves as a warning, however, for policymakers who see military drawdowns solely in terms of potential budget savings. The nature of war in the twenty-first century and evolving national military strategy and foreign policy drive requirements for troops up, rather than down. Political leaders must also consider the force's human capabilities. The U.S. Army that deployed in Operation Enduring Freedom (OEF) and Operation Iraqi Freedom (OIF) was the most technologically advanced one the United States has ever fielded. Training those soldiers to that standard takes time, however, and that training cannot be done quickly.

Finally, the U.S. Army has encountered numerous "liberty dilemmas" throughout its history, and those problems have shaped both the nation's response to crises and the Army's role in them. They have taken many forms, as each era, circumstance, and population reveals a different dilemma. *The American Way of Postwar* describes how the nation and its Army faces those continually evolving dilemmas.

NOTES

1 Quoted in Garry L. Thompson, "Army Downsizing following World War I, World War II, Vietnam, and a Comparison to Recent Army Downsizing," MMAS Thesis (Fort Leavenworth, KS: U.S. Army Command and General Staff College, 2002), 33.

2 See, for example: John Grenier, *The First Way of War: American War Making on the Frontier, 1607–1814* (Cambridge: Cambridge University Press, 2005); Patrick M. Malone, *The Skulking Way of War: Technology and Tactics among the New England Indians* (Lanham, MD: Madison Books, 1991); Thomas G. Mahnken, *Technology and the American Way of War* (New York: Columbia University Press,

2010); Benjamin Buley, *The New American Way of War: Military Culture and the Political Utility of Force* (London: Routledge, 2008); Brian McAllister Linn, *The Echo of Battle: The Army's Way of War* (Cambridge, MA: Harvard University Press, 2009); and most recently, Antulio Echevarria, *Reconsidering the American Way of War: U.S. Military Practice from the Revolution to Afghanistan* (Washington, DC: Georgetown University Press, 2014).

3   The Army currently defines readiness as "the ability of U.S. military forces to meet the demands of the National Military Strategy." See Army Regulation 220-1, *Army Status Reporting and Force Registration—Consolidated Policies* (Washington, DC: U.S. Department of the Army, 2010). For a detailed discussion of the challenges the Army faces in material readiness as it begins to draw down, Michelle M. T. Letcher, "Army Readiness in Preparation for an Uncertain Future," Civilian Research Project, U.S. Army War College/University of Texas–Austin, 2015.

4   "Federal Government Budget Surplus or Deficit," Federal Reserve Economic Data, Federal Reserve Bank of St. Louis, http://research.stlouisfed.org/fred2/series/M318501A027NBEA. Accessed April 1, 2015. Source data from the chart came from U.S. Bureau of Economic Analysis. The last year for which data were available was 2013.

5   The commonly used term until the late twentieth century was "preparedness," a term broadly addressing the nation's ability to go to war. "Readiness" in the twenty-first century has some more specific meanings in military usage. For the purposes of this work and the essays contained herein, the terms "preparedness" and "readiness" are treated as synonyms and apply to the broader context.

6   U.S. Constitution, Article I, Section 8, Clause 12.

7   Alexander Hamilton, *Federalist Papers* no. 8, 44–50.

8   Ethan S. Rafuse, *McClellan's War* (Bloomington: Indiana University Press, 2005), 61–64.

9   C. A. Bach, *The Fourth Division: Its Services and Achievements in the World War* (Garden City, NY: Country Life Press, 1920), 52–59.

10 For detailed discussion, see Richard S. Faulkner, *The School of Hard Knocks: Combat Leadership in the American Expeditionary Forces* (College Station: Texas A&M University Press, 2012).

11 George C. Marshall, "Profiting by War Experience," *Infantry Journal* 18, no. 1 (Jan. 1921): 34–37.

12 For example, see George S. Patton, "Mechanized Forces," *Cavalry Journal* (Sept.–Oct. 1933).

13 For example, the *Infantry Journal* articles included J. S. Switzer, "Concerning Machine Guns," 16, no. 7 (Jan. 1920): 371–429; Franklin T. Best, "The Accompanying Gun," 16, no 10 (Apr. 1920): 834–40; Alexander M. Patch, "Machine-Gun Unit Organization," vol. 17, no. 2 (Aug. 1920): 142–48; Walter C. Short, "Machine Guns of an Infantry Division," 17, no. 3 (Sept. 1920): 261–63; C. A. Dravo, "Machine Guns," 17 no. 4 (Oct. 1920): 319–29; Charles A. Willoughby,

"Machine Gun Known Distance Practice," 17, no. 5 (Nov. 1920): 498–502; and J. A. Doe, "Infantry Machine Guns—The Attack," 17, no. 6 (Dec. 1920): 546–55. Edward M. Almond, "Let Machine Guns Support the Attack," *Infantry Journal* 27, no. 2, (Oct. 1927): 341–54.

14 Henry G. Gole, *The Road to Rainbow: Army Planning for Global War, 1934–1940* (Annapolis, MD: Naval Institute Press, 2003), 29–31.

15 For a complete description and analysis of the color plans, see Gole, *Road to Rainbow*.

16 Gole, *Road to Rainbow*, 122–23.

17 For an analysis of some future senior officers' interwar experience, see, "World War II Division Commanders" (Fort Leavenworth, KS: U.S. Army Command and General Staff College, 1983).

18 Gole, *Road to Rainbow*, 124–35.

19 Marvin A. Kreidberg and Merton G. Henry, Department of the Army Pamphlet 20-212, *History of Military Mobilization in the United States Army, 1775–1945* (Washington, DC: Department of the Army, 1955), 550, table 57; Chief, National Guard Bureau, *Annual Report of the National Guard Bureau, 1941*. The Historical Services Division of the U.S. Army Heritage and Education Center, U.S. Army War College, produced a report in 2014 for the Army staff that examined the World War II experience in detail. See "Myths of Expansibility" (Carlisle, PA: U.S. Army Heritage and Education Center, 2014).

20 Robert R. Palmer, Bell I. Wiley, and William R. Keast, *The Army Ground Forces: The Procurement and Training of Ground Troops* (Washington, DC: Historical Division, Department of the Army, 1947), 489–92.

21 Marvin A. Kreidberg and Merton G. Henry, Department of the Army Pamphlet 20-212, *History of Military Mobilization in the United States Army, 1775–1945* (Washington, DC: Department of the Army, 1955), 594–96.

22 Maurice Matloff, "The 90-Division Gamble," in *Command Decisions*, ed. Kent Roberts Greenfield, repr. 1987 (Washington, DC: Center of Military History, 1958), 373–74.

23 Matloff, "The 90-Division Gamble," 373–74; Palmer, Wiley, and Keast, *Army Ground Forces*, 433–35.

24 Chad L. Williams, *Torchbearers of Democracy: African American Soldiers in the World War I Era* (Chapel Hill: University of North Carolina Press, 2010), 346.

25 Daniel Kryder, *Divided Arsenal: Race and the American State during World War II* (Cambridge: Cambridge University Press, 2000), 37. See also Michael E. Lynch, "'Sic 'Em, Ned': Edward M. Almond and His Army, 1916–1953" (Ph.D. diss., Temple University, 2014).

26 Kent Roberts Greenfield, Robert R. Palmer, and Bell I. Wiley, *The Army Ground Forces: The Organization of Ground Combat Troops* (Washington, DC: Historical Division, Department of the Army, 1947), 216; Palmer, Wiley and Keast, *Army Ground Forces*, 434–38 and chart 1. For a complete treatment of mobilization

difficulties, see John Sloan Brown, *Draftee Division: The 88th Infantry Division in World War II* (Lexington: University Press of Kentucky, 1986).

27 Quoted in John Lewis Gaddis, *The Cold War: A New History* (New York: Penguin Press, 2005), 31.

28 Alice C. Gole, Alfred Goldberg, Samuel A. Tucker, and Rudolph A. Winnacker, eds., *The Department of Defense; Documents on Establishment and Organization, 1944–1978* (Washington, DC: Office of the Secretary of Defense Historical Office, 1978), 35.

29 John B. Wilson, *Maneuver and Firepower: The Evolution of Divisions and Separate Brigades*, Army Lineage Series (Washington, DC: Center of Military History, 1998), 239; Thomas E. Hanson, *Combat Ready? The Eighth U.S. Army on the Eve of the Korean War* (College Station: Texas A&M University Press, 2010), 18–22.

30 James F. Schnabel, *Policy and Direction: The First Year* (Washington, DC: U.S. Army Center of Military History, 1990), 56–57.

31 Frank J. Siltman, "Too Thin on Top: The Under-Resourcing of Headquarters in Force Design," Strategy Research Project, U.S. Army War College, 2006, 2.

32 John Sloan Brown, *Kevlar Legions: The Transformation of the U.S. Army, 1989–2005* (Washington, DC: Center of Military History, 2011), 162–64. See also Lorna S. Jaffee, *The Development of the Base Force, 1989–1992* (Washington, DC: Office of the Chairman of the Joint Chiefs of Staff, 1993).

PART I

Building the American Military Ideal

1

The Art of War

Early Anglo-American Translation, 1607–1643

KEVIN MCBRIDE WITH ASHLEY BISSONNETTE

Two paradigms dominate the historiography of the Pequot War (1636–1637)—the earliest war fought between English colonists and Native Americans in northeastern North America.[1] The first is that Indigenous warfare in southern New England, described as "a Skulking Way of War," was kin based and ritual in nature with limited goals and objectives that were primarily related to revenge, prestige, and captive taking, and resulted in relatively few casualties.[2] A corollary of this perspective is that southern New England was a relatively peaceful place until the arrival of Europeans in the early seventeenth century, after which Native groups began to compete for dominance in the fur and wampum trade. The second paradigm is that New England (primarily Connecticut) colonists who decisively defeated the Pequot, at the time the most powerful tribe in southern New England, were with the exception of a few experienced officers ill trained and inexperienced men drawn from trainbands and provided with weapons they barely knew how to use. In this narrative, the colonists achieved victory over the Pequot largely because of superior military technology and, from a colonial perspective, "Gods Providence."[3]

Neither of these perspectives accurately portrays the events and conduct of the Pequot War, nor how 77 Connecticut soldiers and 250 Mohegan, Wangunk, and Narragansett allies were able to march into the middle of Pequot country and decisively defeat the Pequot, who could field almost a thousand men against the English and allied Indian force. Connecticut's decisive victory over the Pequot in the Mistick Campaign was a radical departure from the existing Anglo-American military-militia system in a number of ways. The campaign drew heavily upon the ranks of combat veterans in the Connecticut settlements, relied heavily on their native allied contingent for support and intelligence, and adapted European weapons and tactics to the enemy and terrain of the New England frontier. The Mistick Campaign (May 18–May 27, 1637) was the decisive campaign of the war, and consisted of two battles fought over an eighteen-hour period. The Pequot lost more than five hundred warriors in these battles, virtually destroying their military capability and leading to their defeat and near annihilation six weeks later.

An analysis of the Mistick Campaign integrating information gleaned from Pequot War battle narratives and recent battlefield archaeological surveys provides important new insights into the campaign and calls into question long-held assumptions about the nature, organization, and experience of Connecticut's militia and the capabilities of its citizen soldiers. Connecticut, as well as the other New England colonies of Plymouth and Massachusetts, had a complex and divisive relationship with the professional soldiers in their respective colonies, and Connecticut's soldiers played an important role in the defense of English settlements. Jason Warren (in this volume and in his recent book *Connecticut Unscathed*) persuasively argues that during King Philip's War/Great Narragansett War (1675–1676), New England's militias formed around the English trainband model, and with the important exception of Connecticut, were woefully inadequate to protect settlers and property from Indian attacks. He argues further that an ill-prepared militia dependent on citizen soldiers and an underfunded military structure based on Anglo-American traditions and beliefs led to near disaster in King Philip's War, proportionally the second most devastating conflict in American history.[4] The same could well have been the case in the Pequot War if not for the constellation of a unique set of circumstances that seemingly argues against Warren's basic premise but in fact fully supports it.

Connecticut achieved victory over the Pequot because of a cadre of experienced officers, noncommissioned officers, and soldiers who served in the Thirty Years' War (1618–1648) in the Lowlands of Europe and settled in the Connecticut River Valley between 1634 and 1636. These veteran colonists were present by both design and circumstance and comprised a fairly high percentage of the English population in the Connecticut colonies on the eve of the Pequot War, contributing as much as one-quarter of the Connecticut soldiers who served in the Pequot War. The officers and men who planned the attack on the fortified Pequot village at Mistick and subsequently led the English allied force through a ten-hour, six-mile fighting withdrawal through the middle of Pequot territory drew upon their collective experiences in the Thirty Years' War. These men also relied upon their recent experiences fighting the Pequot, and designed a tour de force of an offensive campaign that led to the complete defeat of the Pequot. The successful planning and execution of the Mistick Campaign were achieved because of the commanders' ability to successfully translate their experiences from the battlefields of Europe to the terrain and enemies of the New World. In any other circumstance, colonial trainbands, trained and organized for home defense, would have been incapable of planning and executing a complex offensive operation such as the Mistick Campaign. Connecticut and Saybrook colonies' reliance on veteran soldiers during the Pequot War was a significant departure from the English tradition of using trainbands for homeland defense and sending the more undesirable men overseas with the militia. Connecticut's victories forty years later in King Philip's War were built upon the lessons learned in the Pequot War and led to a new frontier mentality characterized by a greater reliance on experienced soldiers and Native allies.[5]

On the eve of the Pequot War, the Pequot numbered approximately four thousand people, reduced by as much as 30–40 percent from the smallpox epidemic of 1633–1634. The Pequot resided in twenty-six villages of varying sizes along the coast and estuaries of Long Island Sound in southeastern Connecticut. The two chief sachems of the tribe, Sassacus and Momoho, resided in the two fortified villages at Weinshauks and Mistick, respectively.[6] In the decades before the Pequot War, the Pequot forged a powerful confederacy of dozens of tributary and allied tribes along Long Island Sound and the Connecticut River Valley.[7] The Pequot gained control of the lucrative fur and wampum (shell beads fashioned from marine shell) trade in southern New England by subjugating dozens of tribes through coercion and warfare.[8] By the eve of the Pequot War, the Pequot were the most powerful tribe in southern New England, and the Pequot military was well organized and highly experienced after decades of warfare with their Native neighbors, and a brief war with the Dutch in 1634.

The Pequot War

The Pequot War was the first sustained conflict between Native Americans and Europeans in northeastern North America. The war lasted eleven months and involved thousands of combatants who fought several battles over an area encompassing thousands of square miles. The most significant battles of the war took place during the Mistick Campaign of May 18–26, 1637, when an expeditionary force of Connecticut soldiers and Native allies attacked and burned the fortified Pequot village at Mistick, killing 400 Pequot (225 men) in less than an hour, half of whom burned to death. The "Mistick Massacre" is widely cited by historians as the major battle of the Pequot War that led directly to the disintegration and defeat of the Pequot tribe as they fled their homeland following the massacre.

The Pequot War began in September of 1636 when a force of twenty soldiers from Massachusetts Bay sailed to the Pequot (Thames) River to demand that the Pequot turn over to English justice the murderers of several English from two years before.[9] The Pequot believed the killings were justified and refused to turn over any of those involved. The English disembarked, and after many hours of fruitless negotiations arrayed themselves in battle formation and attacked the Pequot, killing several and, as the English reported, burning two villages—and "thus began the wars between the Indians and us in these parts."[10]

While the attack was the first time the English confronted Native battle formations, tactics, and weapons in New England, such was not the case for the Pequot, who had fought a brief war with the Dutch two years earlier. Although muskets were superior to Pequot bows in terms of range and penetration, the Pequot were able to use the terrain to their advantage and employ a number of tactics to negate the English advantage in firearms. The English would suffer dozens of casualties in the first six months of the Pequot War before they were able to adapt their Old World military experiences to the battlefields of the New World and win a decisive engagement against the Pequot. The Native allies of the English played an important role in this process as the English relied heavily on their more trusted Mohegan and Wangunk allies (including two Pequot) for guides, intelligence gathering, and scouting. On several occasions, the Native allies helped the English find the enemy under circumstances best suited to effectively utilize European firepower and battle formations.

In retaliation the Pequot laid siege to the nascent Saybrook Fort and colony at the mouth of the Connecticut River, cutting off most of the river traffic to the upriver colonies at Hartford, Wethersfield, and Windsor. Saybrook Fort and colony were settled in late 1635, less than a year before the Pequot War began. The Saybrook proprietors planned a potential refuge for a group of wealthy and influential Puritans whose politics and religious convictions were counter to those espoused by Charles I and the bishop of the Church of England. Fearing for their safety the proprietors contracted with like-minded Puritans such as Reverend Hugh Peters and John Winthrop Jr. for "makinge of fortifications and buildinge of houses at the Riuer Connecticut and the harbor adjoyninge, first for ther owne present accommodation and then such houses as may receive men of quality which latter houses we would have to be builded within the fort."[11] Peters and some of the Saybrook proprietors were also veterans of the Thirty Years' War who knew many of the chaplains, officers, and men serving in English regiments in the Lowlands and drew extensively upon them to plan and settle the fort and colony at Saybrook and a settlement at Windsor twenty miles upriver. In 1634, Saybrook proprietor Sir Richard Saltonstall recruited twenty-one men for his Windsor venture, of which ten would serve in the Pequot War, although it is not known how many of these men were veterans of the Thirty Years' War.[12] In 1635 Sergeant Lion Gardiner (later a lieutenant) was hired by the Saybrook proprietors to oversee "the drawing, ordering, & making of a city, towns, or forts of defense" at Saybrook.[13] Lion Gardiner, an experienced and capable noncommissioned officer, served for several years as an "engineer of fortifications" under Frederick Henry, prince of Orange, during the Thirty Years' War.[14] Of the twenty or so men who served with Gardiner at Saybrook Fort during the Pequot War, at least six are identified as veterans of the Thirty Years' War (see table 1.1).

TABLE 1.1 Saybrook Garrison: Men with Military Experience

Name	Lifespan	Previous Old World Experience	Fort Task
Lion Gardiner[a]	b.1599–d.1663	Military Engineer, Holland	Fort Engineer
Robert Chapman[b]	b.1616–d.1687	Surveyor, under Lion Gardiner, Holland	Sentinel
James Rogers[c]	d.1689	"Soldier, traveler and scholar"	Garrison
John Spencer[d]	b.1595–d.1648	Gunner	Gunner
John Wood[e]	d.1639	Ensign	Garrison
Thomas Pell[f]	b.1608–d.1668	Surgeon, Lieutenant, Holland	Surgeon

a. Lion Gardiner, *Relation of the Pequot Warres*, W. N. Chattin Carlton, ed. (Hartford, CT: Hartford Press, 1901).
b. Anne Sweet, *Robert Chapman, One of Saybrook's First Settlers* (Saybrook, CT: Saybrook Colony History Buffs, 1995); John Winthrop, *Winthrop Papers*, vol. 3 (Boston: Massachusetts Historical Society, 1943), 176.
c. Great Britain Public Record Office, "Letter, April 20, 1629," *Calendar of State Papers Domestic* 141 (London: Her Majesty's Stationery Office, 1860), 521–34.
d. Great Britain Public Record Office, "Letter, July 9, 1630," *Calendar of State Papers Domestic* 170 (London: Her Majesty's Stationery Office, 1860), 298–307.
e. Great Britain Public Record Office, "Letter, May 26, 1627," *Calendar of State Papers Domestic* 64 (London: Her Majesty's Stationery Office, 1860), 184–93.
f. Ruth V. Alley, *Pelliana, Pell of Pelham, Thomas Pell* 1, no. 1 (New York: privately printed, 1962).

For the next seven months the Pequot deployed hundreds of men around Saybrook Fort and the lower Connecticut River, attacking soldiers from the fort as well as any settlers and traders who failed to take adequate precautions against their attacks. By the end of March 1637, almost thirty English had been killed, including half of the fort's garrison. In early March, Massachusetts Bay sent nineteen soldiers under the command of Captain John Underhill, also a veteran of the Thirty Years' War, to help lift the siege. The Pequot then turned their attention to the upriver settlements, and on April 23 they attacked the English settlement at Wethersfield, killing nine settlers, including women and children, and took two girls captive. The attack raised fears among Connecticut colonists of another Virginia massacre, which had occurred in 1622 when the Powhaten Confederacy killed over 350 English settlers in a single day and Jamestown paid a steep price for failing to recruit a sufficient number of experienced soldiers to defend the colony.[15] Jamestown, as did the New England colonies, chose to rely on trainbands of "green" citizen soldiers led and trained by a few experienced soldiers such as John Smith in Virginia, Miles Standish at Plymouth, John Mason in Connecticut, and John Underhill in Massachusetts Bay (all veterans of the Thirty Years' War), recognizing that "safety and peace [cannot] be preserved without military orders and officers."[16] The cadres of experienced soldiers in New England during the Pequot War were better able to protect the colonies than their counterparts in Virginia during the Powhatan Wars (1610–1614). While there were more veterans per capita in the New England colonies than in Virginia, the former region did not observe standard English norms of trainband recruitment, which relied upon social class and standing within a community, and employed as many veterans as were available to fight in the Pequot War. After the war, Plymouth and Massachusetts Bay colonies returned to the largely ineffective traditional trainband model, while Connecticut maintained its "frontier militia tradition," which again proved successful in King Philip's War forty years later.

After the Wethersfield attack, Connecticut leaders recognized that "the eyes of all the Indians in the country are upon the English, to see what they will do," and in response the Connecticut General Court declared an "offensive war" against the Pequot on May 1, 1637.[17] The General Court levied ninety men placed under the command of Captain John Mason and appointed lesser officers and noncommissioned officers all believed to be veterans of the Thirty Years' War. Many of the men who were impressed or volunteered were also believed to be veterans of European wars, including Mason's trusted companion Aaron Stark, a former Scottish mercenary.[18]

English Military Organization

The Puritans who settled Massachusetts and Connecticut in the early 1630s relied on the ancient English tradition of requiring able-bodied men to establish trainbands, drawing from the more desirable members of society, such as yeomen, merchants, and farmers to keep and bear arms only in the defense of the country and to "encounter, expulse, repel, and resist by force of arms" all enemies of the colony.[19] These men were "to be sorted in bands and to be trained and exercised."[20] Militias traditionally were formed largely through impressment of untrained "ruffians, rogues, and vagabonds" and were employed to fight in foreign wars outside of the country.[21]

Reliance on trainbands for homeland defense rather than a professional army reflected a deep-rooted English fear of standing armies that could be employed as a tool of repression. While Puritan leaders recognized the need for an adequate defense, they too harbored grave concerns about standing armies (and marauding militias returned from foreign wars) and even small standing groups of professional soldiers. Colony leaders decided to rely on the time-honored tradition of trainbands comprised of settlers led and trained by a few experienced officers; otherwise "how dangerous it might be to erect a standing authority of military men, who might easily in time, overthrow the civil power."[22]

Colonial New England organized trainbands into companies of sixty and seventy men, who were trained and led by a captain, usually with prior military experience. The amount of time each colony required trainbands to drill varied, ranging from once a week to once a month depending on perceived threats. The captain was assisted by a lieutenant, an ensign, three sergeants, and three corporals. Musketeers generally comprised two-thirds of the company, while the remainder were pikemen. During the Pequot War it appears that all the soldiers, including pikemen, carried muskets. The full pike, in excess of ten feet long, was an effective defense against charging cavalry on the battlefields of Europe. Full pikes were virtually useless in the New World given the wooded terrain and because Native attackers rarely conducted a frontal assault on an English formation. Colonists employed modified "half pikes" during the Pequot War, but these appear to have quickly gone out of use after the war.[23]

The Thirty Years' War brought about a revolution in European military systems as they underwent a series of transformations in tactics and organization due largely to the widespread use of firearms. The events in Europe greatly influenced Charles I, and shortly after his coronation in 1625, he began to make significant reforms to the English military, including modernizing weapons and assigning veterans to the trainbands so they would impart their military knowledge and experience into the militia's training.[24] English monarchs such as Charles I were increasingly willing to become involved in continental wars, which continued to influence the transformation of the English military. It is estimated that eighty thousand Englishmen, or roughly 2 percent of the male population, served in the Lowlands between 1620 and 1642.[25]

Charles I built upon organizational changes in the English militia system first introduced by Queen Elizabeth I, who was the first English monarch to implement sweeping changes in the English militia system. While English law required all men between the age of sixteen and sixty to keep arms for militia service, few knew how to use them. Elizabeth established a system of trainbands drawn from the middle class who mustered on a regular basis for training. However, trainbands were defensive troops that by law and tradition served only in England. The English intended the militias for service overseas, and their ranks were drawn from impressments of untrained men of the lower social classes who were often obtained from prisons and taverns. Charles I impressed thousands of men for deployment, but on their return home they would often range the countryside robbing, pillaging, and raping. These experiences left a deep distrust and fear in the English populace of militias and standing armies, attitudes the colonists transferred to America.[26]

English regimental commanders and lesser officers stationed in the Lowlands were greatly influenced by innovative military thinkers such as Prince Maurice of Nassau (prince of Orange). His outposts served as military colleges, educating his staff in philosophy, new models of warfare, and the latest developments in engineering. This military aspect of the Renaissance attracted men throughout Europe. The Lowlands at this time was the high cultural and scientific mecca of the continent, and the Thirty Years' War, Eighty Years' War, and Anglo-Dutch Wars brought together some of the greatest English and Dutch scientists, military men, and entrepreneurs of the time.[27]

The soldiers who served in English regiments in the Lowlands were bound by "their English speech and English Traditions," but many were also Puritans and further bound by shared religious and political convictions that were often counter to the policies and practices of Charles I and the traditions of the established Church of England.[28] Many exiled English ministers and regimental chaplains formed congregations in cities throughout the Netherlands of like-minded "charges in the Army and/or among the merchants."[29] Spy and agent to The Hague in Holland, William Boswell reported in 1634 that there were at least a dozen English chaplains "ministering to the garrisons or the regiments of the field."[30]

Massachusetts Bay's John Davenport, Connecticut's Thomas Hooker, Rhode Island's Roger Williams, and Saybrook's Hugh Peters were all well-known Puritan ministers who immigrated to New England after serving as English regimental chaplains in the Lowlands. Hugh Peters, who emigrated from Holland to help establish Saybrook Colony, was well known among the merchants and military in Holland, where he recruited many of the men who would settle the colony. He was also an experienced military man, later becoming a principal chaplain to Oliver Cromwell and playing an important role in the creation of the New Model Army during the English Civil War (1642–1651).[31]

Growing political and religious differences with Charles I and the Church of England in the 1630s forced many important Puritan leaders with extensive military and religious connections in Holland to consider emigrating to New England. Peters and the Reverend John Davenport played key roles in recruiting experienced officers and soldiers for Connecticut, and particularly Saybrook.[32] John Mason, commander of Connecticut's forces during the Pequot War, served under Sir Thomas Fairfax during the Thirty Years' War. He was impressed or joined the militia in 1624, attained the rank of sergeant in 1629, and was commissioned a lieutenant in 1632. Shortly after, he emigrated to Massachusetts Bay and then to Windsor, Connecticut, in 1634.[33]

Mason probably met Sir Thomas Fairfax when Fairfax was first sent to the Netherlands in 1628 to train with Sir Horace Vere.[34] Under the prince of Orange, Vere was responsible for the four English regiments that were part of the Kommelijn, troops "constantly entrusted with the most difficult services, and [who] as [such] constantly covered themselves with distinction."[35] Fairfax served with the prince of Orange, as did John Mason, John Underhill, and Thomas Pell at the siege of Bois-Le-Duc (Hertogenbosh) in 1629.[36]

Not all the men who enlisted or were impressed to serve in the Thirty Years' War were ruffians or rogues. Many were upstanding citizens of the lower classes who saw service as an attractive prospect (such as Mason). Social status in Holland could only be determined by military service, not birth. All soldiers had to serve for a prescribed amount of time to attain advanced ranks, such as three years to reach lieutenant and four before they could attain the rank of captain, each rank carrying with it increased status and pay.[37]

More than one hundred Connecticut men are known to have served in one or more campaigns in the Pequot War. Of that number 17 percent were veterans of the Thirty Years' War. Given the limited documentation available for colonists' service, the number is believed to be higher, perhaps as much as 20–25 percent. Most of the men who settled in the Connecticut River Valley between 1634 and 1637 had little or no military experience, and a few were physically unable to participate in the war other than through garrison duty. The Connecticut General Court acknowledged the inexperience of some of the soldiers in the months before the war, as they encouraged trainband captains to provide extra training for the more "unskilled" members of the band.[38] When the Connecticut forces assembled at Saybrook Fort for the Mistick Campaign, twenty "insufficient" Connecticut men were sent back upriver to help defend the Connecticut settlements and replaced by more seasoned soldiers under Captain John Underhill or Lieutenant Lion Gardiner, stationed at the fort.[39] Nonetheless there were still many inexperienced soldiers on the expedition. During the attack on Mistick Fort, John Underhill, second in command of English forces, commented on the initial English volley: "[W]e could not but admire at the providence of God in it, that soldiers so unexpert in the use of their armes, should give so compleat a volley."[40]

Pequot Military Organization

Seventeenth-century Indigenous warfare in southern New England is most often characterized as a "Skulking Way of War"—limited in scope and intensity and consisting primarily of ambushes and raids. Causes of intertribal conflicts cited by anthropologists and historians include feuds between kin groups, vengeance, and warriors seeking to acquire prestige and power and to demonstrate martial skills.[41] Historians rarely mention or ignore references to pitched battles between large numbers of Indigenous combatants and consider these an anomaly.[42] Although archaeological evidence indicates that the Indigenous pre-Contact cultural landscape of southern New England was not peaceful, the evidence also suggests that there were significant changes in Native warfare following the arrival of Europeans (initially the Dutch and later the English) in the early seventeenth century.[43] Dutch sources document significant changes in social, political, and economic patterns as Native tribes responded to new opportunities afforded them by trade with Europeans. One response was increased conflict among Natives groups as they began to compete among themselves to control the fur and wampum trade. As is often the case, cultural change and increasing social and political complexity were embodied in changes in the nature, organization, and complexity of a society's military organization and in the goals and objectives of warfare.[44]

In the two decades following the arrival of Dutch traders in southern New England in 1611, Dutch sources document growing Pequot aggressiveness and military complexity as their political objectives became increasingly regional in scope. In their efforts to control the fur and wampum trade, the Pequot expanded their territorial and political control over large areas of southern New England through warfare, diplomacy, coercion, and alliance building. The Pequot strategy was to gain control over key territory along the Long Island coastline and up the Connecticut River Valley by waging war upon and subjugating Native groups to gain control over their territory.[45]

The Pequot practice of sustained regional warfare for territorial and political control does not fit the model of "skulking" or tribal warfare, but suggests a much higher order of military complexity and organization more akin to a chiefdom than to a tribe.[46] Post-Contact changes in Pequot military and political patterns include construction of fortified villages on defensible hilltops inhabited by the political and military elite, creation of frontiers of uninhabited space between them and their enemies, iconography and objects associated with chiefly "warrior elites," and regional warfare for territorial control.[47] For example, in 1631, the chief sachem of the Pequot and the chief sachem of the Wangunk inhabiting the middle Connecticut River Valley around Hartford

> agreed to meet on the field of battle with their entire forces and to engage in combat, with the condition that the victor would remain, for himself and his successors, forever lord and rightful owner of the aforesaid Fresh River. After three separate battles in open field, Meautiany, chief of the Pequatoos, held the field and was the victor; Sequeen (sachem of the Wangunk) was so beaten and defeated that he became the subject of the Pequatoos. This land Connittekock (Hartford) was bought from the Pequatoos as victors.[48]

The Pequot were the first Native tribe in southern New England to meet Europeans on the battlefield during the Pequot-Dutch War of 1634. The war is one of the least known events in the early colonial history of New England but one with far-reaching effects that directly contributed to the early successes of the Pequot against the English in the first six months of the Pequot War. The causes of the Pequot-Dutch War are obscure, but the conflict began in the winter or spring of 1634 and continued at least through November of 1634. The Pequot probably fought a contingent of seventy Dutch marines known to have been stationed at the Dutch trading post Huys de Hoope, or Fort Hope, near Hartford in December of 1633.[49] A brief but significant piece of information on the conduct of the Pequot-Dutch War was related by John Winthrop, governor of Massachusetts Bay, who commented on the skirmish between twenty Massachusetts Bay soldiers of the Endicott Expedition and the Pequot along the Pequot (Thames) River in September of 1636 that began the Pequot War. As the English disembarked from their ships to form "battalia," the Pequot retreated out of range of the English firearms, attempting to lure the English into an ambush. Winthrop reported, "He [Endicott] marched after them, supposing they [Pequot] would have stood to it awhile, as they did to the Dutch."[50] Winthrop's comment speaks volumes about what the Pequot learned from their first encounters with European battle formations and military technology, and the subsequent tactical adjustments they made.

The Pequot needed to approach within twenty yards of the English through ruse or ambush in order to shoot their arrows at point-blank range to penetrate the weak spots in English armor or buff coats (generally the head, neck, underarm, and legs). Soldiers on the Endicott Expedition reported that "certain Indians conversing with our soldiers did very much observe the armor which was upon them, and would point where they should hit them with their arrows."[51] Other tactics used by the Pequot included enveloping retreating English in a "half moon" formation and sometimes rushing into the "very muzzles of the English guns."[52] During the Saybrook siege, Gardiner grew increasingly exasperated with Massachusetts Bay's lack of support and their lack of appreciation for the effectiveness of Pequot tactics and weapons. After a Pequot ambush that killed five of Gardiner's men, he recovered "the body of one man shot through, the arrow going in at ye right side, the head sticking fast half through a rib on the left side which I took out and cleaned it [rib] and perfumed it to send to the bay, because they said that the arrows of the Indians were of no force" and sent it to Governor Vane of Massachusetts.[53]

The Pequot adjusted far more effectively to English weapons and tactics than the English did to the Pequot in the early months of the war, foreshadowing future New England Native military developments leading up to King Philip's War.[54] During that period the Pequot did not lose a single engagement against the English even though their primary weapon was the bow and arrow tipped with brass points cut from brass trade kettles. On the eve of the Mistick Fort battle, the English reported that the Pequot had only sixteen guns, mostly taken from English killed during the Saybrook siege.[55] These guns were probably flintlocks, as the Pequot appear to have been very selective about the firearms they purchased from the Dutch or took from dead Englishmen. In the same engagement at Saybrook where Gardiner lost five men, he reported that two soldiers dropped their guns as they ran for the safety of the fort (for which Gardiner threatened to hang them). The Pequot won the engagement and controlled the battlefield, yet two days later Gardiner reported that the muskets were still lying where they had been dropped.[56] These guns were probably matchlocks discarded by the Pequot because they were too unwieldy and cumbersome due to their weight and long barrel and could not be "snap shot" because of their ignition system.

Mistick Campaign

The Mistick Campaign lasted from May 18 to May 27, the days when the expedition left and returned to Saybrook Fort. The campaign consisted of two major battles fought on May 26: the Battle of Mistick Fort and the Battle of the English Withdrawal. These battles were fought over a sixteen-hour period through eight miles of Pequot territory and were the longest and most intense engagements of the war, involving more than a thousand combatants.

The Mistick Campaign consisted of four major phases: formulation of the original battle plan, accumulation of men and materials, and subsequent revision of the battle plan at Saybrook Fort; the voyage from Saybrook to Narragansett Bay and the thirty-five-mile march overland from Narragansett to the Mystic River; the attack on the fortified Pequot village at Mistick; and the English allied eight-mile withdrawal and six-mile running battle to the Pequot (Thames) River. The first two phases of the campaign reflect the careful planning and consideration given by the principal commanders (Mason, Underhill, Gardiner, Seeley) to planning, logistics, intelligence gathering, and recruitment of Indigenous allies. The last two phases of the campaign, the battles of Mistick Fort and the English Withdrawal, reflect the professionalism, determination, and experience of the core group of officers, noncommissioned officers, and soldiers who provided leadership during the six-hour running battle.

When the Connecticut General Court declared war against the Pequot, they levied ninety men, thirteen of whom were sailors, to man "one Pink, one Pinnace, and one Shallop."[57] Of the forty-four men whose ages could be determined, 93 percent (n=41) were forty-two or younger, and 82 percent (n=36) were age thirty-seven or younger.[58] Clearly, the men were selected for their youth as the General Court and Mason anticipated a strenuous and lengthy campaign. The General Court requisitioned twenty sets of armor (breastplates or corselets) and sufficient supplies to last the expedition six to eight weeks.[59] Each soldier was ordered to "carry with him 1 lb of powder, 4 lb of shot [and] 20 bullets," while the entire expedition carried "1 barrel of powder from the river's mouth [Saybrook Fort], a light gun if they can."[60]

The General Court appointed John Mason captain and commander of the expedition and "in case of death or sickness under the command of Robert Seeley, Lieutenant, and the oldest Sergeant or military officer surviving."[61] These men planned and organized the campaign in only two weeks, including the selection of soldiers, weapons, equipment, and supplies. The overall strategic design was to use English seapower to bypass Pequot territory where the Pequot held advantages in land forces and movement within interior lines, and to deceive the Pequot by attacking them in the rear, where the English advantages in firepower could be brought to bear.

Subsequent analysis of broken, discarded, and dropped weapons and equipment, personal items, and expended and dropped musket balls recovered from the Mistick Campaign battlefields indicates that the expedition was equipped to anticipate a variety of tactical and logistical contingencies, including construction of defensive works, combat at close and long range, and siege warfare. The types of weapons that the English brought on the expedition were selected to anticipate these contingencies, and do not seem to reflect a random process of selection based on weapon availability of individual soldiers (many may not have owned their own weapons). Weapons recovered from the battlefield included pikes (presumably half-pikes), matchlock and flintlock muskets, carbines, pistols, and possibly a small cannon.[62]

A common misconception among historians is that colonial soldiers in the early seventeenth century (and the Pequot War in particular) were armed primarily with cumbersome matchlock muskets because they were cheaper, readily available, more durable, and easier to maintain than flintlocks. However, Pequot War–era sources suggest that there was growing appreciation and recognition of the utility of flintlock weapons in the New World, including shorter-barreled "bastard" muskets and carbines that were lighter and better suited to maneuver on the terrain and against the potential enemies in the New World. For example, in 1628 Massachusetts Bay ordered weapons for one hundred men, including eighty snaphaunce (flintlocks) and only ten matchlock muskets.[63] Six flintlock (cock arms, sear springs) and three matchlock (serpentines) gun parts were recovered from the Mistick Campaign battlefields, suggesting a two-to-one ratio of flintlock to matchlock weapons.[64] Each type of firearm had advantages and disadvantages depending on the terrain and tactical situation.

Saybrook Fort

Mason arrived at Saybrook Fort on May 16 and showed his commission to Gardiner and Underhill "limiting us to land our Men in Pequot River."[65] While Mason was at Saybrook the General Court sent a letter reaffirming his orders to land on the Pequot River and conduct a frontal assault. Unlike Mason, Underhill and Gardiner had experience fighting the Pequot and understood that European battle formations and tactics would not be effective against the Pequot in spite of the superiority of English weapons:

> [W]hen Captain Underhill and I had seen their [Mason's] commission, we both said they were not fitted for such a design and we said to Mason we wondered he would venture himself being no better fitted and he said the Magistrates could not or would not fend better, then we said that none of our men would go with them neither should they go unless we that were bred soldiers from our youth could see some likelihood to do better than the bay men [Massachusetts Bay] with their strong commission last year [i.e. Endicott Expedition to Pequot River the previous September].[66]

Over the next few days the three commanders and their lesser officers devised an entirely new plan based on their collective experiences in the Thirty Years' War, while utilizing Underhill's and Gardiner's previous experiences fighting the Pequot. Both men knew that a frontal assault against the Pequot had no chance of succeeding.

Fortuitously, the two English girls captured by the Pequot in the Wethersfield raid three weeks before had just arrived at Saybrook the same day as Mason. Dutch traders ransomed them in a prisoner exchange with the Pequot. During their time as captives, the Pequot "carried them from place to place, and shewed them their Forts, and curious Wigwams."[67] The girls were "examined" by the three commanders and provided them with information on the number and disposition of Pequot warriors, the location and nature of their forts, and the type of weaponry they possessed. This information proved critical in the evolution of the Mistick Campaign battle plan. The new battle plan incorporated the intelligence gained from the two girls as well as the experiences of Underhill and Gardiner fighting the Pequot: "& having Stayed there 5 or 6 days before we could agree at last we old Soldiers agreed about ye way . . . and ye Lord God blessed the design & way for yet they returned with victory."[68]

Connecticut Colony continued to rely on veteran soldiers to train and equip the trainbands and to lead Connecticut's militias in subsequent wars. Many of the Connecticut officers who were field commanders during King Philip's War were veterans of the Pequot War and greatly contributed to the overall success of Connecticut's army during the later war.[69] Mason opposed any changes to his orders in spite of overwhelming support for the new plan by all the officers present. Mason eventually embraced the revised plan and later justified his decision:

> But if a War be Managed duly by Judgment and Discretion as is requisite, the Shews are many times contrary to what they seem to pursue: Wherefore the more an Enterprise is dissembled and kept secret, the more facil to put in Execution; as the Proverb, The farthest way about is sometimes the nearest way home. I shall make bold to present this as my present Thoughts in this Case; In Matters of War, those who are both able and faithful should be improved; and then bind them not up into too narrow a Compass: For it is not possible for the wisest and ablest Senator to foresee all Accidents and Occurents that fall out in the Management and Pursuit of a War.[70]

Mistick Fort

The plan the English commanders devised was based on deception, mobility, speed, surprise, and containment. Mason explained the key elements in their decision to forgo a direct frontal attack:

First, the Pequots our Enemies, kept a continual Guard upon the River Night and Day. Secondly, their Numbers far exceeded ours; having sixteen Guns with Powder and Shot. . . . Thirdly, They were on Land, and being swift on Foot, might much impede our Landing, and possibly dishearten our Men; we being expected only by Land, there being no other Place to go on Shore but in that River, nearer than Narragansett. Fourthly, By Narragansett we should come upon their Backs and possibly might surprise them unaware, at worst we should be on firm Land as well as they.[71]

The plan was for the expedition to transit east the hundred miles from Saybrook to Narragansett Bay in full view of the Pequot coast to let the Pequot believe they were afraid to land. The ruse worked, as Mason later reported: "They seeing our Pinnaces sail by them some Days before, concluded we were afraid of them and durst not come near them."[72] From Narragansett the expedition would double back west thirty-five miles to the Mystic River and attack the two Pequot forts at night to catch the Pequot by surprise and fix them within their palisades.

The English plan was a significant departure from the frontal assaults on Block Island and the Thames River the previous fall, which failed to bring the Pequot to open battle. The English learned from these mistakes, and the battle plan for the Mistick Campaign evolved accordingly. Interestingly, the commanders' experience conducting siege warfare in Europe was probably the single most important factor in their decision to conduct a surprise attack on the two fortified Pequot villages in order to contain the Pequot and mitigate their advantages in mobility and use of the terrain.[73]

The expedition spent several days at Narragansett finalizing their plans and enlisting the aid of 250 Narragansett for the attack. Extended negotiations and bad weather delayed the English allied force. Mason grew increasingly anxious with the delays "least they [Narragansett/Eastern Niantic] might discover us to the Enemy, especially they having many times some of their near Relations among their greatest Foes."[74] Mason placed great importance on knowledgeable and ongoing intelligence gathering on the Pequot. At Narragansett he enlisted the aid of two Pequot men, Wequash and Wuttackquiackomin, recently banished from Pequot territory: "valiant men, especially the latter, who have lived these three or four years with the Nanhiggonucks [Narragansetts], and know every pass and passage amongst them [Pequot]."[75] These men were indispensable to the overall success of the expedition, and as the delays at Narragansett continued, Mason sent them to Pequot territory several times to determine whether the element of surprise was still with the English: "[A] friendly Indian that was sent hither as a secret spy, brought word that the Pequots were singing, and dancing, and blessing their God, in that they supposed the English were gone from them."[76] As the expedition approached the Mystic River, the spies were sent out again and "brought us newes that they [Pequot] were secure, having been fishing with many Canoes at sea, and diverse of them walking here and there."[77]

The element of surprise was so important to the potential success of the expedition that on the morning Mason was to depart Narragansett, he declined to wait for Massachusetts Bay Captain Daniel Patrick (also a veteran of the Thirty Years' War who had served with Mason and Underhill), who had just arrived at Providence, thirty-five miles to the north, with forty men. Patrick's men would have been a significant addition to Mason's seventy-seven soldiers, but Mason, guided by his continental military experiences, decided that further delay was not worth risking the element of surprise.

The expedition left Narragansett on May 23 and at dusk on May 25 arrived at Porter's Rocks at the head of the Mystic River, where they spent the night. The English and their Native allies rose just after midnight and began the two-mile march to Pequot Hill, a prominent elevation one-quarter mile west of the Pequot River. The Pequot fort was located at the summit of Pequot Hill and consisted of a circular palisade seventy meters in diameter:

> [H]ere they pitch close together, as they can young trees and halfe trees, as thicke as a mans thigh, or the calfe of his legge. Ten or twelve foote high they are above the ground, and within rammed three foote deepe, with undermining, the earth being cast up for their better shelter against the enemies dischargements. Betwixt these pallisadoes are divers loope-holes, through which they let flie their winged messengers. The doore for the most part is entered sidewaies, which they stop with boughs or bushes as need requireth. The space within is full of Wigwams. This Fort was so crowded with these numerous dwellings, that the English wanted foote-roome to graple with their adversaries, and therefore set fire on all.[78]

The English allied force stopped to make their final preparations at the base of Pequot Hill and split the English into two divisions, with Mason approaching from the northeast and Underhill from the southwest where the two entrances were located. Splitting one's forces in the face of a numerically superior enemy in the heart of the enemy's country speaks to the experience of Mason and Underhill, and their confidence in their veteran force. The commanders did not trust their Native allies, who were afraid of the Pequot and believed that "Sassacus [Chief Sachem] was all one God, and nobody could kill him."[79] The English told their Native allies to form a ring around the fort to prevent anyone from escaping and "that they should by no means fly, but stand at what distance they pleased, and see whether English men would now fight or not."[80] The English plan was to surround the fort and fire an initial volley through the palisade walls, whereupon half of each division would enter the fort "to destroy them by the Sword and save the Plunder" while the remainder of the English waited outside the fort in support.[81] The plan began to unravel when a Pequot sentry discovered Mason and his division as they approached the northeast entrance, and they were forced to begin the attack before Underhill was in position. Mason's men immediately fired a volley through the palisade walls and Mason entered the fort with seventeen men. Mason did achieve a degree of surprise as his entry was not contested, but the Pequot quickly recovered and mounted a ferocious defense inside the fort. Unbeknownst to Mason, the Pequot were aware of the English march through Pequot country and were making preparations to attack them and had reinforced the fort the night before with 150 additional men, bringing the total number of Pequot defenders inside the fort to approximately 225.

Of the seventeen men who entered the fort with Mason, 60 percent were killed or wounded within fifteen minutes. Mason expected approximately seventy-five Pequot defenders inside the fort, the normal complement of men in a village of that size. Instead, the English found themselves fighting 225 Pequot warriors in the close confines of the fort, "strained for room because of the wigwams."[82] The English were in danger of losing the battle, forcing Mason to order the firing of the wigwams inside the fort, and "when the fort was thoroughly fired, command was given, that all should fall off and surround the Fort; which was readily attended by all."[83] Underhill's men forced their way through the southwest entrance only after the fort was already on fire and his division was unable to support Mason's fight inside the fort, although it is doubtful it would have made a difference. A stiff northeast wind fanned the flames and forced the Pequot survivors to the southwest entrance, where they tried to escape the burning fort:

> [M]any courageous fellows were unwilling to come out, and fought most desperately through the Palisadoes, so as they were scorched and burnt with the very flame, and were deprived of their arms, in regard the fire burnt their very bowstrings, and so perished valiantly: mercy they did deserve for their valor, could we have had opportunity to have bestowed it; many were burnt in the Fort, both men, women, and children, others forced out, and came in troops to the Indians, twenty, and thirty at a time, which our soldiers received and entertained with the point of the sword; down fell men, women, and children.[84]

The Withdrawal

The English victory was costly, as two English were killed and twenty to twenty-four wounded in the initial assault, five so severely they had to be carried on stretchers.[85] Forty Native allies were also wounded, largely from English friendly fire.[86] The intensity of the fighting is certainly reflected in the English narratives, but is also evident in the nature and distribution of battle-related objects recovered along the first two miles of the Withdrawal (see figure 1.1).

The English won the battle, but Mason had only sixty combat-effective soldiers, and they faced other obstacles as well:

> And thereupon grew many Difficulties: Our Provision and Munition near spent; we in the Enemies Country, who did far exceed us in Number, being much enraged: all our Indians, except ONKOS [Uncas the Mohegan sachem], deserting us; our Pinnaces at a great distance from us, and when they would come we were uncertain.[87]

The allied force retreated south several hundred meters to a vantage point on Pequot Hill where they could tend the wounded and await sign of their

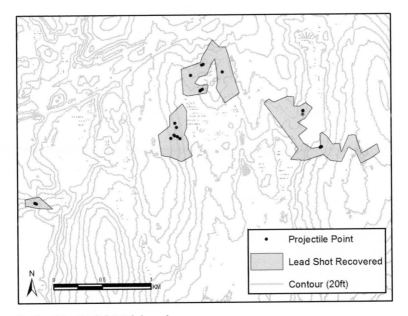

Battle of the English Withdrawal.

ships. Over the next two hours the English fought off three Pequot counter-attacks. The first was repulsed easily "and after five Muskets discharged the Pequots fled."[88] The second attack was an indication of things to come as the Pequot began to abandon the tactics that had proved so successful against the English in their efforts to gain revenge on them. The second attack came when Underhill and thirty English sallied from the vantage point on Pequot Hill to counter a Pequot attack and rescue a contingent of fifty. Underhill reported, "in the space of an hour [we] rescued their [Narragansett] men, and in our retreat to the body, slew and wounded above a hundred Pequots, all fighting men that charged us both in rear and flanks."[89]

As the morning wore on the chief Pequot sachem, Sassacus, gathered hundreds of men from villages throughout Pequot country to attack the English allied force. Three hundred Pequot attacked the English just as they saw their vessels sailing through Long Island Sound on their way to rendezvous in the Pequot River:

> [I]mmediately came up the Enemy from the other fort [Sassacus's fort at Wein-shauks two miles to the southwest]; three hundred or more as we conceived. The Captain lead out a file or two of men to skirmish with them, chiefly to try what temper they were of, who put them to a stand: we being much encouraged thereat, presently prepared to March towards our Vessels.[90]

The route of withdrawal crossed a very challenging terrain with extreme changes in topography and interspersed with glaciated boulder trains and wetlands that were extremely difficult for the English allied column to traverse with their wounded and provided excellent cover and concealment for the Pequot. Mason relates that "some of them lay in Ambush behind Rocks and Trees, often shooting at us, yet through Mercy touched not one of us: And as we came to any Swamp or Thicket, we made some Shot to clear the Passage. Some of them fell with our Shot; and probably more might, but for want of Munition."[91] Although only two miles of the withdrawal have been surveyed during the Battlefields of the Pequot War project, over six hundred battle-related objects have been recovered, including musket balls, brass arrow points, broken gun parts for matchlocks and flintlocks, and a variety of personal items such as knives, pipes, jaw harps, buttons, and aglets. Over three hundred musket balls were recovered along the way, testifying to the intensity of the fighting.

As in the attack on Pequot Hill, Pequot were abandoning the tactics that were previously successful against the English in their rage over the massacre at Mistick. The Pequot continually attacked the English allied column from the front, flanks, and rear and on occasion rushed the column, "sometimes desperately hazarding themselves in open field."[92] In one instance the Pequot "came mounting down the Hill upon us, in a full career, as if they would over run us; But when they came within Shot, the Rear faced about, giving Fire upon them."[93] By the end of the battle the Pequot lost hundreds of men. One English source states that the Pequot lost more men in the Battle of the English Withdrawal than they did at Mistick. If so, Pequot casualties that day may have been as high as five hundred men killed or wounded, more than half of their entire fighting force. It is not known how many English casualties the Pequot inflicted during the Withdrawal. Mason related that upon reaching the Pequot River, "our numbers [were] much weakened."[94]

The Battles of Mistick Fort and the English Withdrawal were significant victories for the English as they eliminated the Pequot as a viable military threat and led to their complete defeat six weeks later at a swamp in southwestern Connecticut outside of present-day Fairfield. The victory at Mistick was won by a carefully planned and executed attack by commanders and officers who had decades of experience in the Thirty Years' War and were able to effectively translate their experience to the battlefields of the New World. The victory over the Pequot in the Battle of the English Withdrawal was not won just through a carefully planned and executed battle plan but through the training and experience of a core of combat veterans who made the necessary tactical adjustments in an unfamiliar terrain against an experienced enemy. The successful employment of an English veteran force in the Pequot War of 1636–1637, whether from design or circumstances, departed from the Anglo-American tradition of trainbands of inexperienced men led by a few veteran soldiers. This pattern presaged Connecticut victory in King Philip's War (1675–1676) and established a New World frontier militia system that relied on veterans, experience, and training more than on mass levees of untrained yeoman farmers.

NOTES

1 Kevin McBride et al., *Battle of Mistick Fort Documentation Plan* (GA-2255–09–017) (Mashantucket, CT: Mashantucket Pequot Museum and Research Center, 2012); Alfred A. Cave, *The Pequot War* (Amherst: University of Massachusetts Press, 1996); Francis P. Jennings, *The Invasion of America: Indians, Colonialism, and the Cant of Conquest* (New York: Norton, 1976) , 146–49, 202–27; Alden Vaughan, "Pequots and Puritans: The Causes of the War of 1637," *William and Mary Quarterly* 21, no. 2 (April 1964): 256–69.

2   Adam Hirsch, "Collision of Military Cultures in the 17th Century," *Journal of American History* 74, no. 4 (March 1988): 1187–1212; Dean Snow, "Iroquoian-Huran War Fare," in *North American Indigenous Warfare and Ritual Violence*, Richard J. Chacon and Ruben G. Mendoza, eds. (Tucson: University of Arizona Press, 2007), 149–59; Patrick Malone, *The Skulking Way of War: Technology and Tactics among the New England Indians* (Madison, WI: Madison Books, 2000).

3   John Mason, *Brief History of the Pequot War,* Thomas Prince, ed. (Boston: Kneeland & Green, 1736).

4   Jason Warren, *Connecticut Unscathed* (Norman: University of Oklahoma Press, 2014); Jason Warren, "Special Commentary: Insights from the Army's Drawdowns," *U.S. Army War College Quarterly Parameters* 44, no. 2 (Summer 2014).

5   Warren, *Connecticut Unscathed.*

6   Kevin McBride, "In the Pequots: The Fall and Rise of an American Indian Nation," *Historical Archaeology of the Mashantucket Pequot* (Norman: University of Oklahoma Press, 1990), 96–116.

7   Kevin McBride, "War and Trade in Eastern New England," in *A Beautiful and Fruitful Place: Selected Rennsslaerwijck Papers*, Margriet Lacy, ed. (Albany, NY: New Netherland Institute, 2013).

8   McBride, "War and Trade in Eastern New England."

9   Cave, *The Pequot War*; Jennings, *The Invasion of America*, 146–49, 202–27; Vaughan, "Pequots and Puritans."

10 Lion Gardiner, *Relation of the Pequot Warres*, W. N. Chattin Carlton, ed. (Hartford, CT: Hartford Press, 1901), 11.

11 John Winthrop, *Winthrop Papers*, vol. 3 (Boston: Massachusetts Historical Society, 1943), 198.

12 Kevin McBride, Ashley Bissonnette, David Naumec, et al., *Site Identification and Documentation: Siege and Battle of Saybrook Fort* (GA-2255-12-011) (Mashantucket, CT: Mashantucket Pequot Museum & Research Center, 2014).

13 Curtiss Gardiner, *Papers and Biography of Lion Gardiner* (St. Louis, MO: Levison & Blythe Stationery Co., 1883).

14 Ruth V. Alley, *Pelliana, Pell of Pelham, Thomas Pell* 1, no. 1 (New York: privately printed, 1962): 15; Gardiner, *Papers and Biography of Lion Gardiner.*

15 Philip Barbour, ed., *The Complete Works of Captain John Smith*, vols. 1 and 2 (Williamsburg, VA: Institute of Early American History and Culture, 1986).

16 Nathaniel B. Shurtleff, ed., *Records of the Governor and Company of the Massachusetts Bay in New England*, vol. 1 (Boston: Press of William White, 1853–1854), 17–18.

17 J. Hammond Trumbull, ed., *Public Records of the Colony of Connecticut, Prior to the Union with New Haven Colony* (Hartford, CT: Brown & Parsons, 1850).

18 Clovis LaFleur, *Aaron Stark, Progenitor of Our Stark Family in North America and the First Three Generations*, Donn Neal, ed. (privately published, 2006); Winthrop,

Winthrop Papers, vol. 3, 405; Trumbull, ed., *Public Records of the Colony of Connecticut*, 9.

19 Shurtleff, ed., *Records of the Governor and Company of the Massachusetts Bay*, 18.

20 Bruce D. Rutman, *A Militant New World, 1607–1640* (PhD dissertation, University of Virginia–Charlottesville, 1959), 25.

21 Kyle Zelner, *A Rabble in Arms* (New York: New York University Press, 2009), 20.

22 John Winthrop, *Winthrop's Journal*, vol. 1, James Kendall Hosmer, ed. (New York: Barnes & Noble, 1908), 260; Hirsch, "Collision of Military Cultures in the 17th Century."

23 Warren, *Connecticut Unscathed*.

24 Zelner, *A Rabble in Arms*, 22.

25 K. L. Sprunger, "Other Pilgrims in Leiden," *Church History* 41, no. 1 (1972): 46–60.

26 Zelner, *A Rabble in Arms*.

27 Ofer Gal and Raz Chen-Morris, *Baroque Science* (Chicago: Chicago University Press, 2013), 3.

28 J. Fiske, *The Beginnings of New England; or, The Puritan Theocracy in Its Relation to Civil and Religious Liberty* (New York: Houghton Mifflin, 1899), 74.

29 Fiske, *The Beginnings of New England*, 74; R. P. Stearns, "The New England Way in Holland," *New Quarterly* 6, no. 4 (1933): 174.

30 "English Preachers in the Netherlands," *1634, Boswell Papers*, I Folio 175 (Kew National Archives); Stearns, "The New England Way in Holland," 752.

31 "Letters, 1624–1636," *Proceedings October, 1908–June, 1909*, vol. 42 (Boston: Massachusetts Historical Society, 1909), 204–35; Winthrop, *Winthrop Papers*, vol. 3; Rev. Samuel Peters, *A History of the Rev. Hugh Peters* (New York: Samuel Peters, 1807).

32 Henry Shelly, *John Underhill, Captain of New England and New Netherland* (New York: Appleton, 1932), 122 ; Davenport Correspondence with Lady Vere, Manuscript (British Museum): MSS 4275.

33 Robert Charles Anderson, *The Great Migration* (Boston: New England Genealogical Society, 1995), 1226, 1225; Shurtleff, ed., *Records of the Governor and Company of the Massachusetts Bay*, 124; Samuel G. Drake, *Result of Some Searches among the British Archives* (Boston: New England Genealogical Register, 1860), 12; Reuben Walworth, *Mason Family*, vol. 15 (Boston: NEHGR, 1861), 117.

34 C. R. Markham, *A Life of the Great Lord Fairfax, Commander-in-Chief of the Army of the Parliament of England* (London: MacMillian, 1870).

35 George Edmundson, "Frederick Henry, Prince of Orange," *English Historical Review* 5, no. 17 (1890): 43.

36 D. Plant, *British Civil Wars and Commonwealth* (2006), british-civil-wars.co.uk; John Mason, *Brief History of the Pequot War*, Thomas Prince, ed. (Boston: Kneeland & Green, 1736), v.

37 D. Campbell, *Puritan in Holland, England, and America*, vol. 2 (New York: Harper and Brothers, 1892), 256.

38 Trumbull, ed., *Public Records of the Colony of Connecticut*, 4.

39 Gardiner, *Relation of the Pequot Warres*, 20.

40 John Underhill, *Nevves from America* (London: Peter Cole, 1638).

41 Snow, "Iroquoian-Huran War Fare"; Malone, *The Skulking Way of War*.

42 Hirsch, "Collision of Military Cultures in the 17th Century"; Malone, *Skulking Way of War*; Wayne E. Lee, "Fortify, Fight, or Flee: Tuscarora and Cherokee Defensive Warfare and Military Culture Adaptation," *Journal of Military History* 68, no. 3 (July 2004); Wayne E. Lee, *Barbarians and Brothers* (New York: Oxford University Press, 2014); Wayne E. Lee, *Empires and Indigenes: Intercultural Alliance, Imperial Expansion, and Warfare in the Early Modern World* (New York: New York University Press, 2011).

43 McBride, "War and Trade in Eastern New England."

44 Don Brothwell, "Biosocial and Bio-archaeological Aspects of Conflict and Warfare," in *Ancient Warfare*, John Carmen and Anthony Harding, eds. (Phoenix Mill, UK: Sutton Publishing, 2004); John Shy, *A People Numerous and Well Armed: Reflections on the Military Struggle for American Independence* (Ann Arbor: University of Michigan Press, 1990).

45 McBride, "War and Trade in Eastern New England."

46 Warren, *Connecticut Unscathed*.

47 McBride, "War and Trade in Eastern New England."

48 *Verbael Gehouden door de Heeren 1725*, Charles Gehring, trans. (Albany, NY: New Netherland Project, 1990), 607.

49 Oliver Rink, *Holland on the Hudson: An Economic and Social History of Dutch New York* (Ithaca, NY: Cornell University Press, 1986), 121–24; McBride, "War and Trade in Eastern New England," 282.

50 Winthrop, *Winthrop's Journal*, vol. 1, 188–89.

51 Increase Mather, *A Relation of the Troubles Which Have Hapned in New England* (Boston: John Foster, 1677), 181.

52 Gardiner, *Relation of the Pequot Warres*, 13.

53 Gardiner, *Relation of the Pequot Warres*, 13–14.

54 Malone, *The Skulking Way of War*.

55 Mason, *Brief History of the Pequot War*.

56 Gardiner, *Relation of the Pequot Warres*.

57 Mason, *Brief History of the Pequot War*, 1.

58 Ashley Bissonnette, "English Soldiers' Biographies," *Battle of Mistick Fort Documentation Plan* (GA-2255-09-017) (Mashantucket, CT: Mashantucket Pequot Museum and Research Center, 2012).

59 Ashley Bissonnette, "Military Ration Analysis," *Battle of Mistick Fort Documentation Plan* (GA-2255-09-017) (Mashantucket, CT: Mashantucket Pequot Museum and Research Center, 2012).

60 Trumbull, ed., *Public Records of the Colony of Connecticut*, 10.

61 Trumbull, ed., *Public Records of the Colony of Connecticut*, 9.

62 McBride et al., *Battle of Mistick Fort Documentation Plan*.

63 Shurtleff, ed., *Records of the Governor and Company of the Massachusetts Bay*, 126.

64 Kevin McBride et al., *Battle of Mistick Fort: English Withdrawal and Pequot Counterattacks* (GA-2287-13-014) (Mashantucket, CT: Mashantucket Pequot Museum and Research Center, 2014).

65 Mason, *Brief History of the Pequot War*, 3.

66 Gardiner, *Relation of the Pequot Warres*, 19.

67 Underhill, *Nevves from America*, 25.

68 Gardiner, *Relation of the Pequot Warres*, 20.

69 Warren, *Connecticut Unscathed*, 100–101.

70 Mason, *Brief History of the Pequot War*, 3.

71 Mason, *Brief History of the Pequot War*, 2–3.

72 Mason, *Brief History of the Pequot War*, 6–7.

73 McBride et al., *Battle of Mistick Fort: English Withdrawal and Pequot Counterattacks.*

74 Mason, *Brief History of the Pequot War*, 5.

75 Winthrop, *Winthrop Papers*, vol. 3, 414.

76 Mather, *A Relation of the Troubles Which Have Hapned in New England*, 68.

77 William Hubbard, *A Narrative of the Trouble with the Indians in New England . . . to Which Is Added a Discourse about the Warre with the Pequods in the Year 1637* (Boston: John Foster, 1677), 126.

78 Philip Vincent, *True Relation of the Late Battle Fought in New England, between the English, and the Salvages* (London: Thomas Harper, for Nathanael Butter, and John Bellamie, 1637), 11–12.

79 Mather, *A Relation of the Troubles Which Have Hapned in New England*, 17.

80 Mason, *Brief History of the Pequot War*, 7.

81 Mason, *Brief History of the Pequot War*, 8.

82 Vincent, *True Relation of the Late Battle Fought in New England, between the English, and the Salvages*, 9.

83 Mason, *Brief History of the Pequot War*, 8.

84 Underhill, *Nevves from America*, 35.

85 Mason, *Brief History of the Pequot War*, 10–11.

86 Roger Williams, *Correspondence of Roger Williams*, I. G. LaFantasie, ed. (Providence: Rhode Island Historical Society, 1988), 83–84; Mather, *A Relation of the Troubles Which Have Hapned in New England*, 47.

87 Mason, *Brief History of the Pequot War*, 10.

88 Vincent, *True Relation of the Late Battle Fought in New England, between the English, and the Salvages*, 11.

89 Underhill, *Nevves from America*, 37–38.

90 Mason, *Brief History of the Pequot War*, 11.

91 Mason, *Brief History of the Pequot War*, 11.

92 Hubbard. *A Narrative of the Trouble with the Indians in New England*, 126.

93 Mason, *Brief History of the Pequot War*, 11.

94 Mason, *Brief History of the Pequot War*, 13.

2

Liberty Paradox

The Failure of the Military System in Mid-Seventeenth-Century New England

JASON W. WARREN

NEW ENGLAND CRISIS: ON FORTIFICATION
AT BOSTON BEGUN BY WOMEN (1676)[1]

A Grand attempt some Amazonian Dames
Controve thereby to glorify their names
A Ruff for Boston Neck of mud and turf
Reaching from side to side from turf to turf
Their nimble hands spin up like Christmas pyes
Their pastry by degrees on high doth rise
The wheel at home counts it an holiday
Since while the Mistress worketh it may play
A tribe of female hands, but manly hearts
Forsake at home their pastry and tarts
To knead the dirt, the samplers down they hurle
The pickaxe one as Commandress holds.
One puffs and sweats, the other mutters why
Can't you promove your work so fast as I?
Some dig, some delve, and others hands do feel
The little wagons weight and single wheel
And least some fainting fits the weak surprise
They want no sack or cakes, they are more wise
These brave essayes draw forth Male stronger hands
More like Dawbers [than] Martial hands
These do the work, the sturdy bulwarks raise,
But the beginners well deserve the praise.

The level of crisis forcing the "Amazonian Dames" of Boston to build bulwarks was such that chronicler Reverend William Hubbard described it as "barbarous and inhumane."[2] The violent end to forty years of tenuous peace between New England colonists and native groups caused heavy casualties and destruction across the region, forcing traditional noncombatants literally to make up ground for preconflict unpreparedness. A dearth of martial readiness, borne of deeply held convictions and just as serious fears, reflected a nascent American dilemma: one in which colonists perceived that the requisite military apparatus would threaten the very religious and political liberty they sought to protect. The history of New England's Great Narragansett War (1675–1676) and that of the decades leading up to the conflict reveal colonial martial attitudes toward standing military structure still present in U.S. political-military discourse.[3] With the notable exception of Connecticut, the militia of New England, modeled on English trainbands, failed to protect settlers and their property from deadly attacks and succumbed to ambushes in the wilderness. After a decisive victory in the Pequot War (1636–1637), the colonists largely rested on their laurels, believing that the traditional English part-time militia system would sufficiently deter or defeat threats from both Europeans and Indians. As future Americans would, New Englanders paid for this overestimation in blood.

This second-deadliest war (per capita) in American history permanently impeded New England's expansion and undermined its economy for a century.[4] An ill-prepared militia and underfunded military structure based on Anglo-American traditions, fears, and beliefs led to military disaster, presaging future U.S. military problems with readiness. Only Connecticut Colony, whose success chroniclers and historians overlooked for almost 350 years, achieved victory due to idiosyncrasies such as experience, geography, capable Indian allies, and inspired leadership.[5] The experience of the other New England colonies during this period typified that of the future United States, where strategic victories often came at a cost due to tactical unpreparedness.

The mid-seventeenth-century New Englanders' attitude toward military apparatuses foreshadowed an inefficient American military policy. Deeply held Anglo-American values of individual political and religious liberty, expressed in New England as Puritan Christianity and its related government, affected military policy. These religious dissenters and separatists from the Church of England understood professional standing military organizations and structure as a danger to religious and political liberty, which, in practice, were intertwined. The English and Dutch had oppressed the Pilgrims and Puritans in the early seventeenth century with the threat of force. The New England colonists were at first sympathetic to Parliament's battle against the Stuart Dynasty, with a tradition of harboring the "regicide" judges Edward Whalley and William Goffe (in the New Haven, Connecticut, area), whose names the local geography and streets still bear. The English civil wars, particularly Oliver Cromwell's dictatorship, however, reinforced early colonists' fear of standing armies. The English military establishment had then only grown in size and authority during Cromwell's reign of political terror in the mid-seventeenth century. Even though they were sympathetic to the revolution's religious bent, the Puritans prepared to restore the Stuart dynasty because Cromwell's (and his heir's) New Model Army–backed reign devolved into tyranny, threatening cherished liberties.[6] Parliament's historic power of the purse, a long-standing English tradition of legislative control over military spending foreshadowed by the Magna Carta, also influenced the New Englander's belief in low taxes, private property, and individual rights. These beliefs did not align with more robust spending on a capable military apparatus.[7]

The restoration of the Catholic-leaning Stuarts after the Cromwells' demise did not temper fears that the English realm would curtail New Englanders' liberties. During this period, the Duke of York sought to limit New England expansion, and his trusted agent Governor Edmund Andros of New York (the colony was named after the duke's title) sought at the outset of the Great Narragansett War to impose the duke's controversial charter on New England.[8] Puritan attitudes based on royal threats, such as this attempt by Andros, continued to reflect the deep-seated fear of military oppression inherited from the time prior to the restored Stuart dynasty under Charles II. These convictions of 1675–1676 created the ironic situation that underfunded and unprepared military resources jeopardized the liberty that the early Americans—and their heirs—sought to defend. U.S. citizens have largely depended on a military model reflecting the attitudes of the king's subjects of America from its earliest settlement, especially during periods of "drawdowns" after military conflict. It has often led to initial military incompetence in conflicts, and the years 1675–1676 were no different.

Fearing another war with Indians (the Narragansetts and their allies) after the defeat of the Pequots in 1637, the Puritans formed the United Colonies of New England as a political and military alliance.[9] This political innovation with military import served to unify, at least in theory, the Puritan colonies' forces into a coherent chain of command. This body met during crises from its inception until after the Great Narragansett War when Andros disbanded it, and the Stuarts revoked the New England colonies' charters in the 1680s.[10] The United Colonies (also called the New England Confederation) achieved a measure of political success given the inadequacy of New England's part-time militia, but it did not always ensure intercolony cooperation. Massachusetts refused to engage its forces in the First Anglo-Dutch War, for example, and the colony squabbled with Connecticut over offensive operations in western Massachusetts and what is now Maine (then part of Massachusetts Bay Colony) during the Great Narragansett War.[11] The United Colonies failed to invest in a more robust military apparatus during times of peace, as its members did not anticipate that the dividends would compensate for this preparation during wartime.

New Englanders continued to maintain a militia system that resembled English trainbands. This required occasional drill in the European fashion on the ubiquitous Yankee town greens. Soon after its founding as a colony, Massachusetts formed the Ancient and Honorable Artillery Company (AHAC) in Boston, which served as a reservoir of military training and knowledge. Though now a nonmilitary service organization, the AHAC still claims members who serve, continuing a heritage as the oldest chartered American military formation.[12] This training served to reinforce rigorous Puritan values and social stratification,[13] as much as it focused on fighting a European enemy in the open field. Although historians criticized this single-mindedness,[14] New Englanders soon determined that the Dutch, French, or Spanish, if allied with nearby native groups, posed the most serious threat to their lives and liberty. As a combined New England army defeated the Pequots, and with the expansion of the colonial population continuing with the Great Migration,[15] the threat of annihilation at the hands of Indians *alone* appeared to recede. Although involved extensively with exclusively Indian-against-Indian encounters, the English feared war with their native neighbors, but not extermination. War scares began to focus on combined Indian-European threats to colonial liberty. The numerous alarms from the end of the Pequot conflict to the beginning of the Great Narragansett War usually maintained an Indian alliance with the Dutch or French as an especially threatening element of violence.[16]

The internecine wars of seventeenth-century Europe continued apace, and previously solid Protestant ties between the English and the Dutch began to deteriorate. The English had even maintained standing English regiments in the Dutch Army for much of the century to fight the Spanish and their allies.[17] Fearing European foes, New Englanders accordingly drilled in linear fashion. They rehearsed volley fire, pike implementation, and the countermarch, the latter of which was the hallmark of European tactics during the early modern era. The training occurred infrequently, however, with the colonies of Connecticut, Massachusetts, and Rhode Island mandating only six training days a year.[18] Although some of the Connecticut colonists were veterans of the

Pequot War and the Thirty Years' War in Europe, six days of training a year was inadequate for any military force, especially one that featured complex training for the integration of musketeers and pikemen. Realizing this short-coming, Connecticut during the first war with the Dutch attempted a general training in Hartford County, under the command of Captain John Mason, the respected military leader from the earlier Pequot War.[19]

With pikemen formed in squares or other linear formations protecting their flanks against cavalry assaults, musketeers maneuvered with the standard countermarch. The first few ranks marched out from the rest of the main body of musketeers and halted within range of the enemy. The first rank would fire in unison, and then pivot to the rear, countermarching through the open-order gaps left vacant by the second and third ranks. The follow-on ranks would march through the first line, and the process would be repeated across the battlefield until the musketeers could close with the enemy, bringing swords (and in Europe, also plug bayonets) to bear.[20] European tactics also featured cavalry as a means to exploit successes achieved by the musketeers' disciplined volleys. Such tactics, first adopted by Maurice of Orange of the Dutch in the early seventeenth century, copied the Roman legion tactics expounded in Vegetius, as the Renaissance had brought his and many other ancient texts to light.[21] These tactics, updated for early modern weaponry, featured movement with the lit matches of the matchlocks, as well as powder bandoleers slung across a musketeer's shoulder and chest. This required training so as not to trigger friendly-fire (literally) incidents. The six training days a year with a half-pound of powder was inadequate, even for veterans, to maintain any meaningful standard of readiness. Pikes also proved useless in the forested terrain against dismounted Indian foes encountered in both the Pequot and Great Narragansett Wars. The colonies would thus have theoretically required more time to retrain pikemen on muskets, requiring nonexistent additional training days.

Compounding a lack of training opportunities was a low supply of powder. The Connecticut General Court attempted to augment this meager supply by increasing its ammunition issue to a half-pound of powder per militiaman per year.[22] The colonists could not easily manufacture powder, although flints and shot were simple enough to fabricate. The Indians mastered flint production and musketball casting techniques as well.[23] Eventually Massachusetts erected a powder mill by the outbreak of the Great Narragansett War and assigned it a guard. Before the mill was erected, New Englanders inefficiently attempted to produce powder in private residences and outbuildings.[24] A half-pound of powder was insufficient to train musketeers to any meaningful level of experience given the amount of powder needed to prime the matchlock muskets and ramrod into the musket barrel (separately) a charge; flint-locks required a similar amount of powder. There were also many training exemptions, such as for the occupations of ministers, magistrates, and other tradesmen deemed necessary for public functions. Massachusetts exempted the entire Harvard College faculty and student body.[25]

The list of those excused from militia training continued to expand in the years after the Pequot War, including those, for example, attending to mills in Middletown, Connecticut, in the late 1650s.[26] Colonial leaders forbade black slaves, indentured servants, and Indians from military exercises, but there were exemptions based on the perceived level of threat. During the First Anglo-Dutch War, Massachusetts allowed to drill "all Scotsman, Negroes, and Indians inhabiting with or servants to the English."[27] Viewing the casualty lists of the other colonies with concern during the Great Narragansett War, the Connecticut Court mandated the training of boys under sixteen years of age.[28] The other New England colonies employed similar training regimens, granted comparable exemptions, and suffered analogous shortcomings.[29]

The colonies created artillery and cavalry arms in the attempt to strengthen militia forces against the combined European-Indian menace, but especially the European threat. Massachusetts constituted a mounted unit in 1652.[30] Six years later, Connecticut followed suit, formally forming a squadron of thirty-seven troopers into the First Connecticut Cavalry, though an informal mounted arm previously had existed in the colony.[31] The Connecticut Court ordered the cavalry, a decade after its constitution, to attend training "in ye respective Townes," but to form into one body for "Generall Traineing," prob-ably once a year.[32] As with the infantry's meager drilling, an annual training event with an entire body of horse was inadequate to achieve mounted profi-ciency by any measure of military effectiveness. All New England colonies by 1675 employed mounted forces of some type and quantity, even in a landscape tangled by swamp and hill, which did not favor the employment of massed cavalry in the European mounted tradition. Multiple accounts also detail that the New England colonists obtained artillery pieces for fortifications.[33]

The colonists' slight upgrade of capabilities focusing on Europeans, how-ever, would prove inadequate to combat native military adaptations over the same period. While the Europeans only marginally increased their meager military resources, the region's American Indians failed to cash in an early version of a "peace dividend," investing instead in adapting to their European adversaries. In the poorly recorded and little understood Pequot-Dutch War of the mid-1630s, the Pequots learned to avoid direct field engagements with a European opponent. The Dutch bested the Pequots in an open-field battle, killing a chief sachem.[34] The Pequots employed these tactics against the English in the Pequot War only two years afterward. Recent battlefield archaeology of the Mystic Fort campaign that destroyed Pequot power in 1637 revealed that the native group would have almost assuredly destroyed the English column that committed the attack during its overextended return march to its ships.[35] This would have been possible had the Pequots maintained the discipline of avoiding standing engagements that they had learned from the Dutch war (the Pequots maintained only sixteen firearms).[36] Enraged from the destruction of over three hundred noncombatants in one of the native group's principal forts, however, the surviving Pequot warriors from the doomed fortress and a nearby bastion massed for an attack on Captain John Mason's beleaguered force and its remaining Indian allies. This single blunder allowed the remaining English and their Indian allies, outnumbered by as many as five to one, to mass dwindling firepower. The action decimated the Pequots as they rashly charged down "Fort Hill" upon the waiting English formation.[37]

During the forty-year interval between Mystic and the Great Narragansett War, the Indians incorporated flintlock muskets into their tactics.[38] These weapons were much better suited than the cumbersome matchlocks to wilderness conditions and to Indians' preference for ambushes and raids. Had the Pequots been armed with flintlocks in 1637, they would have massacred Mason's smaller force. Flintlocks did not require lit matches and thus afforded better concealment for their handlers. The Indians continued intertribal strife during the forty-year period of peace with the English, honing tactical skills. Connecticut's response to ongoing Indian warfare is well preserved in the record, and it usually supported the prerogatives of its chief Indian client, Uncas of the Mohegans, sometimes with military means.[39] Continuing violence between native groups ensured that Indians were much better prepared to fight in 1675 than were their English adversaries. The exception was Connecticut, which employed superior Indian allies.[40]

Indian adaptation did not end with battlefield innovations. After Mystic Fort and the similar destruction of a hilltop fortress of Delaware Indians in what is now Westchester County, New York, during Kieft's War,[41] native northeasterners discontinued the practice of building forts on eminences potential adversaries readily observed. Indians began constructing forts in swamps and thickets in more remote areas. Europeans found it extremely difficult to locate these naturally concealed forts without Indian allies. In the English assault of the Narragansett Fort at Great Swamp in 1675, for instance, a renegade Narragansett led the combined English-allied Indian force to the fort that a dense swamp surrounded. Even with this assistance, the English column only deployed against the fort because the early deep-freeze of the mini–ice age caused the morass to freeze to a depth that supported the movement of troops.[42] Correspondingly, the Indians also abandoned fortresses of a circular design, constructed to thwart arrow-bearing native adversaries from rushing a camp. Having largely adopted firearms by 1675, New England Indians (and Indians along other points of the eastern seaboard) developed small-scale European-style forts with bastions and blockhouses designed to maximize flintlock firepower.[43] These features funneled enemies into areas that the defenders could sweep with musket fire. The Indians within the well-positioned blockhouse in the Narragansett fort at Great Swamp caused most of Connecticut's casualties for the *entire* war. The reconstituted Pequots at the outset of the Great Narragansett War adopted bastions at their Mohantic fort that provided interlocking fields of fire around the fort at the effective range of flintlock muskets.[44] When war came in 1675, Indian preparedness in the realm of tactics and fortifications would further magnify white New Englanders' lack of military readiness during the years 1638–1674.

Always concerned about an oppressive military structure, Massachusetts in 1652 instituted town militia committees that included a civilian town magistrate or deputy. Massachusetts intended the nonmilitary member of the committee to balance military officers' control of the local militias. Over the previous decade, Massachusetts' towns had experienced controversies over elected officers, and the court meant a civilian member to act as a break on potential lawlessness. Further, the committees impressed townsmen to serve as expeditionary soldiers—always a controversial task in New England towns. The English tradition had been to maintain the reliable yeomen at home in trainbands and send the towns' undesirables on offensive operations. This practice carried over to colonial Massachusetts, and including a civilian magistrate on the committee increased the likelihood that militia officers would not impress the politically connected for operations outside of towns. The committees also came to command fortifications in the towns' environs, which hedged against the likelihood of insurrection.[45]

Connecticut followed the example of Massachusetts a year later. In early 1653, during the first war against the Dutch, the Connecticut General Court appointed a group of colony leaders to press men out of "the severall Towns" for a proposed attack on Dutch-controlled Manhattan.[46] Within a month, Connecticut also turned to militia committees to raise soldiers for an expedition ordered by the United Colonies Council. The court ordered the "constables," who pressed soldiers from each town, to take the committee's advice on the pressing of men. Some of the committee members were military officers, such as Captain Mason, who had led the expedition against the Pequots over fifteen years before.[47] The dictates of the New England colonies to assert more civilian control over militia matters attempted to balance military effi-

ciency with the protection of civil society from military interference and potential coups. This watering down of the committees, however, undermined
military readiness by keeping the politically and socially connected at home.
This highlighted the continuation of the Anglo-American liberty dilemma
from the earlier founding era of New England and traditions inherited from
England.

The seventeenth-century New England military system risked serious
damage to property and loss of life, especially at the hands of local native
groups that the English began to underestimate in martial matters. The un-
guarded and unfortified nature of New England towns at the onset of violence
in 1675 testified to the colonists' overconfidence, both in their perceived relationships with local Indians and in their ability to adopt quickly a wartime
posture. The insufficient military apparatus of New England could avoid total
defeat, however, as European large-scale-power-projection capabilities were
deficient in the mid-seventeenth century,[48] and Indians lacked artillery to
reduce major strongholds. When tested by the Dutch on Long Island in 1674,
the colonial military establishment proved sufficient for a part-time army to
hold off a reduced European expeditionary force. The Connecticut militia
prevented the Dutch from seizing English towns on eastern Long Island, and
perhaps, in southwestern Connecticut. The Dutch force of approximately
three hundred marines operated on extended lines of operation from Europe and had to garrison recaptured New York (some local Dutch militia was
also available), as well as fight the New Englanders.[49] If other such invasions
occurred, invaders would have similarly suffered strategic consumption exacerbated by the North American weather of a mini–ice age. Strategic consumption, or the reduction of forces over the course of a campaign due to
various factors, would have weakened already-stretched power-projection
capabilities. Invaders of New England would have lost combat strength when
forced to garrison a supply line through the wilderness to ward off raids;
requisition fodder for its horse-drawn artillery, wagons, and troopers; offset
losses from disease; and replace casualties from battle. It would then have had
to continue to fight the Yankee militia, perhaps with Indian allies, in a weakened state.[50] These tasks would have been exacerbated during this period of
climate turbulence, where there were years without summers, shortening a
campaign season. Tree-ring samples from southeastern Canada to the Chesapeake Bay region indicate that there were no summer temperatures for the
period 1675–1676.[51] The small colonial standing force structure would suffice
to counter this threat, reduced by the intricacies of campaigning and unusu-
ally harsh weather during the mini–ice age.

The Great Narragansett War one year after the Dutch incursion of the Third Anglo-Dutch War, however, proved the ultimate arbiter of New England's lack of a suitable military apparatus. In little more than a year, the bodies of over six hundred colonial soldiers rotted in the fields and forested trails of the region's southern stretches.[52] The Indian coalition had annihilated column upon column of New England militia. The anti-English Indian coalition surrounded Captain Richard Beers's ill-fated troop on a knoll and destroyed it outside of Northfield, Massachusetts; overran Captain Thomas Lathrop's command on the marshy plain broken by a creek thereafter named Bloody Brook near Deerfield in the same colony; pinned Captain Michael Pierce's soldiers to a river and annihilated them near Providence, Rhode Island; and smoked out Captain Samuel Wadsworth's unit from its commanding position atop a hill and wiped out his militia at Sudbury, Massachusetts.[53] All across New England the warriors raised the victorious war-whoop along with the bloody scalps of their victims. Ill suited to the non-European conditions in which they found themselves without suitable Indian allies, colonial troops blundered as much in the deep primordial forests as they had in reckoning the military adaptation of their adversaries.

Defeat, the harshest of teachers, forced the colonists to adapt. Although engaged in ancillary fashion with the wars of the Indians since 1637, white New Englanders had failed to discover the Indian military incorporation of the flintlock into their traditional tactics, which historian Patrick Malone described as an Indian revolution in military affairs.[54] These tactics constituted irregular warfare, featuring ambush, stealth, and speed, which the Indians used to great effect against Beers, Lathrop, Pierce, Wadsworth, and other English commanders. It is a misunderstanding, however, that Indians did not occasionally mass to fight in the open field, as they did at Pierce's defeat and at Great Swamp. The colonists' reference to a "skulking way of war" was hence an inadequate description of native tactics, although contemporaries of the conflict and most historians alike trumpeted the idea. The "skulking way" misinterprets Indian selectivity as the unwillingness to fight pitched battles and implies cowardice. The colonists applied the term out of frustration in their attempt to combat the anti-English coalition.[55] After suffering grievous losses borne of ill-preparedness, the colonists of the other New England colonies followed Connecticut's example, as did Benjamin Church of Plymouth, and began to employ larger numbers of allied Indians, some of whom switched sides.[56] Fighting on the other side was not unusual either for Europeans of the early modern era before the birth of the Enlightenment ideal of a nation state. Connecticut had mainly overcome its similar lack of preparedness by employing more Indians with better tactical wherewithal from the onset of the conflict.[57] The tactically dominant and closely related Mohegans, Pequots, and Western Niantics often constituted more than 40 percent of Connecticut's field forces.[58]

Famed military theorist Carl Von Clausewitz cautioned repeatedly that commanders should maintain numerical superiority, either at the tactical point of decision or through a strategic reserve, in order to hedge against surprise.[59] This argument for mass aimed at ensuring flexibility to counteract uncertainty. In the case of mid-seventeenth-century New England, the colonists failed to anticipate the Indians' incorporation of the flintlock musket into their tactical system, and without the more robust force structure that Clausewitz cautioned was necessary to prepare for the unknown, suffered the bloody consequences. A return to traditional part-time training reduced the capabilities developed during the Pequot War, thereby reducing the flexibility of New England forces to adapt to Indian wherewithal with overwhelming numbers. Even a modicum of retained Pequot War structure would have served as a buffer against the unknown, what Clausewitz later termed the "fog of war."[60] Undesirables manned the ranks of many colonial field forces, and many of the well connected in the non-Connecticut colonies remained at home. As a result, Indians often outnumbered the colonists at the point of attack, the place where numbers matter most, although the colonists outnumbered natives in the aggregate five to one.[61]

In addition to these militia inadequacies, New England's fortresses exemplified the region's unpreparedness and lack of investment in standing military structure. In the case of Saybrook Fort at the mouth of the Connecticut River, it also revealed a developing relationship between public and private military interests that would span U.S. military history. Tracing the ebb and flow of the region's forts according to perceived military threats testifies to a Yankee belief in peace dividends and thrift. For example, Connecticut reconstituted its sole European-style fortress at the mouth of the Connecticut River during times of crisis only to allow its decay in subsequent years. In 1635, the English improved upon Saybrook Fort from an earlier Dutch fort. Its next commander, Lion Gardiner, a Dutch-trained engineer of Thirty Years' War service, hastily improved the fort as the threat of Pequot attack increased. He prepared it enough to ward off a siege from the Pequots and their allies.[62]

When danger threatened again with the Narragansetts in the early 1640s, the court in Hartford obtained an agreement with one of the original proprietors of Saybrook Colony to repair the fort, which had fallen into a state of disrepair after the Pequot War. Connecticut levied a tax to pay Captain George Fenwick for this effort.[63] This established a public-private partnership until Fenwick's death. Fenwick's repairs were not transpiring as quickly as the court had planned, and it inquired about this soon after the original arrangement.[64] Establishing a private-public military relationship that often characterized the colonial era of warmaking in America, the court allowed Fenwick to collect two pence per bushel of grain and six pence per "biskett" for a period of ten years.[65] As every free white male member of New England society was technically a de facto member of the militia (minus the above mentioned exemptions), there was never a clear demarcation between private and public military affairs. Connecticut's funding of a private individual to maintain the most important fortification in the colony, if not New England, highlighted this unique relationship. The public funding of private military ventures, a situation still in existence as recently as Blackwater's involvement in the Iraq War,[66] has been one American attempt to ameliorate the liberty dilemma. The overreliance on private enterprise in warfare has proven inefficient (and sometimes immoral) in U.S. military history, however, and the maintenance of the fort at Saybrook was no exception.

A year later, in the summer of 1645, the colony enlisted Captain Mason and two others to assist Fenwick in erecting further fortifications at the fort site.[67] This foreshadowed the court's charge for Mason to rebuild the fort and command the guns, the ammunition, and the citizens of the town of Saybrook.[68] The original fort then burned to the ground in 1647. Understanding the importance of the fort at the river's mouth and the able navigation of sloops to the Massachusetts border beyond Hartford, the colony rebuilt the fort at the water's edge to improve cannon accuracy. The Indian threat of siege had dissipated since 1637, obviating the need to control the entrance neck to Saybrook Point. The court reinstituted the earlier funding scheme.[69] Fenwick was nominally in charge of the rebuilt fort, now removed to the southeast corner of the point, and the court charged an advance fee to the towns. The colonists had been trading and transporting a lot of the corn ("grain" and "corn" were often used interchangeably) before the payment deadline, and hence Fenwick was not collecting substantial fees to cover his costs and presumably profit from the enterprise.[70] The court authorized an interior dwelling house, probably similar to one in the center of the original fortress, as well, which could theoretically support a permanent staff.[71] Some months after this authorization, the court was again displeased at the lack of progress for both the interior house and the fortifications at the new site.[72]

The outbreak of the First Anglo-Dutch War renewed emphasis on the fort at Saybrook, and Connecticut once again turned to its trusted veteran, Captain Mason. The court charged Mason with fixing and laying six of the "great guns" at the fort and with calling forth the militia and even pressing unwilling inhabitants for the "defence of the said place."[73] Connecticut Colony later reached a more formal relationship with the inhabitants of Saybrook, reflecting a prior agreement, which previously had subsumed the town, fort (including the fort and its weaponry), and uninhabited lands authorized to Fenwick by a former charter. The fort's defenses consisted (at least) of two demiculverns, two sakers, a murderer, two "hammered pieces," forty matchlocks with accoutrements, four carbines, and an unknown quantity of swords. This was no mean complement of weaponry for that time period in New England. The court authorized Fenwick to inhabit the fort for ten years, as long as he provided living arrangements for a gunner and his family.[74] This agreement appeared to end the previous private-public payment regimen in which Connecticut allowed Fenwick to collect taxes on agricultural exports discharged through the mouth of the river. In 1660, the heirs of Fenwick formerly terminated any remaining claim on income or land associated with previous arrangements.[75] Although a later disagreement over this settlement surfaced,[76] this ended a security partnership between a private individual and a colonial governmental body, a practice that would regularly revive, especially during wartime, throughout American history. Around the time of the settlement of Fenwick's estate, the court also granted two influential Connecticut residents three hundred acres of land for their previous service in "incouragemt to ye Artillery," again demonstrating a private-public military partnership.[77]

The state of Saybrook Fort symbolized the lackadaisical nature of upkeep for colonial military apparatuses, which became structural victims of Anglo-American antimilitary attitudes. The fort at Saybrook continually fell into disrepair, and portions required reconstruction in 1676 during the Great Narragansett War, when progress was temporarily made: "the fort house, together, with the fortification, is near finish."[78] That progress was nearly too late, as Andros, with a larger armada, would have seized the fort in July 1675, to enact the Duke of York's charter.[79] Choking off commerce and transportation generally would have disabled Connecticut, perhaps leading to its merger with Royal New York. By 1680, Saybrook Fort had again decayed, as it did in 1689—a process that continued throughout the bastion's history. An inspection in 1693 detailed a state of ill repair:

> Wee find that such are the Ruinous decayes of ye said fort . . . the Gates are all down but one, and one of them gone, both Wood and iron therrof ye hooks of the greate Gate stole; most of ye Iron of one of ye Carriages with all the iron of another, taken away; the Platformes all Rotten and unserviceable; part of ye stone wall yt supports the mount fallen down, most of the mud wall decayed,

with the Palasados agt itt; abuott Four Rodd of plank Wall on the north that never was done, and Lyes open. . . . most of ye great shott pilfered and gone.[80]

Connecticut was less fortunate during the latter wars against Britain, when enemy forces destroyed or circumvented coastal fortifications, including Fort Saybrook, during the War of 1812.[81]

The upkeep of major fortresses at Castle Island in Boston Harbor, and on Burial Hill in the town of Plymouth, followed this same inefficient pattern. Plymouth, the site of initial English settlement in New England, rebuilt its main fortifications in 1632, 1635, 1642, and 1675. Massachusetts Bay Colony renewed its major fortification guarding the mouth of Boston Harbor at Castle Island (original 1633) in 1638, 1644, 1653, 1663, 1673–1674, and several times during the wars with France after 1676. The colonial expenditures to repair these bastions during crises weighed heavily on the towns and men of means in the colonies. The required effort needed to rebuild structures was also significant, as the role of the "Amazonian Dames" signified in the fortifying of Boston Neck, when much of the town's manpower was deployed on campaign. Anglo-American attitudes, even with significant native and European threats lurking in early colonial America, prevented a minimal investment to man key strongholds with a small standing garrison, which would have been more efficient than the episodic larger rebuilding costs associated with repairs.

During the Great Narragansett War, the forts at Saybrook, Plymouth, and Boston remained unscathed, as did most of the colony of Connecticut, but the rest of the region lay devastated. Had the European forces, other than Andros's modest armada, simultaneously invaded the region, these ill-prepared bastions would have been reduced or bypassed, leading to the collapse of Puritan New England. As it was facing Indians alone, New Englanders had seventeen towns smoldering as ruins and another fifty damaged. Individual losses amounted to more than 150,000 English pounds, an enormous sum in 1676.[82] A system of garrison defense, relying on strongpoints, usually survived assaults, but the rest of the afflicted towns remained exposed to destruction.[83] New Englanders' pecuniary ways, though based on powerful cultural precedents, ultimately proved shortsighted. Peace dividends reflect what economists call "hyperbolic discounting," which refers to citizens' weighing immediate gain over long-term efficiencies.[84] Maintaining a minimum of fortification upkeep and garrisons would have saved the colonists money by obviating the costly rebuilding of dilapidated structures. Some improvements, like the addition of brick and stone inner fortifications at the Castle in Boston

Harbor, occurred with improvements in technology,[85] but the vast amount of fortification design, if maintained at a usable level, would have been sufficient throughout the seventeenth century.

The successful emergence of Connecticut from the Great Narragansett War does not serve as a counterpoint for robust standing forces and structures. The main reason for the colony's success was its employment of the Mohegans and Pequots—the best native fighters in New England. Though discussing their fighting ability is beyond the scope of this chapter, they enabled English victory, along with other contributing factors.[86] One such factor was recent combat experience a year prior to the conflict, when Connecticut successfully forayed against Dutch regular forces on Long Island. Experience also mattered in this case, as the only other major English-Indian war in the region to 1675—the Pequot War—occurred exclusively within Connecticut's borders. A surprising number of veterans survived the forty-year interlude to lead the colony during the Great Narragansett War. Connecticut also employed its towns' leading sons in combat roles, a marked difference from Plymouth and Massachusetts, which kept its Puritan heirs safely in the rear. The colony employed more volunteers, who were motivated by the prospect of plunder, than its Puritan counterparts. Connecticut's more compact population density along waterways enabled a more sound defensive posture than Massachusetts Bay's distributed population. With its geographically tenuous position on the New England frontier, Connecticut's towns maintained a trace of fortresses from earlier threats since 1637, and these were more readily rebuilt in 1675–1676. Finally, Connecticut too would have suffered more from a lack of standing troops and fortresses, but the hostile coalition deemed the colony a secondary objective until after the Great Swamp Fight of December 19, 1675, which brought the powerful Narragansetts openly into the fray.[87] Connecticut succeeded where Plymouth and Massachusetts failed due to a combination of factors that superseded its similar Puritan-English cultural, political, and military background. The colony's successes in 1675–1676 represented more the idiosyncrasies of the colony's situation than a lasting model for modern military success at low cost. Connecticut's experience does demonstrate that in certain cases, however, motivated volunteers, who are more representative of the population, when aided by competent native allies, can conduct successful operations with positive strategic outcomes.

It took three hundred years for Americans to jettison an amateur military mindset based on suspicion and perceived cost savings. In 1950, until National Security Council Memorandum 68 signaled for the first time a major commitment to a permanent professional peacetime force to face down an apparent worldwide Communist threat, the United States' underfunded and undersupplied part-time militia system, grounded in deeply held Anglo-American values and experiences, failed to prevent initial military fiascos in nearly every conflict from America's initial English settlement until Vietnam.[88] In the case of seventeenth-century New England, the militia system required expansion and fiscal attention before it met with battlefield success in 1676, after the lean military years between the Pequot War and the Great Narragansett War. Until the fall of Quebec a century later, with the serious projection of British military power of James Wolfe's fleet during the French and Indian War (Seven Years' War in Europe),[89] a system relying on part-time colonial militias failed to counter the French and their Indian allies during the period 1689–1763. Only France's commitment of a fleet and ground forces at Yorktown in 1781 sealed a decisive outcome for the colonists in the next war, which witnessed General George Washington relying heavily on militia units that could not alone achieve victory.[90] A hastily concocted force to fight Indians in the old Northwest in 1791 met with singular destruction and caused a reevaluation of American forces that led eventually to victory in 1794.[91] British disinterest during the War of 1812 allowed the fledgling United States to claim victory despite military shortcomings, while the eastern successes of the Confederacy in 1861–1863 resulted from an enervated federal standing force.[92] The Spanish-American War, beginning in 1898, again demonstrated the weakness of an underfunded and -resourced U.S. military, particularly its land component. Both World Wars began poorly for U.S. forces in terms of casualties and the inability to plan higher-level operations. The industrialization and mass production of war, although it had its beginnings with the U.S. Civil War, had rendered the amateur forces and force structure of the U.S. military obsolete by 1950. Only after the Korean War were U.S. forces prepared to fight initial campaigns with some level of competency, and this too did not lead to victory in Vietnam or Somalia, and seemingly not in Afghanistan (though arguably the defeat of ISIS may eventually lead to a U.S.-friendly Iraqi state). These failures were often partially the result of the continued hollowing of professional forces during interwar periods.[93]

As the current drawdown signifies, however, the distaste for large standing forces remains a vestige from the early colonial era. Americans' continued belief in the viability of the part-time citizen soldier, rooted in the early colonial militia and its English antecedents, is a risky model to maintain efficient capabilities. The sparsely trained, pressed field forces of the Puritan colonies and apostate Rhode Island stood little chance without Indian allies against an adaptable, artful enemy—the very enemy the modern U.S. Army should anticipate. As part-time militia, it was difficult enough for New Englanders to maintain an approximation of common European-style tactical proficiency, let alone train for other martial possibilities such as irregular warfare.

Although the Indian coalition's power was broken forever by 1676, the traditional New England militia system did not succeed. Rather, colonial success rested on the effectiveness of Connecticut's Indian-supported offensive operations, and those of the other colonies that eventually copied it. The United States has relied on three different kinds of force structure since the emergence of American military power in the first third of the seventeenth century. The first was the seventeenth-century underfunded military apparatus, which best reflects traditional Anglo-American values and experiences, and encompasses most years in American military history. If this system were to make its return today, Americans would have to become comfortable with the risk inherent in relying on part-time soldiers, which incurred full-time slaughter in 1675. The second, during the periods of 1917, 1941–1942, 1950, and 1991–present, was a reliance on a middle-ground system, where the United States depended upon a relatively small but more robust standing force structure than the traditional militia system, which Americans increased through cadre and funding during times of crisis. This model, although presently less successful, reflects Connecticut's employment during 1675–1676 of a small professional force reliant on competent native support and frequent combat experience. The third trend is the 1863–65, 1918, 1943–45, and post–WWII (1951–1991) model of a relatively well-funded and large standing U.S. military apparatus, which usually gained strategic success, winning battles and campaigns to do so. All of these military systems maintained an element of risk to American values and lives, however, as there is neither a panacea for potential military challenges in peace nor a silver bullet for victory in war.

NOTES

1 Benjamin Tompson, *New England Crisis; or, A Brief Narrative of New England's Lamentable Estate* (Boston: John Foster, 1676), 30–31, courtesy Ashley Bissonnette, Mashantucket Pequot Museum and Research Center, Foxwoods, CT.

2 William Hubbard, *History of the Indian Wars in New England* (Boston: John Foster, 1677), 15. Jill Lepore references Hubbard's quotation for her acclaimed *Name of War: King Philip's War and the Origins of American Identity* (New York: Knopf, 1998), describing the influence of the conflict on American memory and attitudes, especially as they relate to American Indians.

3 Jason W. Warren, *Connecticut Unscathed: Victory in the Great Narragansett War, 1675–1676* (Norman: University of Oklahoma Press, 2014), demonstrates how the Great Narragansett War is a more appropriate naming convention for the conflict than the traditional "King Philip's War."

4 Daniel R. Mandell, *King Philip's War* (Baltimore, MD: Johns Hopkins University Press, 2010), 137, considers the war's effect on the economy and Warren, 4, describes the war as America's second-bloodiest conflict.

5 Warren, 173–82.

6 Wayne E. Lee, *Barbarians and Brothers: Anglo-American Warfare, 1500–1865* (Oxford: Oxford University Press, 2011), 118, references Anglo-Americans' fears of standing armies after Cromwell's "military rule." The Connecticut governor's son, Fitz-John Winthrop, prepared to return to fight in 1658 for Charles II. Warren, 102.

7 Kyle F. Zelner, *A Rabble in Arms: Massachusetts Towns and Militiamen during King Philip's War* (New York: New York University Press, 2009), 22, 28–29, 42 for Charles I's subjects' military fears pre-Cromwell.

8 J. H. Trumbull, ed., *Public Records of the Colony of Connecticut*, vol. 2. (Hartford, CT: Brown & Parsons, 1850–1890), 334–35; hereafter referred to as PRCC.

9 See Mandell, 18, for the formation of the United Colonies.

10 Mandell, 143.

11 PRCC, 260; Warren, 152.

12 George M. Bodge, *Soldiers in King Philip's War* (Boston: 1906, reprint 3rd ed., Baltimore, MD: Genealogical Publishing, 1967), 472; www.ahac.us.com, accessed 28 March 2015.

13 Zelner, 28–29, 157; John Shy, *A People Numerous and Armed: Reflections on the Military Struggle for Independence* (Ann Arbor: University of Michigan Press, rev. ed., 1990), 2.

14 Warren, 12–13.

15 Mandell, 11.

16 See for instance PRCC, 240, 242, 244.

17 Warren, 99–100.

18 PRCC, 97, and in Connecticut's case even during a time of alarm; Zelner, 30, for Massachusetts; J. R. Bartlett, ed., *Records of the Colony of Rhode Island and Providence Plantations*, vol. 2 (New York: Adamant Media, 2005), hereafter RCRPP, 114, 568.

19 PRCC, 246.

20 Warren, 164.

21 John Childs, *Warfare in the Seventeenth Century*, Smithsonian History of Warfare, series ed. John Keegan (Washington, DC: Smithsonian Books, 2001), 47–48.

22 PRCC, 165.

23 Kevin McBride, "Fort Mohantic, Connecticut: The Pequot in King Philip's War," in *Native Forts of the Long Island Sound Area*, ed. Gaynell Stone (New York, Sheridan, 2006), 331.

24 Nataniel B. Shurtleff, ed. *Records of the Governor and Company of the Massachusetts Bay in New England, Printed by Order of the Legislature* (Boston: William White, 1853–1854), 51.

25 Zelner, 32.

26 PRCC, 333.

27 As quoted in Zelner, 32.

28 PRCC, 451–52.

29 Plymouth was still electing officers for field missions, Warren 138–39, as was Rhode Island, RCRPP, 51–53, 114, 171–72, 539.

30 Zelner, 34.

31 PRCC, 299; Bodge, 466.

32 PRCC, 381.

33 PRCC, 104, 138, 155–56, 237–38, 267, 344, for Connecticut; for Plymouth, Robert Arthur, "Coast Forts of Colonial Massachusetts, *Coastal Artillery Journal* 58, no. 2 (23 February 1923): 103, 105–6; for Massachusetts, ibid., 108–13; for Rhode Island, RCRPP, 197, 536–

34 McBride, "Fort Island: Conflict and Trade in Long Island Sound" in *Native Forts*, 260–61, and conversation with author.

35 I conducted a terrain analysis with McBride and his research team covering a couple of miles of the ground that the English and their remaining Indian allies traversed, and concluded that the narrow trail surrounded by wood and hillocks would have disadvantaged the English. The colonists would have been unable to form easily, especially when low on ammunition and having to carry the wounded, and the Pequots could have picked off many of the English with accurate arrow fire to exposed arms, legs, and faces, eventually disabling and overwhelming the column in close combat, before the English reached the rendezvous point with the sloops.

36 John Mason, *Brief History of the Pequot War*, Thomas Prince, ed. (Boston, MA: Kneeland & Green, 1736).

37 See McBride's associated chapter.

38 Patrick M. Malone, *Skulking Way of War: Technology and Tactics among the New England Indians* (Baltimore, MD: Johns Hopkins University Press, 1991), 126.

39 For Connecticut's support of Uncas see Michael Oberg, *Uncas, First of the Mohegans* (Ithaca, NY: Cornell University Press, 2003). For record of conflict see PRCC, 94, 106, 128, 138, 294, 295, 299, 302–6, 346, 371.

40 For discussion, see Warren, chapter 6.

41 John W. De Forest, *History of the Indians of Connecticut from the Earliest Known Period to 1850* (Hartford, CT: Wm. Jas. Hamersley, 1851), 207–8.

42 Warren, 165; for mini-ice age in New England see Geoffrey Parker, *Global Crisis: War, Climate Change, and Catastrophe in the Seventeenth Century* (New Haven, CT: Yale University Press, 2013), 445–83.

43 McBride, "Fort Mohantic," 322–36; Warren, 135–36 for Narragansett forts; Wayne Lee, *Empires and Indigenes* (New York: New York University Press, 2011), 62–65, for discussion of native fortress adaptations. Lee, 63–64, describes how the Squakheags (near present-day Northfield, Massachusetts) transformed their fortress to European design to ward off Iroquois with European weapons, in similar manner to the Pequots, Narragansetts, and Delaware, further to the south.

44 Warren, 167; McBride, "Fort Mohantic," 322–27.

45 Zelner, 35–39.

46 PRCC, 241.

47 PRCC, 242–43.

48 Warren, 145–47.

49 Warren, 47.

50 Warren, 46.

51 Parker, 763 n.30 on how tree rings from Quebec to the Chesapeake demonstrate that there were essentially no summer temperatures for this period.

52 Warren, 4.

53 Warren, 140–41.

54 Malone, 117.

55 For "cutting off way of war" see Lee, 151–59; for massing to fight at Pierce's fight and Great Swamp, see Warren, 141, 165.

56 Mandell, 115–17.

57 Warren, 172–82.

58 Warren, 156–57.

59 Carl Von Clausewitz, *On War*, ed. and trans. Michael Howard and Peter Paret (New York: Knopf, 1993), 228–32, 247–49.

60 Clausewitz, 161.

61 Warren, 39.

62 Warren, 21.

63 PRCC, 95.

64 PRCC, 113.

65 PRCC, 119.

66 Dexter Filkins, *The Forever War* (New York: Vintage, 2008), 220, 230–31.

67 PRCC, 128.

68 PRCC, 155–56.

69 PRCC, 156.

70 PRCC, 170.

71 PRCC, 187.

72 PRCC, 200.

73 PRCC, 237–38.

74 PRCC, 267–69.

75 PRCC, 329.

76 PRCC, 345.

77 PRCC, 344.

78 As quoted, no author named, "Coast Forts in Colonial Connecticut," *Coastal Artillery Journal* 69, no. 3 (Sept. 1928): 239.

79 "Coast Forts in Colonial Connecticut," 239.

80 "Coast Forts in Colonial Connecticut," 240.

81 Christopher Ward, *The War of the Revolution*, ed. John R. Alden, vols. 1–2 (New York: Macmillan, 1952), 492–95, 626–28; "Coast Forts in Colonial Connecticut,"

243; 1812 artifacts associated with Pequot War excavation, National Park Service American Battlefield Protection Program Site Identification and Documentation: Siege and Battle of Saybrook Fort; Technical Report: (GA-2255-12-011), McBride, David Naumec, Bissonnette, Noah Fellman, Laurie Pasteryak, et al., Mashantucket Pequot Museum and Research Center, 1 January 2015.

82 Warren, 4–5.

83 Warren, 98–99.

84 David I. Laibson, "Hyperbolic Discount Functions, Undersavings, and Savings Policy National," NBER Working Paper Series, Working Paper 5635, Bureau of Economic Research (Cambridge, MA: June 1996); also on impulse control see G. W. Ainslie, "Impulse Control in Pigeons," *Journal of the Experimental Analysis of Behavior* 21, no. 3 (May 1974): 485–89.

85 Brick could better absorb accidental explosions. Arthur, "Coast Forts of Colonial Massachusetts," 112–13.

86 Warren, 154–56.

87 Warren, 60, 64–65.

88 Charles E. Heller and William A. Stofft, eds., *America's First Battle's, 1776–1965* (Lawrence: University of Kansas Press, 1986), discusses this phenomenon. Contributors do not always consider first battles as defeats, but indicate second battles were sometimes losses due to overconfidence from initial success.

89 Fred Anderson, *The War That Made America: A Short History of the French and Indian War* (New York: Penguin Books, 2006), 200.

90 David H. Fischer, *Washington's Crossing* (Oxford: Oxford University Press, 2004), 275, 346–62.

91 Colin G. Conway *Victory with No Name: The Native American Defeat of the First American Army* (Oxford: Oxford University Press, 2014).

92 See associated chapters in this volume.

93 Jason W. Warren, "Insights from the Army's Drawdowns," Special Commentary, *U.S. Army War College Quarterly, Parameters* 44, no. 2 (Summer 2014).

3

Surprisingly Professional

Trajectories in Army Officer Corps Drawdowns, 1783–1848

SAMUEL WATSON

Congress "reduced" (the contemporary term) the early national Army in 1783, 1796, 1802, 1815, and 1821—roughly once every decade, even if we discount the disbandment of the stillborn Federalist armies in 1800. Although the absolute numbers involved—like the size of the Army—were minuscule by today's standards, the proportions were at least equal (in 1796, 1802, and 1821) to, and sometimes far greater (in 1783 and 1815) than, those in the current, post-Vietnam, or post–Cold War drawdowns. These frequent drawdowns suggest great instability in the land forces of the early republic, but the national standing Army sustained a surprising degree of stability in its core officer cadre during this era, through the war with Mexico until the great national mobilization of the Civil War. Indeed, the officer corps of the national standing Army gradually became one of the most stable institutions of the early republic, and the government agency with the greatest autonomy from partisan influence, especially after the stabilization of international relations and Army missions and force structure after 1821.[1]

These assertions probably come as a surprise to most students of American military history, since most of the nonspecialist scholarship—and most of the specialized scholarship for the Federalist and Jeffersonian periods—maintains otherwise. So it is important to set out terms and caveats. By "national standing Army" I mean the small force, effectively permanent after the Jeffersonian Republicans accepted its existence in 1796, that served primarily in the West before 1812 and would serve on the borders and frontiers thereafter.[2] I will briefly address the forces raised for temporary service during crises, but these were almost universally regarded as temporary: neither their officers nor their political sponsors, nor policymakers of either party (with the possible exception of a few authoritarian Federalists), intended or expected these forces to be retained after the crises that impelled their creation had passed. Thus, one can speak of a tale of two forces, not making the usual distinction between regulars and citizen-soldier militia or volunteers but one between the standing Army—composed of regulars, whom contemporary policymakers did not regard or treat as citizen-soldiers—and temporary forces, whether volunteers, militia, or expansions of the regular component. This is also a distinction between federal and state control over officer accessions and retention. Regular officers were appointed and confirmed entirely by federal officials, although the executive branch did select nominees with regional and sectional balances in mind, and sought recommendations from men of reputation and influence in localities throughout the nation.

By "core officer cadre" I mean field-grade and senior company-grade officers: captains, majors, and colonels. Reductions in the enlisted force occasioned little debate among national policymakers, of either party, during this era: they were either citizen-soldiers, who expected, and were expected, to go home once an emergency ended, or regulars, regarded as something akin to mercenaries by Americans across the political spectrum. Within the standing Army, career-minded lieutenants enjoyed substantial security, for there were plenty of lieutenants (and not a few captains) who resigned for individual reasons or were already returning to civilian life when each reduction began. Prior to the War of 1812, the average officer served about five years. Only when officers reached the grade of captain, which usually took five to ten years, did they really become invested in the Army as a career. Thus the routine turnover in junior officers, a dimension of the more general flux in life courses and career patterns in the early American republic, actually ameliorated the impact of drawdowns: the instability of peacetime officer careers, though certainly an obstacle to developing professional expertise and institutional capability, served to calm the individual and political passions that a drawdown spurs today. Officers who sought military careers were usually able to pursue them, with the constraint that promotion past captain often took more than a decade in peacetime.[3]

This essay is a comparative one, spanning nearly a quarter of the nation's history. Fortunately for both author and reader, several of the drawdowns of the period are easily addressed, so the essay will focus on the reductions in 1802, 1815, and 1821. In 1783, George Washington proposed retaining five of the Continental Army's eighty-six regiments, but the Confederation was hardly able or willing to do so, especially after an exhausting generation of protest, tension, and war.[4] Essentially *everyone* was sent home: the seven hundred soldiers (an infantry regiment and two artillery companies) who remained to guard military posts and supplies were so small a fraction of the Continental Army, or of the fledgling nation's military potential, that attempting to parse why a handful of specific officers were retained is meaningless in political, and indeed institutional, terms. There does not appear to have been any concerted effort to select specific officers for retention, and doing so would not have meant much for the nation's military capability, in comparison to the reservoir of experience among the men who returned home.[5]

Since this essay addresses so many reductions, it cannot explore the social, political, and economic consequences of America's early drawdowns, such as the role veterans played in both rebellion and constitutional formation during the 1780s. These important stories have been told elsewhere.[6] Here I can only suggest the broad context for the drawdowns, and some specifics about the processes and criteria employed and their outcomes, with the focus on those who hoped to make the Army a career. Given the poor conditions of enlisted service, the lack of opportunity for enlisted soldiers to advance, and the disdain for long-term enlisted service shared even among enlisted soldiers, a career in the Army meant service as an officer—and only officers had the connections to secure or dispute retention during reductions.

In addition to social and cultural attitudes, a second context was international, and together these shaped the political and economic environment in which drawdowns took place. The fledgling nation faced an unstable security situation—a postcolonial, or semicolonial, relationship with overbearing European powers during the French Revolutionary and Napoleonic wars, which pushed national security policy to the forefront of politics and partisan divisions. As the Federalists leaned toward accommodation with Britain, and the Republicans opposed doing so, national security policy became highly politicized. Americans shared a revolutionary ideology that stressed the threat of concentrated power, which meant widespread suspicion of standing armies, no matter how small. And Federalist efforts to concentrate power—to develop "energy in the executive," largely for national security purposes, much like that in the British fiscal-military state—spurred Republican fears of authoritarianism. Finally, Republicans, and ultimately most Americans, resisted the imposition of taxes sufficient to create a substantial national security establishment or fiscal-military state. As a result, both the size and the composition of the national Army and its officer corps were partisan questions.[7]

Nevertheless, within the constraints of a small standing force, the executive branch, and indeed the Army officer corps itself, secured a surprising autonomy in selecting officers for retention during reductions in force. In 1783 and 1796, the numbers involved were small enough that this meant little, and the disbandment of the Federalist armies in 1800 had little direct effect on the regular component, whose personnel had remained distinct from the much larger forces legislated, but only partially recruited and officered, by the Federalists for the crisis with France. In 1802 Thomas Jefferson proceeded almost unilaterally, probably with some advice from Secretary of War Henry

Dearborn, but without significant input from the Army's only general, James Wilkinson, or veteran field-grade officers. In 1815 and 1821, Presidents Madison and Monroe permitted the Army's senior leaders remarkable autonomy in shaping the officer corps, and they did so through an organized process, with explicit criteria for officer assessment. Comparing the 1815 and 1821 reductions demonstrates a shift in the way the Army attempted to address some persistent dilemmas, in officer qualifications, officer career persistence and stability, institutional accountability and capability, and ultimately civil-military relations. These informal but successful shifts in policy prefigured and underlay the professional development I demonstrate in my books *Jackson's Sword* and *Peacekeepers and Conquerors*.

Even more surprisingly, given the fierce partisan divisions of the time, neither partisan nor sectional considerations dominated the reductions. In 1796, every officer had been appointed by a Federalist president and confirmed by a Federalist, or at least pro-administration, Senate. Yet despite Federalist strength in New England—or perhaps because of growing Republican strength in the South—the proportion of officers from the former region numbered only about 70 percent of that region's share of the nation's free population, while the proportion from the South was equal to its population share. The disproportion came in officers from the mid-Atlantic states, located close to the capital and still concerned to protect their western frontiers.[8] Nor has any evidence been found that the emerging Republican Party in Congress sought the dismissal of officers who may have held more extreme Federalist attitudes in 1796: such views only came to the fore during the crisis over French aggression in 1798 and 1799. The debate over Jay's treaty with Britain proved far more rancorous and partisan than that over the reduction.

Although Jefferson feared rampant Federalism in the officer corps before he took office, and sought assessments of each officer's political views from his advisers, the evidence of his choices demonstrates that anti-Federalism was not his principal criterion for retention or disbandment in 1802. And by 1815 and 1821, most officers had been appointed and confirmed by Republicans, and the few remaining Federalists were older veterans, tested by long service, who posed no threat to military subordination to the government. Similarly, by 1815 the officer corps, which came largely from the Northeast during the 1780s and 1790s, had become balanced between northern and southern men. President Madison did request the retention of field-grade officers from west of the Appalachians, but the generals who recommended officers for retention had already recognized that that was desirable, and had no difficulty finding qualified westerners like Zachary Taylor.[9]

The first drawdown that really distinguished among career officers, or those in a position to aspire to military careers, came in 1802. To summarize, in 1783 Congress disbanded virtually the entire Army; in 1796 it disbanded only 34 out of about 220 officers (15 percent)—virtually all of them captains and lieutenants;[10] and in 1800 it disbanded all of the Federalist forces raised since 1798. In the standing Army, stationed almost entirely on the western frontier, the four "sublegions" created in 1792 became four infantry regiments in 1796 and remained so until 1802. (Throughout the era of this essay, statutes usually authorized an infantry regiment about thirty-three officers: a colonel, a lieutenant colonel, a major, ten captains, ten first lieutenants, and ten second lieutenants. Artillery regiments often had more lieutenants, but eight rather than ten companies.) Given these scales, and general contemporary agreement that peace made them reasonable, historians have written little about the reductions before 1802. In contrast, the 1802 drawdown has been the most debated, or perhaps misunderstood, of the early national reductions in force, largely because of the ideologically charged language often employed by President Jefferson, and by many historians who have studied his policies. In recent years, Jeffersonian scholars have tended to stress the president's calculated and often effective use of national power, rather than his ideological antipathy toward it. In response to both patterns, other historians, myself included, have criticized the many disparities between ends and means in Jeffersonian national security policy.[11]

The Republicans had some reason to be concerned about Federalist partisanship in the nation's standing Army. On February 4, 1801, President Adams nominated eighty-seven men to vacancies in the Army's permanent regiments, a number nearly one-third their total complement. (The lame-duck Senate debated but confirmed them before Jefferson's inauguration.) Forty-four of these men had served in the forces established for the crisis with France, and fourteen of the fifteen whose political allegiances appear to be known (according to a list made for President Jefferson that July) considered themselves Federalists. Though there was no immediate Republican hue and cry like that over Adams's judicial appointments, this infusion of Federalists doubtless encouraged Republicans to view the old frontier army more as they had the temporary Federalist armies. In the opinion of historian Theodore Crackel, "events [between 1798 and his inauguration] convinced [Jefferson] that the existing army would constitute an illegitimate opposition to his regime." Yet the frontier army had not initiated any of those events (the Alien and Sedition Acts, for example), and played little role in the intimidation and repression that did occur. Indeed, Jefferson accepted the need for a standing force to patrol the frontiers, which he expected to move westward in accordance with his overarching vision of a self-replicating agrarian republic. Thus, despite the participation of some regular companies in the suppression of Fries's Rebellion (in Pennsylvania in 1799), "for Jefferson and the more moderate [i.e., majority] Republicans," Crackel observes, "the events of 1798–1800 demonstrated not the necessity of dissolving the army, but the necessity of creating a Republican army." Since Republicans believed that they embodied republicanism, in contrast with what they considered Federalist aristocracy, this conclusion could have led to wholesale dismissals (then referred to as "removals"), as it did in the civil service.[12]

According to Crackel (the leading historian of the Army during the Jeffersonian era), the new administration followed three paths to reach its goal, a "chaste Republican reformation":[13] discharging some Federalist officers during the reduction of the standing Army in 1802, choosing only Republicans or those known to be politically neutral for new commissions, and courting moderate Federalists and officers without strong political beliefs in order to redirect their sympathies. Ultimately, the three-fold expansion of the officer corps in 1808 made Republicans the majority within the Army, though military preparedness against British aggression was the primary motive for the build-up that year. William Skelton has questioned Crackel's thesis of political intent as applied to the reduction of 1802 and the role of West Point in new officer commissions, but it does seem that political considerations were significant, though less decisive than Crackel suggests. The Military Peace Establishment Act of 1802 reduced the standing force to one artillery and two infantry regiments, with a single brigadier general—James Wilkinson—at its head. Although the actual strength of the Army as a whole decreased by only three hundred men (to a total of about thirty-three hundred), eighty-eight officers—just over a third of the total—were discharged. Adams's lame-duck appointees were not discharged *en masse*, despite the coincidence of numbers involved.[14]

After Congress passed a law restructuring the Army and its officer corps, executive branch officials selected, or did not select (in effect dismissing), specific officers for retention. (Since these men were not being commissioned or promoted, their retention did not require senatorial confirmation, although the retention of specific individuals in specific positions sometimes aroused controversy, usually from rival officers rather than Congress.) Jefferson ultimately prioritized military ability as a criterion for retention, and his administration retained numerous officers known for Federalist opinions. In 1801 the War Department compiled a list of all 258 serving officers (not including surgeons, surgeons' mates, and other personnel without command authority), on which someone, probably Jefferson's private secretary, Captain

Meriwether Lewis, noted the perceived military ability, and much less often the political allegiances, of 230. Lewis's list of officers' political leanings is actually quite incomplete, or perhaps tentative. Although virtually every officer in the Army had been appointed by a Federalist president, only nine officers out of the 230, 4 percent of the officer corps, were considered "opposed most violently to the Administration, and still active in its vilification," or "strong Federalists," as Crackel terms them. Only forty-eight, less than a quarter, were considered Federalists of any sort, though Crackel includes those "opposed to the Administration more decisively" among his "moderate Federalists." The vast majority (171 of 230, or indeed 197 of 256, nearly 75 or 80 percent) were politically neutral, were apathetic, or had not expressed sufficient partisanship for their affinities to be known. The numbers make it clear that the officer corps was not Republican—hardly surprising given Republican orientation toward the states and the corresponding aversion to central institutions, and that Federalist administrations had appointed the officer corps throughout the 1790s—but they present no evidence that the officer corps as a body was ardently Federalist, much less a threat to the Republicans. This was hardly the violently partisan bastion of Federalist aristocracy and authoritarianism, the potential threat to American democracy, sometimes intimated by Jeffersonian scholars who focus on the president's rhetoric.[15]

In Crackel's opinion, "the Military Peace Establishment Act of 1802 was not [primarily] intended to reduce the Army [i.e., for budgetary reasons]; rather, it provided the administration with a means to accomplish a political catharsis of the military establishment." Crackel maintains that "officers considered 'unworthy' were forced out with little reference to other measures," but that "among those who were dismissed despite being found militarily qualified, political affiliation was clearly an important factor." The sample size is too small to say this with certainty, but it is hard to doubt that there was some politicization; there is little reason to suspect otherwise given the strictures of Republican rhetoric and ideology and the intense experience of partisan tension between 1798 and 1800. Nevertheless, the proportion of Federalist and neutral or apathetic officers dismissed was virtually equal, at 28–29 percent (14 of 48 vs. 9 of 32). That of Republican partisans was significantly lower, but based on much smaller numbers. The largest proportion of officers discharged (63 of 139, or 45 percent) came from among those whose politics were unknown, usually because they were young lieutenants with little time in grade. These men comprised three-fifths of the total list and nearly three-quarters of those deemed professionally (or perhaps morally or ethically) unworthy. One-third of the officers rated "second class, respectable as Officers," were discharged, suggesting that the Republican desire for fiscal economy had some influence. On the other hand, the stated standard of evaluation was respectability as an officer—not partisanship, or even republicanism in the broader ideological sense.[16]

Excepting Crackel's emphasis on the "chaste republican reformation," all commentators agree that military merit was the most influential criterion for retention. The very fact that the administration did not attempt to assess the political loyalties of 165 of the 256 officers suggests limits to its partisanship, though most such officers were very junior, and letters recommending them for commissions may have been destroyed in the fire in the War Department offices at the end of 1800. Partisanship played a surprisingly small role given the tensions of the preceding decade. Only fourteen of the forty-eight officers (30 percent) listed as confirmed Federalists were discharged, versus seventy-two (42 percent) of those known to be neutral or whose politics were not known. Six of the dismissed Federalists had also been rated unworthy in terms of military proficiency, so only eight officers out of 256 may be said to have been disbanded on primarily partisan grounds. On the other hand, two men "opposed to the Administration most violently . . . and still active in its vilification" were actually promoted. The most senior Republican officer, a major, was first considered and rejected for promotion to a staff post—which would certainly have been a political move—and then dismissed because he was considered morally or militarily "unworthy," although he was the only one of eleven confirmed Republicans so rated. Overall, 85 percent (thirty-five of forty-one) of those deemed "unworthy of the commissions they bear" were discharged, and another resigned, although one was promoted to lieutenant colonel through the operation of the seniority principle. In contrast, the administration dismissed only seven (12 percent) of the fifty-eight officers rated "1st Class, as esteemed from a superiority of genius & Military proficiency." These ratings and proportions suggest that the officer corps of 1801 was less partisan than the Republicans feared, though less able than they wished.[17]

Jefferson's evaluation process left much to be desired, despite a much less politicized outcome than might have been expected given Republican rhetoric during the crisis between 1798 and 1800, or his extensive dismissal of civilian officials on partisan grounds.[18] The assessments of officers' military merit were made by a captain, a company-grade officer with only six years in the Army when he compiled the list. Lewis's biographers have sometimes argued that he had extensive knowledge of his peers from his service as a paymaster, but those short, intermittent interactions could indicate little about an officer's military expertise. William Skelton has suggested that James Wilkinson worked with Lewis to arrive at the evaluations, a reasonable hypothesis to explain the assessments of politics as well as merit, but Jefferson's correspondence contains no evidence that he consulted the general. Perhaps Secretary of War Dearborn did so, but Jefferson's papers contain no correspondence from the secretary on the issue, after Dearborn's initial proposal for reducing the structure of the standing force.[19]

Jefferson could hardly trust Wilkinson for unbiased advice, for the general had worked closely with Alexander Hamilton on military issues amid the partisan tensions between 1798 and 1800. (The same considerations would have applied to any contact between Dearborn and Wilkinson. Indeed, the general was moving about the west at the time, and his official letterbooks contain no comment on the reduction.)[20] Nor, apart from relying on his Virginia protégé and private secretary, could Jefferson bypass the general to seek the opinions of Wilkinson's subordinates. Nor did Dearborn, a Revolutionary War veteran, have any personal knowledge of the vast majority of officers. Thus the president of the United States had to rely on a junior officer, with less than a decade's service, for advice on the professional qualifications of the Army officer corps. Lewis had no specific professional qualifications for judging his peers (and his superiors), and he did not explain whatever criteria he may have employed, or how individuals met them. Since he had neither seen combat nor been charged with inspecting unit drill, he probably had to rely on reputations stated to him in offhand ways in casual garrison talk.

Following the reduction, Jefferson appointed twenty new officers at the newly created rank of ensign, the lowest in the commissioned hierarchy. The Republicans wanted to remake the officer corps, but not at the cost of an expensive increase in the officer corps that would apply the Federalist precedent of overtly partisan appointments (in the forces authorized in 1798 and 1799) to the national standing Army. Similarly, the Republican leadership chose not to seek a loyal military command structure by promoting enlisted men or appointing new officers (particularly senior ones) *en masse* from civilian life. Thus, at the end of 1802, nearly three-quarters of the officer corps were still men who had been appointed by Federalist administrations.[21] By maintaining the status quo in officer accessioning, the Republicans reaffirmed the social and cultural criteria of gentility, which most Republican leaders (and especially the Virginians) shared with the Federalists, along with the institutional principle of promotion by internal seniority, which provided certainty for officers and effectively excluded men who had not committed themselves to an extensive period of military service. Regular officers supported this preference in promotion opportunities as a key guarantee of occupational autonomy throughout most of the century.

Besides discharging regimental officers, the act eliminated several senior staff posts created in 1798 and held by Federalists. It was here that the Republicans truly damaged the Army's ability to perform the missions assigned to it. Despite the Army's repeated problems supplying the expeditions of the 1790s, the Military Peace Establishment Act cut the positions of quartermaster general, deputy quartermaster general, and the deputy inspectors, whose duties were to enhance efficiency and accountability in the Army's supply system. Considering staff officers' placement prone to political if not personal corruption, believing that Secretary of War Dearborn could handle the Army's administration almost single-handedly, and fearful of alienating the officer corps should seniority be ignored, the administration destroyed the staff instead. During the Jeffersonian era, Army logistics would largely be handled by private businessmen, who had to bid low to win least-cost contracts. They often cut corners in order to make profits, or delivered insufficient supplies late.[22]

The transportation and distribution of supplies became an entirely civilian matter left to frequently unreliable contractors subject neither to military discipline nor to financial bonds for good behavior. The quartermaster general's duties were divided among the secretary of war and three civilian agents, and the regimental quartermasters were returned to their line assignments and replaced by civilians. Unit commanders were permitted to make purchases in case of deficiencies, and sometimes did so with their own money, but the administration's economy drive discouraged them from doing so. This proved a significant change: not only was the original provision of supplies contracted out; so was their transportation and distribution to the troops in garrison and field. Congress abolished the inspectorate responsible for pursuing accountability; the adjutant and inspector general served primarily as an assistant to the secretary of war in Washington. The inadequacy of the staff, and especially the lack of quartermaster services, damaged the Army severely when it was concentrated in large formations, first at Terre aux Boeufs in 1809, when hundreds of soldiers died of disease, and then through much of the War of 1812, when inadequate supplies routinely delayed offensives and compelled retreats. Logistical expertise and accountability both suffered without a staff formally committed to public service and subject to sanctions beyond those available through lengthy civil court proceedings.[23]

Jefferson's officer corps led only three regiments, and remained as unstable in officer career persistence (though it appears that there were fewer duels and courts-martials) as the officer corps of the 1790s. Fortunately, it did not have to fight. When war threatened, as with Spain over the Louisiana-Texas boundary in 1805 and 1806, Wilkinson realized that the Army lacked the logistical capability to sustain offensive operations, and he backed away from his own predisposition toward precipitating international conflict. The standing Army did prove capable of occupying New Orleans in 1803 and arresting Aaron Burr in 1807, but neither operation tested it against armed opposition. The War of 1812 proved a much more arduous test, but that meant an officer corps with far more experience and potential when peace brought another reduction in 1815.

The officer corps that fought the war was fashioned in the build-up of 1808 and during the war itself, when Congress authorized nearly sixty regiments of regulars. The standing Army Congress retained in 1815 was slightly larger than the force authorized in 1808: eight infantry regiments, a rifle regiment, a light artillery regiment, and thirty-two artillery companies. This numbered a dragoon regiment less but twelve artillery companies and an infantry regiment more than seven years before.[24] Thus, when the conflict ended, the officer corps had to be reduced by about 80 percent, to 674 of the 3,495 total officers in service, and about 489 of the 2,271 combat arms officers.[25] Since probably 90 percent of the officers were Jeffersonian Republicans, partisan affinity could not serve as a discriminator, but the administration could have tried to rely on sectional balancing or personal patronage, whether political, social, or familial. Fortunately, President Madison hoped to rely on demonstrated merit. But what experiences would qualify as meritorious, and who would evaluate officer experience?

The result became the Army's first institutional attempt at evaluations for the officer corps as a whole. Madison did not have to rely on a friendly captain, a deceitful commanding general, or an elderly secretary of war, as Jefferson had done. He entrusted the six generals who were intended to remain in the Army—Jacob Brown, Andrew Jackson, Winfield Scott, and three others—with acting as a committee to assess the reports the War Department required all regimental and higher commanders to make about their subordinates. (William Henry Harrison had left the Army a year before.) These reports were to rank officers in three classes, principally according to "competen[ce] to engage an enemy in the field" and "distinguished military merit and approved moral character."[26]

One's assessment of the level of standardization and uniformity in the review process, particularly in 1815, is largely a matter of perspective, dependent on whether one chooses to stress the fact that the process—unprecedented in the U.S. government, and not repeated until after the Civil War—was undertaken or the limits of its execution. Reporting proved spotty, undermined by the speed of the process, which lasted no more than a couple of months during the spring of 1815, and by the lack of information many commanders had about their subordinates. Many regiments had been only partially officered; many officers had not reported for duty, or had served only short periods, or had been on detached staff or recruiting service; and many commanders had served short periods or had been detached themselves. The eagerness officers of all ranks felt to return home led many to leave their regiments as soon as they could, and many regiments' reports were perfunctory, or were not submitted at all.[27]

Fortunately, the Army had a core of regiments tested in battle during the Niagara campaign the previous summer, in which four of the six generals on the retention board had served. The process was further simplified because only a couple of the six generals were actually present in Washington to assess the reports. Andrew Jackson remained in New Orleans in the months just after the war; Edmund Gaines had already been sent to join him. Alexander Macomb, representing the Right Division of the Northern Army, which had been engaged in the short Plattsburgh campaign in the late summer of 1814, did not arrive in Washington until April 18. Nor was Jacob Brown, commander of the Left Division of the Northern Army and the highest-ranking general (promoted to major general before Jackson) to be retained, present until April 25. Thus it seems probable that Brown's former brigade commanders Winfield Scott and Eleazar Wheelock Ripley, who were already in the capital when the secretary issued their instructions on April 8, prepared preliminary lists that were reviewed by Brown and Macomb. No assessments of individual officers by Brown, Scott, or Ripley have survived, and given their hurry it seems probable that they simply made a list, which could be quickly copied into the form of a new Army Register. Gaines and Jackson did send extensive reports on the officers concentrated at New Orleans, but there were only four regular regiments there, a small fraction of the Army and its officer corps.

In sum, commanders evaluated about a third of the officer corps. Although personal knowledge often meant personal friendship and solicitude, commanders condemned 252 officers, approximately 27 percent of those evaluated, to third-class status and near-certain discharge. Of the 908 infantry, rifle, and dragoon officers evaluated in terms comparable to the three classes, 360 (40 percent) were rated first- and 296 (one-third), second-class. With the majority of the reports coming from Brown's Left Division or units under Macomb's command, the generals could select men personally known to them. They did so primarily on grounds of merit demonstrated through battlefield gallantry. Although the reports frequently referred to officers' energy, intelligence, and zeal, bravery under fire proved by far the most important quality that can be correlated to retention. Under the circumstances, this was to be expected. Military education remained too rare to serve as a common criterion: West Point—the only institution of professional military education at the time—had only graduated eighty-nine officers before the war, of whom less than forty remained in service in 1815, and those (thirty more) graduated during it were still lieutenants. Indeed, graduation from the fledgling Military Academy was not mentioned once in evaluation reports from the field. Nevertheless, the Army's senior leaders do not seem to have found the academy's spotty efforts to teach military science irrelevant, for the correlation between graduation from West Point and retention proves so strong that it must have been decisive. About 75 percent of those who had graduated before the war and were still in service, twenty-nine of the thirty-one graduates from 1813 and 1814, and all of the thirty cadets graduated in March 1815 were selected for retention. In sum, 92 of 102 graduates still in the Army that month were retained—making roughly one-seventh of the new officer corps—and only two of them declined to remain in the postwar establishment.[28]

Combat was a surprisingly simple discriminator for the majority of officers. Though we might consider bravery subjective, many of the officers commissioned in 1808 and 1812 had seen little combat. Few regular units had served in the Washington-Baltimore campaign, the Creek and New Orleans campaigns, or the western campaigns in 1812 and 1813, while the Niagara campaigns of 1812 (Queenston Heights) and 1813 had brought little luster to American arms. Brown and Scott knew the reputations of their subordinates, who had fought in the Army's most intensive campaign, on the Niagara frontier in the summer of 1814. Indeed, the forces deployed in the Niagara theater fought through four campaigns (including the advance toward Montreal in the autumn of 1813), over a period twice that of the wars in the South and West. Scott had served in all four campaigns, and Brown (and Ripley) in the last two. With Left Division commanders dominating the retention board, substantial numbers of officers were retained from the force that fought the campaign of Chippawa, Lundy's Lane, and Fort Erie. Indeed, as a rule of thumb, if a Niagara officer wanted to remain in service, and had not failed to show courage, he was almost sure to be retained.[29]

Officers rated first-class made up about 80 percent of those retained in 1815. Nevertheless, although experienced military professionals oversaw the drawdown, without any of even the limited politicization of the 1802 reduction, it did depend on a handful of key leaders, their opportunities for identifying potential and shaping the permanent force constrained by the rarity of formal military education and the moral (and potentially political) claims of combat experience. Enough officers from Jackson's southern army and Macomb's Right Division were retained to prevent angst or controversy rising to the level of factionalism from those portions of the Army. But was battlefield gallantry sufficient to make good officers? The board rejected numerous officers for problems with alcohol, but the evaluations provided little evidence of how brave officers would take care of their soldiers, uphold financial accountability, treat civilians respectfully and work smoothly with local leaders along the frontiers, or deal diplomatically with Indians when diplomacy was desired. Was gallantry a guarantee of genteel behavior—the ideal early-nineteenth-century approach to smoothing interpersonal relationships?

Too often it was not. The 1815 evaluations placed so much emphasis on combat performance that factors that might have enhanced group cohesion were neglected. Indeed, the very aggressiveness valued in battle became a liability in peacetime, as officers hungry for the fame and glory they had received during the war turned their frustration with boring duty and slow promotion on one another. The Army of the following half-decade was plagued by discord and neglect—neglect of soldiers, supplies, and accountability to the citizenry, whether personal, financial, or even constitutional, as in Jackson's invasions of Florida, supported by his subordinates, who led or advocated similar adventures unauthorized by Congress or the executive. The Army of that era was a mess, and many of its officers seem to have been primarily concerned with quarreling, with peers, superiors, subordinates, and civilians, or with personal prospects and comfort. Indeed, between 1815 and 1821 the Army was probably more disorderly than in any period of similar length before or after, with the possible exception of the 1970s. Even worse, the Army's officers were prime contributors to the discord that followed the War of 1812, despite—or perhaps, in their belligerent pride, because of—their sense of validation in the Niagara campaign. Indeed, approximately half the officers retained in 1815 left the Army voluntarily by 1821. Yet another 15 percent of those retained were dismissed (usually the consequence of courts-martial) during the intervening years or disbanded in the second reduction, suggesting that many of the brave officers retained in 1815 lacked long-term dedication and commitment to the Army as a career and profession.[30]

The standing Army—which was more "General Jackson's Army" than Mr. Madison's or Mr. Monroe's, at least where it counted, on the southern frontier—proved an effective instrument of national power, pressuring Spain to surrender Florida and advancing up the Mississippi River against Native American opposition. But it was not a sustainable effectiveness—not sustainable logistically, financially, institutionally, or politically. Desertion rates rose to and exceeded 20 percent of the Army's soldiers each year, and an equal proportion of officers were absent from their duty, some on authorized leave but many not. The records of the era are rife with officers failing to render timely and accurate returns, with general and standing orders uncommunicated or disobeyed, and with violence by officers and enlisted soldiers against civilians and by officers against soldiers and each other. Andrew Jackson made power projection work through the force of his will (and the similarity between his objectives and those of President Monroe), but the expedition Monroe intended to advance up the Missouri River to the Yellowstone country in 1818 only got about a hundred miles before its supply network collapsed, and it did not complete its mission until 1825. Fortunately, the international situation calmed during the 1820s, and the Army had a respite in which Scott's General Regulations could become normative and Thomas Sidney Jesup could reform the Quartermaster Department and Army logistics. But in 1820 the Army was unreliable, institutionally (in its treatment of its own personnel), financially, and constitutionally.[31]

The 1821 drawdown proved an important, perhaps crucial, step in the officer corps' professional development: the process in which it began to become a profession based on more than hands-on experience and aptitude in one dimension of its potential mission set. By 1821 tensions with Britain and Spain had declined, an economic depression had begun, and the republican ideology of limited government was encouraging a new wave of congressional demands to reduce spending and taxation. This time the standing force would shrink from fourteen regiment-equivalents to eleven. This limited reduction—at 20 percent of the officer corps, the smallest of those during the early republic—meant that Army leaders could eliminate dysfunctional officers without worrying about having to cut many capable ones.

It also meant an officer corps that served as a cadre for the development of military expertise, to provide experienced staff officers and large-unit leadership in wartime. Yet most modern accounts suggest that the reduction was a defeat for military professionalism. Scholars have long debated the exact form and intent of Secretary of War John C. Calhoun's plan for an "expansible army." Was Calhoun's primary objective to provide the skeleton for a larger force, with each unit to be filled out to raise an expeditionary army several times larger than the peacetime one, as happened during the Second Seminole War and the Canadian border crises in 1838? Was it to maintain a cadre of experienced officers who would be able to develop professional expertise in preparation for war? The reduction in 1821 numbered about 20 percent of the officer corps (versus approximately 80 percent in 1815), and the number of officers per company and regiment remained the same. Although the Ordnance Corps and several much smaller staff organizations were disbanded, each artillery company (approximately forty enlisted soldiers in peacetime) was authorized four lieutenants. (Infantry companies retained two lieutenants.) It could be argued that this was due to the dispersion of artillery regiments in a large number of coastal forts, but the excess lieutenants enabled the Army to maintain an ordnance organization and provide officers from outside the small Corps of Engineers for fortification construction and for topographical engineer work under the General Survey Act of 1824.[32]

Indeed, for the next forty years, Military Academy graduates were assigned to units as supernumerary "brevet" second lieutenants, even if there was no place for them in the Army's statutory force authorizations. In other words, West Pointers were allowed (and paid) to serve as officers, commonly for several years, before permanent commissions became available due to deaths or resignations. (There was no system of retirement until the Civil War.) Indeed, during Andrew Jackson's presidency, these officers averaged nearly triple their number under John Quincy Adams. In 1829 the Army Register listed forty-one such men—more than a regiment's complement of officers and half as many men as all the second lieutenants required by the regiments of either infantry or artillery. In 1830 there were sixty-five—the equivalent of two infantry regiments of officers. This surplus persisted—and Congress allowed it to persist, essentially recognizing West Point graduates' claim to commissions, despite all the Jacksonian rhetoric about limited government, monopoly, and privilege—until a wave of resignations in 1835 enabled those graduates to take up permanent commissions.

Thus, whatever the specific legislation and consequent numbers, the post-1821 Army *was* expansible in terms of potential combat power, it *was* expanded by increasing the authorization of enlisted men (to a hundred for each company) in 1838, and it *did* provide a cadre for the development of greater war-fighting capability. Congress, the executive branch, and the Army officer corps effectively sustained Calhoun's vision, a concept largely developed by career officers. Congress rejected only one specific version of expansible military organization, while the new system effectively maintained and developed a cadre of expert professionals. Though often criticized by Jacksonian demagogues for not serving with troops in the field, these cadre officers—today we would call them the "institutional army"—taught others at West Point and in the infantry and artillery schools established in the mid-1820s; planned and supervised the construction of the system of coastal fortifications, the centerpiece of American defense planning; maintained the Army logistically and developed administrative experience essential for projecting power on a larger scale in Mexico and the Civil War; and performed civil duties sought by the public by surveying transportation routes, providing the Army with an additional *raison d'être* during the international peace of the 1820s.

Jacob Brown and Winfield Scott dominated the selection process in 1821 to an even greater degree than they had six years before. Eleazar Ripley had left the Army in 1820, and Jackson had expressed his intent to do so. Alexander Macomb was commanding in Detroit, Edmund Gaines along the Florida frontier. The War Department's criteria for evaluation were no more specific in 1815 or 1821 than Jefferson's had been in 1802. (Indeed, they were less specific, in not referring to officers' political attitudes.) However, while Army leaders did not write the criteria themselves, they shared the values and expectations embodied in the language promulgated by the War Department. Unit commanders were given wide latitude in making and expressing recommendations according to standards they rarely felt compelled to articulate, and they responded with a wide range of language and widely varying degrees of thoroughness and precision. This lack of standardization, combined in 1815 with late reports and some commanders' failure to report, illustrates the limited reach of bureaucratic routines and accountability in the Army, as in government and society as a whole, during the early postwar years. However, with less urgency and fewer officers moving about, commanders were much more responsive than in 1815.

Officers were again rated in three categories (though the standards were tightened, and only the first class was truly sought after), and again most of the third-tier officers were dismissed. The difference lay in the criteria, both stated and unstated, employed by reporting officers and the selection board. This time, many combat veterans were dismissed, and there proved much less wiggle room for combat veterans who had shown irresponsibility, lack of accountability, or disrespect for authority. The criteria issued by the War Department were now "intelligence, habits, and military skill."[33] The evaluations continued to emphasize energy, zeal, and intelligence, but there was a good deal more reference to intelligence, and far more to "habits" of reliability: calm and steady deportment, genteel manners, and moderation in the use of alcohol. Now the clearest correlation with retention became education at West Point, and after the reduction, the proportion of Military Academy graduates surged to nearly a third of the corps.[34]

Few of these graduates were combat veterans. Did this mean that the Army's senior leaders devalued military capability? No. Virtually none of the 1815 reports had actually referred to tactical capability, at, say, battlefield maneuver. They referred to bravery alone—to leadership by example. Few of the 1821 reports mentioned tactical capability either, though Brown and Scott may have accessed the reports of the Army's inspector generals, who assessed units' and officers' performance in drill. Instead, education meant socialization and habituation as much as math or military engineering. The latter were crucial for artillery and ordnance as well as engineer officers—in sum, about two-fifths of the officer corps. But socialization in deportment and manners, and habituation to timeliness, accuracy, and accountability, were critical for every officer. (Cadets also did a great deal of infantry and artillery drill, far more than many would do in their units after graduating.) The selection of officers who could calibrate their behavior to different situations began to ameliorate the problems that had plagued the postwar Army:

- the inattention to police and discipline; to orders, reporting, and record-keeping; to soldier health and welfare;
- the lack of respect for superiors, peers, and subordinates, for soldiers and civilians;
- the discord and malaise that seemed pervasive whenever the Army was not engaged in active campaigning.

Variations in the respondents' terminology may obscure the essential similarity of their assumptions about the qualities that made a good officer. Their appraisals had a fundamental consistency and coherence founded in assumptions widely shared among the early national gentry from which the officer corps came. Perhaps most significantly, the authors of these evaluations thought the social values shared by civil society just as important as military expertise; indeed, terms signifying social values were used substantially more often, especially in 1821, while there were virtually no references to tactical ability (rather than gallant behavior under fire) per se. Commanders responded to the demand for judgments in highly individual terms, but their criteria were clearly derived from a common social origin and vocabulary. Their evaluations were not overtly politicized, yet neither were they made in isolation from the values of their society, or at least from those of the genteel portion of society they had been socialized to identify with.[35]

Indeed, a symbiotic relationship between civilian "social" and militarily "functional" criteria was clearly evident in the conceptions of military capability suggested by the language of these reports. Much more emphasis was placed on battlefield experience and gallantry in 1815 than in 1821, but in both years the focus centered on officers' behavior rather than knowledge or expertise in the abstract. Aside from battlefield distinction, commanders usually referred to military ability as a matter of attentiveness—of energy, industriousness, enterprise, and zeal—evidence of responsible behavior and initiative rather than knowledge or expertise per se. Indeed, they rarely mentioned the specific behaviors, or duties, in which officers could physically demonstrate responsibility: comments on aptitude at drill and troop discipline were quite rare in either year, though common in inspection reports on unit readiness during the period between the reductions.

Command, and troop handling, were apparently envisioned as products, or even expressions, of one's personal charisma and presence, the coolness and calm under fire commonly labeled gallantry. But the weight given to experience and potential changed between 1815 and 1821. In 1815, both gallantry and experience had been demonstrated by past behavior; indeed, references to "experience" and "distinction" normally signified gallantry in battle. With the resignation of so many combat-tested officers between 1815 and 1821, one might expect to see combat experience and gallantry referred to *more* often as a means of distinguishing between officers in the latter year, but this did not prove true. Instead, socialization at the Military Academy—evidence of military bearing and command presence, but only of *potential* for gallantry in combat—was apparently accepted as a substitute for combat experience in indicating leadership capability. This substitution was presumably acceptable because that socialization inculcated the republican norms of selfless duty (meaning subordination to group norms and objectives), honor (meaning both personal integrity and ambition for reputation), and country (meaning disinterested public service and leadership), along with physical and mental endurance, self-discipline and denial, mental steadiness, and moderation in manners and temperament. Indeed, West Point habituated aspiring officers from any background to the values and practices of self-discipline, calm, and moderate deportment, which gentry leaders saw as the constituent elements of effective command presence, sustained institutional leadership, and the potential for battlefield gallantry.[36]

The virtual absence of overt politicization is remarkable. Politics, personal friendships, and the desire to protect older men who had devoted their lives to the service of their country certainly influenced the selection process behind the scenes, and these personal connections meant that a few older officers were retained despite diminished capacity. Yet there were no notations about officers' political affinities, or the intensity of their allegiances, as there had been on the list President Jefferson used in 1802, or in the appointments process during the build-up between 1808 and 1812 (or those for the Federalist armies in 1798 and 1799), when the administration routinely consulted congressmen and local notables on the allegiances of prospective officers. Indeed, only *one* out of the more than sixty reports made in 1815 and 1821 mentioned politics, and it did so in reference to enlisted men rather than officers. In those years, the "politics" of retention took the diffuse form of preexisting personal and social connections among the national elite and its local dependencies, and the general social and cultural bias in favor of "gentlemen," rather than partisan or factional consciousness. Within the Army the selection process sometimes provided commanders with limited opportunities to promote the fortunes of favored subordinates, but this modest patronage can be considered functionally rational because it was based on first-hand observation and personal compatibility (meaning effective teamwork) in military settings, rather than political affiliations extrinsic to the Army.[37]

No doubt much of the reason for this lack of politicization lay in the dominance of the Republican Party, for factional allegiances within that broad alliance could be addressed through social connections and criteria rather than overtly political ones. By 1815 most avowedly Federalist officers (who had generally entered the Army before 1801) had reached an age when they could be evaluated and discharged on functional grounds of infirmity or inability to endure the rigors of the field. Their more junior counterparts—those few who remained, given promotions and the Republican dominance of appointments during the previous decade—could hardly be damned for their partisan affinities after "having shared in the privations, sufferings, and toils incident to active service" in the war.[38]

Sectionalism seems to have played as limited a role as politics, although similar caveats should be made. That is, there were no references to sectional origin or identity in the reports from units, though it seems probable that the generals received private appeals that mentioned these characteristics, and in 1815 Secretary of War Dallas assured Madison that "local claims" (clearly meaning those of state pride, and probably those of state politics) were not "disregarded in the search for distinguished military merit."[39] The 1815 reduction did privilege one group of officers on the basis of *military* geography, for the test of combat made merit manifest, and as the source and demonstration of ability and merit, gallant leadership and experience under fire led to patronage for the veterans of the Army's successful campaigns. This was most true of those who had served in the Left Division of the Northern Army during the Niagara campaign in 1814, for four of the six members of the 1815 board (and all three of that convened for the next reduction six years later) had held senior commands at Chippewa, Lundy's Lane, or Fort Erie. Only General Macomb had served in the Right Division, and a disproportionate number of its regiments (mostly those of Major General George Izard, which did little when sent to reinforce Brown that fall) did not send in reports.

In 1815 only Andrew Jackson represented the southern army. His report mentioned only seventy-seven officers, a number of them volunteers who neither sought nor were likely to be offered retention, and he was not formally consulted in 1821, when he accepted the governorship of Florida rather than reduction to brigadier or a destructive fight with Brown. Gaines's 1815 report was very extensive but very late, and his recommendation that the board

SURPRISINGLY PROFESSIONAL | 93

favor men tried in the Niagara campaign probably outweighed the mere list-ing he gave to the officers of the southern regiments he had just been sent to command in New Orleans. Yet this imbalance, which might have appeared awkward if publicized, was hardly dysfunctional or unmerited, insofar as the regular units at New Orleans had not fought an extended campaign or of-fensive battles against their British counterparts in the open field, nor had they trained a tactically proficient force like the officers of the Left Division. In other words, the Army's senior leaders believed that the most important threat to American national security remained conventional warfare with Britain, so the southern army's successes against the Creeks, won with the aid of often-unreliable volunteers and militia and Native American allies, counted little in their assessment. Apparently the nation's political represen-tatives shared this assessment, for there was no hue and cry over the favor shown to the veterans of the northern campaign. Indeed, many of these of-ficers were southern in origin, which must have deflected or deterred impu-tations of sectional favoritism, as did Jackson's retention as commander of a new Southern Division on equal terms with Brown's northern one.

The advantages, disadvantages, and extent of the officer corps' autonomy as a professional body were all apparent in the tenacity and success with which the 1815 and 1821 selection boards sought to maintain the principle of seniority in promotion. In 1815, the value placed on experience inevita-bly meant that the reports sent from the regiments tended to recommend a higher proportion of captains than of lieutenants. Yet the very fact that the evaluating officers rated subordinates in all grades implies that they expected the majority of the selections to be made within each grade independent of the others, a practice that became official policy in 1821. Not only did the boards avoid reordering seniority among the officers from within each war-time grade; they also attempted to make the selections and reductions at each grade from within, rather than retaining all the higher-ranking officers at the expense of their subordinates. Doing so required deciding between compet-ing priorities: seniority measured by time in service expressed the claims to preference of men who had sacrificed substantial portions of their lives in the nation's service, while maintaining seniority measured in time in grade re-mained essential to the institutional stability that assured officers of some cer-tainty in their careers, an important incentive for them to remain in service.

Maintaining seniority in length of service would have been counterpro-ductive given the desire for officers vigorous enough to lead troops in the field, and selecting men simply by moving from the highest ranks on down was impossible, since the mass of field- and general-grade officers would refuse to accept "degradation" to more junior rank. The demand for merit and ability, which contemporaries thought measurable only by experience (meaning time in service and behavior in battle), did mean that a substantial number of the officers selected in 1815 were reduced in grade at the expense of their juniors. Doing so spurred controversy from all angles, leading a number of officers to decline retention and others to a festering resentment of men with less time in grade, or later dates of commission, who had been retained at their wartime ranks. Such demotions were expedient and individual, however, and the discord that followed did not produce any substantial reversal of the board's decisions. The controversy did encourage the 1821 board to recommend that all reductions occur from within the separate grades of rank, a constraint more easily accepted that year due to the limited scale of the drawdown and the commitment demonstrated by officers who had remained in the Army since the war. As a result, in 1821 demotion was only resorted to in a few cases where there were insufficient slots for senior officers at their prereduction ranks, as in the cases of brigadier generals Henry Atkinson and Alexander Macomb, who accepted reduction to colonel, but in specific positions they valued. These demotions did not lead to a lasting reevaluation of the seniority principle, nor did they undermine the expectations that undergirded the security aspiring officers sought from public service in the profession of arms.[40]

The operation of the selection process also suggests that the national standing Army, now effectively permanent, had secured a substantial degree of autonomy in its internal functioning. The boards were able to decide officers' futures with relatively little intervention from the president, the War Department, Congress, or interested private parties. With the exception of a few field-grade and senior staff positions in 1821, when Andrew Jackson's desire to advance his protégés clearly made a difference, the Madison and Monroe administrations accepted the generals' recommendations (which were not closely supervised by civilian officials) almost without hesitation. Generals, field-grade officers, and senior staff officers were not dismissed against their will, and the disputes over rank, position, and seniority that got into Congress were rare exceptions to the smooth confirmation of the new lists.[41]

The national standing Army grew by three mounted regiments (and one of infantry) between 1821 and 1846, essentially restoring its 1816 strength by the eve of the war with Mexico. Congress added another nine regiments to the federal Army during the war, but disbanded all of them, along with the volunteers recruited by states, at its conclusion. Despite President Polk's reputation for antipathy toward the regulars, his administration dismissed the officers of the wartime regiments *en masse*, while disbanding virtually none of the career officers from the prewar Army. The handful of officers commissioned during the war who were retained in 1848 remained because of ordinary individual casualties and resignations that West Point, which did not expand during the war, could not fill. Despite a quarter-century of Jacksonian egalitarianism and antagonism toward monopoly, historians have found no evidence of substantial political debates over the composition of the postwar officer corps: as Winfield Scott said of West Point, the war with Mexico had proven the standing Army and its officer model. Thus, unlike the build-ups of 1808 and 1812, or the Civil War a generation in the future, that of 1846 had virtually no effect on the composition of the postwar officer corps. The standing Army was taken as the basis for the peacetime force, and no retention board was deemed necessary. Although some meritorious wartime officers were compelled to abandon military careers, Polk and his fellow Jacksonians were unwilling to fight for a substantial diffusion of officer commissioning. (Some of these men did reenter the Army when it expanded beyond what West Point could supply in 1855.) "Mr. Polk's Army" reverted to General Scott's Army, an institution remarkable for its autonomy from partisan and democratic influence at the very height of partisanship and egalitarianism (at least rhetorically) in American politics.[42]

The reduction of 1821 proved one of the most critical steps in the process by which the national standing Army gained professional autonomy. It did not end intemperance, though dueling began to decline (for a number of reasons) and officers became less quarrelsome. The drawdown enabled the regulars to rely on a less diverse set of commissioning sources, permitting an end to routine commissions directly from civilian life, or from the ranks of noncommissioned officers, until the Civil War. As a result, the Army and its officer corps became more rigidly hierarchical and authoritarian, more class-bound. Not surprisingly, illegal violence by individual officers against enlisted soldiers continued unabated until the massive influx of citizen-soldiers in 1861. But the Army became much more accountable to representative government, individually, financially, and constitutionally.[43]

This was not solely due to the reductions. Most accounts of the Army's reform during the 1820s center on Brown, Scott, Thomas Jesup, Sylvanus Thayer, and Secretary of War Calhoun, or on Jackson's departure from the force. Yet the Army's senior leaders needed junior officers who would implement reforms. The officers of 1815–1821, like their predecessors, often proved unreliable, a threat to their institution as well as their Constitution. Those of the following decades did not. In 1815 Brown and Scott were able to base retention on military criteria, setting a precedent against partisanship or sectionalism and in favor of professional autonomy, but they had few educated officers to choose from, in a national security situation where war still seemed likely. By 1821 they had many educated lieutenants, while they retained combat veterans for most slots of captain and above. Thus experience could mentor education, until education acquired experience. The result was the beginning of the professional officer corps.

NOTES

1 For this later stability, see William B. Skelton, *An American Profession of Arms: The Army Officer Corps, 1784–1861* (Lawrence: University Press of Kansas, 1992), chs. 6–11; Samuel J. Watson, *Jackson's Sword: The Army Officer Corps on the American Frontier, 1810–1821* (Lawrence: University Press of Kansas, 2012), ch. 7 and conclusion; and idem, "How the Army Became Accepted: West Point Socialization, Military Accountability, and the Nation-State during the Jacksonian Era," *American Nineteenth-Century History* 7 (June 2006): 217–49.

2 See Richard H. Kohn, *Eagle and Sword: The Federalists and the Creation of the Military Establishment in America, 1783–1802* (New York: Free Press, 1975) and Lawrence Delbert Cress, *Citizens in Arms: The Army and the Militia in American Society to the War of 1812* (Chapel Hill: University of North Carolina Press, 1982).

3 Skelton, *An American Profession of Arms*, 35, provides a nuanced assessment of the balance between stability and instability in the early officer corps. There was limited educational or career specialization in the early republic, where there were few complex, large-scale institutions—military officers were unusual in having any formal career hierarchy at all. Officer careers grew much longer after the stabilization in force structure during the 1820s: the officers on the 1830 Army Register examined by Skelton averaged a bit more than twenty years—the *average* officer on the 1830 list served the full span of today's career to retirement with a pension. See ibid., tables 11.1–11.4 and figure 11.1, for statistics on officer career lengths, promotion rates and timing, and reasons for attrition.

4 Washington to Congress, May 1, 1783, "Sentiments on a Peace Establishment," at http://founders.archives.gov/?q=Sentiments%20on%20a%20Peace%20 Establishment%20Author%3A%22Washington%2C%20George%22&s=1111311111& sa=&r=7&sr.

5 Russell F. Weigley, *History of the United States Army* (New York: Macmillan, 1967), 586 n.21, points out that there was an infantry regiment in addition to the eighty artillerists guarding ordnance stores at West Point and Fort Pitt. That regiment was replaced by a new one of similar strength in mid-1784.

6 See especially Kohn, *Eagle and Sword*, which is the only monograph focused on Federalist military policy.

7 See ibid.; Cress, *Citizens in Arms*; and Max M. Edling, *A Revolution in Favor of Government: Origins of the U.S. Constitution and the Making of the American State* (New York: Oxford University Press, 2003), who most explicitly articulates the historiographical concept of the fiscal-military state for the early United States.

8 Skelton, *An American Profession of Arms*, table 2.1. Ibid., figure 1.1, shows the authorized strength of the officer corps across this era (including those for the Federalist "Additional Army" in 1798–1799).

9 Ibid., 62 and 139. Ibid., 35, notes that of 149 officers commissioned by the Jefferson administration between 1803 and 1807, only 70 remained in the Army in 1812, and by 1816 a mere 27 (18 percent of the original group) were still in service, in an Army of approximately 600 officers. Only nineteen officers first commissioned in the eighteenth century remained after the 1815 reduction, less than 3 percent of the postwar corps (p. 62).

10 James Ripley Jacobs, *The Beginning of the U.S. Army, 1783–1812* (Princeton, NJ: Princeton University Press, 1947), 193. In 1796, the Army's authorized officer strength was 240–250, depending on how the staff was counted. The reauthorization of that year, replacing the twelve four-company infantry and rifle battalions of the Legion with four regiments of ten companies apiece, cut the authorized number of captains and lieutenants by about a third, but casualties and resignations prior to the reduction meant that the actual impact was about half what it might have been. Despite the 1792 law that underpinned the Legion of the United States (as the Army was called for the next four years), lieutenant colonels (who were not authorized by the law) rather than brigadier generals had commanded the four sublegions (saving the government money, and meaning younger men in command), and several brigadier generals commissioned during the era of the Legion had resigned in 1793 and 1794, so that James Wilkinson was the only brigadier. The number of majors was reduced from sixteen to twelve. The laws regarding Army organization, which include authorized strengths at each rank, are summarized in Charles K. Gardner, comp., *A Dictionary of the Officers of the Army of the United States* (New York: Putnam, 1860). Army registers for 1797 and 1802 are in Thomas H. S. Hamersly, comp., *Complete Regular Army Register of the Unites States, for One Hundred Years (1779 to 1879)* (Washington, DC: Hamersly, 1880).

11 See Samuel Watson, "Trusting to 'the Chapter of Accidents': Contingency, Necessity, and Self-Constraint in Jeffersonian National Security Policy," *Journal of Military History* 76 (October 2012): 973–1000.

12 Skelton, *An American Profession of Arms*, 24–25; Theodore J. Crackel, *Mr. Jefferson's Army: Political and Social Reform of the Military Establishment, 1801–1809* (New York: New York University Press, 1987), 13. The controversy over Adams's "midnight appointments" and the Judiciary Act of 1801 is discussed in Richard E. Ellis, *The Jeffersonian Crisis: Courts and Politics in the Young Republic* (New York: Oxford University Press, 1971). Early national political culture was overtly antipartisan, yet each party claimed to embody the political nation against illegitimate (Francophile, Anglophile, "mobocratic," or aristocratic) factions. Thus each party claimed to be the only true representative of public opinion and the public interest, and hence, not a party in the pejorative sense used at the time,

while their opponents were ideologically, and ultimately morally, illegitimate, at least in their antipartisan rhetoric.

13 Crackel, *Mr. Jefferson's Army*, 14. Crackel's book is the only monograph focused on the Army during the Jeffersonian era.

14 Ibid., 44–45, and passim; Skelton, *An American Profession of Arms*, 99, 368, and 377. The Army was significantly understrength when the law was passed, so few enlisted soldiers had to be discharged. See also Crackel, "Jefferson, Politics, and the Army: An Examination of the Military Peace Establishment Act of 1802," *Journal of the Early Republic* 2 (April 1982): 21–38. Skelton acknowledges that political considerations were involved in Jefferson's appointment policies, but dates this to the expansion of 1808 (p. 27). Crackel's suggestion that the administration sought to convert political moderates through persuasion seems to rest primarily on the memoirs of Joseph G. Swift, then a captain (*Mr. Jefferson's Army*, 51). On the other hand, there is little reason to suspect that Jefferson and Dearborn would not have used such methods, though perhaps with less personal attention to individual officers than Swift's example would suggest. The discharged officers received a minimum of three months' severance pay depending on their time in service. The number of officers disbanded and retained is somewhat unclear. On December 19, 1801, Secretary of War Dearborn reported that there were 248 officers; American State Papers: Documents, Legislative and Executive, of the Congress of the United States, Class V, Military Affairs (Washington, DC: Gales and Seaton, 1832–1861), vol. 1: 139–41. The "Organization of the Army," dated June 1, 1802, in Hamersly, *Complete Regular Army Register*, 49–51, lists only 146 officers: five in the staff and engineers (discounting the paymaster, who had no military rank), 66 in the artillery, and 75 in the infantry (including nine ensigns, a rank not employed in the artillery). There were also 28 surgeons and surgeon's mates, double the number on the 1801 list. Skelton says that there were 191 officers in the Army, a number "only slightly greater than the membership of the two houses of Congress" (*An American Profession of Arms*, 25)—a valuable point—but does not provide a source. Weigley, *History of the United States Army*, 109, cites Jacobs, *The Beginning of the U.S. Army*, 252, who cites the Hamersly list, coming to a number of 172 officers, which is only two off from the 146 plus the 28 medical personnel. Crackel notes that 88 of the 230 officers evaluated on the 1801 list were disbanded, but that twenty new ensigns were commissioned. This would add up to 162 officers, and the 1802 list in Hamersly includes only nine ensigns; the consequent subtraction would leave 151 officers. Crackel does not address the disposition of the 26 officers the Jefferson administration listed as "unknown to us" on the 1801 list.

15 The list is dated July 24, 1801, in the Jefferson Papers, Series 1, Library of Congress, http://hdl.loc.gov/loc.mss/mtj.mtjbib010336; see also Donald Jackson, "Jefferson, Meriwether Lewis, and the Reduction of the United States Army," *Proceedings of the American Philosophical Society* 124 (April 1980): 91–96. Crackel refers to 256 officers; there are 258 on the list, including James Wilkinson and

Meriwether Lewis, neither of whom was evaluated. (There were also fourteen surgeons and surgeons' mates.) The 26 officers listed by Lewis as "unknown to us" were, therefore, not known Federalists.

16 Crackel, *Mr. Jefferson's Army*, 45, 49–51, and table 2.1.

17 Edward M. Coffman, *The Old Army: A Portrait of the American Army in Peacetime, 1784–1898* (New York: Oxford University Press, 1986), 9–10; Crackel, *Mr. Jefferson's Army*, 49–50; Skelton, *An American Profession of Arms*, 61. The figures presented by Coffman and Crackel differ in minor respects; I have used Crackel's as they are slightly more complete. Of the 230 officers assessed, 55 were New Englanders, 54 southerners, and ten westerners. Pennsylvania, Virginia, Maryland, and Massachusetts led the states as sources of officers, with 46, 36, 31, and 30, respectively. Pennsylvania was slightly overrepresented compared to its share of the free population, and Maryland substantially so. The reduction did not affect any one region disproportionately, despite New England's Federalism—though this may have been because Jefferson hoped to develop Republican strength in that region, and did not want to alienate potential supporters with imbalanced removals.

18 For context, see Carl E. Prince, "The Passing of the Aristocracy: Jefferson's Removal of the Federalists, 1801–1805," *Journal of American History* 57 (December 1970): 563–75, which examines a similar process in the civil service. Leonard White notes that as president, Jefferson removed 109 out of 433 civil officials subject to such action on his part. Forty had been Federalist "midnight appointments," and by the summer of 1803 only 130 of the 316 civil officials subject to presidential appointment were identifiably Federalists. All the new appointees were Republicans. With few Federalists left to remove, Madison and Monroe removed a grand total of twenty-seven officials apiece; Leonard D. White, *The Jeffersonians: A Study in Administrative History, 1801–1829* (New York: Macmillan, 1959), 354–55 and 379. See also Sidney H. Aronson, *Status and Kinship in the Higher Civil Service* (Cambridge, MA: Harvard University Press, 1964); Noble E. Cunningham Jr., *The Jeffersonian Republicans in Power: Party Operations, 1801–1809* (Chapel Hill: University of North Carolina Press, 1963), chs. 2–3; idem, *The Process of Government under Jefferson* (Princeton, NJ: Princeton University Press, 1978), ch. 8; Dumas Malone, *Jefferson the President: First Term, 1801–1805* (Boston: Little, Brown, 1970), chs. 5–8 and 25; and Crackel, "The Military Academy in the Context of Jeffersonian Reform," in Robert M. S. McDonald, ed., *Thomas Jefferson's Military Academy: Founding West Point* (Charlottesville: University Press of Virginia, 2004), 99–117.

19 Skelton, *An American Profession of Arms*, 377 n.91.

20 Official Letterbooks, Wilkinson Papers, Chicago Historical Society.

21 Crackel, *Mr. Jefferson's Army*, table 2.1.

22 Ibid., 46–47 and 80–81. There was only one Republican field-grade officer available to fill all these posts, and he was so ill that he sought retirement.

23 Erna Risch, *Quartermaster Support of the Army, 1775–1939*, rev. ed. (Washington, DC: Center of Military History, 1988), 118; Skelton, *An American Profession of*

Arms, 8. See the U.S. Statutes at Large, 2 *Stat.* 132–37, for the text of the Military Peace Establishment Act. Risch, *Quartermaster Support*, ch. 4, discusses supply operations during the first decade of the nineteenth century. In general, see White, *The Jeffersonians*, chs. 15–18, and Cunningham, *The Process of Government under Jefferson*, ch. 6, on the structure and operations of the War Department and the Army staff during this era.

24 Gardner, comp., *Dictionary of the Officers of the Army*, 14–16 and 22; Adjutant and Inspector General's Office, General Order, May 17, 1815, in William A. Gordon, *A Compilation of Registers of the Army of the United States, from 1815 to 1837* (Washington, DC: Dunn, 1837), 57. See James E. Lewis Jr., *The American Union and the Problem of Neighborhood: The United States and the Collapse of the Spanish Empire, 1783–1829* (Chapel Hill: University of North Carolina Press, 1998) and Michael S. Fitzgerald, "Europe and the United States Defense Establishment: American Military Policy and Strategy, 1815–1821" (Ph.D. diss., Purdue University, 1990), for the most complete explorations of diplomatic and political context.

25 The most detailed examination is in William B. Skelton, "High Army Leadership in the Era of the War of 1812: The Making and Remaking of the Officer Corps," *William and Mary Quarterly* (3rd series) 51 (April 1994): 253–74.

26 Acting Secretary of War Alexander J. Dallas to the selection board, April 8, 1815, in Gordon, *A Compilation of Registers*, 53–54. The initial circular, sent to the regimental commanders, was dated March 14, 1815, in Confidential and Unofficial Letters Sent by the Secretary of War (Microform Series 7), Record Group 107, National Archives. The "average" date of responses sent from the infantry regiments was April 9, which suggests that the average commander wrote his evaluations over the course of about two weeks.

27 The regimental reports for 1815 are collected in Letters Received, Office of the Secretary of War, Unregistered Series (Microform Series 222), Record Group 107, National Archives, filed alphabetically by author. Apparently, nine of the forty-six infantry regiments, as well as one of the four rifle regiments, did not respond. Indeed, only twenty-four of the forty-two colonels of infantry regiments actually reported; four regiments had no colonel in the spring of 1815. (Thus, in thirteen of the forty-six infantry regiments, a major or the lieutenant colonel made the officer evaluation report.) The only extant reports from artillery unit command- ers came from lieutenant colonels (battalion commanders) William Macrea, at New Orleans, and James House, from the harbor of New York City. House ranked only seventeen officers (and only four captains), and commented only on the two he judged third-class. Macrea ranked only eighteen men, praising only the senior captain in the corps. However, as noted in the text, Gaines and Jackson reported on most of the officers in their commands, which included artillery, Macomb knew the artillerymen of his Right Division, and Brown, Scott, and Ripley knew the artillerists of the Left Division, while there was little regular army artillery in the West. Presumably lack of familiarity led most commanders to rank only the officers they were willing to recommend, and the reports on twelve regiments,

none of which provided significant comments regarding individuals, rated an average of slightly less than half of their company officers. Indeed, six of these units' reports rated a third or less of their officers, as did three other regiments whose reporting officers provided individual comments. The intersection of military and social geography probably had much to do with these difficulties: most of these units were in the West, or had been hastily raised along the coast in 1814, producing personnel turbulence and thus unfamiliarity between officers. Given their limited combat experience and time in service, most of the officers of these regiments must have expected to be disbanded in any case, and more often than not, they probably intended going home, having only joined the Army late in the war, essentially as citizen-soldiers. Thus a total of no more than forty-three (including the Regiment of Light Dragoons) out of fifty-eight regiments (counting the artillery proportionally) have left reports, and only thirty-one of fifty-eight were actually reported on in substance or detail and in time for use by the board. Breaking the numbers down according to patterns in the distribution of first-, second-, and third-class ratings (or their equivalents), eight regiments averaged 15, 7, and 5.5 officers in these classes (55, 25, and 20 percent); nine regiments averaged 11, 9.5, and 3.5 (45, 40, and 15 percent); twelve regiments averaged almost precisely equal proportions (totals of 100, 104, and 100 officers per class, respectively); and five regiments averaged 3.5, 8, and 13 (15, 33, and 52 percent). Six of the first eight regiments had been distinguished in extensive combat, all in the Niagara campaign. Of the units in the fourth group, one was evaluated by an officer who had just been transferred into the regiment, and two by officers from outside. Sixteen (or 40 percent) of the regiments' reports also went on to rate surgeons and surgeons' mates, often with specific comments in addition to rankings, usually positively and with much more praise than damnation. A few officers also reported on the number of "five-year" enlisted men (those with several years remaining to serve at the war's end) under their command, and a few made general estimates of the state of their regiments as fighting units, comments that went beyond the demands of the War Department circular.

28 Of eighty-nine men who had graduated from the academy before the declaration of war, approximately 20 percent had resigned before the war, about 12 percent of those remaining resigned during it (and a quarter died, in battle or otherwise), and about a quarter of the remainder were discharged in 1815. (One declined retention.) The largest element, thirty-two men (36 percent of the initial group, and more than 75 percent of those still available at the time of the reduction), were retained.

29 The Twenty-first Infantry Regiment provides perhaps the best single example, both because of its distinguished wartime performance at Chippewa and Lundy's Lane on the Niagara and because of its officers' significant place in the retained force. Colonel James Miller singled out three severely wounded officers from outside his regiment, along with a captain (his aide) who had been brevetted twice

for gallantry. (Miller did not put much emphasis on the brevets themselves, nor did the other respondents, who stressed combat experience, apparently taking brevets as the proper reward for gallantry.) Miller saw little real distinction among the three classes of captain and the first and second classes of lieutenants, all of whom he praised for their experience and behavior under fire. The three first lieutenants Miller labeled third-class were "Moderate in Duty, good for nothing," "Moderate in sobriety, *Dissipated*," and "Moderate in *Honesty*," suggesting that the rare cases of incapacity in this combat-tested unit were attributed to social rather than military failings. The officers of the Twenty-first became the core of the post-reduction Fifth Infantry, with Miller as colonel, Josiah Vose (a major in the Twenty-first, reduced to captain) and four of the Twenty-first's captains (including three of those from the four Miller rated first-class) as half of the new unit's complement of company commanders, and five lieutenants (three of four first-class first lieutenants and two of three first-class second lieutenants) from the Twenty-first as a quarter of the Fifth's complement in that grade. Overall, nine of the thirteen officers Miller judged first-class were retained in the Fifth, making nearly a third of its total complement; another captain he rated first-class was retained in the artillery. One of the three regimental medical officers, all rated first-class by Miller, was also retained in the Fifth, as was Major John McNeil of the Eleventh Infantry, one of the officers outside the Twenty-first whom he had praised. Of course, this does mean that three of the thirteen officers he rated first-class were disbanded, but 80 percent of those he so rated were retained, in a reduction of 80 percent of the Army's officers.

30 Statistics from Skelton, "The United States Army, 1821–1837: An Institutional History" (Ph.D. dissertation, Northwestern University, 1968), 40–42, and Ronald Spiller, "From Hero to Leader: The Development of Nineteenth-Century American Military Leadership" (Ph.D. dissertation, Texas A&M University, 1993), 38–39. Wartime officer turmoil is explored in Alan Taylor, *The Civil War of 1812: American Citizens, British Subjects, Irish Rebels, and Indian Allies* (New York: Knopf, 2010); J. C. A. Stagg, "United States Army Officers in the War of 1812: A Statistical and Behavioral Portrait," *Journal of Military History* 76 (October 2012): 1001–34; and idem, "Freedom and Subordination: Disciplinary Problems in the U.S. Army during the War of 1812," *Journal of Military History* 78 (April 2014): 537–74.

31 See Watson, *Jackson's Sword* and "How the Army Became Accepted," for discussion of the Army's lack of accountability, particularly to representative civilian government, during the half-decade after the war. On the other hand, some 30 percent of the line officers listed on the Army Register in May 1816 served for twenty years or more, helping to provide unprecedented continuity in the Army's leadership.

32 See Roger J. Spiller, "Calhoun's Expansible Army: The History of a Military Idea," *South Atlantic Quarterly* 79 (Spring 1980): 189–203, and for context Michael S. Fitzgerald, "Rejecting Calhoun's Expansible Army Plan: The Army Reduction Act of 1821," *War in History* 3 (Summer 1996): 161–85. Fitzgerald is primarily concerned

with the reasons for the reduction; he does not address the actual impact on the Army's force structure or capability. Spiller does not take a clear stand, observing that the plan was remembered as a model for professional military development; however, because Congress substituted its own plan, requiring greater reductions in the officer corps, he states that Calhoun's "plan foundered," "failed to win the support of Congress," and was "stillborn" (200, 202, 203). These statements are factually correct but convey a fundamentally inaccurate sense of the outcome and consequences. See Skelton, *An American Profession of Arms*, 126–35, for what I think was the first clear recognition of Calhoun's intent and the success of the cadre concept.

33 War Department circular, March 10, 1821, in Letters Sent by the Secretary of War Relating to Military Affairs, 1800–1889, Microfilm 6, Record Group 107, National Archives.

34 Of the 111 officers who graduated from West Point in the years between the reductions, thirteen (12 percent) left the Army before the 1821 reduction, but 94 of the remaining 95 were retained in 1821. Similar proportions prevailed among the graduates of earlier years who were still in the Army: fifteen of the eighteen remaining officers who had graduated during the war and 21 of 23 of those trained before the war were retained in 1821 (83 and 91 percent). In sum, 93 percent (143 of 153) of the Military Academy graduates who remained in service in 1821 were retained that year. Thus, after the reduction, nearly two-thirds of the lieutenants of artillery (97 of 147) and more than 40 percent of those of infantry (55 of 132) were West Point graduates. See Skelton, "The United States Army, 1821–1837," 40–42. Combined with the de facto Military Academy commissioning monopoly instituted by Calhoun and Monroe in 1821, the proportion of West Point graduates in the Army officer corps surged, from 15 percent in 1817 to 40 percent six years later and 60 percent in 1830.

35 See Samuel P. Huntington, *The Soldier and the State: The Theory and Practice of Civil-Military Relations* (Cambridge, MA: Harvard University Press, 1957), ch. 9, for the classic statement of the thesis that American military professionalism developed in isolation from, and to a substantial degree in opposition to, civilian society and its values. Weigley, *History of the United States Army*, and Marcus Cunliffe, *Soldiers and Civilians: The Martial Spirit in America, 1776–1865*, 2nd ed. (New York: Free Press, 1973), extended this theme to the antebellum era, and William Skelton frequently implies some agreement, though he qualifies the argument by referring to separation and distinctiveness rather than isolation or alienation. Allan R. Millett, *Military Professionalism and Officership in America* (Columbus, OH: Mershon Center Briefing Paper, 1977), on the other hand, stresses the parallels between civilian and military professionalization, and doubts "that even long-term professional socialization produced a coherent philosophical point of view that was uniquely military" (15).

36 Samuel Watson, "Developing 'Republican Machines': West Point and the Struggle to Render the Officer Corps Safe for America," in McDonald, ed., *Thomas Jefferson's Military Academy*, 154–81.

37 To some extent, this "personal politics" anticipated what William B. Skelton has labeled "Army politics": the essentially nonpartisan pursuit of individual (or unit or branch) objectives focused within the Army's organizational structure, employing personal civilian friends with political influence but with the outcome usually determined by institutional factors. See Skelton, "Officers and Politicians: The Origins of Army Politics in the United States before the Civil War," *Armed Forces and Society* 6 (Fall 1979): 22–48.

38 Major Willoughby Morgan, report of the Twelfth Infantry, April 2, 1815, Letters Received, Office of the Secretary ofWar, Unregistered Series (Microform Series 222), Record Group 107, NationalArchives.

39 Raymond Walters Jr., *Alexander James Dallas: Lawyer—Politician—Financier, 1759–1817* (Philadelphia: University of Pennsylvania Press, 1943), 225. Aside from satisfying Andrew Jackson, the most delicate political matter was Madison's desire to appoint a Kentuckian to field rank, since the president noted that "the want of a Western member of the Board at Washington will not fail to excite attention." Several western officers reassured the secretary, who then reassured the president that "the western portion of the country has a full portion of the peace establishment." The next day the secretary wrote to Madison that "Lieutenant Spotts, who is strongly recommended by General Jackson, and for whom I ask a brevet, says that the Army Register will give the highest satisfaction to the South," the only mention of sectional interest in these letters apart from those concerning the West. John D. Morris, *Sword of the Border: Major General Jacob Jennings Brown, 1775–1828* (Kent, OH: Kent State University Press, 2000), 188, maintains that Eleazar Ripley was retained as one of the six general officers largely in order to represent New England, where he had served as Republican speaker of the Massachusetts House of Representatives before the war (p. 95). However, Ripley had served as one of the three brigade commanders in Brown's Left Division on the Niagara (and had been a regimental commander at the battle of Crysler's Field in 1813) and was badly wounded in the sortie from Fort Erie. He had lost Brown's confidence after Lundy's Lane and was beginning to engage in disputes with virtually every senior officer in the division, but, complementing Morris's point, this may have played a part in his retention, because Madison hoped to avoid the uproar Ripley would raise if he were disbanded. The troubled general finally resigned in 1820, though not before he had accepted the presidency of James Long's filibustering expedition into Texas. This colorful story notwithstanding, Ripley's career is evidence of an officer corps becoming less politicized through self-selection, as men chose whether to accept the responsibilities and constraints of the army. See Samuel Watson, "Soldier, Expansionist, Politician: Eleazer Wheelock Ripley and the Dance of Ambition in the Early American Republic," in Gene A. Smith and Sylvia L. Hilton, eds., *Nexus of Empire: Loyalty and National Identity in the Gulf Borderlands, 1763–1835* (Gainesville: University Press of Florida, 2009).

40 Jacob Brown, April 1, 1821, file B-239, Letters Received by the Secretary of War, Registered Series, 1801–1870, Microfilm 221, Record Group 107, National Archives.

See Skelton, *An American Profession of Arms*, 62, on the reactions from officers involuntarily disbanded in 1815. Although a fair number of the officers disbanded in 1815 were reappointed to fill vacancies opened by officers who resigned in 1815 (after the reduction) and 1816, most of them left the army (voluntarily or involuntarily) by 1821, or were disbanded in the reduction of that year.

41 Only thirty-four officers are mentioned in the Madison-Dallas letters collected in George Mifflin Dallas, *Life and Writings of Alexander James Dallas* (Philadelphia: Lippincott, 1871), regarding approximately twenty-five positions; in only seven cases—about 1 percent of the total slots available—did Dallas or Madison decide contrary to the board's recommendations. On May 7, Madison wrote to Dallas that he would not allow disputes about seniority to outweigh the recommenda- tions of the board, though of course the board had stuck largely to the seniority principle, reducing any overt conflict between priorities or criteria. Three days later the president observed that some of the officers he had expected to be retained were not on the board's final list, but he told the secretary that he would make no changes. Madison then made a series of observations about individual cases: that it was alright to leave the colonels of the First Rifle and Twenty-eighth Infantry regiments out of the army, though the former was being pushed by his father, the powerful Representative John Sevier of Tennessee, and the latter had strong support in his home state of Kentucky. Madison also asked Dallas to check on Colonel Charles Todd, previously of William Henry Harrison's staff, with whom Madison shared mutual friends in Virginia, but the president specifically left the decision on Todd up to the secretary of war, and all three officers were discharged. On May 13 Dallas wrote to Madison suggesting the substitution of two surgeons and a judge advocate for those recommended by the board. He also reported that Secretary of State Monroe thought it wise to retain another surgeon because the circumstances (a personal dispute between the surgeon and his colonel) would produce "suggestions of a disagreeable kind if [he were] struck off." The president agreed with these changes, and the latter surgeon became assistant surgeon general in 1818, though he was discharged in 1821. (The secretary's pick for judge advocate resigned in May 1816 and was replaced by the man recommended by the selection board.) On May 14, Dallas sent a final list of emendations, providing a replacement for an officer who had accepted appoint- ment as U.S. consul in London, a replacement for Lieutenant Colonel George Croghan if that officer pursued his proffered resignation, and four substitutions of one officer for another, one because Winfield Scott had reported that a mistake had been made and another at the request of the selection board. One of the officers (a captain) substituted for was then placed at the head of the first lieutenants in his branch, while the lieutenant with the least seniority was dropped from the retention list. Dallas suggested Franklin Bache as surgeon of the Second Infantry, a slot left open by the selection board, observing that Bache's appointment "will have a good effect," presumably politically. (The Baches were a leading Republican family in Philadelphia.) Madison responded affirmatively two

days later, with one final suggestion to retain an officer spoken well of around Charlottesville, whom Dallas sought to replace. (That officer declined retention.)

42 The four new regiments created for western service in 1855 were officered in substantial part by commissions directly from civilian life, as the dragoon and mounted rifle regiments had been in 1833, 1836, and 1846. This was unavoidable since West Point only graduated a quarter of the officers necessary for the new regiments, but Democratic partisanship, and sectional favoritism shown by Secretary of War Jefferson Davis, certainly played a part in the selection of the new officers. This backlash against General Scott's army was then engulfed by the Army's immense expansion during the Civil War, which certainly reshaped the officer corps, as the Army retained after Reconstruction numbered twice that in 1860, while West Point had only grown incrementally. See Mark R. Grandstaff, "Preserving the 'Habits and Usages of War': William Tecumseh Sherman, Professional Reform, and the U.S. Army Officer Corps, 1865–1881, Revisited," *Journal of Military History* 62 (July 1998): 521–45. Nevertheless, the top of the officer corps remained dominated by Military Academy graduates, who commanded the armies on both sides in fifty-five of the sixty largest Civil War battles (and on one side in the other five).

43 See Watson, *Jackson's Sword*, 247–52, for a discussion of possible alternative commissioning patterns—from enlisted soldiers, directly from civilian life, or from additional military academies—which the Jacksonians chose not to pursue unless West Point was unable to provide sufficient officers.

PART II

Managing Industrial-Era Warfare

4

Challenged Competency

U.S. Cavalry before, during, and after the U.S. Civil War

JOHN A. BONIN

In the spring of 1857, President James Buchanan, facing a rebellion to federal authority from the Mormons in Utah, ordered Governor Brigham Young removed from office. He directed Brevet Lieutenant General Winfield Scott to send "such an imposing force as to convince these deluded people that resistance would be in vain and thus avoid the effusion of blood."[1] On May 28, 1857, Scott ordered some twenty-five hundred U.S. Army regulars to be assembled as the Army of Utah.[2] On October 9, Colonel E. B. Alexander, commanding the lead infantry elements, reported that his advance into Utah had stalled due to resistance from the over-two-thousand-strong Mormon Nauvoo Militia and because "the want of cavalry is severely felt, and we are powerless . . . to effect any chastisement of the marauding bands that are constantly hovering about us."[3] By November 1857, the expedition, now under Colonel Albert S. Johnson, commander of the Second U.S. Cavalry, who had arrived with six companies of the Second U.S. Dragoons under Lieutenant Colonel Phillip St. George Cooke, sought winter quarters. In January 1858, concerned that the Regular Army might be too small for the Mormon crisis, Senator Jefferson Davis submitted a bill to increase its size by six thousand men, which stimulated little more than a congressional debate.[4] Fortunately for Buchanan, presidential negotiators ended the crisis and Johnston's Army peacefully entered Salt Lake City on June 26, 1858, to install a new governor and restore federal control.[5]

Less than three years later, the small United States Regular Army failed to prevent another conflict and would prove totally ill prepared for the task of suppressing a larger rebellion and restoring the union. When on April 12, 1861, southern secessionists fired on federal troops in Fort Sumter, South Carolina, the U.S. Regular Army consisted only of some sixteen thousand widely dispersed personnel with less than four thousand (mostly coast artillerymen) east of the Mississippi.[6] Unlike with the Mormons, two days after President Abraham Lincoln's inauguration, the Confederate Congress voted to authorize a massive force of one hundred thousand militia on March 6, 1861.[7] The

U.S. Army was totally disorganized and untrained for large-scale operations, and led by old men, many of whose sympathies lay with the South. It consisted of only ten infantry, four artillery, and five mounted regiments, plus nine staff departments with only four general officers. However, it completely lacked operational headquarters above regiment.[8] The five regiments comprising the U.S. Army mounted force (First and Second Light Dragoons, Regiment of Mounted Rifles, and First and Second Cavalry) constituted a minor auxiliary to the established infantry and artillery branches that would absorb years of casualties and setbacks until it provided the North with a mobile arm capable of decisive results. This chapter will focus on events before, during, and after that wartime cavalry transformation, to include the impact that postconflict drawdowns had on this force as a microcosm of the larger phenomenon of Army drawdowns.

Background

The concept of mobility in warfare is several thousand years old. Men riding in chariots or mounted on horses have for centuries provided relative mobility, range, and tactical striking power in comparison to men fighting on foot, but at far greater expense.[9] By the Napoleonic era, European cavalry organized in independent units as large as corps had become standardized as light, heavy, and dragoons. Light cavalry (hussars or chasseurs) provided the most numerous types of mounted forces performing the roles of reconnaissance, security against surprise, and pursuit of retreating enemy forces. The heavy cavalry (often named "cuirassiers" for their plate armor) were normally held in reserve and utilized the shock effect of a mounted saber charge to destroy enemy formations. Dragoons, which earlier had been mounted infantry using horses for enhanced mobility, retained a carbine for dismounted action but were now employed predominantly mounted like other cavalry.[10]

In America, a rather different practice than that of Europe evolved. During the Colonial era, the lack of roads and broken terrain in America eliminated the need for traditional European cavalry except for a few troopers serving primarily as escorts, messengers, or scouts. As early as 1658, Connecticut formed a small militia cavalry troop of some thirty-seven men for multirole duty as light dragoons and employed a force of three hundred light dragons during King Philip's War.[11]

At the start of the American Revolution, some colonies had volunteer mounted militia units of troop size. The First Troop Philadelphia City Cavalry, originally formed on November 17, 1774, as the Philadelphia Troop of Light Horse with twenty-eight of the city's gentlemen, famously participated in numerous local actions.[12] In 1776, the Continental Congress considered the idea of adding mounted units to the Continental Army. Major Elisha Sheldon's small detachment of Connecticut militia troopers proved useful for reconnaissance during the later phases of the 1776 campaign. Also, the intimidation of Continental infantry by British light dragoons caused General George Washington to ask Congress to authorize cavalry for the Continental Army. A resolution of Congress called for up to three thousand light dragoons, but Washington formed only four small regiments. Major Elisha Sheldon's Connecticut troops and six Virginia troops of light horse formed the basis of the first two regiments. Congress authorized 280 officers and men organized into a headquarters and six small troops of forty-four each for four regiments of light dragoons. These never reached full strength, and Washington eventually converted them into smaller and less expensive mixed cavalry and infantry "legions."[13] By war's end, Congress discharged all the light dragoons, and for the next fifty years, mounted units existed only fleetingly in the U.S. Regular Army.

General Arthur St. Clair's disaster of 1791 in the Northwest Territories revealed the need for cavalry when fighting Native Americans. Consequently, Major General Anthony Wayne's legion included a regular squadron of four troops of light dragoons in addition to a Kentucky mounted militia brigade. On August 20, 1794, at the Battle of Fallen Timbers, the dragoon's sabers contributed significantly to the rout of the Indians.[14] During the War of 1812, two small regular dragoon regiments participated with detachments in several battles. Mounted militia units proved more numerous and successful. After these wars, Congress, dedicated to a minimum standing army, again disbanded the regular dragoons.[15] Congressional opposition, primarily because of the increased cost, had eliminated regular mounted units in the Army's drawdown after every crisis during this period, placing total reliance on mounted militia units for cavalry.[16]

By 1832, as the frontier moved west, the Army finally activated permanent mounted units to provide a more mobile response to the hostile Plains Indians. In June 1832, Congress authorized the Battalion of Mounted Rangers and within a year converted it into the Regiment of Dragoons. Congress mounted it for speed, but for economy trained and equipped it to also operate dismounted. In 1836, Congress authorized a second regiment of dragoons to assist with the Seminole War. However, in 1843, with the end of the Seminole War, Congress voted to unhorse the Second Dragoons to save money. But due to pressure from the West, Congress remounted the Second in 1844. For the Mexican War, Congress in 1846 authorized a new regular Regiment of Mounted Riflemen as well as seven regiments of volunteer cavalry.[17] Illustrative of the popularity of militia in the South as compared to the North, all seven of these regiments hailed from slave states (two Texas, two Missouri, one Arkansas, one Kentucky, and one Tennessee).[18] After the Mexican War and the usual postwar reductions, the Army retained three regular mounted regiments and returned them to duty on a greatly expanded frontier.

Throughout this period, the small U.S. mounted force attempted to adapt conventional European cavalry tactics to the realities of dispersed combat on the frontier without adequate guidance from the War Department. Although Indians constituted the main opponents of this period, the Army's mounted doctrine consisted of an 1841 adoption of a French cavalry manual that emphasized conventional mounted combat.[19] As Brevet Lieutenant General Winfield Scott, the commanding general of the Army, stated in 1850, "The great extent of our frontiers, and the peculiar character of the services devolving on our troops, render it indispensable that the cavalry element should enter largely into the composition of the Army."[20] Operational demand caused Secretary of War Jefferson Davis in 1855 to obtain approval for two additional mounted regiments.

Also in 1855, Davis dispatched a three-man military commission led by Major Richard Delafield to observe changes in the art of war during the Crimean War. Davis specified in his instructions to Delafield, "[T]he arms and equipment of cavalry of all kinds will claim your particular attention."[21] However, the lavishly prepared primary report of over 280 pages focused on changes to fortifications and artillery. Delafield in his cover letter stated that "the Secretary of War will do a great service to the nation by increasing the material and munitions means of defense . . . preparatory to that great struggle which sooner or later may be forced upon us, and to resist which, with our present means, we are comparatively unprepared."[22] As for cavalry, the report stated, "We have at present five mounted regiments, and as yet have made no suitable permanent provision for this arm."[23] Upon returning as the junior member of the commission, Captain George B. McClellan, First U.S. Cavalry, in his separate report found "the nature of cavalry service in the United States . . . quite different from that . . . in Europe."[24] He recommended the development of both real dragoons equally capable of mounted and dismounted combat; and light cavalry capable of matching Indian mobility, thereby forcing Indians into combat in which the U.S. Army's "superiority of weapons and discipline" could be brought to bear.[25]

At the War's Start

One day after the evacuation of Fort Sumter, President Lincoln enacted the Militia Act of 1792 to call for seventy-five thousand militia for three months of federal service to augment the small regular Union forces. In January 1861, the federal government had only five understrength regiments of horse (about 20 percent of the Regular Army) with some 82 officers and 3,123 enlisted men present for duty, all stationed in the West.[26] Between January and April 1861, resignations by a majority of southern officers significantly reduced the numbers of regular mounted officers, including four of five regimental commanders and two seconds-in-command.[27]

Two weeks after the shelling of Fort Sumter in Charleston Harbor, Carl Schurtz, German émigré and Republican Party activist, sought permission to raise a regiment of volunteer cavalry in New York City as part of the seventy-five thousand volunteers. He obtained an audience with both General Scott, still commanding general of the Army at age seventy-five, and Secretary of War Simon Cameron. Both rejected his offer. General Scott argued that despite its Napoleonic significance in traditional war, cavalry would lack usefulness during the impeding Civil War. He believed that cavalry should serve only in auxiliary roles to infantry and artillery. Scott based his beliefs on the marked improvements of rifled firearms, which would render a cavalry charge too costly, as well as the restricted nature of the wooded terrain throughout the potential theater of operations. Since he believed the war would terminate quickly, the expense of arming, training, and equipping more cavalry would prove unnecessary. Experts of the period opined that it took two years to properly train a cavalryman.[28] Only one company of volunteer cavalry gained government approval in April 1861, and only because its commander, Captain Samuel W. Owens, had funded the unit. The company, consisting of Unionists from the District of Columbia, patrolled the streets and suburbs of D.C. for three months.[29]

To expand the existing Regular Army, Congress eventually did authorize one new cavalry regiment (of twelve companies), as well as nine infantry regiments in July 1861. General Scott successfully rebuffed all attempts to add more than one cavalry regiment in the initial call for forty regiments of ninety-day volunteers. Scott had no faith in volunteer cavalry; it was a very expensive arm and would open an immense field for fraud and corruption.[30] Consequently, at the Battle of Bull Run, the first major battle in the East, Brigadier General Irwin McDowell had only seven small companies of regular Union cavalry in his army of forty thousand.[31] The U.S. Army had neither adopted the European concept of cavalry nor developed a native alternative.

During the First Battle of Bull Run on July 21, 1861, the South fielded some fourteen militia cavalry companies, including two small regiments under Colonel R. C. Radford and Lieutenant Colonel J. E. B. Stuart. As Union forces facing General Thomas Jackson's brigade faltered, Stuart's cavalry on the left and Radford's on the right conducted devastating charges that panicked northern recruits. As much of the Union cavalry had been distributed for courier duty at various headquarters, only a rump battalion of four regular companies had been held in reserve to cover the rout of the Union Army.[32]

During the next two years, the South gained and maintained cavalry superiority over the Union forces and effectively utilized this factor to offset southern inferiority in manpower and industrial potential. The South rapidly formed large numbers of volunteer mounted units composed primarily of men accustomed to riding. These men also provided their own weapons and horses, and were organized into increasingly larger independent formations as brigades, divisions, and corps. Initially, southern cavalry served under dynamic commanders such as J. E. B. Stuart, Turner Ashby, and Wade Hampton in the East; and Nathan B. Forrest, John Hunt Morgan, Earl Van Dorn, and Joseph Wheeler in the West. Early in the conflict, Confederate senior commanders employed their cavalry more effectively for obtaining intelligence and screening troop movements. In addition, Confederate cavalry conducted occasional independent raids into the North that disrupted communications, tied down Union forces, and obtained or destroyed supplies.[33]

In comparison with the Confederates, the Union cavalry remained ineffective in battle for a variety reasons. After Bull Run, the War Department realized the need for mounted troops in a longer war and transferred all the regular cavalry from the West, as well as raised eighty-two volunteer cavalry regiments by the end of 1861.[34] Initially, Congress accepted volunteer regiments with only ten companies per regiment, but by mid-1863 all were directed to the new regular design of twelve companies with over twelve hundred men authorized. However, the North faced competing demands for the employment of horses to mount its cavalry, as the Army also needed the muscle power of horses to pull hundreds of supply wagons and ambulances. In addition, Major General George B. McClellan, in organizing the Army of the Potomac, took advantage of northern industry by emphasizing the use of horse-drawn firepower by allocating approximately twice as many horses to his artillery as to his cavalry. In March 1862, the Army of the Potomac had 520 guns in 92 batteries with some 11,000 horses while his cavalry had only some 5,000 horses.[35]

Organization of Union Cavalry Regiments: 1861

	Union Cavalry Regiment	Regiment Headquarters
Authorized Strength: 55 Officers 249 Non-commissioned officers 984 Soldiers Total: 1,288		• Colonel- Commander • Lieutenant Colonel- Second in Command • Captain-Adjutant • Captain- Quartermaster • Captain-Commissary • Surgeon • Assistant Surgeon • Chaplain • Two Chief Buglers

1st Battalion	2nd Battalion	3rd Battalion
Major-Commander Lieutenant-Adjutant Lieutenant-Quartermaster Lieutenant-Commissary Six Sergeants	Major-Commander Lieutenant-Adjutant Lieutenant-Quartermaster Lieutenant-Commissary Six Sergeants	Major-Commander Lieutenant-Adjutant Lieutenant-Quartermaster Lieutenant-Commissary Six Sergeants

Companies A, B, C, D	Cavalry Company	Companies E F, G, H	Cavalry Company	Companies I, K, L, M	Cavalry Company
	Captain-Commander 1st Lieutenant 2d Lieutenant First Sergeant Four Sergeants Eight Corporals Two Buglers Two Farriers One Saddler One Wagoner 82 Privates		Captain-Commander 1st Lieutenant 2d Lieutenant First Sergeant Four Sergeants Eight Corporals Two Buglers Two Farriers One Saddler One Wagoner 82 Privates		Captain-Commander 1st Lieutenant 2d Lieutenant First Sergeant Four Sergeants Eight Corporals Two Buglers Two Farriers One Saddler One Wagoner 82 Privates

Figure 4.1: Organization of Union Cavalry Regiments: 1861

In addition, unlike the more rural South, Union cavalry initially faced significant problems in the training of large numbers of urban recruits and the acquisition of suitable cavalry horses and adequate weapons. Major General David McM. Gregg commented after the war that

[t]hese regiments had been hastily formed . . . [with] many improper [officer] appointments. . . . [R]esult was the failure of many of the regiments to make any progress in preparing themselves for the duties of cavalry in the field. . . . The condition of the horses . . . when received were totally unfit for cavalry service, having been taken . . . from dishonest contractors.[36]

A unit formed in Trenton, New Jersey, in August 1861 exemplified this situation. After moving to Washington, D.C., the unit's poor discipline and lack of camp sanitation prompted Private F. Rodgers to complain directly to General McClellan about "the disorganized condition of the 1st New Jersey Cavalry."[37] Perhaps the worst shortage affecting Union cavalry was that of weapons. In addition to a desperate shortage of cavalry equipment in 1861, the Ordnance Bureau under Brigadier General James Ripley placed almost no orders for cavalry weapons or equipment in the first few months of the war.

As a result, it was not until 1863 that Union cavalry became fully equipped. Until then, many cavalry units received a variety of inadequate and nondescript weapons that ranged from obsolete single-shot horse pistols to foreign muskets.[38]

Early Operations in the East

Without a clear conception of mounted operations, the Union armies failed to properly organize their cavalry. Because of inadequate headquarters support elements, Union commanders fragmented many of their new cavalry regiments to perform this duty.[39] As Major General Wesley Merritt wrote after the war, "[T]he smallest infantry organization had its company or more of mounted men, whose duty consisted of supplying details as orderlies for mounted staff officers . . . or in camp acting as grooms and bootblacks. . . . [T]his treatment demoralized the cavalry."[40] During the Peninsular Campaign of 1862, General McClellan, rather than massing his numerous volunteer cavalry regiments, assigned them to infantry formations to perform picket duty, escort wagons, and conduct limited patrolling.[41] McClellan appointed Brigadier General George Stoneman as his chief of cavalry to serve as a staff officer at headquarters to supervise these fragmented mounted elements, but not to exercise independent command.[42] Stoneman had a dyspeptic nature and proved an unfortunate choice as a cavalry leader due to hemorrhoids, which prevented his sitting in a saddle for long periods.[43]

As for the regular cavalry, McClellan concentrated most of his five small regiments into a cavalry reserve under Brigadier General Cooke so as to "have a reliable and efficient body on which to depend in a battle."[44] General Gregg commented that unlike the volunteers, "regular regiments were in their habitual state of efficiency."[45] During the Battle of Gaines Mill, General Cooke infamously ordered five companies of the 5th U.S. Cavalry with 220 troopers under Captain Charles Whiting to charge a Confederate infantry brigade across a 250-yard open field in order to save several Union batteries. Most of the saber-wielding troopers never reached the enemy, suffering at least fifty-eight casualties in the attack.[46]

When McClellan's Army of the Potomac departed for the Peninsular Campaign, he directed several Union forces to guard the Shenandoah Valley against Confederate Major General Thomas "Stonewall" Jackson and his cavalry commander, Colonel Turner Ashby. The rolling terrain of the valley would require good cavalry for information. Unfortunately, these Union forces had an assortment of poorly trained and equipped cavalry units. Major General John C. Fremont reported that his cavalry horses were "so nearly starved and broken down as to be nearly useless."[47] Major General James Shield referred to the 1st West Virginia as "good for nothing" and the 1st Rhode Island as "rubbish cavalry . . . an encumbrance."[48] The 1st New Jersey in its first combat exemplified Union problems with employing cavalry. Near Harrisonburg, Virginia, on June 6, 1862, the regiment blundered into an ambush set by Turner Ashby and escaped from "the field of their defeat, leaving their colonel, three captains, one-twelfth of their troopers, and the regimental colors in the hands of the enemy."[49]

McClellan again demonstrated his misuse and lack of confidence in Union cavalry in the Antietam Campaign of 1862. General Orders No. 155, Headquarters, Army of the Potomac, September 9, 1862, directed that "Provost Marshals will send cavalry where they have it, on all roads to their rear to hurry up stragglers."[50] During Antietam, the war's single bloodiest battle, he failed to employ his reserve cavalry and assigned them only to the missions of "supporting the artillery . . . driving up stragglers."[51] According to Marcus A. Reno, "Our organization was so incomplete that the operations of the cavalry during the Antietam Campaign were almost insignificant . . . so much so that . . . it was a joke to offer a reward for a dead cavalryman."[52]

After the battle, Major General J. E. B. Stuart conducted a raid from 10 to 13 October with eighteen hundred troopers selected from across his three-brigade cavalry division through the rear of the Union Army. Shortages of horses resulted in McClellan ineffectively responding with only eight hundred mounted soldiers.[53] During the raid McClellan complained to the War Department, "It is absolutely necessary that some energetic means be taken to supply the cavalry of this army with remount horses."[54] The quartermaster-general of the Army, M. C. Meigs, replied that since September 1, 1862, he had provided over ten thousand horses to McClellan, at a cost of over $1.2 million. But the abuse of the animals by ill-disciplined troops caused such wastage of horses as to render the cavalry ineffective. When he learned of McClellan's concern over "fatigued horses," President Abraham Lincoln retorted, "[P]ardon me for asking what the horses of your army have done since the battle of Antietam that fatigue anything?"[55] McClellan used his lack of sufficient cavalry as an excuse not to comply with the president's order to advance into Virginia, for he claimed,

> My experience has shown the necessity of a large and efficient cavalry force. . . . [But] without more cavalry horses our communications, from the moment we march, would be at the mercy of the large cavalry forces of the enemy, and it would not be possible for us to cover our flanks properly. . . . Under the foregoing circumstances I beg leave . . . to await the reception of new horses.[56]

According to General Merritt, McClellan had demonstrated "ignorance of the proper use of cavalry" and had completely failed to provide "management of this important arm of service."[57] Within three weeks, Lincoln replaced McClellan largely for his failure to advance aggressively after Antietam.

After taking command of the Army of the Potomac on November 7, 1862, Major General Ambrose Burnside moved against Fredericksburg in late November to force his way to Richmond. Burnside reorganized the Army of the Potomac into three "grand divisions" each of two infantry corps and a cavalry brigade or division. While this action split his force of some six thousand cavalry for infantry support, its weakness hardly mattered during the ensuing bloody Battle of Fredericksburg. Once again, playing mere spectators, the Union cavalry suffered only two killed and six wounded.[58]

Belatedly, the Union Army recognized the importance of a mounted arm. On February 6, 1863, shortly after assuming command of the Army of the Potomac, Major General Joseph Hooker consolidated most of his cavalry into a single corps of three divisions under Brigadier General Stoneman.[59] In April, Hooker chose Stoneman's corps of almost ten thousand cavalrymen to pry General Lee out of his Fredericksburg defensive position at the start of what would become the Chancellorsville Campaign. Hooker only retained Colonel Thomas Devin's small cavalry brigade when he realized that his daring plan would have left the Army without any cavalry screens. Later referred to as Stoneman's raid, this operation failed to accomplish Hooker's objectives, as it only minimally disrupted Lee's communications. However, the raid ensured the Union cavalry corps' absence during most of the Battle of Chancellorsville where it could have screened Hooker's flanks attack and resulted in heavy casualties to Devin's overworked unit.[60]

After Chancellorsville, 1863 became the turning point when Union "cavalry became a powerful and effective force" as it achieved parity with its southern counterparts in the East.[61] The cavalry corps, now commanded by Brigadier General (later Major General) Alfred Pleasonton, conducted an effective reconnaissance in force against Stuart's cavalry that turned into a classic cavalry battle at Brandy Station in early June. When Major General George Meade took command of the Army of the Potomac on June 28, Meade and Pleasonton reorganized the cavalry into a larger three-division corps incorporating Julius Stahel's small cavalry division from the defenses of Washington, D.C.[62] General Pleasonton also used this opportunity to promote three of his more aggressive young aides, George A. Custer, Elon J. Farnsworth, and Wesley Merritt, to brigadier general over older volunteers.

During the start of the Gettysburg Campaign, Union cavalry effectively screened the advance of the Army of the Potomac during its movement north.

While General Stuart took his Confederate cavalry on another raid around the Union Army, Major General John Buford's 1st Cavalry Division screened the Union left flank, making initial contact with Lee's army on July 1. Fighting dismounted, Buford effectively delayed the rebel advance upon the town until supporting infantry could arrive. On July 3, Brigadier General Custer's Michigan Brigade attached to Major General Gregg's 2nd Cavalry Division stopped Stuart's attempted attack on the rear of the Union Army, which was made in conjunction with Major General Pickett's direct infantry assault.[63] General Pleasonton's failure to concentrate his pursuing cavalry stymied Meade's attempt to destroy Lee's army during its subsequent retreat.[64] In addition, Stuart's cavalry partially reclaimed its reputation with hard fighting in covering Lee's retreat.[65]

Another major factor in the further improvement of the Union cavalry occurred in July 1863, when Secretary of War Edwin M. Stanton established the Cavalry Bureau. This was a unique organization that oversaw procurement and a series of depots empowered to improve the efficiency of Union cavalry and reduce the enormous wastage of horses.[66] After the first two heads of the bureau proved unable to unsnarl bureaucratic problems, Stanton in January 1864 selected a member of Major General U.S. Grant's staff, James H. Wilson. As bureau chief, Brigadier General Wilson adopted the breech-loaded Spencer seven-shot magazine carbine as the standard arm for the cavalry service over the objections of the fiscally conservative chief of ordnance. In addition, he reformed the previously corrupt system of horse procurement operated by the Quartermaster Department and improved cavalry recruit training. By April 1864, Wilson had succeeded in mounting and arming the Union cavalry to a high professional standard.[67]

Early Cavalry Operations in the West

In the Western Theater of Operations, Union cavalry also suffered early inferiority to Confederate cavalry. In the first year of the war, the Union raised and disposed of volunteer cavalry in an atmosphere of utter confusion; units lacked proper missions, they frequently fought outnumbered, and senior commanders fragmented units to support the infantry.[68] For example, on April 2, 1862, Major General U.S. Grant, commander of the Army of the Tennessee, parceled out his three regiments and eight separate companies of cavalry among his six divisions of infantry at Shiloh Landing, Tennessee. In addition, Grant's subordinate division commanders, such as Major General William T. Sherman, failed to properly employ their cavalry for security, contributing to the Confederates achieving surprise on April 6.[69] A notable exception to the poor employment of Union cavalry in the West proved to be Colonel Philip H. Sheridan's conduct at the Battle of Booneville, Mississippi, on July 1, 1862. Sheridan, who only six weeks earlier had been a captain in the 13th U.S. Infantry, succeeded in defeating a numerically superior Confederate cavalry force using a combination of firepower from five companies of dismounted troopers with Colt revolving rifles, and a mounted flank attack by four saber companies.[70]

In late 1862, Confederate generals N. B. Forrest and Earl Van Dorn stopped General Grant's first attempt to take Vicksburg through central Mississippi with devastating cavalry raids on his rear. Grant claimed that these raids "demonstrated the impossibility of maintaining so long a line of road over which to draw supplies for an army moving in an enemy's country."[71] The one bright spot for Grant occurred when Colonel Benjamin Grierson's long-range raid with a brigade of less than one thousand men severed Vicksburg's rail connections with the East in April–May 1863.[72]

Similarly, Major General William Rosecrans, commanding the Army of the Cumberland in early 1863, believed he could not advance toward Chattanooga in the face of General Braxton Bragg's superior Confederate cavalry. His endless requests for additional cavalry resulted in his receiving permission from Secretary of War Stanton to mount five thousand infantry on horses or mules.[73] A senior Union cavalry officer called Colonel Abel D. Streight's ill-fated mule-mounted infantry raid that resulted "the most senseless thing I saw done during the war to waste men and material."[74] Conducted simultaneously with Grierson's raid in April and May 1863, Streight's objective was to break the Western & Atlantic rail line south of Dalton, Georgia, and force Bragg to withdraw. Unfortunately for the federals, General Forrest outmaneuvered Streight's brigade of some fifteen hundred saddle-sore men and forced them to surrender.[75]

For the 1863 Chickamauga Campaign, General Rosecrans increased his mounted forces by permitting additional units to become mounted infantry. Colonel John T. Wilder converted his infantry brigade and then obtained private funding to purchase Spencer rifles. During the ensuing campaign, Wilder's brigade became the workhorse of the Army. In June 1863, this brigade led the advance through the Hoover Gap, where Major General George Thomas awarded them the nickname of the "Lightning Brigade" for their rapidity of fire.[76] Partially because of improved Union mounted elements, two Confederate cavalry corps under Generals Forrest and Wheeler, despite their numerical superiority, failed to properly coordinate their actions, keep their commander informed, or effectively conduct a pursuit of Rosecrans's defeated army.[77]

Sheridan in the East

Shortly after Lieutenant General Ulysses S. Grant took command as general-in-chief of all the Union armies in early 1864, he faced several problems in preparing the Army of the Potomac for his envisioned operations. Finding a shortage of infantry and an excess of artillery, Grant converted several heavy artillery regiments that had manned the fortifications around Washington into infantry.[78] Grant also sought an officer to transform the effectiveness of the cavalry of the Army of the Potomac. According to historian Russell Weigley, "Grant believed they needed an exceptional leader to mold them into the clearly superior arm necessary to win the war."[79] Grant chose from the western armies Major General Phillip Sheridan. General Meade, retained in command of just the Army of the Potomac, considered Sheridan's role to be "an adjunct at Army Headquarters—a sort of chief of cavalry" supervising picket duty, protecting rear areas, covering infantry movements, and screening the flanks.[80] Sheridan, on the other hand, insisted that cavalry should "be kept concentrated to fight the enemy's cavalry" so that "the flanks and rear of the Army of the Potomac would require little or no defense."[81] After the bloody, indecisive battle during the Wilderness Campaign on May 8, 1864, Sheridan and Meade argued over an independent role for the cavalry. As Grant sided with Sheridan, Meade ordered Sheridan to concentrate his corps of three divisions to "proceed against the enemy's cavalry."[82]

Sheridan began to achieve decisive results with his concentration of the cavalry of the Army of the Potomac. While none of the major cavalry battles of 1863 had resulted in a clear Union victory, Sheridan obtained clear cavalry superiority over Stuart's cavalry at Yellow Tavern on May 11, 1864. This battle proved an "indisputable defeat" for the Confederate cavalry, including General Stuart being mortally wounded in action with General Custer's Michigan Brigade.[83] Sheridan then conducted devastating raids into Virginia and screened the Army of the Potomac's crossing of the James to Petersburg during the Overland Campaign.[84] During the ensuing savage fighting, the firepower provided by Sheridan's dismounted troopers proved critical.[85] Despite the failure of General Burnside's corps at the Battle of the Crater in late July, Grant thought that "if our cavalry should get well round the enemy's right . . . we may yet take Petersburg."[86]

Desperate to avoid stalemate at Petersburg, General Lee saw an opportunity to divert Grant and sent Lieutenant General Jubal Early to the Shenandoah Valley with a quarter of his Confederate forces. In July 1864, Early twice threatened Washington, D.C., and sent cavalry to burn Chambersburg, Pennsylvania. These actions forced Grant to reluctantly postpone decisive operations around Petersburg. He first sent elements of the Seventh Corps to protect Washington and then to reorganize Union forces with Major General Sheridan placed in command of the new Army of the Shenandoah.[87] Sheridan detached a provisional cavalry corps with two of his veteran cavalry divisions, the 1st (under Brigadier General Merritt) and the 3rd (initially commanded by Brigadier General Wilson, but later under Brigadier General Custer) from the Army of the Potomac. Sheridan's subsequent Shenandoah Valley Campaign not only crushed Early in a series of battles utilizing the firepower of his carbines and the flexibility of his troops to fight mounted or dismounted but also deprived the Confederacy of this fertile area.[88] Under Sheridan, the cavalry became the equal of the infantry and artillery, and the spearhead of his offensives at Winchester and Cedar Creek.[89]

Departing Winchester on February 27, 1865, Sheridan and his cavalry hastened the end of the war. First, he conducted a devastating raid through Charlottesville, Virginia, before rejoining Grant outside Petersburg on March 26. Sheridan then employed the mobility of his reformed Cavalry Corps to turn Lee's flank at Five Forks, and to conduct a relentless pursuit to Saylor's Creek ending with Lee's surrender at Appomattox.[90] Historian Russell F. Weigley provides a summary of this action: "This had not been simply a cavalry corps, but a highly mobile striking arm, capable of standing to fight infantry as well as of moving with the fastest speed possible. In the final campaign against the Army of Northern Virginia, Sheridan's striking arm had become the decisive factor."[91]

Wilson in the West

After a series of defeats of Union cavalry at the hands of General Forrest during the 1864 Atlanta Campaign, General William T. Sherman complained to Grant, "Our cavalry is dwindling away . . . [and] is always unable to attempt anything. Garrard is over-cautious, and I think Stoneman is lazy."[92] As Sherman lacked trust in his cavalry commanders, he wired Grant for "a good cavalry officer to command."[93] In September 1864, Sherman obtained the commander of Sheridan's 3rd Cavalry Division, General Wilson.

Wilson applied Sheridan's cavalry concepts as he reformed Sherman's cavalry in late 1864. According to Wilson, he "had already reached certain conclusions, not only from the study of military history, but from observation in the field, as to the proper functions of cavalry and the necessity of handling it in masses against the enemy's front, flanks, and communications."[94]

Promoted to major general, Wilson obtained Sherman's approval to collect, mass, remount, and re-equip with Spencer carbines sixty-one of the seventy-two cavalry regiments under Sherman's command into a single cavalry corps of seven divisions. Of this force, Wilson provided one division to accompany Sherman's march through Georgia and another to participate in the attack on Mobile, Alabama.[95] Wilson inherited the political challenge represented by twelve regiments of one-year Tennessee (Union) Volunteer Cavalry raised by Andrew Johnson, the Union governor and vice-president elect. Finding rampant desertion, poor horses, and a lack of leadership, Wilson replaced all of Johnson's regimental commanders and seized numerous privately owned horses, including Johnson's own carriage horses.[96]

With the remaining divisions of this corps, Wilson demonstrated the professionalism and tactical flexibility of Union cavalry. During November–December 1864, Wilson successively delayed Confederate general John B. Hood's advance on Nashville, conducted counterattacks upon Hood's flanks, and performed a mounted pursuit of the defeated Confederates for over 175 miles. The following spring, beginning on March 22, 1865, Wilson, with three divisions, including the Lightning Brigade of mounted infantry, comprising some twelve thousand well-mounted and well-equipped troopers (plus fifteen hundred men without horses to guard his trains), conducted an independent strategic penetration of the deep South. Historian James Jones has referred to this anachronistically as a Yankee Blitzkrieg.[97]

In less than two months, Wilson's corps delivered the strategic *coup de grace* to the remaining southern heartland that ended any possibility of continued resistance. Wilson's troopers rode more than 525 miles; defeated General Forrest at Selma; occupied Montgomery; destroyed numerous industrial facilities, including those at Columbus, Georgia; and reoccupied central Georgia, capturing Confederate President Jefferson Davis near Irwinville on May 10, 1865. The corps captured nearly 7,000 Confederate militia while suffering only 99 killed and 626 wounded or missing.[98] In contrast to previous Union problems with horses, Wilson had been able not only to replace all unserviceable horses at Confederate expense but also to mount his men without horses.[99] While the mobility for these successes depended on serviceable horses, the firepower to enable Wilson's cavalry to overcome entrenched infantry came from the Spencer carbine that every trooper carried. As he later declared, "To the perfection of this carbine and the rapidity with which it could be fired, I attribute the uniform success of the assaults made against the enemy's entrenchments at Nashville, Selma, West Point and Columbus."[100] In his memoirs, Wilson wrote that he believed not only that his mobile corps were invincible but also that his men "justly regarded themselves equal to any task."[101] Historian Jerry Keenan speculates on what could have been accomplished if the Union cavalry had been able to function at its full potential years earlier.[102]

While Sheridan and Wilson's cavalry corps achieved decisive results against the Confederates, militia cavalry exclusively served in the West against the Native Americans. On November 29, 1864, in the absence of regular U.S. Cavalry, militia colonel John M. Chivington commanded some seven hundred short-term volunteer militia of the 1st Colorado Cavalry, the 3rd Colorado Cavalry, and a company of the 1st Regiment of New Mexico Volunteer Cavalry that conducted a brutal massacre of Black Kettle's Cheyenne encampment. Some two hundred Native Americans, mostly women and children, died at Sand Creek, Colorado.[103]

Russell Weigley argues that "[a] reliable mobile arm is invaluable, even indispensable, to the combination of forces that permit elevating tactical pressure against an enemy into wider threats encompassing an entire theater of war."[104] By April 1865, the Union Cavalry had been transformed from a minor auxiliary branch into just such a reliable mobile combat arm capable of decisive results. The Civil War provided the U.S. Army with an opportunity to develop a conceptual model of a mounted arm not only appropriate to the tactical conditions it faced but also capable of providing both decentralized support of infantry formations and the conduct of independent strategic missions. The Union Cavalry proved to be more than just mounted infantry, as it could fight equally well mounted or dismounted, as circumstances dictated. This transformation had not been possible with extemporaneously formed short-service militia. It required aggressive leaders, such as Sheridan, Wilson, Custer, and Merritt. This transformation also required management by the Cavalry Bureau to acquire the most appropriate and expensive technology of the day (Spencer repeating carbines), to procure serviceable horses, and to ensure well-trained cavalrymen who knew how to fight as well as how to maintain their horses.

Sheridan in Texas, 1865

As the Civil War ended in the East in May 1865, there remained one more strategic task for a large mounted force of the wartime volunteer Union Army. Confederate Lieutenant General Edmund Kirby-Smith's Trans-Mississippi Department in Texas contained "the only organized rebel army left in the Confederacy," with over fifteen thousand troops, including many experienced Texas cavalrymen.[105] General Grant sent Major General Sheridan from Virginia to Texas with instructions "to operate against this command, to break it up or destroy it."[106] Sheridan also had the mission of restoring Texas to Union control as well as of being in a position to "aid [President Benito] Juarez in expelling the French from Mexico."[107] Grant assigned Sheridan an

Army of Observation of over forty thousand men in three infantry corps that would primarily enter Texas using ports along the Gulf of Mexico.[108] In addition, "because of a desire of Grant to make a strong showing of force in Texas," Sheridan "decided to transverse the State with two columns of Cavalry."[109] To command the cavalry, Sheridan specifically requested from his Cavalry Corps of the Army of the Potomac Major General Wesley Merritt's 1st Cavalry Division headquarters and Major General George Custer's 3rd Cavalry Division headquarters. However, the units for these divisions had to be collected from volunteer cavalry regiments in Louisiana, West Tennessee, Mississippi, and Alabama. "Very few of these troops had been in action" and "almost without exception, were clamoring to be discharged and sent home."[110] Merritt's division of five thousand departed Shreveport, Louisiana, on July 9 on a model thirty-three-day, six-hundred-mile march to San Antonio; while Custer's division of four thousand departed on August 8 from Alexandria, Louisiana, to Houston and then to the state capital at Austin.[111] Perhaps because of these overwhelming numbers, no resistance was encountered, even by large numbers of ex-Confederates, who had gone home armed and unrepentant.[112]

With the surrender of Kirby-Smith's forces, the aggressive Sheridan relished the possibility of confronting the some thirty-one thousand French forces of Emperor Maximilian in battle.[113] He felt that the Union Army at the close of the Civil War, and especially its cavalry, was the finest in the world, and hoped for any opportunity to prove it. After arriving in Texas, he proclaimed IV Corps and Merritt's cavalry division in San Antonio to be ready for combat; positioned a pontoon train at the Rio Grande; opened communications with the Mexican patriot Juarez; dispatched scouts to inquire about roads and forage in Mexico; and deposited some thirty thousand surplus rifled-muskets on the Rio Grande for use by Juarez's forces.[114] French and imperial forces were very much dispersed, and General Thomas Mejia had no more than 3,500 men in northern Mexico across from Texas.[115]

Frustrated with the pace of diplomacy, Sheridan liberally interpreted his orders, which directed him to preserve neutrality. In November 1865, Sheridan reported to Grant,

> My own idea is that if our Government means to take the contract [to intervene] only 6,000 cavalry is required, and a demand for the surrender of Matamoras, which would be given up. This cavalry could be started into the country from Fort Duncan, and the whole of Northern Mexico would rise with it. . . . The French cannot concentrate in this part of Mexico against a cavalry force, on account of supplies.[116]

Ironically, Sheridan's "saber rattling" received backing in the reporting of French Colonel Francois de Chenal as an official observer from 1864 to 1865 with the Army of the Potomac on the increased combat effectiveness of the Union Army. De Chenal specifically noted the superiority of Union cavalry, especially fighting dismounted, which could "throw up entrenchments like the infantry"[117] in comparison with the obsolete Napoleonic-style French cavalry that preferred mounted charges with *l'arme blanche* than to dismount with carbines.[118]

The presence and maneuvers of Sheridan's veteran Army of Observation, with its two divisions of cavalry, significantly contributed to U.S. diplomatic pressure and the French decision in 1866 to withdraw their forces, abandoning Maximilian. But, these would be the last corps and division-sized formations in the U.S. Army for over thirty years. As the Army discharged Sheridan's volunteers in Texas during late 1865 and early 1866, the Army replaced them with a few regular units, including the 4th and 6th U.S. Cavalry.[119] Even George Custer, mustered out as a major general of volunteers in Houston, Texas, in March 1866, reverted to his permanent grade as a captain in the 5th U.S. Cavalry.

Reconstruction and Postwar

In addition to Texas, the U.S. Army in the spring of 1865 also faced the unprecedented task of occupying ten conquered southern states and administering "Reconstruction." The Army initially conducted this duty with the large numbers of volunteers already in the South.[120] However, in the first week of May 1865, days after the surrender of Confederate armies in the East, the adjutant general of the U.S. Army issued an order for the muster-out of all volunteer cavalry troopers whose enlistments would expire in the next four months, since the cost of horses, tack, and fodder made cavalry expensive to maintain. The remaining men would reorganize as full-strength regiments. This order did not affect the black cavalry regiments, as most enlistments would not begin to run out until late 1866, but it reduced drastically the size of the mounted force available to patrol the occupied South.[121] Throughout the summer of 1865, as the War Department continued to disband mounted regiments, pleas for cavalry increased. One frustrated officer on Reconstruction duty in South Carolina reported that while his infantry was efficient, "a small force of cavalry would be of infinite service."[122] By January 1866, the occupation force in the South shrank from some 270,000 to only 87,500 while the War Department had mustered out more than 800,000 soldiers.[123]

During the Civil War, the Union Army raised over two thousand regiments of all branches, including 1,696 infantry and 78 artillery.[124] The 272 regiments, 45 separate battalions, and 78 separate companies of Union cavalry faced a Confederate cavalry estimated at 137 regiments, 143 separate battalions, and 101 separate companies.[125] Civil War cavalry historian Stephen Z. Starr estimates that nearly three hundred thousand men had served in the Union cavalry and mounted infantry during the war.[126] By July 1866, this massive Union volunteer force of over one million men in all arms had been mustered out. It had also became apparent even to Congress that the previous small Regular Army would not be large enough to perform all of its duties, such as in the South for Reconstruction, along the Mexican border, and the usual frontier duties out west. Congress approved an initial postwar Regular Army of fifty-seven thousand, more than double what it had been in 1861. For the first time, the regular establishment had been increased substantially immediately after a war. Reflecting its increased significance, the Army permanently added four cavalry regiments to the previous six. Two of these, the 9th and 10th Cavalry, composed of white officers with black enlisted men, the Army formed out of volunteers from the U.S. Colored Troops. The newly mustered 7th Cavalry received George Custer as its lieutenant colonel.[127] Unfortunately, the men who composed the regiment were "decidedly bad, as was the case with all regular regiments at the close of the war."[128] By 1868, ninety-two cavalry companies were stationed among fifty-nine posts in a vast area west of the Mississippi, while twenty-eight still occupied the South.[129] Such fragmentation made serious training for large unit operations or foreign war impossible, but the highly successful concepts developed by Union cavalry commanders permeated military thought even if they were not immediately codified into Army doctrine.

According to frontier historian Robert M. Utley, "The Army tried to perform its unconventional mission with conventional organization and methods."[130] The prevailing Army technique dispersed small detachments in frontier posts for defense and then concentrated them for offensive use. This concept placed a premium on mounted troops, for as General William T. Sherman declared, "Cavalry is the most efficient arm of the service for the . . . existing condition of things in the Indian Country."[131] Once in combat, the cavalry depended on superior organization, discipline, and especially firepower to prevail. Adoption of a modification of Colonel Emory Upton's *Infantry Tactics* of 1867 as the cavalry tactical manual in 1874 emphasized dismounted firepower.[132] For several years after the Civil War, cavalry units remained equipped with the Spencer carbine, because "a unit armed with it could deliver devastating sustained firepower, as Custer's Seventh demonstrated at the Washita in 1868."[133] However, in 1873 a cost-conscious arms board selected the .45 caliber single-shot breech-loaded Model 1873 Springfield as the standard weapon for both infantry and cavalry because it made maximum use of surplus weapons and possessed allegedly better reliability.[134]

With Reconstruction in the South also ended by 1873, Congress once again placed greater reliance on traditional state militias. Accordingly, Congress reduced the Regular Army by half, to some twenty-eight thousand, but retained ten cavalry regiments, or 20 percent of the total personnel of the Army. The Army essentially remained at this strength until 1898.[135] In June 1876 came the shock of the Battle of Little Big Horn. A more numerous and better-armed Sioux-Cheyenne coalition of Native Americans wiped out five companies of Lieutenant Colonel George Custer's 7th Cavalry.[136] The 7th had recently turned in their Spencer carbines and been re-equipped with the trapdoor Springfield Model 1873, which utilized copper cartridges that expanded and became stuck in the breech when rapidly fired.[137] As a result, Congress added twenty-five hundred men back to the cavalry, but this came only by reducing existing infantry units.[138]

In 1890 with the end of the Indian Wars, the Army again reduced the size of its mounted force by 50 percent, to only six thousand troopers. At the same time, the Army began to reemphasize conventional warfare. Earlier in 1881, General Sherman had established the School of Application for Infantry and Cavalry at Fort Leavenworth, Kansas, as the beginning of the Army school system.[139] Later in 1892, Congress established a separate cavalry school at Ft. Riley, Kansas.[140] In 1896, *Drill Regulations for Cavalry* became the first official postwar cavalry doctrine. This regulation drew heavily upon Civil War, not Indian War, experience. Operationally, this regulation made a distinction between "corps cavalry," or those regiments attached directly to infantry formations, and independent cavalry formations capable of conducting strategic raids to "destroy his communications, to destroy his depots and sources of supply; to gain information, to cause alarm in the enemy's country or create a sentiment unfavorable to the prosecution of the war."[141]

War with Spain in 1898 found the Regular Army once again unprepared. In the absence of preexisting staffs, the Army rapidly created brigade, division, and corps headquarters. Congress called upon volunteers and invoked the Militia Act of 1792 for state-organized militia to help conduct the war. While the Army mustered some 125,000 militia, only three regiments and nine separate troops of cavalry came from eight states. Most of these units were not fully manned, trained, or equipped, and thus only three cavalry troops served overseas. Two New York troops served mounted in a brigade under (recalled)

Major General Wilson in Puerto Rico, and a Nevada troop saw action in the Philippines as part of Major General Merritt's new VIII Corps. The Army also recruited three regiments of U.S. Volunteer Cavalry at large. The First U.S.V., better known as the "Rough Riders," served dismounted in Cuba in former Confederate Major General Wheeler's Cavalry Division along with five dismounted Regular Cavalry regiments. Only one squadron of the 2nd U.S. Cavalry served mounted in Cuba.[142]

Conclusion

Prior to 1832, the United States lacked permanent cavalry in its small Regular Army primarily due to attitude and cost. A changing strategic environment combined with the challenges of employing militia led to the Regular Army having five mounted regiments by 1855. Prior to the Civil War, the U.S. Army used overwhelming force to include effective mounted units to back diplomacy in resolving the Mormon Rebellion of 1857–1858. Again after the Civil War, the United States used overwhelming force and effective mounted units to reoccupy Texas and encourage French departure from Mexico in 1865–1866. In both cases, the U.S. Army prevailed without serious fighting. But these would be exceptions to the normal state of unpreparedness of the U.S. Army for a crisis in the nineteenth century, primarily due to rapid drawdowns immediately after each major conflict. In order to prevail over the Confederate States by 1865, the Union needed not only to mobilize its industrial base and raise a large army but also to develop an effective mounted arm capable of decisive results employing firepower and maneuver. Unfortunately, transforming the inadequate U.S. Cavalry from its prewar auxiliary status into a significant mobile arm took at least three hard years and thousands of lives lost as well as lost opportunities for early success. At the cusp of the American century in 1898, the repercussions of post–Civil War Army unpreparedness would receive greater attention than in previous periods. During the twentieth century, the United States would learn once again that it required both a large army and, despite the cost, a large mobile force capable of decisive action.

NOTES

1 James Buchanan, 8 December 1857, as quoted in David L. Bigley, *The Mormon Rebellion: America's First Civil War, 1857–1858* (Norman: University of Oklahoma Press, 2012), 3.

2 Circular; Instructions from General Winfield Scott, Headquarters of the Army, 28 May 1857, from *The Utah Expedition, 1857–1858: A Documentary Account of the*

United States Military Movement under Colonel Albert Sydney Johnston and the Resistance by Brigham Young and the Nauvoo Legion, edited by LeRoy R. Hafen (Glendale, CA: Clark, 1982), 27–30.

3 Colonel E. B. Alexander's Report, Headquarters Army for Utah, 9 October 1857, to Colonel S. Cooper, Adjutant General, USA, from *The Utah Expedition*, 73.

4 *The Utah Expedition*, 247.

5 Bigley, *The Mormon Rebellion*, 315–25; and Gregory J. Urwin, *The United States Cavalry: An Illustrated History* (New York: Blandford, 1984), 105–6.

6 Clayton R. Newell and Charles R. Shrader, *Of Duty Well and Faithfully Done: A History of the Regular Army in the Civil War* (Lincoln: University of Nebraska Press, 2011), 3 and 10. For a recent account of the prewar U.S. Army, see Clayton R. Newell, *The Regular Army before the Civil War, 1845–1860* (Washington, DC: Center of Military History, 2014).

7 Russell F. Weigley, *A Great Civil War: A Military and Political History, 1861–1865* (Bloomington: Indiana University Press, 2000), 15; and Russell F. Weigley, *History of the U.S. Army*, enlarged ed. (Bloomington: Indiana University Press, 1984), 198.

8 Newell and Shrader, *Of Duty Well and Faithfully Done*, 3 and 50. U.S. Army generals and their ages on 1 January 1861 included Commanding General, Brevet Lieutenant General Winfield S. Scott (seventy-five); Commander of the Department of the East, Brigadier General John E. Wool (seventy-seven); Commander of the Department of Texas, Brevet Major General David E. Twiggs (seventy-one); and Commander of the Department of the West, Brigadier General William S. Harney (sixty-one). Twiggs would infamously surrender all of his forces to the state of Texas on 18 February 1861 while still on active federal service.

9 David D. Dorondo, *Riders of the Apocalypse: German Cavalry and Modern Warfare, 1870–1945* (Annapolis, MD: Naval Institute Press, 2012), 3. Dorondo provides a recent assessment of horse cavalry in modern warfare.

10 For a classic history of horse cavalry up to the American Civil War, see George T. Denison, *A History of Cavalry from Earliest Times*, 2nd ed. (London: Macmillan, 1913); and for Napoleonic Cavalry see David Chandler, *The Campaigns of Napoleon* (New York: Macmillan, 1966), 352–56.

11 George Madison Bodge, *Soldiers in King Philip's War: Being a Critical Account of That War* (Boston: New England Historical-Genealogical Society, 1906), appendix.

12 Samuel J. Newland, *The Pennsylvania Militia: The Early Years* (Annville: Pennsylvania National Guard Foundation, 1997), 126–27.

13 Robert K. Wright, *The Continental Army*, Army Lineage series (Washington, DC: Center of Military History, 1983), 105–7.

14 Alan D. Gaff, *Bayonets in the Wilderness: Anthony Wayne's Legion in the Old Northwest* (Norman: University of Oklahoma Press, 2004), 36, 306–12.

15 Mary-Lee Stubbs and Stanley Russell Connor, *Armor-Cavalry, Part I*, Army Lineage series (Washington, DC: Center of Military History, 1969), 7.

16 Stubbs and Connor, *Armor-Cavalry*, 3–7; and Robert M. Utley, *Frontiersmen in Blue: The United States Army and the Indian, 1848–1865* (New York: Macmillan, 1967), 19–20. During this period a cavalry regiment cost at least double the cost of an infantry regiment to maintain.

17 Stubbs and Connor, *Armor-Cavalry*, 8–10.

18 Stephan Z. Starr, *The Union Cavalry in the Civil War*. Vol. 1, *From Fort Sumter to Gettysburg* (Baton Rouge: Louisiana State University Press, 1979), 58; Albert C. Brackett, *History of the U.S. Cavalry: From the Formation of the Federal Government to 1 June 1863* (New York: Harper, 1865), 60.

19 See J. R. Poinsett, *Cavalry Tactics* (Philadelphia: Lippincott, 1841).

20 Winfield Scott, as quoted in U.S. War Department, *Secretary of War, Annual Report, 1850* (Washington, DC: GPO, 1850), 114–15.

21 Richard Delafield, *Report on the Art of War in Europe in 1854, 1855, 1856* (Washington, DC: Bowman, 1860), xiii.

22 Letter to the Secretary of War, from Major Richard Delafield, 11 August 1856, in Delafield, *Report on the Art of War in Europe*.

23 Delafield, *Report on the Art of War in Europe*, 257.

24 George B. McClellan, *The Armies of Europe: Comprising descriptions in detail of the military systems of England, France, Russia, Prussia, Austria, and Sardinia; adapting their advantages to all arms of the United States service; and embodying the report of observations in Europe during the Crimean War, as military commissioner from the United States government, in 1855–1856, originally published under the direction of the War Department by order of Congress* (Philadelphia: Lippincott, 1862), 386.

25 Ibid. See also pages 208–9 for McClellan's discussion of types of cavalry and how frontier Indians could provide partisan troops equal to Cossacks.

26 Stubbs and Connor, *Armor-Cavalry*, 12–13; Newell and Shrader, *Of Duty Well and Faithfully Done*, 4. Another 100 officers and 482 enlisted were listed as "absent" on 1 January 1861.

27 Newell and Shrader, *Of Duty Well and Faithfully Done*, 245. Colonels Thomas T. Fauntleroy, William W. Loring, Robert E. Lee, and Albert S. Johnson and Lieutenant Colonels George B. Crittenden and William J. Hardee resigned to follow their states.

28 Edward G. Longacre, *Lincoln's Cavalrymen: A History of the Mounted Forces of the Army of the Potomac* (Mechanicsburg, PA: Stackpole, 2000), 1–3.

29 Ibid., 14–15.

30 Starr, *Union Cavalry*, vol. 1, 69.

31 Ibid., 14; Brackett, *History of the U.S. Cavalry*, 209–18. See also Longacre, *Lincoln's Cavalrymen*, 12–27.

32 Longacre, *Lincoln's Cavalrymen*, 25–27; and Edward G. Longacre, *Lee's Cavalrymen: A History of the Mounted Forces of the Army of Northern Virginia, 1861–1865* (Norman: University of Oklahoma Press, 2002), 17–24.

33 Starr, *Union Cavalry*, vol. 1, 209–33; Longacre, *Lee's Cavalrymen*, 25–49.

34 Ibid., 128–29. A Union Cavalry regiment was authorized by act of Congress on 21 July 1861 to consist at full strength of 12 companies of 104 men, plus battalion and regimental staff for a total of 1,288. After a few months of active service, most regiments averaged 400–500. See also Starr, *Union Cavalry*, vol. 1, appendix.

35 George B. McClellan, *Complete Report on the Organization and Campaigns of the Army of the Potomac* (New York: Sheldon, 1863), 8.

36 David McMurtie Gregg, "The Union Cavalry at Gettysburg," in *Annals of the War, Written by Leading Participants, North and South* (Philadelphia: Times Publishing, 1879), 372.

37 Private F. Rodgers to Major General George McClellan, 17 October 1861, Records of the First New Jersey Cavalry, National Archives, as quoted in Francis C. Kajencki, *Star on Many a Battlefield: Brevet Brigadier General Joseph Karge in the American Civil War* (Cranberry, NJ: Associated University Presses, 1980), 30.

38 Starr, *Union Cavalry*, vol. 1, 66, 124–28.

39 Ibid., 240–41.

40 Wesley Merritt, "Personal Recollections—Beverly Ford to Mitchell's Station, 1863," in Theophilus F. Rodenbough, ed., *From Everglade to Canon with the Second Dragoons* (New York: Van Nostrand, 1875), 284.

41 Starr, *Union Cavalry*, vol. 1, 262–63.

42 McClellan, *Complete Report*, 6–7.

43 Eric J. Wittenburg, *The Union Cavalry Comes of Age: Hartford Church to Brandy Station* (New York: Brassey's, 2003), 14.

44 McClellan as quoted in U.S. War Department, *The War of the Rebellion: A Compilation of the Official Records of the Union and Confederate Armies*, Series I, vol. 1 (Washington, DC: GPO, 1881), 622.

45 Gregg, "The Union Cavalry at Gettysburg," 372.

46 Longacre, *Lincoln's Cavalrymen*, 91–92.

47 As quoted in Starr, *Union Cavalry*, vol. 1, 283.

48 As quoted in ibid., 285.

49 Henry R. Pyne, *The History of the First New Jersey Cavalry* (Trenton, NJ: Beecher, 1871), 56; see also Kajencki, *Star on Many a Battlefield*, 46–50. Turner Ashby was killed the same day subsequent to the cavalry action by federal infantry.

50 U.S. War Department, *The War of the Rebellion: A Compilation of the Official Records of the Union and Confederate Armies*, Series I, vol. 19, part 2 (Washington, DC: GPO, 1881), 226–27.

51 Starr, *Union Cavalry*, vol. 1, 316–17. Cavalry casualties on 17 September 1862 consisted of only seven killed and twenty-three wounded.

52 Marcus A. Reno, "Boots and Saddles: The Cavalry of the Army of the Potomac," *National Tribune*, April 29, 1886.

53 McClellan, *Complete Report*, 123.

54 McClellan to Halleck, 12 October 1862, in McClellan, *Complete Report*, 126.

55 As quoted in Longacre, *Lincoln's Cavalrymen*, 112.

56 McClellan to Halleck, 21 October 1862, in McClellan, *Complete Report*, 129.

57 Merritt, "Personal Recollections," 284.

58 Starr, *Union Cavalry*, vol. 1, 323–26.

59 General Order No. 6, 6 February 1863, U.S. War Department, *The War of the Rebellion*, Series I, vol. 25, part 2, 51. "All cavalry scattered about the Army were called in and each infantry corps was left with one squadron only to serve as orderlies and messengers."

60 Wittenburg, *The Union Cavalry Comes of Age*, 136 and 170–71; and Starr, *Union Cavalry*, vol. 1, 351–62.

61 Ibid., xiii.

62 Ibid., 416. Stahel had been commanding the division from a covered wagon drawn by four white mules, and was subsequently relieved of his command by General Pleasonton.

63 Edward G. Longacre, *The Cavalry at Gettysburg: A Tactical Study of Mounted Operations during the Civil War's Pivotal Campaign, 9 June–14 July 1963* (Lincoln: University of Nebraska Press, 1986), 180–92 and 220–39.

64 Eric J. Wittenburg, J. David Petruzzi, and Michael F. Nugent, *One Continuous Fight: The Retreat from Gettysburg and the Pursuit of Lee's Army of Northern Virginia, July 4–14, 1863* (New York: Savas Beatie, 2008), 153–54.

65 Ibid., 317.

66 Longacre, *Lincoln's Cavalrymen*, 221–22.

67 James H. Wilson, *Under the Old Flag*, vol. 1 (New York: Appleton, 1912), 331.

68 Stephan Z. Starr, *The Union Cavalry in the Civil War*. Vol. 3, *The War in the West, 1861–1865* (Baton Rouge: Louisiana State University Press, 1985), 5 and 20–21.

69 Ibid., 43–49.

70 Phillip Henry Sheridan, *Personal Memoirs of P. H. Sheridan, General, United States Army* (New York: DaCapo, 1992), 85–90. As a result of this action, Major General William S. Rosecrans recommended Sheridan be promoted to brigadier general and, shortly, command of an infantry division.

71 Ulysses Simpson Grant, *Personal Memoirs of U.S. Grant* (New York: Dover, 1995), 169.

72 Starr, *Union Cavalry*, vol. 3, 185–95.

73 Ibid., 205–14.This contributed to the creation of Colonel Wilder's "Lightning" Brigade of Mounted Infantry equipped with Spencer repeating rifles.

74 Major General David Stanley as quoted in Starr, *Union Cavalry*, vol. 3, 221.

75 Starr, *Union Cavalry*, vol. 3, 214–21.

76 Glenn W. Sunderland, *Wilder's Lightning Brigade: and Its Spencer Repeaters* (Washington, IL: BookWorks, 1984), 43.

77 See David A. Powell, *Failure in the Saddle: Nathan Bedford Forest, Joseph Wheeler, and the Confederate Cavalry in the Chickamauga Campaign* (New York: Savas Beatie, 2010).

78 David W. Hogan, *The Overland Campaign: 4 May–15 June 1864* (Washington, DC: Center of Military History, 2014), 15. In a reversal of General McClellan's

priorities, the Army of the Potomac on 3 May 1864 had 16,311 cavalry horses and only 5,158 artillery horses. Starr, *Union Cavalry*, vol. 2, 87.

79 Weigley, *A Great Civil War*, 369.

80 Sheridan, *Personal Memoirs*, 193.

81 Ibid.

82 Ibid., 200.

83 Stephan Z. Starr, *The Union Cavalry in the Civil War*. Vol. 2, *The War in the East from Gettysburg to Appomattox, 1863–1865* (Baton Rouge: Louisiana State University Press, 1981), 107.

84 For a recent summary of this campaign see Hogan, *The Overland Campaign*.

85 For a discussion of these events, see Longacre, *Lincoln's Cavalrymen*, 268–98.

86 General Grant as quoted in Starr, *Union Cavalry*, vol. 2, 232.

87 Jeffrey D. Wert, *From Winchester to Cedar Creek: The Shenandoah Campaign of 1864* (Carlisle, PA: South Mountain Press, 1987), 6–16; and Raymond K. Bluhm Jr., *The Shenandoah Valley Campaign, March–November 1864* (Washington, DC: Center of Military History, 2014), 28–41.

88 For an in-depth discussion of these events see Starr, *Union Cavalry*, vol. 2, 245–321.

89 Wert, *From Winchester to Cedar Creek*, 249.

90 For a discussion of these events see Starr, *Union Cavalry*, vol. 2, 365–85, 421–88.

91 Russell F. Weigley, *Towards an American Army* (New York: Columbia University Press, 1962), 193.

92 Starr, *Union Cavalry*, vol. 3, 458. See also David Evans, *Sherman's Horsemen: Union Cavalry Operations in the Atlanta Campaign* (Bloomington: Indiana University Press, 1996).

93 Ibid., 533.

94 Wilson, *Under the Old Flag*, vol. 2, 7.

95 Edward G. Longacre, *Grant's Cavalryman: The Life and Wars of General James H. Wilson* (Mechanicsburg, PA: Stackpole, 1996), 159–64.

96 Ibid., 179–81.

97 James Pickett Jones, *Yankee Blitzkrieg: Wilson's Raid through Alabama and Georgia* (Athens: University of Georgia Press, 1976).

98 Ibid., 185–86.

99 Jerry Keenan, *Wilson's Cavalry Corps: Union Campaigns in the Western Theatre, October 1864 through Spring 1865* (Jefferson, NC: McFarland, 1998), 176; and Starr, *Union Cavalry*, vol. 1, 43. Wilson captured over two thousand Confederate horses at Selma alone.

100 Wilson, *Under the Old Flag*, vol. 1, 332.

101 Ibid., vol. 2, 274.

102 Keenan, *Wilson's Cavalry Corps*, 222.

103 Utley, *Frontiersman in Blue*, 293–97; see also Ned Blackhawk, "Remember the Sand Creek Massacre," *New York Times*, November 28, 2014, A31.

104 Weigley, *A Great Civil War*, 369.

105 Report of Major General Phillip H. Sheridan, "Operations in Texas and on the Rio Grande, 14 November 1866," in U.S War Department, *The War of the Rebellion: A Compilation of the Official Records of the Union and Confederate Armies*, Series 1, vol. 48, part 1, chapter 60 (Washington, DC: GPO, 1896), 298.

106 Ibid.

107 Grant, *Personal Memoirs*, 459.

108 William A. Dobak, *Freedom by the Sword: The U.S. Colored Troops, 1862–1867* (Washington, DC: Center of Military History, 2011), 423 and 434. XIII Corps came from Mobile; IV Corps from Tennessee; and over sixteen thousand U.S. Colored Troops of the XXV Corps arrived in Texas to remove them from occupation duties in Virginia.

109 Sheridan, *Personal Memoirs*, 403.

110 Frederick Whitaker, *A Complete Life of General George A. Custer.* Vol. 1, *Through the Civil War* (Lincoln: University of Nebraska Press, 1993), 317, 321 (reprint of the 1876 version).

111 Sheridan, "Operations in Texas and on the Rio Grande, 14 November 1866," U.S. War Department, *The War of the Rebellion: A Compilation of the Official Records of the Union and Confederate Armies* (Washington, DC: GPO, 1896), Series 1, vol. 48, part 1, chapter 60, p. 299; and William L. Richter, *The Army in Texas during the Reconstruction, 1865–1870* (College Station: Texas A & M University Press, 1987), 14–19. Custer's division had five regiments: the 1st Iowa, 2nd Wisconsin, 5th and 12th Illinois, and 7th Indiana.

112 Richter, *The Army in Texas*, 18.

113 Rene Chartrand, *The Mexican Adventure, 1861–1867* (Oxford: Osprey, 1994), 18.

114 Sheridan, *Personal Memoirs*, 404–10.

115 Percy F. Martin, *Maximilian in Mexico: The Story of the French Intervention, 1861–1867* (New York: Scribners, 1914), 209 and 214.

116 Major General Phillip Sheridan to Lient. Gen. U. S. Grant, November 5, 1865, in U.S War Department, *The War of the Rebellion: A Compilation of the Official Records of the Union and Confederate Armies*, Series 1, vol. 48, part 2 (Washington, DC: GPO, 1896), 1252.

117 Francois de Chenal, *The American Army in the War of Secession*, translated by Lt. M. J. O'Brien (Leavenworth, KS: Spon, 1894), 28. For other foreign views of the Civil War, see Jay Luvaas, *The Military Legacy of the Civil War: The European Inheritance* (Lawrence: University Press of Kansas, 1988).

118 According to Rene Chartrand, *The Mexican Adventure*, 18–20; the French cavalry in Mexico comprised some thirteen squadrons of less than four thousand total light cavalry: hussars, *chasseurs a cheval*, and *chasseurs d'afrique*. Their primary equipment included a sabre and a single shot percussion pistol or carbine, with only officers having revolvers. No French or imperial troops had breech loading, repeating carbines (such as the U.S. Cavalry's Spencer carbines) nor the famous French *Chassepot*.

119 Richter, *The Army in Texas*, 25–28.

120 Mark L. Bradley, *The Army and Reconstruction, 1865–1867* (Washington, DC: Center of Military History, 2015), 7

121 Ibid., 15; and Dobak, *Freedom by the Sword*, 471. Orders disbanding volunteer cavalry and horse-drawn artillery between May and October 1865 are in *Official Records*, ser. 3, 5: 11–12, 48–49, 94–97, 516–17.

122 Captain H. S. Hawkins as quoted in Dobak, *Freedom by the Sword*, 472.

123 Bradley, *The Army and Reconstruction*, 15.

124 Weigley, *History of the U.S. Army*, 227.

125 Stubbs and Connor, *Armor-Cavalry*, 14–15.

126 Starr, *Union Cavalry*, vol. 2, 505.

127 Ibid., 19–23; and Weigley, *History of the U.S. Army*, 266–67.

128 Whitaker, *A Complete Life of General George A. Custer*, vol. 1, 347.

129 Stubbs and Connor, *Armor-Cavalry*, 20.

130 Robert M. Utley, *Frontier Regulars: The United States Army and the Indian, 1866–1891* (New York: Macmillan, 1973), 47.

131 Ibid., as quoted on 51.

132 Walter E. Kretchik, *U.S. Army Doctrine: From the American Revolution to the War on Terror* (Lawrence: University Press of Kansas, 2011), 85; Weigley, *History of the U.S. Army*, 275–76; and Emory Upton, *Cavalry Tactics* (New York: Appleton, 1874).

133 Utley, *Frontier Regulars*, 72.

134 Justin G. Prince, "'Thanks to God and Lieutenant General Sherman': The United States Army in the Breechloader Era, 1864–1892," master's thesis (Norman: Oklahoma State University, May 2010), 71–74; and Weigley, *History of the U.S. Army*, 268.

135 Weigley, *History of the U.S. Army*, 267.

136 Numerous accounts of this battle exist, however. See Robert M. Utley, *Custer Battlefield: A History and Guide to the Battle of the Little Big Horn* (Washington, DC: U.S. Department of the Interior, 1988); Robert M. Utley, *Custer: Cavalier in Buckskin* (Norman: University of Oklahoma Press, 2001), 132–53; Jeffrey D. Wert, *The Controversial Life of George Armstrong Custer* (New York: Simon & Schuster, 1996), 340–55; and James S. Hutchins, "The Cavalry Campaign Outfit at the Battle of Little Big Horn," in *The Custer Reader*, edited by Paul Andrew Hutton (Norman: University of Oklahoma Press, 1992), 327.

137 Prince, "'Thanks to God and Lieutenant General Sherman,'" 76–77.

138 Stubbs and Connor, *Armor-Cavalry*, 23.

139 Weigley, *History of the U.S. Army*, 273. This school would evolve into the U.S. Army Command and General Staff College.

140 Stubbs and Connor, *Armor-Cavalry*, 22.

141 U.S. War Department, *Drill Regulations for Cavalry* (Washington, D.C.: GPO, 1896), 365.

142 Stubbs and Connor, *Armor-Cavalry*, 26–28. These were the First, Third, Sixth, Ninth, and Tenth U.S. Cavalry Regiments.

5

The Elusive Lesson

U.S. Army Unpreparedness from 1898 to 1938

EDWARD A. GUTIÉRREZ WITH MICHAEL S. NEIBERG

A native of Portland, Maine, Captain John Clifford Brown found himself a stranger in a foreign land. During his first year on hostile ground, he reflected,

> We have no real right to be here, we ought all to be dead by the side of some mud hole or impassable ford, as we wandered in the jungle, or by some mountain pass. . . . Curious sensation walking down the track in the pitchy darkness with a detail of four or five men, knowing there are 300 insurgents in the neighborhood who are anxious to shoot you and who may be laying behind the next clump of cane or behind the rice paddies for all you know. . . . Personally I, and I think all thinking people here agree, cannot help seeing that the country will amply repay the United States for their trouble in subjugating it.[1]

Upon returning home, Captain Anson T. McCook concluded, "I have a sense of indignation at the needless loss of time, money, and life caused by the Administration's refusal to prepare after war had long become inevitable; in addition, I regret that the war's lessons will so soon be forgotten."[2]

Although their remarks are modern in tone, Captains Brown and McCook did not fight in Vietnam, Afghanistan, or Iraq, but in the Philippines and Flanders Fields. The years 1898 to 1938 are an invaluable four decades for modern policymakers and commanders to examine because they challenged the U.S. Army with both conventional and unconventional warfare, as well as several drawdowns. More importantly, these years show the dangers a drawdown and stagnation can produce when an unprepared nation finds itself entwined in a conflict where war becomes inevitable.

This chapter examines U.S. Army unpreparedness before, during, and after the Great War, but it is vital to address several other conflicts in the years prior to 1917. The years before the United States entered World War I constructed a false sense of preparedness not only within the Army but also within American society. America stumbled into battle against opponents it did not understand and underestimated. Although the U.S. Army sustained casualties against Spanish and indigenous foes, their naivety would cost them dearly against the battle-hardened Germans along the Western Front.[3]

After years of political tension, the sinking of the USS *Maine* on 15 February 1898 in Havana Harbor drove America toward war with Spain on 25 April. Unprepared for the conflict, the U.S. Army sent troops into a stifling climate with cowhide boots, flannel shirts, and winter trousers. Since many were forced to sleep on the ground due to the lack of supplies, tropical diseases ravaged the men.[4] After a disorganized embarkation from Tampa, Florida, the Army's D-Dayesque landing at Daiquirí, Cuba, on 22 June 1898 was a fiasco. Daiquirí featured no wharf or port facilities as sixteen thousand men attempted to land on the Cuban coast.[5]

General Joseph Wheeler noted the problem as he approached Daiquirí aboard the USS *Allegheny*. "With the aid of our glasses we could see the town of Daiquirí, the place selected for our landing. The place has no harbor. . . . It was, therefore, evident that we would be obligated to land on the beach, or else at the end of a small dock that extended some twenty yards from the shore," commented Wheeler.[6] After two days, only six thousand men made it ashore. During the landing, two African American cavalrymen drowned, and the Army dumped hundreds of horses and mules into the water—more than fifty drowned, including Rain-in-the-Face, one of the two horses Teddy Roosevelt had brought to Cuba with him.

In a letter to his wife, Major Batson of the Ninth Cavalry wrote, "It is pitiful to see the poor brutes swim from one boat to another. Sometimes they get near the shore, then turn around and swim to sea. Of course a great many of them are drowned, and the beach is covered with dead horses and mules."[7] While waiting to go ashore, also writing to his wife back home, Leonard Wood noted, "You can hardly imagine the awful confusion and lack of system which meets us on every hand in this business. Somehow everything seems to go in a happy-go-lucky-way."[8]

The situation was utter chaos, yet fortune favored the Americans during the landing: the Spanish had abandoned their coastal defenses and overall the weather remained pleasant. With the aid of the U.S. Navy, Spanish forces, exhausted from years of fighting against Cuban revolutionaries, succumbed to the offensives launched by the U.S. Army. In addition, rather than concentrating his forces, Spanish commander General Arsenio Linares y Pombo dispersed his ten thousand troops around Santiago de Cuba and San Juan Heights, where the decisive battle of the campaign occurred. As with any war, it is important to note why the victors won, but also why the defeated lost. The latter is the deciding factor in the Spanish-American War. The U.S. Army overcame its unpreparedness against the Spanish because of overwhelming force, but more notably, an exhausted and miscalculating enemy ensured American victory in the battle for Cuba.

The war in the Philippines transpired in similar fashion. Worn down by Filipino revolutionaries and with the aid of Commodore George Dewey, the Spanish once again proved too enervated to pose a serious threat to the U.S. Army. Once Spain surrendered Manila on 13 August 1898, U.S. Army size became static. In the minds of American military leaders, however, this stagnation in Army growth was not a problem, but a logical preservation of Army force structure. A year later, Army strength stood at sixty-four thousand; however, German and French armies dwarfed this number. Both countries commanded armies of over a half-million men, and Britain maintained an army of 250,000.[9]

U.S. Army size remained small as a new conflict erupted in the Philippines against Filipinos, known as *insurrectos* to American troops. The popular notion of the war remains one where both sides waged a vicious campaign to defeat the other, with the U.S. Army obtaining victory using concentration camps and a brutal operation that crushed all resistance in the Samar province of the eastern Philippines. Brian McAllister Linn effectively debunks this myth and concludes, "Unfortunately for the historical record these last campaigns are now perceived as typifying the entire war. Even more distressing, many Americans, particularly in academia, interpret the Philippine War through an ideological perspective developed during the 1960s."[10] Moreover, Linn argues that with around twenty-five thousand combat-ready troops, the U.S. Army "soldier in the Philippines was probably as good or better than any in the nation's history."[11]

The U.S. Navy once again played a crucial role in enabling the Army to obtain victory in the campaign. In addition, the Army succeeded through a combination of superior technology, especially the Krag-Jorgenson rifle, and effective tactical-level doctrine. *Insurrecto* errors aggrandized U.S. Army success on the archipelago. Several of the most vital reasons why the *insurrectos* lost were revolutionary leader Emilio Aguinaldo's poor leadership and other insurgent commanders' ineffectiveness, and *insurrecto* terrorist tactics, which alienated the population rather than converting them to the revolutionary cause.[12] The war officially ended in 1902, although sporadic fighting would continue until 1913.

A year later, on the eve of the Great War in 1914, the U.S. Army numbered less than 98,000, compared to Germany's 620,000, France's 560,000, and Britain's 250,000.[13] In the spring of that year, due to an ongoing diplomatic dispute between America and Mexico, the U.S. Army's 5th Infantry

Brigade landed in Veracruz, Mexico, and took control of occupational duties from U.S. Marines and sailors attempting to wrest control of the city from revolutionaries. The Army established a successful military government and brought order to Veracruz. The greater enemy for the Army in Veracruz was not the revolutionaries, but disease. After Mexican dictator Victoriano Huerta resigned and the new president, Venustiano Carranza, guaranteed the citizens of Veracruz's safety, the U.S. Army left the port on 23 November 1914.[14]

Two years later the U.S. Army would reenter Mexico on a manhunt to capture Mexican revolutionary Pancho Villa. On 8 March 1916, Villa and five hundred of his men attacked Columbus, New Mexico, killing seventeen Americans.[15] A U.S. Army expeditionary force, led by General John J. Pershing, spent a year engaged in the Punitive Expedition from March 1916 to February 1917 in an unsuccessful attempt to hunt down the elusive Villa in northern Mexico. The Punitive Expedition devoured supplies, leaving insufficient materiel for the American Expeditionary Forces (AEF) when America declared war with the Central Powers in April 1917. The Army trained Pershing's troops in some modern tactics, such as trench warfare, but they soon forgot those lessons, as they played cat and mouse with Villa across the vast terrain of Chihuahua, Mexico. More important, the Army's attention focused on Mexico rather than on preparations for possible intervention in Europe; homeland defense and open-field battle remained the hallmarks of Army doctrine.[16]

The U.S. Army's total strength was only 107,000 in 1916.[17] The U.S. Navy consisted of many outdated battleships and was ill prepared to face the German u-boat menace or to transport the Army across the Atlantic Ocean. In the air, America was also far behind; the U.S. Air Service (USAS) possessed only fifty-five trainer planes, almost all of which were outdated and not combat ready.[18] Although the Wright brothers had introduced the airplane to the world in 1903, as late as 1911, the U.S. Signal Corps had only one plane and one pilot.[19] In addition, the military did not officially distinguish pilots until 1912, and from 1908 to 1913, the United States spent only $430,000 on aviation, compared with the $22 million spent by France and Germany.[20]

The National Defense Act of 1916 had cut the Army General Staff to the bare minimum; as a result, it appeared that the United States was incapable of coming to the aid of the European Allies. Although Congress had established the Council of National Defense to prepare American industries for war, it actually worked against preparedness. The council, comprised of engineers, academics, and industrialists, created advisory networks that operated in each state, but this type of state and national organization proved unwieldy. In addition, the Council of National Defense limited itself to compiling data and taking inventory of the resources necessary for wartime. The U.S. Army was thus an inefficient operation with limited funds in 1916; Congress was not willing to provide the resources needed to ensure its growth, and in general, the populace did not support military preparedness.[21]

Secretary of War Newton D. Baker favored the decentralization of government, as did the rest of Wilson's administration, and Baker disregarded Army officers, who warned that the military lacked staff and supplies. This situation continued even after the United States declared war. Troops had no uniforms; weapons and supplies of every sort were scarce. Only when Congress questioned Baker in January 1918 did the Wilson administration react to the lack of military supplies. North Carolina senator Lee S. Overman sponsored the Overman Act, passed by Congress on 20 May 1918, which enabled Wilson to consolidate six agencies into one and gave him greater power to spend money for wartime purposes.[22]

Prior to the Overman Act, the U.S. Army scrambled to prepare for war. During the summer of 1917, the Army had to construct temporary quarters to house the new soldiers, having to build both wooden barracks and tents, along with roads and sewer systems. There was no time for Army officials to follow the usual procedure of soliciting bids for the construction of camps, since the Allies needed soldiers at the front immediately. Therefore, the Army expanded old camps and set up new ones to accommodate the growing number of troops. Camp construction in the southern states did not take into account the possibility of cold winter weather, and the men assigned to these quarters suffered the effects.[23]

Supplies for the AEF were another problem. The doughboys needed uniforms, weapons, medical supplies, field glasses, helmets, ammunition, mess kits, horses' equipment—the list went on. There was little surplus due to the 1916–1917 mission to Mexico and the lack of industrial preparation for war. Demand for uniforms, ammunition, and food was especially high. The Army turned to American executives for advice on where to obtain the best quality for their money. To supply such a vast number of soldiers in such a short time took a great deal of effort by the various bureaus of the Army. The Quartermaster Corps alone supplied the Army with 17,000,000 woolen trousers and breeches, 22,198,000 flannel shirts, and 26,423,000 shoes.[24]

The Regular Army was small, the National Guard was limited in size, and both forces were sorely underequipped. Units had no tanks, no gas masks, only 742 field pieces, a mere 43 heavy guns, and 2,000 antiquated machine guns.[25] Just as it had been in the Spanish-American War, ammunition was also in short supply.[26] During their training at Army camps, some men drilled with broomsticks and wooden weapons instead of real rifles and artillery.

Many of the doughboys sent overseas had never even fired a rifle. Men of the 82nd Division dubbed their wooden rifles the "Camp Gordon 1917 Model Rifle."[27] Although most camps provided training in going over the tops of trenches, grenade throwing, and bayonet practice, many soldiers did not experience live-fire exercises. "As regards preparation for meeting the enemy, I consider the training at Camp McClellan below par. We were only trained in discipline and in Civil War tactics. Very few of our men saw an automatic rifle, live grenade or had any idea of formations for a modern attack," emphasized Captain Charles T. Holtzman Jr.[28] Lieutenant Joe Roddy described his unit's training: "Our trench mortar battery was organized at Camp Jackson where we did practically all of our training with wooden sticks. It was not until the last of our training that we got a chance to use the guns themselves which we fired once or twice with a small charge and dummy shells."[29]

Officer training posed an additional difficulty. When the United States declared war, the number of officers and men in the Regular Army and the National Guard was low. Even the General Staff had only forty-one officers.[30] Although draftees and volunteers filled the shortage of troops, the deficiency in experienced commissioned officers was problematic. Prior to World War I, General Leonard Wood had initiated the Military Training Camps Association, also known as the Plattsburgh training camps, where aspiring young officers, most of them from upper-middle-class families, spent a month in training.[31] When the United States declared war, the Plattsburgh camps served as models for the officer training camps established across the country. Potential commissioned officers spent ninety days in training and then, in most cases, joined military units. These officers, often called ninety-day wonders by the soldiers they commanded, were not always prepared for the realities of combat.[32]

Many doughboys complained about these new officers and criticized their ability to lead. Artilleryman Private Harold T. Lyons observed, "The older Regular Army officers were fine officers and knew what they were doing. I was disgusted with the conduct of the 90-day officers."[33] General Pershing, now commander of the AEF, requested that American troops receive six months of training in the United States and two additional months of training when they arrived in France, followed by a month in a quiet sector before taking part in combat. Pershing ignored his own timetable for training when the Allies pressed the United States for troops; he called for a large American force to arrive at the front as quickly as possible.[34] As Richard S. Faulkner argues, "The sad reality was that the AEF was an army of 1914 thrust into 1918."[35] The AEF lacked time, technology, and training. The United States' unpreparedness would be measured by the number of lives lost in Europe.[36]

While the Army ensured that its soldiers would be physically strong, it did not harden their minds to the horrors of the front. These men had never heard the sounds of a Maxim machine gun or the rumble of the earth during an artillery shelling. They barely had time to learn the fundamentals before the Army shipped them off to France. This was basic training at its most basic. But their inadequate training did not worry most soldiers; they were too eager to cross the Atlantic and win the war. Many doughboys believed the Germans were inept brutes who would be easy to defeat.[37]

General Johnson Hagood, chief of staff of the Services of Supply, lamented the War Department's lack of preparation: "The fourteen years, 1903 to 1917, during which the General staff had been in existence had not been spent in making plans for war, the purpose for which it was created, but in squabbling over the control of the routine peace-time administration and supply of the Regular Army and in attempts to place the blame for unpreparedness upon Congress." Hagood also charged that, from 1914 to 1917, the War Department had not anticipated the country's entry into the war and had failed to plan. "Hindsight is better than foresight," he commented, "and I, like all the rest, did not have the brains—or the genius—to see preparedness in its true light."[38]

After the war, many returning veterans also lamented the lack of preparation. Infantry captain George W. Cheney stated,

> My experience was that the American Army never did reach the point of being completely equipped and organized as had been contemplated in War Department plans. This goes to show that we were woefully unprepared in spite of repeated warnings, and the fact that we entered the war three years after it started. We should have a standing army of 500,000 and compulsory military training for one year for each boy reaching age 18.[39]

"I am a strong advocate of preparedness. If the U.S. Army had had the proper equipment and some trained officers our losses would have been less and the Army better managed," said infantry sergeant Marcel W. Rice. He determined, "We should keep a large well-trained National Guard and fair-sized regular army. The volunteer is the better soldier. We should develop a strong air service so that in future wars our infantry will not suffer for lack of eyes."[40] When Second Lieutenant John M. Ross returned home, he expressed "[a] hope that our United States will never again be caught unprepared and that our military program will be adequate for its full protection, both on land and on the sea."[41] Yet in spite of its many deficiencies, the United States mobilized and prepared a large fighting force in a remarkably short time. The nation's strong industrial foundation, along with its vast population, enabled the rapid creation of a formidable military force and America sent two million men to Europe.[42]

General Pershing believed the AEF could end the stalemate on the front. The infantryman, Pershing assumed, was still the backbone of an army, and the United States could show its European counterparts how war was supposed to be waged. Pershing and the AEF soon learned the hard truth: America was unprepared. The trenches, modern technology, and artillery were the champions, and infantrymen alone could not win the war—a lesson the Europeans had learned after three years of vicious combat. The Allies believed it would take more than American bravado to achieve victory in Europe. Much to Europe's surprise, however, with the aid of Allied (especially French) technology, the United States rescued the Allies. Although the cost was high, doughboy élan and numbers saved the Allies from defeat against the Germans' spring offensives.[43]

Americans who craved battle did not realize the barbarity of industrialized warfare. But even with hindsight, the majority of American soldiers still supported their initial patriotic enthusiasm for the war, the draft, and enlistment after the Armistice. What these men did not know was that their country had been poorly prepared to train, equip, or transport them to the front. Throughout the war, in fact, American forces depended on the Allies for almost all their heavy artillery, machine guns, tanks, airplanes, and other supplies.[44]

American casualties were high—but would have been higher had German combat effectiveness been at its 1914 level. Captain Clarence M. Thompson remarked, "It was mighty fortunate we entered the war after the enemy was weary. The dash of the American carried him thru but at terrible expense for what was accomplished. What would it have cost if our untrained men had met that enemy two years earlier?"[45] The AEF lost far fewer lives than the European forces, but given the short time the U.S. Army engaged in combat, the cost was dear: 320,518 casualties, including 116,516 dead.[46] For the AEF, the cost of being on the winning side—with only one year at the front (beginning with Cambrai on 20 November 1917)—was 53,402 killed in action, or an average of 146 men killed each day. By contrast, the French Army lost 1,397,000 in four years—an average of 895 French soldiers killed each day.[47] As doughboy William L. Langer reflected, "Fortunately for us, we were spared the ordeal of the French, British, Germans, Russians, and Italians. Our term of service under fire was short. We got just enough of blood, sweat, and tears to satisfy our craving for adventure. And then, we were lucky enough to be on the winning side."[48]

After the Armistice on 11 November 1918, the U.S. Army once again began a drawdown in fighting capability. America's strategic leaders would not have understood the term "drawdown," at least not in the sense that we use it today. With only a few exceptions, as they had done after the Spanish-American War, the leaders of the American military in the years immediately after the Great War did not think that they were reducing the Army or drawing it down. They thought instead that they were returning the Army to its proper and normal state within the American system. They had raised a large and powerful force to meet a specific contingency, and now, with that contingency gone and that enemy beaten, the Army could return to its regular peacetime mission of guarding frontiers and training for future contingencies.[49]

Dissenting voices existed, of course. Men like Theodore Roosevelt and former Army chief of staff General Leonard Wood argued for introducing Universal Military Training (UMT) in order to ensure that the nation would not need to start from scratch again to meet a future emergency.[50] But UMT never did take hold in the American mind, and it remained an unpopular idea, especially in the South and the West.[51] Roosevelt's death in January 1919 and Wood's defeat in the 1920 Republican primary contest for the presidency silenced the two voices that had argued most strenuously for it. As a result, World War I did not produce any radical changes in the American system for personnel procurement.

Although the phrase is often overused and misunderstood among scholars, the "Return to Normalcy" that Warren G. Harding promised while campaigning for president and that most Americans advocated in 1920 applied to the military as well.[52] To Americans, normalcy in military terms meant a small army, raised by volunteers, and garrisoned far away from the great industrial cities of the eastern seaboard. Perhaps for the final time in American history, a postwar world meant not staying on guard and on watch, but returning to a state of mere existence, and at low cost.

Nevertheless, there are many important lessons we can learn by looking at the years 1919–1920 and the debates in those years about the best way to prepare the Army, and the armed services more generally, for the task of defending America. When American policymakers and commanders cast their eyes back almost a century, they can find echoes of many of the same debates, rooted in the same basic American constructs, that military planners face today. The end of the First World War shows in stark relief some classic American patterns, especially those from the previous twenty years. The three most essential patterns seen after the Armistice were the debates about America's role in the world; the tensions between the Regular Army on the one hand and the National Guard and Reserves on the other; and the debate over whether the Army or the Navy could best defend American interests.

It is essential to note that the term "drawdown" is relative. The leaders of 1919–1920 would have been quite content with even a tiny fraction of the resources, influence, and prestige enjoyed by the U.S. Army of today. Unlike today, the Army of those years could not even depend on the rhetorical support of friendly congressmen, and the notion of a budget in the billions of dollars would probably have rendered them speechless. In some ways, the Army has truly come a long way.

But in other ways, the debates remain largely the same. At the highest level, the end of World War I raised a debate about America's proper role in the world. President Wilson's idealistic vision of a world connected by common law and international organizations had (at least in theory) little need for large, standing armed forces. America's power in this system would derive from its moral suasion and its place in the vanguard of history.[53]

Wilson's conservative opponents disagreed with much of his ideology, but not with the desire to reduce armaments expenditures. The world they saw involved no entangling alliances, least of all with the ever-feuding Europeans. Led by Senator Henry Cabot Lodge, they sought to keep American freedom of diplomatic maneuver absolute. When Lodge and his fellow thinkers spoke of "isolationism," they meant not ignoring the world, but keeping America free to interact with that world unencumbered by treaties, alliances, or international organizations.[54]

It appears that Lodge and his followers had the pulse of America about right. "The Return to Normalcy" meant, for most Americans, a return to America's traditional approach of not joining alliances and not intervening directly in European affairs. Congress's rejection of the Treaty of Versailles and the League of Nations underscored that point dramatically.[55] Especially after the frustration of the Paris Peace Conference, many Americans looked at Europe as a place of hopeless ancient feuds likely to draw the United States in once again. A return to a foreign policy light on Europe and heavy on traditional interventions closer to home in Latin America seemed the appropriate response.

Even Wilson, his internationalism notwithstanding, took careful steps to limit America's international profile. He did send troops to Latin America, and he did order the ill-starred Northern Russian and Siberian expeditions, but he understood the limits of American military power.[56] He clearly and carefully limited American involvement in the Allied occupation of Germany, much to the annoyance of the French and the British. He also firmly refused European attempts to involve America directly in the affairs of Armenia and would not accept a mandate over large parts of Turkish territory. In this sense, at least, 1919–1920 offers one stark contrast to the world of today: the American system stated clearly and unequivocally what missions it would not pursue.[57]

Thus, one way to look at the period after the First World War would be to see it as a conscious attempt to return to the world of 1914. In that sense, a policymaker or military commander might draw the analogy that America today is trying not so much to draw down but to return to the levels of 10 September 2001 or even perhaps to 1 August 1990. Just as in the 1920s, such a logic forces choices about strategic policy and military leaders as well as the need to develop a fundamental understanding of what has changed in the intervening years and what has not. The world of the 1920s looks stable in retrospect, but contemporaries felt repeated aftershocks from the great seismic events of 1914–1918, including the spread of bolshevism, a huge growth in Japanese power, the probability of a continued failed state in Mexico, the beginning of the end of European imperialism, and the first stirrings of fascism. Boozy Gatsby-like images of F. Scott Fitzgerald and the Jazz Age notwithstanding, we must not assume that their world was any less unstable or unpredictable than our own. For serious strategists, the world looked dangerous, unstable, and capable of producing almost anything except lasting peace.[58]

The end of the First World War led to a reinvigoration of a debate as old as the republic itself.[59] In the years before the war, Progressive reformers both inside and outside government sought to modernize the Army by centralizing control of it in Washington, D.C. In effect, they wanted to bring the forty-eight National Guard and militia units under direct federal control. They wanted to take training, supply, and promotion out of the hands of the governors and put them in the hands of the professionals inside the Army. As long as the nation's defense rested in the hands of locals, they argued, it remained subject to parochialism, petty politics, and nepotism of the worst kind. Just as political progressives sought to take down the urban machines, military progressives sought to eliminate what they saw as an antiquated military model better suited to the age of the minuteman than the age of the Maxim gun and the airplane.[60]

Woodrow Wilson's first secretary of war, Lindley Garrison, and his assistant secretary of war, Henry Breckenridge, led this fight. In 1916, they proposed a Continental Army Plan that would have vastly increased the number of men in a federally controlled reserve while reducing the role of the National Guards significantly. In their eyes, and the eyes of the Army staff, the plan recognized the increased complexity of modern warfare and acknowledged the basic fact that war, like medicine or the law, should thereafter remain exclusively in the hands of professionals.[61]

The Continental Army Plan ran into intense opposition from those Americans fearful of the concentration of power in Washington that would result. The governors and the National Guard lobby, with powerful congressional allies on their side, moved quickly to squash it. The final 1916 National Defense Act gave the reformers almost none of what they wanted. Instead, the forty-eight National Guard units remained under state control.[62] The bill did, however, earmark federal defense dollars for modernizing National Guard equipment, thus drawing away precious money for the Regular Army. The only victory for the reformers came in the act's authorization for the president to federalize the National Guard in the event of a national emergency. Garrison and Breckenridge were so furious with the act that they both resigned rather than work under its provisions. The amateurs, they argued, had won, leaving America unable to defend itself for the foreseeable future.[63]

Supporters of the National Guard disagreed. They argued that the First World War experience had proven the essential wisdom of their approach. Although the professionals continued to disparage the performance of the National Guard throughout the war, several National Guard had units that fought well as part of the larger American Expeditionary Forces. They included the 28th "Keystone" (Pennsylvania) Division that fought in almost every major action of the AEF; the 27th "Empire" Division (New York) and 30th "Old Hickory" (Tennessee and North Carolina) divisions that broke the Hindenburg Line; and Douglas MacArthur's famous 42nd "Rainbow" Division with regiments from across the country. The National Guard system, its supporters argued, had worked.[64]

The debate continued after the war. The progressive reformers again wanted to increase federal control and reduce the influence of local politics. Once again, the National Guard lobby and sympathetic politicians pushed back. Once again, they won. The so-called Palmer reforms (named for Brigadier General John McAuley Palmer) aimed for a Regular Army of 288,000 men, most of whom would serve as training cadre for the National Guard. The Guard itself, twice the size of the Regular Army, would serve as the core of any force to fight a future war. Palmer sought to bring elements of the Swiss militia model to the United States. He envisioned dividing the United States into nine regions, each with one Regular Army division, two National Guard Divisions, and three reserve divisions in a kind of preview of the Abrams reforms of the post-Vietnam period.

The 1920 National Defense Act aimed to form a "total force" half a century before the term was coined. The act divided American land forces into a Regular Army, a National Guard, and an Organized Reserve. It also put National Guard officers on the Army staff and formed joint planning committees with officers from all three parts of the force. Congress kept the basic concept, but slashed the size of the Regular Army to 130,000 men, about half of what Palmer had requested. As a result, as Brian McAllister Linn notes, "Without resources to accomplish any of its missions, the Army pretended to do them all," and the Army became, in Linn's characterization, "little more than a collection of skeleton units devoting their time to maintenance, administration, and the desultory training of the National Guard and reserves." In other words, the Army went back to normalcy as defined by a small army, a decentralized National Guard, and political constraints imposing on the Army's desires to determine its own fate.[65]

Some reformers doubted even the need for that large an Army. In 1916, President Wilson had signed two huge naval bills, amounting to more than $300 million in new construction. Navalists tended to argue that the Army could not meet the future strategic challenges of the nation as the well as the Navy could. They contended that the Army's primary defensive role, coastal artillery, no longer sufficed. Thinking of both European and Asian threats, and aware of the strategic implications of the Panama Canal, they advocated putting shrinking defense dollars into a fleet that could protect and project on two coasts.

The rising Japanese threat symbolized a debate on the pivot to Asia *avant la lettre*. The United States and Japan were the only two states stronger in 1918 than in 1914. Japanese growth, combined with the relative decline in resources that the Europeans could thereafter put into defending their East Asian colonies, radically changed the dynamic between the United States and Japan. These fears predated the war, but the unexpected results of the war vastly increased them. Then, as now, policymakers who worried about the shifting balance of power in Asia argued that the Navy, not the Army, held the key to maintaining American interests across the vast Pacific Ocean.[66]

Another challenge soon arose in the air-minded approaches of strategists like William "Billy" Mitchell who came back from France convinced that ground forces now lay at the mercy of air forces. By 1925 Mitchell had made himself a national celebrity by challenging the conventional wisdom of both the generals and the admirals. He argued that neither coastal artillery nor surface fleets could protect America from any future combination of threats.[67]

Thus the first lesson from the "drawdown" of 1919–1920 may well be that there is not a great deal that is truly new. The same pressures on leaders today—uncertain global environments, rapidly changing technology, interservice rivalry, and a decline in resources—acted on leaders a century ago. If that insight provides comfort, however, the next insight will not. In the 1920s the missions and range of operations of the United States remained largely limited to what Americans would today call homeland defense. Aware that it had limited resources, the nation asked the Army to do little. The generals of the 1920s planned for a frightening variety of contingencies, but they never had to execute any of them.

Yet somehow, out of this disorder the Army managed to educate a new generation of leaders who would indeed see the nation through the next national emergency. They included well-known names like George C. Marshall, George S. Patton, Dwight D. Eisenhower, Douglas MacArthur, and many others. In addition to these famous commanders were the anonymous staff officers of a system that, in the recollections of British air marshal Charles Portal, generated the ideas that shaped Allied strategy in World War II.[68] Somehow, perhaps without even knowing it had done so, the Army made the right decision in an age of austerity and uncertainty: it had, in fact, made the only investment certain to pay dividends, the education of its people. Nonetheless, these educated officers faced enemies who had spent the 1930s honing their military prowess for the next conflict. America's foes were primed for war.

The two decades prior to and after World War I provide an instructive model for the future of the U.S. Army. These years tested the Army with amphibious landings, manhunts, a counterinsurgency, city occupation, conventional warfare, and the Interwar Years—a period of Western reluctance to prepare for future war. Regardless of whether military leaders believe that the age of conventional or unconventional warfare is at an end, these forty years illustrate that it is critical for the Army to be prepared and malleable enough to respond to whatever the future might bring. It is essential to remain at the forefront of technology and combat effectiveness. Only with great hubris do policymakers and commanders assume that they know what future missions and conflicts will be asked of the U.S. Army.

NOTES

1   John Clifford Brown, written on 23 August, 17 September, and 20 December 1899, in *Gentleman Soldier: John Clifford Brown and the Philippine-American War*, ed. Joseph P. McCallus (College Station: Texas A&M Press, 2004), 158, 88, and 99.

2   Anson T. McCook, 27 March 1920, box 11, Military Service Questionnaires, 1920–1930, War Records Department, Record Group 12, State Archives, Connecticut State Library (hereafter CSL).

3   America lost 2,446 servicemen during the Spanish-American War, from which the U.S. Army lost 2,430 men: 369 were killed in action, and 1,594 soldiers were also wounded during the conflict. Nese F. DeBruyne and Anne Leland, *American*

War and Military Operations Casualties: Lists and Statistics (Washington, DC: Congressional Research Service, 2015), 2.

4   The Army believed yellow fever to be the greatest danger; however, more men suffered from malaria and dysentery. Kenneth E. Hendrickson, *The Spanish-American War* (Westport, CT: Greenwood, 2003), 38.

5   Joseph Smith, *The Spanish-American War: Conflict in the Caribbean and the Pacific, 1895–1902* (London: Longman, 1994), 123.

6   G. J. A. O'Toole, *The Spanish War: An American Epic, 1898* (New York: Norton, 1986), 265.

7   David F. Trask, *The War with Spain in 1898* (Lincoln: University of Nebraska Press, 1996), 213–14.

8   Trask, *War with Spain*, 213.

9   Edward M. Coffman, *The Regulars: The American Army, 1898–1941* (Cambridge, MA: Belknap Press of Harvard University Press, 2004), 27.

10   Brian McAllister Linn, *The Philippine War, 1899–1902* (Lawrence: University Press of Kansas, 2000), 327–28.

11   Linn, *Philippine War*, 326.

12   Linn, *Philippine War*, 322–28. See also, Brian McAllister Linn, *The U.S. Army and Counterinsurgency in the Philippine War, 1899–1902* (Chapel Hill: University of North Carolina Press, 1989) and David Silbey, *A War of Frontier and Empire: The Philippine-American War, 1899–1902* (New York: Hill and Wang, 2007).

13   Coffman, *Regulars*, 27.

14   For a taut description of the conflict and occupation see Max Boot, *The Savage Wars of Peace: Small Wars and the Rise of American Power* (New York: Basic Books, 2002), 148–55. See also Jack Sweetman, *The Landing at Veracruz, 1914: The First Complete Chronicle of a Strange Encounter in April, 1914, When the US Navy Captured and Occupied the City of Veracruz, Mexico* (Annapolis, MD: Naval Institute Press, 1987).

15   Friedrich Katz, *The Life and Times of Pancho Villa* (Stanford, CA: Stanford University Press, 1998), 546, 566.

16   Edward A. Gutiérrez, *Doughboys on the Great War: How American Soldiers Viewed Their Military Experience* (Lawrence: University Press of Kansas, 2014), 28. Mark Ethan Grotelueschen stresses the Punitive Expedition's effect on the Army's artillery branch, which closed its School for Fire at Fort Sill, Oklahoma, and shut down the Field Artillery Board. Mark Ethan Grotelueschen, *The AEF Way of War: The American Army and Combat in World War I* (Cambridge: Cambridge University Press, 2007), 24–25.

17   Coffman, *Regulars*, 27.

18   James J. Hudson, *Hostile Skies: A Combat History of the American Air Service in World War I* (Syracuse, NY: Syracuse University Press, 1968), 2–3. By 1915, the airplane had become a necessity on the Western Front, mostly for reconnaissance and artillery spotting. In a short time, Europe realized the true power of the airplane, and the modern military role of the fighter and bomber materialized. As

in many other areas of wartime supply, the AEF depended on the Allies to provide airplanes. American ace Eddie Rickenbacker and every other American pilot flew French and British airplanes, predominantly the French SPAD 13 and Nieuport 28. Besides being short on planes, the Army had only twenty-six pilots. See Roger G. Miller, *A Preliminary to War: The 1st Aero Squadron and the Mexican Punitive Expedition of 1916* (Honolulu: University Press of the Pacific, 2005), 53, and Herbert A. Johnson, *Wingless Eagle: U.S. Army Aviation through World War I* (Chapel Hill: University of North Carolina Press, 2001), 157–216.

19 Tami Davis Biddle, *Rhetoric and Reality in Air Warfare: The Evolution of British and American Ideas about Strategic Bombing, 1914–1945* (Princeton, NJ: Princeton University Press, 2002), 49.

20 Biddle, *Rhetoric and Reality*, 319.

21 Gutiérrez, *Doughboys*, 28.

22 Gutiérrez, *Doughboys*, 29.

23 Gutiérrez, *Doughboys*, 65.

24 Edward M. Coffman, *The War to End All Wars: The American Military Experience in World War I* (Lexington: University Press of Kentucky, 1998), 35. Gutiérrez, *Doughboys*, 71.

25 John P. Finnegan, *Against the Specter of a Dragon: The Campaign for American Military Preparedness, 1914–1917* (Westport, CT: Greenwood, 1974), 189.

26 Gutiérrez, *Doughboys*, 29.

27 Richard S. Faulkner, *The School of Hard Knocks: Combat Leadership in the American Expeditionary Forces* (College Station: Texas A&M University Press, 2012), 107.

28 Charles T. Holtzman Jr., 25 June 1921, box 8, World War I History Commission, series I: Individual Service Records (Questionnaires), 1919–1924, Library of Virginia. The French Army issued the first automatic rifle, the 8 mm. M1915 CSRG (Chauchat), called the "Show-Show" by doughboys. Holtzman might be referring to the Chauchat or to the .30-caliber M1918 Browning Automatic Rifle (BAR), which did not appear on the battlefield until September 1918. By that time, the war was nearly over, but the Army made extensive use of the BAR until the late 1960s.

29 Quoted in Harold Elk Straubing, ed., *The Last Magnificent War: Rare Journalistic and Eyewitness Accounts of World War I* (New York: Paragon House, 1989), 221. Gutiérrez, *Doughboys*, 61–62.

30 Donald Smythe, *Pershing: General of the Armies* (Bloomington: Indiana University Press, 1986), 8.

31 At the time of the Great War, Plattsburgh was spelled without the *h* at the end. For purposes of consistency, it is spelled Plattsburgh throughout this chapter.

32 Gutiérrez, *Doughboys*, 63.

33 Harold T. Lyons, box 59, CSL.

34 David M. Kennedy, *Over Here: The First World War and American Society*, 2nd ed. (Oxford: Oxford University Press, 2004), 198–99.

35 Faulkner, *School of Hard Knocks*, 327.

36 Gutiérrez, *Doughboys*, 63.

37 Gutiérrez, *Doughboys*, 63.

38 Johnson Hagood, *The Services of Supply: A Memoir of the Great War* (Boston: Houghton Mifflin, 1927), 22–23, 27. Gutiérrez, *Doughboys*, 29.

39 George W. Cheney, 10 July 1919, box 15, CSL.

40 Marcel W. Rice, 21 July 1919, box 35, CSL.

41 John M. Ross, 6 October 1919, box 35, CSL.

42 Gutiérrez, *Doughboys*, 30.

43 Gutiérrez, *Doughboys*, 40.

44 Gutiérrez, *Doughboys*, 40.

45 Clarence M. Thompson, 26 April 1921, box 14, CSL.

46 DeBruyne and Leland, *American War*, 2. A casualty is defined as a combatant lost to the military, which includes dead, wounded, missing, captured, ill, and status unknown. The number of deaths, 116,516, includes all deaths: killed in action and died from wounds, diseases, and accidents. As a point of comparison, the total casualties for other major belligerents were as follows: Austria-Hungary, 6,920,000; Germany, 6,861,950; Russia, 6,761,000; France, 3,844,300; Britain, 2,556,014. Niall Ferguson, *The Pity of War* (New York: Basic Books, 1999), 295.

47 American figures calculated from DeBruyne and Leland, *American War*, 2. French figures calculated from Jean-Baptiste Duroselle, *La Grande Guerre des Français: L'incompréhensible* (Paris: Perrin, 1994), 7.

48 William L. Langer, *Gas and Flame in World War I* (New York: Knopf, 1965), xix. Gutiérrez, *Doughboys*, 132.

49 Scholarship on this period is thin. One survey (albeit outdated) is Russell Weigley, *History of the United States Army* (New York: Macmillan, 1967), chapter 17.

50 See Jack C. Lane, *Armed Progressive: General Leonard Wood* (San Rafael, CA: Presidio Press, 1978).

51 See Finnegan, *Against the Specter of a Dragon*, which covers this area of the UMT well.

52 John A. Morello, *Selling the President, 1920: Albert D. Lasker, Advertising, and the Election of Warren G. Harding* (Westport, CT: Praeger, 2001), 6. See also Wesley M. Bagby, *The Road to Normalcy: The Presidential Campaign and Election of 1920* (Baltimore, MD: Johns Hopkins Press, 1962).

53 Lloyd E. Ambrosius, *Wilsonianism: Woodrow Wilson and His Legacy in American Foreign Relations* (New York: Palgrave Macmillan, 2002), 35–36, and A. Scott Berg, *Wilson* (New York: Putnam, 2013), 24–29.

54 William C. Widenor, *Henry Cabot Lodge and the Search for an American Foreign Policy* (Berkeley: University of California Press, 1983), 67–68.

55 John Milton Cooper, *Breaking the Heart of the World: Woodrow Wilson and the Fight for the League of Nations* (Cambridge: Cambridge University Press, 2001).

56 Carl J. Richard, *When the United States Invaded Russia: Woodrow Wilson's Siberian Disaster* (Lanham, MD: Rowman and Littlefield, 2013).

57 An excellent assessment of the tragedy of the gap between Wilsonian rhetoric and action is in Erez Manela, *The Wilsonian Moment: Self-Determination and the International Origins of Anticolonial Nationalism* (New York: Oxford University Press, 2007).

58 One insight into this era comes from a biography of Henry Stimson, who served in both Republican and Democratic administrations in the First and Second World Wars. See Henry L. Stimson and McGeorge Bundy, *On Active Service in Peace and War* (New York: Harper, 1947).

59 The best summary of the origins of this debate is Lawrence Cress, *Citizens in Arms: The Army and Militia in American Society to the War of 1812* (Chapel Hill: University of North Carolina Press, 1982).

60 Peter Karsten, "Armed Progressives: The Military Reorganizes for the American Century," in Peter Karsten, ed., *The Military in America: From the Colonial Era to the Present* (New York: Free Press, 1986), chapter 24.

61 John Garry Clifford, *The Citizen Soldiers: The Plattsburg Training Camp Movement, 1913–1920* (Lexington: University Press of Kentucky, 2015), 111–12.

62 Nelson Lloyd, *How We Went to War* (New York: Scribner's, 1919), 14.

63 Frederick Palmer, *Newton D. Baker, America at War*, vol. 1 (New York: Dodd, Mead, 1931), 2–5.

64 David Woodward covers this debate in some detail in David Woodward, *The American Army and the First World War* (Cambridge: Cambridge University Press, 2014).

65 Brian McAllister Linn, *The Echo of Battle: The Army's Way of War* (Cambridge, MA: Harvard University Press, 2007), 118–19.

66 Walter LaFeber, *The Clash: U.S.-Japanese Relations throughout History* (New York: Norton, 1997), 128–59, and John Davidann, "Citadels of Civilization: U.S. and Japanese Visions of World Order in the Interwar Period," in Richard Jensen, Jon Davidann, and Yoneyuki Sugita, eds., *Trans-Pacific Relations: America, Europe, and Asia in the Twentieth Century* (Westport, CT: Praeger, 2003), 21–44.

67 William Mitchell, *Winged Defense: The Development and Possibilities of Modern Airpower* (Tuscaloosa: University of Alabama Press, 2009), originally published in 1925. See also Biddle, *Rhetoric and Reality*.

68 Edward M. Coffman, *The Embattled Past: Reflections on Military History* (Lexington: University Press of Kentucky, 2014), 158. Coffman notes that Portal told Forrest Pogue that "none of the top military leaders [of World War II] were great strategists. Rather, the ideas came from the colonels and lieutenant colonels who prepared the papers that the leaders discussed."

6

When the Smoke Clears

The Interwar Years as an Unlikely Success Story

MICHAEL R. MATHENY

Since the founding of the Republic, political sensitivities and financial common sense mandated a small professional army that would shape and lead much larger citizen levies called to arms in moments of national crisis. The Army surged during war, feasting on the nation's resources, before shrinking and enduring fiscal famine in peace. Although this pattern was significantly modified during the Cold War, in which the nation found itself permanently semimobilized with a peacetime draft and a growing military industrial complex, the Army nonetheless swelled and then shrank after major conflicts. Meeting the challenges of postwar drawdowns and the inevitable fiscal challenges that follow is critical as the Army seeks to draw both operational and institutional lessons from every conflict. The Army drawdown after World War I and the extreme fiscal constraints imposed during the interwar period from 1919 to 1940 offer great lessons in how to meet these challenges in preparing for an unknown future. After the carnage of the Great War, great power conflict did not look likely through much of the twenties, but by the thirties it became increasingly probable. The Army's interwar investment in professional military education, the study of war, and cultivation of talent paid huge dividends in preparing for what turned out to be its greatest challenge—World War II.

Most historians view the interwar period as a time of stagnation for the U.S. Army. The consequence of this extended, almost twenty-year postwar drawdown hangover was unpreparedness for World War II. In one study of the interwar period, a prominent historian concluded, "[T]he Army, in short, was responsible for its own unpreparedness. Tight budgets and an isolationist-minded Congress and public were powerful constraints, but the Army would not have been ready even with adequate resources."[1] Another military historian agreed that the Army "failed to develop a viable doctrine during the ensuing period of extended peace."[2] Contrary to these rather well-established views, given the circumstances, the Army, in fact, managed the post–World War I drawdown in a fairly effective manner, which significantly contributed to its future success in the coming global conflict.

The drawdown from the Great War beginning in 1919 forced the Army to make hard choices based on ever-decreasing resources. Army leadership chose to focus on its human capital and the study of war. Brought together in a rejuvenated professional military education system, this focus allowed the Army to identify and cultivate talent while it studied the lessons of World War I. Specifically, this new sense of professionalism focused on the study of national mobilization and the projection, maneuver, and sustainment of large forces over great distances. All of these were crucial to the global expeditionary warfare that would be necessary in the next war. The great economic power of the United States had to be transformed into great armies, fleets, and air forces that had to be raised, deployed, sustained, and maneuvered on a global scale. This required military professionalism of a high order. The Army leadership in a bleak period of fiscal constraint invested in professional military education as the best and perhaps the only real possible preparation for future war. It was the right choice and significantly contributed to victory in World War II.

Unlike previous contractions and drawdowns that would come afterwards, when the smoke cleared in 1918, the U.S. Army faced a new realization that future war would include total national mobilization projecting landpower on a continental, indeed global, scale. How might the Army develop or even retain the necessary capabilities to project power in an era of extreme fiscal and organizational constraint? Confronted with an insignificant small Army armed with aging World War I equipment, the Army's leadership pondered the possible as well as the lessons of the Great War. Their choices would have long-term consequences for the Army and national security.

The U.S. Army came home to a very brief period of celebration that quickly turned into an extended period of financial retrenchment and public indifference. During the war, the Army swelled to more than twenty-two times its prewar strength, which meant that the inevitable drawdown would be equally drastic.[3] It was not only drastic but long lasting. In fact, it may be considered in two phases: the initial postwar drawdown followed by an extended period of tough choices as the Army struggled through twenty years of persistent fiscal constraint. In the first phase, as in earlier wars, the American Army rapidly shrank as the citizen soldiers were quickly demobilized. Within six months of the Armistice, the Army discharged 2,736,218 officers and men. Two years after the war, the regular Army was reduced to 204,292 officers and men. Within seven years, it mustered only 134,829 soldiers.[4]

Anxious to reduce expenditures in the wake of wartime debt, Congress quickly lost interest in funding the military. Although the National Defense Act of 1920 authorized a regular Army of 280,000 officers and men, Congress never appropriated the money to fill the ranks. Unfortunately, the Army commissioned over five thousand officers, expecting to reach the authorized strength. Officers commissioned in 1920 became part of a group known as the "hump." This year group of officers suffered extremely slow promotion rates.[5] When combined with promotion by seniority, the "hump" plagued earlier year groups as well. Future general Albert C. Wedemeyer, commissioned in 1919, spent fifteen years as a lieutenant. Chronic underresourcing was felt throughout the Army. Within four years of the end of the war, Secretary of War John Weeks noted, "Economy has literally become the primary consideration in every departmental undertaking."[6] By 1924, the total budget for national defense had declined from $11 billion in 1919 to $500 million.[7] Well before the belt tightening brought on by the Great Depression, the Army lacked money to maintain its authorized peacetime strength, let alone train or modernize.

Beginning in 1929, the Great Depression further aggravated the Army's ability to maintain any pretense of readiness or preparation for war. It was very much a hollow army, so much so that Douglas MacArthur, chief of staff of the Army in 1930, noted that "in many cases there is but one officer on duty with an entire battalion; this lack of officers has brought Regular Army training in the continental United States to a virtual standstill."[8] In 1932 MacArthur reminded the secretary of war in his official report that "the universal and inescapable influence" of the economic depression had rendered the Army "below the point of safety."[9] To add insult to injury, President Hoover's administration mandated a 10 percent across-the-board pay cut for the Army in 1930.[10]

Regardless of the reductions in military strength, constant lack of funding, and public indifference, U.S. Army officers of the interwar period soldiered on while the senior leadership struggled to keep the Army in some state of readiness. The first task the Army faced, indeed should always face, was learning and incorporating the lessons of the last war to ensure its preparation for the next conflict. These often took the form of tactical, operational, or institutional lessons, which were integrated into doctrine and training. Tactical lessons are the most perishable, as their utility fades with advances in technology and when the nature of the adversary or conflict dictates applicability. Operational lessons are difficult to establish, for they inevitably cast long shadows on generalship in particular, and policy in general. Perhaps the most important, but often overlooked, lessons are those that may be gained to inform institutional strategies, which may best prepare the Army to meet future challenges. Although often criticized, the U.S. Army in the interwar period did much better in learning and adapting operational and particular institutional lessons than is generally recognized.

The Army began to examine the lessons from World War I soon after the smoke cleared. General Pershing established twenty military boards to consider the lessons from all aspects of the American Army's performance in France. Pershing also established the Superior Board on Organization and Tactics to review all the findings and make its own recommendations. The Superior Board reached conclusions not only about organization and tactics but also about the larger lessons of the American Army in modern war. The board highlighted the importance of unity of command, logistics, and the effectiveness of the American Expeditionary Force (AEF) staff organization.[11] With regard to tactics and organization, the Army did make changes over the next twenty years, attempting to incorporate new technology in the form of tanks, aircraft, and other new or improving instruments of war. However, the real and lasting advantage the Army gained was not in purchasing or experimenting with the few new weapons or vehicles it could afford, but with an investment in human intellectual capital. The chief of staff of the Army, who was responsible for handling much of the drawdown, was General John J. Pershing. It was Pershing who decided that the most practical response was to invest in officer education by revitalizing the military school system.[12]

Pershing became the chief of staff in 1921 and determined to utilize his wartime experience to shape the Army for the postwar period. The one great lesson from World War I that was seared into Pershing's mind was the woeful unpreparedness of the American Army for war.[13] Unable to quickly mobilize American industry or harness it to war needs, the American Army depended largely on French and British artillery, airplanes, and tanks. In terms of leadership and management, the massive four-million-strong citizen army eventually raised by the nation had to make do with only 432 graduates of the Command and General Staff School available to lead it and provide some basis for professional staffs.[14] Pershing found it necessary to establish a staff school in France to cover the gap in expertise on staffs, seeking to shape and direct the newly forged mass American Army.

Pershing returned from the war determined to avoid the lack of preparedness that characterized American participation in World War I, but what could be done in an era of extreme fiscal constraint?[15] The interwar years was a period in which it seemed useless to train impossibly understrength units. Line units were grossly understrength, with many infantry companies, for example, consisting of only seven or eight men for training.[16] As commander of the American Army in France, Pershing recognized the value of Leavenworth graduates. As chief of staff of the Army, he pinned his hopes on a school system that would provide the engine of professionalism for the American Army in the twentieth century.[17] With a small-budget-starved peacetime Army, he realized that true preparation for modern war could occur only in the military schools.

The schools most responsible for senior military education in the interwar period were the Leavenworth Schools and the Army War College (AWC). The Command and General Staff School (CGSS) was modestly established as the School of Application for the Infantry and Cavalry at Fort Leavenworth in 1881. Eventually, this school morphed into a staff college with the purpose of not only educating promising officers but also identifying officers suitable for duty on the Army staff. Prior to 1917 Leavenworth turned out a limited but talented number of staff officers and commanders that Pershing found invaluable in shaping and leading the AEF. The Army closed the Leavenworth schools during the war, but opened the doors again in the summer of 1919. For the next three years, Leavenworth separated military education into the School of the Line and the Staff School. The School of the Line provided instruction on brigade and division tactics. The Staff School focused on the organization, maneuver, and sustainment of corps and armies. The two schools combined in 1922 to become the Command and General Staff School (CGSS). This new school reduced student attendance to one year, allowing for greater throughput of officers. In 1928, the Army reestablished a two-year course to allow students more time and greater opportunity for rigorous study. The two-year course lasted until 1935, when once again the need for more trained officers reduced the Staff School to twelve months.[18]

The Command and General Staff School in the twenties studied the lessons of World War I. Historical case studies, lessons on functions of the staff, and tactical instruction centered on divisions, corps, and the field army comprised most of the curriculum. The instructors drilled students in campaign planning, the Army problem-solving process, logistics, and combined arms tactics. After 1936, the one-year course focused exclusively on division and corps tactics. Larger unit and Army operations became the sole responsibility of the Army War College.

Originally established in 1903 at Washington Barracks in Washington, D.C., the Army War College, like the Leavenworth Schools, closed its doors in 1917 for the duration of the Great War. Reestablished in 1919 as the General Staff College, it was renamed the War College in 1921 to avoid confusion with the Command and General Staff School at Fort Leavenworth. The mission of the War College differed from that of the CGSS at Leavenworth. The War Department mandated that the War College "train officers in the conduct of army and higher echelons; . . . instruct in those political, economic and social matters which influence the conduct of war; . . . train officers for joint operations of the army and navy; [and] . . . instruct officers in the strategy, tactics, and logistics of large-unit operations in past wars, with special reference to the World War."[19] The great lesson absorbed from World War I was that modern war for the United States Army meant national mobilization to enable force projection over great distances. The Army's decision to invest in and rely on the professional military schools to cultivate and prepare future senior leaders paid huge dividends. Together the schools addressed the key issues necessary to fight and win the nation's next war: cultivation of talent, national mobilization, power projection, maneuvering, and the global sustainment of large forces.

Cultivating Talent

Officers worked and lobbied hard for selection to attend the Command and General Staff School. Selection to attend the course and its successful completion were the keys to promotion. Students were rank-ordered according to merit, and the commandant wrote individual efficiency reports on each officer, indicating those suitable for service on the General Staff. It was a rigorous course that generated significant pressure on the students. Lectures, conferences, and problem solving filled the class day from 8:30 a.m. until 5:00 p.m., five days a week. Dwight D. Eisenhower attended the school in 1926, enduring a curriculum that called for seventy-eight map problems and terrain exercises worth a total of one thousand points. Eisenhower worked hard and benefited from advice and notes offered by George Patton, who had attended the course the previous year.[20] After graduating number one in his class, Eisenhower wrote an anonymous article for *Infantry Journal* to advise future students on how to reduce their anxiety and succeed in their studies. All the officers recognized that success at Leavenworth was important to their success in the Army.

Unlike Leavenworth, the War College focused more on education than training. Col. H. B. Crosby, assistant commandant of the War College, informed the students in 1924,

> [T]his is distinctly a college—where we learn from an exchange of ideas and not by accepting unquestioned either the views of the faculty or the views of the student. At Leavenworth we accepted the principles and doctrines laid down

by the faculty of that school. Here we reach our own conclusions, faculty and student, following a full and free discussion.[21]

Free inquiry, an absence of school solutions, and time for professional reflection marked the year at the War College. There was time not only for reflection but also for developing long-lasting friendships. Omar Bradley, future Army group commander in Europe, attended the War College in 1933. He found the time to organize a baseball team with Jonathan Wainwright as umpire, William F. Halsey as shortstop, and himself as pitcher.[22]

Army leadership recognized that attendance at both the Command and General Staff College and the Army War College was a quality cut and a necessary milestone for success. During World War II, all Army group and field Army commanders attended both the CGSS and the AWC. Of the thirty-four generals who commanded corps, all but one graduated from Leavenworth, and twenty-nine also graduated from the War College.[23] Getting the right officers into the school system was the first step. The next step was ensuring that through a mix of rigor and reflection, officers deepened their professional knowledge and understood the requirements for victory in the next war.

National Mobilization

The United States entered World War I without a detailed plan concerning how to contribute to the Allied cause or to expand and harness national industry for military needs. No national plan even existed detailing the organization and expansion of the War Department for such a global crisis. The prewar professional military education system as a whole was immature, lacking sufficient military expertise to create a modern mass army. President Woodrow Wilson had forbidden prewar contingency planning, considering it provocative to the warring powers. As a result, the Army General Staff was overwhelmed and unprepared for the scale of mass modern industrial warfare. Arriving in Washington and surveying the situation, Pershing was astonished at the "apparent lack of foresight in administration circles."[24] In reflecting on American unpreparedness in World War I, George C. Marshall, who would later shape the Army build-up for World War II, likewise recalled, "[I]t is inconceivable that we should have found ourselves committed to a war while yet in such a complete state of unpreparedness."[25]

As a result of this painful experience, the War Department undertook a series of mobilization plans during the interwar period. To ensure that officers were prepared to participate and direct this national effort, mobilization planning became a matter of special attention at the Army War College. By 1925, the Army War College instructed students that there were four types of plans responsible for organizing and directing military action from the national level down to a campaign plan within a theater of war. Of these, the Army staff was responsible for developing the Army Strategic Plan, which directed mobilization.[26] In the Preparation for War Course, War College students attended lectures on national mobilization, prepared individual case studies, and developed mobilization plans for major exercises. The Army was particularly concerned with mobilizing manpower.[27]

The Army was also concerned with mobilizing national industry to sustain and equip the mass armies required to win in modern industrial warfare. In 1924, the War Department created the Army Industrial College to study and prepare officers for the challenges of industrial mobilization. Starting with only nine students in its first course, the five-month course eventually grew "in scope and prestige until by the middle 1930's it had become in its field a complement to the Army War College."[28] By addressing this major shortcoming with plans and education after World War I, the Army greatly reduced the time it took to intervene effectively in World War II. From the time America declared war in April 1917, it took the U.S. Army almost a year and half to field an army capable of effectively intervening in the conflict. Within nine months of the declaration of war in World War II, the American Army invaded North Africa, engaging Vichy French and Axis forces.

Solid planning and preparation made an arsenal of democracy possible. The United States got off to an early start by ramping up industry and the armed forces in 1940 with the introduction of the draft and the refinement of mobilization plans. In the Second World War, the U.S. armed forces would not utilize Allied equipment, but provide it to them. By the end of the war, American industry provided U.S. and Allied forces with forty-six thousand aircraft and over sixty thousand tanks. Although there were many reasons for this astounding success, military leaders' acknowledgment of the problems so evident in World War I and their attempt to address them through education and planning within the military school system and the War Department proved decisive on the fields of Europe and the jungles of the Pacific.

Projecting Force

Geography made force projection a geostrategic imperative for the United States. The German Army was designed to attack its proximate neighbors and for a time was imminently successful. The American Army, however, needed to leverage both air and sea power in order to come to battle and defeat its adversaries. The Army War College from its inception was specifically charged to study joint operations and prepare officers to conduct them.[29] In the early twenties the Naval War College and Army War College exchanged both students and faculty and initiated a series of joint exercises. Unlike the Command and General Staff College, the War College used exercise scenarios based on the real-world contingency plans designated by various colors.

Some of the color plans, such as War Plan Red, which involved a conflict with Great Britain, were unrealistic, but War Plan Orange, or war with Japan, proved not only realistic but prophetic.[30] Because of the U.S. commitment to defend the Philippines, War Plan Orange was the most frequently exercised color plan scenario at the Army War College. Every year the students studied, briefed, and planned in some detail the requirements for projecting force across the Pacific. At the heart of the problem was how to leverage land-, sea-, and airpower to concentrate force within the theater to defeat the enemy. The Navy would secure sea control, allowing the transport and support of land and airpower. Landpower would secure and build naval and air bases from which to further extend American power throughout the theater. All was done under the umbrella of airpower, which constantly extended American operational and strategic reach across the Pacific. All this required joint command and staffs, which, although not doctrinally authorized, became the preferred student "solution." The emphasis on logistics and amphibious operations became both obvious and necessary in any study of future war in the Pacific.

In 1928, for example, Major Simon B. Buckner, while a student at the Army War College, insisted that the unity of command requiring a single commander for both Army and naval forces was essential in joint operations. He went on to note in his committee's study of joint operations that the Army was behind in developing techniques for amphibious operations, recommending the adoption of methods employed by the Marine Corps.[31] Buckner went on to command the Tenth Army, responsible for seizing Okinawa in 1945. He eventually organized the Tenth Army as a joint task force complete with an integrated joint staff of Marine, Navy, Air Corps, and Army officers. Even for those officers not destined for command in the Pacific, the War Plan Orange exercises were useful. Omar Bradley remembered that "another group wargamed the operation of a half-million-man field army in the Philippines. I found that lecture valuable background later in the European War."[32]

The 1936 student plan for War Plan Orange consisted of twelve incredibly detailed volumes, which included a joint estimate, mobilization plans for both the Army and the Navy, and a Western Pacific theater joint plan; it even addressed a joint basing plan. The students also called for a joint commander and staff. Noting the tremendous logistics challenges, the student committee also provided for the joint commander to direct logistics for all the services, which was a significant innovation in military thinking. Of the twenty-four officers participating in this committee, nineteen would become generals, including the briefer, Lieutenant Colonel Orlando Ward.[33]

The study and exercise of War Plan Orange allowed the students to consider and plan for the challenges of that theater, but other exercises also allowed them to contemplate global war. Beginning in 1934, a student committee was routinely involved in preparing war plans for coalition warfare. One of the first war plans involved the United States, Great Britain, China, and the Soviet Union combating the Japanese empire. By 1935, War College students were developing and exercising coalition plans against a Nazi confederation of Germany, Italy, and Austria. By 1937, students were developing war plans against a global enemy coalition of Germany and Japan. All of these specific and general war plans anticipated the challenges in projecting combat power over continental distances.

Maneuvering

The Command and General Staff School focused on combined arms—cooperation between branches of the Army and staff planning processes. Staff estimates, the military decision making process, and the five-paragraph field order were all necessary for the deployment and maneuver of American forces. These staff processes were drilled into the students and subsequently used at all levels of command, from the Joint Chiefs of Staff in Washington down to battalion level. The staff processes were also used at the Army War College in the study of joint operations, and became standard throughout the services. This common approach to problem solving and managing large forces was essential, but the key feature in the ability to maneuver large forces was the development of campaign planning.

Commanders exercise operational art, or the arrangement and sequencing of battles and major operations to achieve strategic objectives, through campaign planning. During the interwar years, the senior military schools made great strides in establishing a framework for campaign planning that was frequently exercised, particularly at the Army War College. In World War I, the generals' persistent pursuit of the single decisive battle was unable to break the bloody stalemate of the Western Front. War College students studying the Great War noted that the theater commander, often responsible for several armies, no longer managed single battles but became a director of operations.[34] Colonel C. M. Bundel, director of the War Plans Division, lectured the students that war "is divided into several distinct steps or phases which, while inherently distinct, nevertheless are interdependent and in some cases overlapping. It is believed that the differentiation of these phases is essential to clear understanding and correct solution of the many problems involved."[35]

In 1934, the War College established a faculty war plans division that included air corps and Navy instructors. The school settled on the five-paragraph field order format for campaign plans, blossoming soon with detailed intelligence and logistics annexes; formatting improved through constant exercises. Phasing was a key improvement as it became obvious that maneuver in large-scale operations demanded synchronization.[36] By the midthirties, the operations paragraph listed major subordinate forces with assigned tasks by phase.[37] These campaign plans also synchronized operations with air and naval forces.

One of the revolutionary developments arising out of World War I was airpower. During the interwar period, airpower still belonged to the Army and the War Department. Airpower seemed unique in its potential to operate simultaneously at the tactical, operational, and strategic levels. Despite fervent airpower advocates such as Billy Mitchell's argument for airpower's strategic role, the Leavenworth schools and the Army War College tied airpower to tactical and operational support of ground maneuver. At Leavenworth and the War College, students planned for the employment of landpower in which airpower was an ever-present and necessary reality in the theater of operations. Typical missions assigned in exercises included gaining air superiority, reconnaissance, ground support, and, most importantly, "shaping" theater operations.[38] In shaping theater operations, planners employed airpower to attack the enemy's lines of communication, as well as to isolate the battlefield. General Eisenhower's Transportation Plan for Operation Overlord, the invasion of France in 1944, used airpower to target the Germans' ability to rush forces to the invasion area. In essence, Eisenhower used a typical War College solution to isolate the lodgment area and win the battle to build up forces on the continent. Despite the growing utility of airpower, one of the most consistent features of professional military education during the interwar years was an emphasis on logistics.

Sustaining

"You need very few Napoleon Bonapartes in war, but you need a lot of superb G-4's," lectured Major General Fox Connor to the Army War College class of 1931.[39] As Pershing's wartime assistant chief of staff for operations (G-3), Connor had a good deal of credibility with the class. As Connor's lecture prescribed, logistics was consistently stressed at both the Staff and War colleges. At the War College, the faculty insisted that "[e]very phase of military operations, every strategic or tactical conception is inextricably interlocked to a greater or lesser extent with some phase of supply and transportation."[40] At the Staff College in the 1920s, logistics made up 10–15 percent of the instruction. When compared to the 25–29 percent consumed by tactical instruction, the amount of time the faculty devoted to logistics was considerable.[41] At the Army War College, the G-4 Course absorbed even more of the curriculum, where instructors stressed the integration of logistics in campaign planning and exercises.

Logistics was not just a matter for logisticians. Though most of the students at the college were combat arms officers, instructors required them to write detailed logistic annexes for exercises. Logistics determines the art of the possible, and planning for sustainment was critical at the operational level of war. The students learned to anticipate the challenges that logistics could alleviate. In planning for a War Plan Orange scenario, for example, one student committee noted that the "magnitude of the logistics involved [in a Pacific war] is appalling."[42] By 1931, the War College reduced the number of exercises so that "more time was given for the careful working out of the logistic features of operations."[43]

The U.S. Army needed to pay attention to the massive logistics necessary to support modern mass industrial warfare. Over time, logistics planning became ingrained at all levels in the Army. General Marshall reorganized the Army in 1942 into the Army Ground Forces, the Army Air Forces, and Army Services of Supply. Unlike their adversaries in World War II, who prized tactical expertise, in the U.S. Army, a logistician could rise to the highest ranks. In theater, commanders created their own logistics command. No Allied operation after 1942 failed due to logistics. The preparation and planning for the kind of logistical excellence that could transform and apply American industrial power into military power was in large part the result of anticipating and studying the challenges afforded by professional military education in the interwar period.

The Pay-Off

With America's entry into World War II, the U.S. Army faced the daunting prospect of projecting armies across vast oceans to face well-equipped and victorious enemies. Fortunately for the Allies, the German and Japanese armies over time demonstrated significant deficits in conducting and sustaining joint operations. In its assault on Europe, the German Army consistently failed to balance ends, ways, and means at either the operational or the strategic level. General Eisenhower concluded "that throughout the struggle, it was in his logistical inability to maintain his armies in the field that the enemy's fatal weakness lay."[44] Additionally, the Germans failed to develop any effective joint or combined command and staffs to direct their military efforts.

In the Pacific, the Japanese not only suffered from the same tactical bias that prejudiced attention to logistics but failed miserably to develop any joint approach to the conduct of operations. Japanese Army-Navy rivalry precluded effective joint planning from the highest to the lowest levels. At the strategic level, the Imperial General Staff "was a facade to cover two separate organizations with strong competing interest and rivalries."[45] The Japanese Army and Navy developed individual plans and issued orders separately through their own chains of command. Coordination between the services was based on cooperation, not a formal command structure. Additionally, Japanese emphasis on fighting spirit and offensive operations always kept them operating at the margins of logistical risk.

In contrast, the U.S. Army fared much better in its ability to master modern industrial warfare to project, maneuver, and sustain forces on a global scale. The investment in professional education during the lean years must not be underestimated. Major General Ernest N. Harmon, wartime commander of the 1st and then 2nd Armored Divisions, reflected,

> A Military historian recently asked me how the United States, indifferent and even contemptuous of the military in peacetime, had been able to produce a group of generals, proficient enough to lead armies successfully against German might. I am now convinced that the intensive and imaginative training at the Command and General Staff College had a great deal to do with it.[46]

Likewise, there were many testimonials to the Army War College. After serving as a corps commander in World War II and later as chief of staff of the Army, General J. Lawton Collins reflected on the value of his year at the Army War College: "These studies were of value to the students," he remarked, "in that they learned what constituted a war plan, the scope of military intelligence that would be required, the logistical support that would have to be provided, the combined Army, Navy, and Air operations that would have to be planned and the political and economic factors that would have to be considered."[47]

With little money for equipment, unit training, or organization, the senior leadership of the U.S. Army in the post–World War I drawdown recognized that the best investment of limited resources was in officer education, the intellectual capital of the Army. With few units to command or train, the Army emphasized professional education to prepare officers. Lieutenant General Robert Eichelberger, commander of the Eighth Army in World War II, remembered, "I kept being sent back to school. In 1925, at the age of thirty-nine, I became a student at the Command and General Staff School at Fort Leavenworth. I learned more at thirty-nine than I ever learned at twenty-one."[48]

The second and extended phase of the Army drawdown did not end until 1938, when the U.S. government could no longer ignore growing international tensions. Japan's assault on China in 1937, coupled with Germany's march into Czechoslovakia and Austria in 1938, attracted congressional attention. That year Congress finally authorized and paid for an increase in Army strength to 165,000. The Navy and Air Corps benefited most from this awakened interest in national security. The Vinson Naval Parity Act authorized the Navy to acquire one hundred ships and one thousand aircraft. The 1938 budget also included $500 million for ten thousand airplanes.[49] For the Army it was a slow build until 1940 when the fall of France sent shock waves through the government.

Postconflict drawdowns are an inevitable part of the operational cycle and institutional life of the Army. The one thing the generation of senior Army leaders understood in the interwar years was that the investment in human intellectual capital provided a hedge against the inevitable fog, friction, and complex problems that the unknown future will surely bring. The Army cultivated institutional adaptability in a rigorous and well-supported school system that insisted on critical and creative thinking in its most promising officers. Professional military education was the one answer, the one response to the lingering drawdown from World War I that enabled the interwar Army to prepare for the even greater challenges that emerged in the 1930s. As summed up by Lieutenant General "Lightning Joe" Collins when reflecting on the interwar period, "[I]t was our schools that saved the Army."[50]

NOTES

1 David E. Johnson, *Fast Tanks and Heavy Bombers: Innovation in the U.S. Army, 1917–1945* (Ithaca, NY: Cornell University Press, 1998), 229.

2 William O. Odom, *After the Trenches: The Transformation of U.S. Army Doctrine, 1917–1939* (College Station: Texas A&M University Press, 1999), 9.

3 Russell F. Weigley, *History of the United States Army* (Bloomington: Indiana University Press, 1984), 599.

4 Ibid.

5 Edward M. Coffman, *The Regulars: The American Army, 1898–1941* (Cambridge, MA: Harvard University Press, 2004), 239, 240.

6 U.S. War Department, *Report of the Secretary of War to the President for 1922* (Washington, DC: Government Printing Office, 1922), 13.

7 U.S. War Department, *Report of the Secretary of War to the President for 1923* (Washington, DC: Government Printing Office, 1923), 4.

8 Quoted in C. Joseph Bernardo and Eugene H. Bacon, *American Military Policy: Its Development since 1775* (Harrisburg, PA: Stackpole, 1955), 388.

9 "Report of the Chief of Staff of the United States Army to the Secretary of War for 1932," extract in *Annual Report of the Secretary of War for 1932* (Washington, DC: Government Printing Office, 1932), 54, 46.

10 The Franklin Roosevelt administration mandated a further cut in 1933. Carlo D'Este, *Eisenhower: A Soldier's Life* (New York: Holt, 2002), 213.

11 The United States Army, American Expeditionary Force, "Superior Board on Organization and Tactics" (United States Army Military History Institute [hereafter USAMHI], 1919), 5, 6, 7.

12 Pershing's emphasis on the school system led to the increased importance attached to attendance and a dramatic increase in the number of graduates. Prior to World War I, there were only 432 Leavenworth graduates. During the interwar period, 3,677 officers graduated from the Command and General Staff School. Coffman, *The Regulars*, 280, 281.

13 John J. Pershing, *My Experiences in the World War* (New York: Stokes, 1931), 1:16.

14 Timothy K. Nenninger, *The Leavenworth Schools and the Old Army: Education, Professionalism, and the Officer Corps of the United States Army, 1881–1918* (Westport, CT: Greenwood, 1978), 157.

15 Pershing, *My Experiences in the World War*, 1:16; and George C. Marshall, *Memoirs of My Service in the World War, 1917–1918* (Boston: Houghton Mifflin, 1976), 8.

16 Coffman, *The Regulars*, 2004, 234.

17 Military historian Edward M. Coffman noted,
> The spectacular row over air power and the development of an armored force in the postwar period were indications of change, but more basic was the new professionalism of the army. In part this was a result of the war experience, but there was a greatly increased emphasis on the schools and professional training. Although a few officers attended the Leavenworth schools and the Army War College before 1917, many did not think this training was essential. After the war, it was.

Coffman, *War to End All Wars* (Lexington: University of Kentucky Press, 1981), 361–62.

18 Boyd L. Dastrup, *The U.S. Army Command and General Staff College: A Centennial History* (Manhattan, KS: Sunflower University Press, 1982), 60–65.

19 "Summary of Courses," Course 1928–1929, 12, AWC Curricular File 1–105, USAMHI.

20 Carlo D'Este, *Eisenhower: A Soldier's Life* (New York: Holt, 2002), 178.

21 Col. H. B. Crosby, "Orientation Lecture," delivered to the AWC, September 3, 1924, AWC Curricular File 294–2, USAMHI.

22 Jonathan Wainwright became a major general who commanded and surrendered American forces in the Philippines in World War II. William F. Halsey became a four star admiral and commander of U.S. forces in the South Pacific. Omar N. Bradley and Clay Blair, *A General's Life: An Autobiography of General of the Army Omar N. Bradley* (New York: Simon & Schuster, 1983), 74.

23 Robert H. Berlin, *U.S. Army World War II Corps Commanders: A Composite Biography* (Fort Leavenworth, KS: Combat Studies Institute, 1989), 10, 12. Additionally, in terms of cultivating talent, "Of the thirty-four generals who commanded corps (in WWII), twenty-five spent ten or more years at schools during the interwar period." Coffman, *The Regulars*, 281.

24 Pershing, *My Experiences in the World War*, 1:8.

25 Marshall, *Memoirs of My Service in the World War*, 8.

26 WPD Committee No. 8, "Joint Plans, Army Plans, GHQ Plans," September 26, 1925, War Plans Course, AWC Curricular File 310–11, 1–9, USAMHI.

27 Weigley, *History of the United States Army*, 406.

28 Ibid., 407.

29 "Summary of Courses," Course 1928–1929, 12 AWC Curricular File 1–105, USAMHI.

30 As a result of the Spanish-American War, American interests and forces were pushed further into the Pacific with the occupation of the Philippines. Anti-Japanese riots in California and increasing tensions over immigration provoked President Theodore Roosevelt in 1906 to ask the Navy to prepare plans for a possible conflict with Japan. For the next thirty years, War Plan Orange generally considered three phases to such a conflict: Japanese forces overrun the Philippines, U.S. forces advance across the Pacific and retake the islands, and, finally, U.S forces blockade Japan, resulting in negotiations or surrender. In 1939 the color plans were replaced by the Rainbow Plans, which involved planning against multiple threats. Rainbow 5 called for Anglo American cooperation in defeating the Axis and led directly into specific wartime coalition planning following American entry into the war. Regardless, War Plan Orange provided the conceptual blueprint for the American offensive in the Central Pacific in World War II. See Maurice Matloff and Edwin M. Snell, *Strategic Planning for Coalition Warfare, 1941–42: The United States Army in World War II* (Washington, DC: Office of the Chief of Military History, Department of the Army, 1953).

31 Subcommittee No. 3, "Training System of the Navy Including the Marine Corps with a View to More Effective Cooperation between the Army and Navy in Joint Operations," October 4, 1928, G-3 course, AWC Curricular File 352–4B,1.10, USAMHI.

32 Bradley and Blair, *A General's Life*, 74.

33 Orlando Ward became a major general and commanded the First Armored Division in North Africa. War Plans Group No. 2, "Subject: War Plan Orange," April 11, 1936, AWC Curricular File 5–1936–19/1–2, 33, USAMHI.

34 Committee No. 11, "Command and Organization of Large Units," February 23, 1926, Command Course, AWC Curricular File 338–1, 28, USAMHI.

35 Colonel C. M. Bundel, "Orientation and Outline for the War Plans Course," lecture delivered to the AWC, April 1, 1926, AWC Curricular File 310A, WPD #14, 2, USAMHI.

36 The development of phased operations was critical in campaign planning as it allows the commander to synchronize forces and operations in time, space, and purpose. In World War I, ground operations became phased to coordinate the advance of the infantry with artillery support. I maintain that during the interwar period this tactical phasing was extrapolated into operational phasing as American officers contemplated the challenges of projecting force across the Pacific in any conflict with Japan.

37 Committee No. 1, "Subject: War Planning," February 19, 1936, AWC Curricular File 5–1936A-19/1–12, USAMHI.

38 Conduct of War: Part II Map Maneuver, Group 2, Red Coalition, May 20, 1938, AWC Curricular File 6–1938–9B, 2, USAMHI.

39 Major General Fox Connor, "Organization and Function of the G-3, AEF," lecture delivered to the AWC, September 18, 1931, AWC Curricular File 383-A-98, G-3 Course 6, USAMHI.

40 Major C. C. McCornack, "The G-4 and Some of His Problems," lecture delivered to the AWC, November 15, 1926, G-4 Course, AWC Curricular File 334A-3, 1, USAMHI.

41 See U.S. Army, "Instruction Circular No. 1" (Fort Leavenworth, KS: General Service School Press), for the years 1922–1930, Combined Arms Research Library at Leavenworth, Kansas.

42 War Plans Group no. 2, "Subject War Plan Orange," April 11, 1936, AWC Curricular File 5–1936-19/1–12, 33, USAHMI.

43 Summary of Courses at the Army War College since the World War, AEX Curricular File 1–105, 19, USAMHI.

44 *Report by the Supreme Commander to the Combined Chiefs of Staff on the Operations in Europe of the Allied Expeditionary Force, 6 June 1944 to 8 May 1945* (Washington, DC: Government Printing Office, n.d.), 121.

45 Louis Morton, *Strategy and Command: The First Two Years* (Washington, DC: Office of the Chief of Military History, Department of the Army, 1962), 235.

46 Ernest N. Harmon, *Combat Commander: Autobiography of a Soldier* (London: Prentice International, 1970), 49.

47 J. Lawton Collins, *Lightning Joe: An Autobiography* (Baton Rouge: Louisiana State University Press, 1974), 94.

48 Robert L. Eichelberger, *Our Jungle Road to Tokyo* (Nashville, TN: Battery Press, 1989), xv.

49 Weigley, *History of the United States Army*, 417.

50 Coffman, *The Regulars*, 289.

PART III

Conceptualizing Cold War Framework

7

Searching for the Greatest Generation's Army in 1950

SCOTT BERTINETTI AND JOHN A. BONIN

Following the Allied victory in World War II, the United States found itself in a position unique in its 169-year history. America's geographic location, combined with its vast resources and intact industrial base, relative to the wartime destruction in Europe and Japan, meant that the United States was unquestionably the world's economic superpower. After fully mobilizing its manpower and forcing the eventual surrender of the Axis powers, the United States was ready for its service members to come home. Significantly, the United States also maintained a monopoly on the greatest weapon created during World War II—the atomic bomb. The atomic bomb enabled the United States to demobilize the majority of its Army, and it served as an insurance policy as part of its national defense.[1] The United States' economic might and its geographic location, combined with the notion that it retained the most devastating weapon available to defend its borders, enabled it to assert its influence across the globe.

Following World War II, the United States quickly demobilized upon the conclusion of hostilities in Europe and the Pacific. This was not an unusual phenomenon, especially for the U.S. Army. It was ready to revert to maintaining a relatively small peacetime Army, relying on the power of atomic weapons and the time and space that geography enabled to defend its borders.

The requirement for maintaining a large standing Army during peacetime, not for war but as a deterrent to war, was an unknown concept in the early-twentieth-century United States. The need for a large standing military ground force post-1945 fundamentally changed the way Americans viewed and employed their Army. This realization by Americans occurred as the role of the United States in the world changed following World War II. This new requirement for a standing Army, forward deployed and prepared to conduct military operations, evolved over a six-year period (1945 to 1950). During this time, the United States' decision to rearm its Army was influenced by a series of outside and unforeseen influences that directly confronted American political ideology and America's role as one of the world's superpowers. This chapter will focus on the events following World War II that led the United States to reassess its political position in the world and the role of the U.S. Army leading up to 1950. This reassessment, combined with external events and subsequent U.S. decisions, would directly impact the need for the United States to have a large, combat-ready, standing Army and to position a significant portion of those forces in Germany by 1951.

The post–World War II world continued to change politically. Previous colonial holdings sought their independence, while the war's destruction relegated previous world powers, such as Great Britain and France, to secondary positions. Like many of the other nations of Europe, the French and British economies were in tatters following World War II. In an effort to reboot their economies, European countries focused much of their effort internally, and in the cases of Great Britain and France, sought to reassert themselves in their prewar colonial holdings. In light of the "peace" that followed, the United States and many of the Western European nations demobilized sizeable portions of their military.

For the United States, "The great demobilization of the Armed Forces that had fought and won World War II was officially over by 1947, but the problems the military faced of readjusting to peacetime were just beginning."[2] During this period, the U.S. Army fell from a peak strength in 1945 of 8,267,958 men in uniform (including the U.S. Army Air Force) to 1,891,011 by the following year. The war's end consigned the U.S. Army largely to occupation duty in both Europe and the Far East, while it maintained a minimal strategic reserve within the United States.[3] By June 1946, the U.S. Army had twelve of its sixteen remaining divisions engaged in occupation duty: three in Germany, one in Austria, one in Italy, one in the Philippines, four in Japan, and two in Korea.[4] In combat units, the Army reduced from a wartime high of ninety divisions to only ten by 1948.[5]

Maintaining a large standing Army appeared expensive in terms of personnel and equipment and often conflicted with other domestic priorities. In addition, the U.S. political and military leadership believed that America's geographic position, combined with its industrial might, would help mitigate the risk of required military mobilization time for future conflicts. Shortly after World War II, President Truman advocated the need for Universal Military Training (UMT) to shorten the time required in the event of full mobilization. Truman and others believed that UMT would enable the nation to rapidly mobilize in the event of a large-scale war. Congress questioned the need for a large-scale Army, however, when the United States maintained the atomic bomb as a deterrent. Once the United States developed the atomic bomb, it hinged its defense strategy on the capability that no other country possessed. Indeed, for "most Americans, including most of the government, the U.S. Army in the late 1940's seemed almost irrelevant to the Communist challenge."[6]

The reasons for this American attitude were threefold: the initial threat of conflict in Europe appeared to diminish since the Europeans had been at war for six years and their will and capabilities were exhausted; the high cost of maintaining large military organizations ran contrary to domestic priorities; and the United States maintained the world's only nuclear arsenal, thus negating the need for a large standing army. Also, the apparent inclination of the Soviet Union to revert to prewar manning levels influenced this calculus: "The strength of the immediate post-war Soviet Army was put at about two and a half million men."[7] By 1950, the estimate remained roughly the same.[8] The Soviet Union's subversive activities of promoting Communist ideology across the globe combined with the West's unclear understanding of its intentions to further justify the reduction in U.S. conventional forces.

Following World War II, the United States was in the preeminent position of power in a world transitioning to the postcolonial and modern era. American industrial capacity had remained untouched from the terrible destruction of World War II. America's allies, however, were not as fortunate. The economies of Europe were devastated as internal infrastructures had collapsed and many polities had fallen under Soviet occupation or control. In the shadows of World War II, the European nations focused on rebuilding economically, and leaders perceived that demobilizing their nations' wartime structures aided this effort.

In part as a result of the economic chaos in the aftermath of the war, European nations contended with the political ideologies of "Communism, Socialism, and Social Catholicism."[9] Previously unpopular ideologies advocating social and political change, such as communism, were gaining momentum. Marxist ideology promised a needed balm for economic reconstruction, and thus loomed as a haunting specter for the capitalistic, Western democratic nations. Greece and Turkey dealt with a more overt threat, and were eventually aided by the Truman Doctrine. France and Italy had to contend politically with Communist parties enticing voters to form Marxist-socialist governments. The increasing popularity of Marxist ideology following the war signaled that many people in Europe desired change from the prewar politics of their countries. The significance of these groups gaining popularity increased the likelihood of political takeover, which would not be beneficial to the United States, politically or economically.

The United States did not initially view the Soviet Union, its wartime ally, as a threat. However, in the latter half of the 1940s, the United States began to question Soviet intentions. Many Americans viewed communism as a threat emanating from the Soviet Union. From the United States' point of view, there was very little differentiation between apparent Marxist political subversion and the foreign policy of the Soviet Union. The West increasingly considered a global Communist threat monolithically, as a single ideology controlled by the Kremlin.

Prior to World War II, the United States maintained an isolationist approach toward world affairs. During the conflict, the United States was able to maximize its latent industrial base to produce armaments not only for itself but for many of the Allies fighting the Axis Powers. The United States' industrial capability supported reconstruction efforts throughout Europe following the war, through initiatives such as the Marshall Plan. Providing equipment and supplies continued as a large part of American foreign policy following World War II. However, by 1949 the United States realized that being able to produce weapons and war material alone to support its allies was no longer a viable strategy for achieving its foreign policy objectives. If the United States were going to embody its "superpower" position to further its own interests, it would have to apply all of the elements of national power toward a new world order, shedding its previous isolationist attitudes.

As it was, the United States was unprepared for its role as leader of the free world. It at first underestimated the overt strength of the worldwide Communist threat. The peacetime United States was untested in employing all of its elements of national power (diplomatic, military, economic, and informational resources) in mutually supporting fashion on a global scale as part of a comprehensive national strategy. The United States, however, did grow into this role, at first utilizing its economic and informational capabilities toward achieving foreign policy objectives. The Marshall Plan and Truman Doctrine, for instance, supported U.S. objectives by providing funds and equipment to assist struggling friendly nations recover economically and militarily, which also assisted in the containment of communism.

In the immediate postwar aftermath, prior to the Soviet's development of an atomic bomb, President Truman's emphasis on domestic issues had enervated conventional forces by levying a tight budget on the Army: "The administration had little choice but to rely upon its atomic monopoly as a means of deterring the Russians."[10] Furthering this approach, "Truman had not sorted out the competing priorities of public opinion, domestic economy, constitutionality, morality, and the national-security state."[11]

The United States' defensive plans to counter Soviet military threats prior to 1950 rested on the use of atomic weapons. However, from 1945 through 1948, the era of the American nuclear monopoly, the nation's stockpile and delivery capability remained extremely limited. According to David Rosenberg, "[T]here were only two weapons in the stockpile at the end of 1945, nine in July 1946, thirteen in July 1947, and fifty in July 1948. None of these weapons were assembled."[12] In addition, through 1948, there were only approximately thirty B-29s in the Strategic Air Command that had been modified to release atomic bombs, and all of these aircraft remained stateside in Roswell, New Mexico.[13] Through 1950, the U.S. nuclear stockpile remained too small and the weapons too large and unwieldy to be used against potential Soviet tactical targets, such as troops and transportation nodes.[14]

Strategic planning in 1948 acknowledged that due to geographical proximity, the Soviets would probably achieve initial military success in Western Europe. Planning called for the United States to counter Soviet geographic advantage by attacking Soviet military forces and urban-industrial targets with nuclear weapons.[15] Although military planners recognized that employment of nuclear weapons would not negate the use of ground forces, they doubted the overall effects that nuclear weapons would achieve militarily and economically. The U.S. Weapons System Evaluation Group assessed the United States with a significant loss of aircraft in such an attack: "The evaluation expected that at least one-third would be lost during night attacks and up to half in daylight attacks."[16] The military plan, called OFFTACKLE, hinged on the United States maintaining access to Europe via Great Britain, and after mobilizing and assembling forces for two years, embarking on a continental campaign similar to the one conducted in World War II.[17]

Domestically, the United States focused priorities at home rather than abroad with programs such as the G.I. Bill. Reflecting traditional peacetime military attitudes and beliefs and fiscal priorities, the defense budget declined steadily through 1949. Manpower requirements were also reduced during this same time period. In 1950, "Congress cut the authorized strength of the Army from 677,000 to 630,000 men. By June, actual Army end-strength bottomed at 591,487."[18]

While developmental and production priorities were allocated to the other services, the Army remained relatively static in terms of its weapons and doctrine between 1946 and 1950. The Army struggled with its narrative and its role in the nation's defense, a historic problem given Anglo-American attitudes ranging back to the colonial era. Although Army leadership believed their institution would play a significant role in a future war, they did not develop a clear vision on how it would do so. This lack of vision failed to counter budgetary restraints that prevented much modernization or updating of operational doctrine within the service. The advent of nuclear weapons provided the United States with a monopoly on a weapon that appeared to obviate land power requirements. The Army maintained that it would still be needed in phases following the employment of nuclear weapons in order to perform its traditional role of engaging the enemy and holding terrain.[19] According to the 1949 Field Service Regulation, the Army's role remained relatively unchanged. The new manual was a compilation of the lessons learned from World War II, continuing to focus on the types of terrain or environments in which the Army could expect to operate. In light of the advent of strategic weapons, the Army continued to expect to fight similarly to the way it did during World War II. The 1949 manual, however, did address "the dangers of radiation and of radioactive materials and said nothing about tactics on the atomic battlefield."[20] As General Mathew Ridgway described 1950 Army doctrine, "I don't think that at that time American doctrine contemplated limited war. The concept had always been all-out war, where everything is used in order to achieve victory."[21]

The 1950 combat strength of the U.S. Army consisted of "ten divisions, a division-size European Constabulary, and nine separate regimental combat teams."[22] Within these organizations, reduced authorizations and manning shortages resulted in combat units operating at two-thirds of their assigned strength. The divisions were maintained as frameworks for mobilized soldiers to fill in the event of an increased defense requirement. This was not a departure from American peacetime military structure, as discussed elsewhere in this volume.

In the summer of 1950, U.S. Army Europe lacked the capability to conventionally defend Germany or any other West European nation. The years following the Second World War found the U.S. Army in Germany performing various types of constabulary missions that prohibited training for conventional operations. In addition to the division-sized U.S. Constabulary, the 1st Infantry Division remained as the lone U.S. combat division in Germany. Unlike most other U.S. Army divisions in the postwar period, it maintained its fully authorized structure, but like others was not maintained at full strength. In addition, the Army neither organized units for combat nor trained them for war. It was not until the advent of the Korean War that the United States realized the possibility that the Soviets could also threaten Western Europe with military action. The only deterrent to the Soviet threat was a unified counterforce from an untested North Atlantic Treaty Organization (NATO).

Even with atomic weaponry, operationally and doctrinally, the United States Army continued to plan to operate under the conditions of World War II. The Army believed that it would have time to build divisions and train soldiers in the event they were needed for a large land war against the Soviet Union. This continued to be the prevalent view of the Army even after North

Korea's attack on South Korea in June 1950. General Mark Clark, chief of U.S. Army Field Forces, during an inspection of units at Fort Devens, Massachusetts, said he believed that American soldiers continued to be of high quality but that "their numbers in Europe were inadequate," and further stated "[t] hat the Army could build a division from scratch in nine months."[23] Unfortunately, by the time the Army trained and deployed to the potential European theater, it would have been too late to combat a Soviet offensive directed at Western Europe.

Soviet intentions became more apparent in the late 1940s, with the Berlin Blockade of 1948, the coup in Czechoslovakia that same year, and the Soviet attainment of atomic weapons in 1949. The Soviet Union confronted the United States with a military threat driven by the ideology of Marxism and the economic power of the Russian state, translating these factors into an aggressive, expansionist drive.[24] The threat of monolithic global communism became more apparent when China fell to Mao Tse Tung's Communists in 1949. The combination of these events introduced a significant challenge to the United States and its postwar role in the world. Additionally, the Soviet Union had armed itself during the war and maintained its wartime strategy throughout this period. Its industrial priorities remained producing military weapons and continued buildup of its armed forces. By the late 1940s, "It was estimated that the Soviets maintained 175 to 200 army divisions."[25] Once the Soviets also gained atomic technology, well ahead of the American projections, the period of American security based on its own nuclear capability and geographic position ended.

In January 1950, President Truman directed the Departments of State and Defense to reexamine the U.S. strategy in light of the Soviets' development of the atomic bomb. The State Department's NSC-68 drastically changed the United States' worldview and with it, the traditional small American peacetime military establishment. It recognized that the Soviet Union and communism posed an existential threat to the West. For containment as outlined by George Kennan and others to work, the United States and its allies would have to respond in a method that the Soviets understood: with a prepared conventional military force.[26] In response to Soviet overtures, NSC-68 presented President Truman with four options: "do nothing, initiate a preventative war, retreat into the Western Hemisphere, or bring its military strength and its allies up to equal out the balance."[27] The Soviets appeared to be gaining strength as America reconsidered its reliance on the atomic bomb: "The Soviets would be able to mount a variety of threats: general war, limited war, subversion, rupture of the Western alliance, undermining the American will."[28] The fact that the United States had the atomic bomb had not deterred the Soviets' intentions or shifted their national objectives, foreshadowing that nuclear weaponry was not a panacea for military conflict.

There were others within government who supported the NSC-68 assessment of the Soviets. The State Department's Chinese Affairs section voiced concern over Chinese and Soviet diplomatic moves: "Military moves in European and Asiatic sectors of the Communist camp [lead] U.S. intelligence to conclude that both the USSR and China are capable of launching war across their frontiers without further notice."[29] The U.S. ambassador to the Soviet Union further supported NSC-68's findings: "[W]e did not need to match them man for man, gun for gun, and tank for tank, but . . . we must be so strong as to make the Soviets pause and give careful consideration to the risk that they would run in engaging in a general war with the Western world."[30]

Not everyone within the U.S. government supported NSC-68's assessment of world affairs. The assistant secretary of state for economic affairs, Willard L. Thorp, cautioned the president on the economic statistics used by the NSC-68 planning committee. Thorp believed that "the broader economic case is clearly not proven. In fact, all the evidence in the report points the other way that the actual gap is widening in our favor."[31] Thorp, however, was viewing the total capacity of the United States compared to that of the Soviet Union, rather than estimates of pure military spending. General Omar Bradley, the chairman of the Joint Chief of Staff, proved to be concerned as to the effect of increased defense spending on the U.S. economy and Americans' standard of living. Some in the Senate questioned the policy of a forward-deployed standing Army. Many Americans believed that this would provoke the Soviets to military action on the continent. This lobby had a point, as there was no overt conventional military posturing from the Soviets toward Western Europe at this time, other than its large standing Army of "22 Soviet divisions poised a few miles from the zonal boundary opposed by four weak Anglo-American divisions."[32] From 1950 through 1952, U.S. dependents and noncombatants were neither evacuated from Europe nor prevented from flowing into it.[33] The events leading to NSC-68 and the arming of NATO would place the United States on a path that would endure for more than sixty years.

Korea remained another zone of confrontation with communism. Although the United States did not fight on the peninsula in World War II, the U.S. Army XXIV Corps, consisting of three divisions, arrived in 1945 to occupy the southern portion of Korea and repatriate the Japanese Army.[34] The United States reduced this force to only the 5th Regimental Combat Team (RCT) by December 1948. With the departure of the 5th RCT by July 1949, the defense of South Korea rested completely in the hands of the nascent South Korean Army, backed by only a handful of U.S. Army advisors.[35]

Consequently, when the North Koreans attacked South Korea on June 25, 1950, the violence exposed a hollow U.S. Army. General Douglas MacArthur, commanding general of the U.S. Far East Command, had only the Eighth Army with four divisions on occupation duty in Japan, all at reduced manning and equipment levels. When the South Korean Army rapidly collapsed and air and naval forces failed to stop North Korean T-34 tanks, President Truman responded on June 30 to the United Nations resolution to stop Communist aggression by ordering the U.S. Army into Korea. By the end of July, Eighth Army had three of his four understrength Army divisions fighting in Korea. General Matthew Ridgway believed that the U.S. Army's initial performance in Korea "was a miserable performance, really, in the first place, because the Congress of the United States had insisted upon tearing down this magnificent machine at the end of World War II."[36] More apparent in June 1950 was the failure of atomic weapons to prevent a full-scale North Korean attack on its southern neighbor.

In light of Soviet support for North Korea, the United States came to the realization that it would have to commit forces abroad to be prepared to fight if necessary. However, the U.S. Army was not the same Army that had concluded combat operations in both Europe and the Pacific theaters a little over five years earlier. The commitment of U.S. Army divisions to stave off the North Korean attack, combined with the requirement for a ground forces deterrent in Europe, finally enabled the Army to regain relevance at the advent of the nuclear age.

As events unfolded in 1950, it became apparent that a planned military build-up would not meet the near-term objectives that the national leadership desired or that NSC-68 predicted. In addition to the four divisions already in MacArthur's command, during 1950, the Army deployed the 2nd and 3rd Infantry Divisions from its strategic reserve.[37] The Army had to depend on standing force structure to satisfy its drastically increased manpower requirements and to restore a reserve capability. In order to bring existing active divisions up to strength, the Army filled those units with individual reservists and with soldiers assigned to the National Guard. Initially, four National Guard divisions were federalized with the 28th and the 43rd divisions assigned to Europe, while the 40th and 45th divisions saw service in Korea.[38] The Army ordered active divisions serving as training divisions to be reorganized into operational divisions like the 4th Infantry Division, which would later be assigned to Europe.

Although the Army lacked combat capability in its ten active divisions of 1950, it also lacked capacity in its higher headquarters to provide direction and synchronize division efforts in both Korea and Germany. When North

Korea attacked, the U.S. Army maintained only V Corps headquarters at Fort Bragg, North Carolina, and only at 75 percent effectiveness. As early as July 19, 1950, General MacArthur, who had been forced to deactivate I and IX Corps in Japan on March 28, 1950, as part of budget cuts, requested two corps headquarters.[39] Again, the Army looked internally to source this often-overlooked command and control requirement. V Corps was manned at strength and redesignated I Corps before deploying to the Pusan perimeter of South Korea by September 13, 1950. The newly formed IX Corps, outfitted with cadre from Fifth Army, followed shortly.[40] In addition, for the invasion of Inchon, on August 21, 1950, MacArthur activated X Corps, initially formed from his own Far East Command staff.[41] Simultaneously, the Army activated a new V Corps in August, followed by the reactivation of VII Corps at Fort Meade, Maryland, in January 1951. The Army would assign both headquarters to West Germany, where on November 24, 1950, the U.S. Constabulary headquarters in Stuttgart became Headquarters, Seventh Army. [42] Consequently, within one year, in addition to Korean War commitments, the Army deployed four divisions to Europe from the United States, along with two corps headquarters.[43]

The United States' nuclear capability may have been the undeniable deterrent preventing Soviet military operations from moving into Western Europe. The U.S. Army, however, was not initially prepared for conventional military operations against the Soviets. Many of the lessons it learned from the Second World War had departed along with wartime veterans. Doctrinally, the Army remained unchanged and was expected to function at corps levels and below, much as it did during the war years. Due to budgetary reasons, the Army relied on much of the same equipment designed and developed during the previous war.

The 1950 American nuclear war plan called for the use of at least 133 nuclear devices, and that plan remained in effect until 1952.[44] As America began to rearm, it did not go unnoticed by many that the Soviets may have indeed missed an opportunity to attack. Retired General Lucius D. Clay, the former head of the U.S. Military Government in Germany, expressed his belief, in late October 1950, that "the fact that Russia has not moved to date indicates to me she is not ready."[45] Clay's remark was significant since he was U.S. military governor for Germany during the 1948 Berlin Airlift and because he believed that any delay by the Soviets would allow the United States and its allies the time needed to build military strength.

Time was an important factor that the United States believed was an acceptable risk regarding mobilizing, training, and deploying ground forces. Strategically, the United States overestimated the amount of time before the Soviets would acquire nuclear capabilities. Another significant risk regarding time and space was that Western Europe was left undefended from a Soviet ground attack during this period. Arguably, this would place the Soviets on the European Atlantic Coast more rapidly than the United States could adequately respond with its own ground forces. Because of the geographical location of the United States compared to the trouble spots around the globe, combined with the significance of the demilitarization of its forces, Army leadership always envisioned the United States having the time to rebuild. The Army's leadership eventually realized that it no longer could afford a small, unprepared force, as had been the nation's experience since 1775.

The United States could not alone be responsible for the defense of Western Europe. The significant numbers maintained by the Soviet military and its allies dictated that the only means to defend Western Europe rested in an alliance of nations to counter potential Soviet aggression. NATO, established at the time the Soviets achieved atomic armament, had by necessity begun to arm itself with dedicated units. However, the economic strain hindered the participating nations from contributing adequate forces, as was required for each country by NATO. By 1950, Europeans were concerned with regional security and were looking to the nascent superpower capabilities of the United States for assurance and defense, due to the advent of Soviet atomic capability and its large standing army. As concerned with security as the Europeans were, they were equally unsure of America's response in the event of a confrontation with the Soviet bloc: "From where we sit, the administration seems in danger of erring very badly in the direction of 'Let's wait and see' and 'Let's not do anything until we are absolutely sure of it.' The people of Western Europe seem, on the one hand, to be frightened to death that we are going to bluster into a general war."[46]

Due to the Korean War and the decision to commit troops to NATO and Europe, Army manpower steadily began to increase, and in 1951, stood at 1,531,774, while peaking in 1952 at 1,596,419.[47] It would remain over the million-man mark through 1956 due largely to the conflict over Korea and the realization that a fully prepared standing Army was a necessity to deter Soviet aggression. It was only after Korea that the possibility of Soviet aggression appeared to resonate with the American political leadership. It must be noted that the 1950s build-up provided a large standing U.S. Army with a focus that the nation was prepared to fund, departing from its traditional antipathy of large-scale ground forces. The Army mission became tied to a viable threat reflected by national objectives.

Undergirding this shift in policy was a concomitant budget allocation toward national defense to support a forward-based Army. The requirements for facilities such as barracks, supply depots, ammunition holding facilities, dining facilities, headquarters, recreational facilities, exchanges, schools, and family quarters, to outline a few, received funding—not to mention the allocation of funds for modernization of equipment and training requirements. The concept of forward basing symbolized the United States' evolution from an isolationist nation to superpower status. The positioning of combat troops in Europe provided a viable deterrent and signaled to both friends and potential adversaries its commitment to Europe. Basing enabled American forces forward in Europe reduced the mobilization-time factor, and symbolized de facto American commitment to both friend and foe alike: "In 1947, within Germany there were 99 bases, from 1947 through 1967, the number of bases numbered 278."[48]

As this period indicates, nations' priorities continue to evolve. The United States today can take note of the difficulty in formulating a strategy in uncertain times. Assessing the threat in 1950 arguably was no simpler than it is today. A historical insight from this early period of the Cold War was to maintain a balance between governmental domestic priorities, while adequately maintaining military preparedness. In terms of military strategy, it is impossible to predict how the next war will be fought; thus the maintenance of military structure is necessary for strategic flexibility, when unpredicted crises arise. The smart implementation of technology and the positioning of forces in troubled areas may hedge against poor policy and unpredictable events.

This short period of time during the Cold War illuminates several reoccurring themes that resonate with an "American way of war." The United States Army following World War II, in a situation similar to those of many of its previous wars outlined in this volume, quickly demobilized and suffered budget cuts reducing its size and capabilities (preventing the upgrading of its equipment). While it conducted after-action reviews following World War II in order to assess performance, many of the lessons were not directly translated into consideration of how the U.S. Army would conduct the next war. Generally, the Army remained unchanged in terms of doctrine and equipment. It believed that if it had to fight a conventional war, it would use the same type of equipment and fight in a similar manner as it did during the previous war, while relying on atomic weapons. The reliance on technology as the panacea for general unpreparedness is dangerous in the conduct of war, as the opening stages of the Korean War demonstrated. The utilization of technology to enhance capabilities rather than to dictate doctrine is a critical consideration for defense preparation.

The post–World War II era for the United States served as a significant strategic watershed in terms of world politics and how the nation would interact in an altered world landscape. By early 1950, the Truman administration and leaders within the U.S. Army believed that ground forces would be utilized in ways similar to the Second World War. However, the Truman administration also did not view the U.S. Army as being as strategically relevant to the needs of the contemporary world as the other services. As a consequence, Army capabilities deteriorated (roles, missions, organizations), creating a mismatch with national objectives. Flaws in the Truman administration's strategic approach were exposed after the North Korean invasion. Although the North Korean attack against South Korea that year can be labeled as the trigger, the Korean War was the penultimate event capping four years of the United States acquainting itself with its new role as a world superpower. While a large standing Army does not guarantee success in terms of assurance, deterrence, coercion, or combat, the degree of success in future conflicts can be enhanced if the U.S. Army's roles, missions, and organizations are synchronized with national strategy and sourced to support that strategy.

NOTES

1   This would change in 1949, with the Soviet Union exploding its first nuclear device. Defense planning groups had acknowledged that the Soviets were working on an atomic bomb, but these groups believed that the Soviets would not have the capability until 1954.

2   Jeffrey A. Larsen and Erin R. Mahan, *Establishing the Secretary's Role: James Forrestal,* Historical Office, Office of the Secretary of Defense (Washington, DC: National Defense University Press, 2011), 11.

3   Russell F. Weigley, *History of the United States Army* (New York: Macmillan, 1967), 569.

4   John B. Wilson, *Maneuver and Firepower: The Evolution of Divisions and Separate Brigades* (Washington, DC: U.S. Army Center of Military History, 1998), 208.

5   Robert A. Doughty, *The Evolution of US Army Tactical Doctrine, 1946–76* (Fort Leavenworth, KS: Combat Studies Institute, U.S. Army Command and General Staff College, 1979), 1; and William W. Epley, "America's First Cold War Army, 1945–1950," *AUSA Land Warfare Paper,* no. 32 (August 1999): 4.

6   Weigley, *History of the United States Army,* 501.

7   Albert Seaton and Joan Seaton, *The Soviet Army: 1918 to the Present* (New York: Meridian, 1986), 160.

8   James Dobbins, *America's Role in Nation-Building: From Germany to Iraq* (Santa Monica, CA: Rand, 2003), 11.

9   Derek W. Urwin, *Western Europe since 1945: A Political History,* 4th ed. (New York: Longman, 1989), 6.

10 John Lewis Gaddis, *We Now Know: Rethinking Cold War History* (New York: Oxford University Press, 1997), 92.

11 Ibid.

12 David Alan Rosenberg, "The Origins of Overkill: Nuclear Weapons and American Strategy, 1945–1960," *International Security* 7, no. 4 (Spring 1983): 14–15.

13 Ibid., 15.

14 Ibid., 16.

15 Robert R. Bowie and Richard H. Immerman, *Waging Peace: How Eisenhower Shaped an Enduring Cold War Strategy* (New York: Oxford University Press, 1998), 14–15.

16 Ibid., 14–15.

17 Ibid., 15.

18 Weigley, *History of the United States Army*, 502.

19 Doughty, *The Evolution of US Army Tactical Doctrine*, 1.

20 Ibid., 2–3.

21 Oral History Interview with General M. B. Ridgway conducted April 18, 1984, by Maurice Matloff, OSD Historical Office, Pentagon, Washington, DC, 16.

22 Weigley, *History of the United States Army*, 502.

23 "Gen Clark Terms Troops in Europe 'Cream of Crop,'" *Stars and Stripes*, November 1, 1950, European edition.

24 Russell F. Weigley, *The American Way of War: A History of United States Military Strategy and Policy* (Bloomington: Indiana University Press, 1973), 380.

25 Senate Committee on Foreign Relations and Committee on the Armed Services, *Assignment of Ground Forces of the U.S. to Duty in the European Area*, 81st Cong., 1st sess., February 26, 1951, S. Res. 8, 610.

26 See John Lewis Gaddis, *The United States and the Origins of the Cold War, 1941–1947* (New York: Columbia University Press, 1972).

27 "A Report to the President Pursuant to the President's Directive of January 31, 1950: United States Objectives and Programs for National Security, April 7, 1950," in U.S. Department of State, *Foreign Relations of the United States*. Volume 1, *1950* (Washington, DC: Government Printing Office, 1950), 272.

28 Weigley, *The American Way of War*, 380.

29 "Memorandum by the Director of the Office of Chinese Affairs (Clubb) to the Assistant Secretary of State for Far Eastern Affairs (Rusk), Subject: Estimates of Moscow-Peiping Time-Table for War, December 18, 1950," in U.S. Department of State, *Foreign Relations of the United States*. Volume 1, *1950* (Washington, DC: Government Printing Office, 1950), 479.

30 "Memorandum of Conversation by the Ambassador in the Soviet Union (Kirk), Subject: Report to the President, December 19, 1950," in U.S. Department of State, *Foreign Relations of the United States*. Volume 1, *1950* (Washington, DC: Government Printing Office, 1950), 483.

31 "Memorandum by the Assistant Secretary of State for Economic Affairs (Thorp) to the Secretary of State, April 5, 1950," in U.S. Department of State, *Foreign*

Relations of the United States. Volume 1, *1950* (Washington, DC: Government Printing Office, 1950), 218.

32 Dobbins, *America's Role in Nation-Building,* 11.

33 Evident from articles in the European version of the military paper, *Stars and Stripes,* announcing arrivals.

34 Wilson, *Maneuver and Firepower,* 211.

35 Allan R. Millet, *The War for Korea, 1945–1950: A House Burning* (Lawrenceville: University of Kansas Press, 2005), 186–90.

36 Oral History Interview with General M. B. Ridgway, 34.

37 Wilson, *Maneuver and Firepower,* 240–41.

38 Ibid., 242–43.

39 James F. Schnabel, *Policy and Direction: The First Year* (Washington, DC: U.S. Army Center of Military History, 1990), 134–35.

40 Ibid.; and Gordon L. Rottman, *Korean War Order of Battle: United States, United Nations, and Communist Ground, Naval, and Air Forces, 1950–1953* (Westport, CT: Praeger, 2002), xxi, 10, and 11.

41 Schnabel, *Policy and Direction,* 158.

42 John B. Wilson, compiler, *Armies, Corps, and Divisions, and Separate Brigades* (Washington, DC: Center of Military History, 1987), 30, 64, and 72.

43 Mary Ellen Condon-Rall, *NATO and the Army Family in Europe,* http://www. history.army.mil/html/bookshelves/resmat/backups/a19990331nato5.html, October 5, 2011.

44 Bowie and Immerman, *Waging Peace,* 15.

45 "Gen Clay Sees No War Soon," *Stars and Stripes,* November 1, 1950, European edition.

46 "Memorandum by the Assistant Secretary of State for Public Affairs (Barrett) to the Secretary of State and the Under Secretary of State (Webb), Subject: Current Emergency, December 5, 1950," in U.S. Department of State, *Foreign Relations of the United States.* Volume 1, *1950* (Washington, DC: Government Printing Office, 1950), 423–24.

47 Ibid., 569.

48 James R. Blaker, *United States Overseas Basing: An Anatomy of the Dilemma* (New York: Praeger, 1990), 43.

8

The Post–Korean War Drawdown under the Eisenhower Administration

RAYMOND MILLEN

To avoid the precipitous demobilization reminiscent of the World Wars, the Dwight D. Eisenhower administration sought to down-size the U.S. Armed Forces over a period of years following the end of the Korean War. To this end, the administration sought to base military force ceilings and force distribution on the Basic National Security Policy (BNSP), popularly known as the New Look. This approach, however, was by no means universally accepted or without rancor. Parting from the American tradition of full-scale demobilization, Eisenhower reasoned that in the modern era, U.S. national security could no longer depend on vast oceans for protection. He made this point clear during congressional testimony as the supreme allied commander for NATO in 1951 when he asserted "that the preservation of a free America required our participation in the defense of Western Europe; that success was attainable, given unity in spirit and action; and that our own major role should be as a storehouse of munitions and equipment, although initially a fairly heavy commitment of American troops would be required [i.e., two divisions]."[1] In his view, the old notion of "Fortress America" was not only outdated but also foolhardy.

As the Cold War became increasingly global and antagonistic, two camps emerged in U.S. policy circles on how to confront the Soviet threat. Associated with the first camp, the Truman administration adopted a mobilization strategy pursuant to NSC-68 and the outbreak of war in Korea.[2] Viewing the Soviet Union as intent on world domination through military aggression, on a par with the Third Reich, NSC-68 recommended a massive expansion of military capabilities. Under the air of crisis, the U.S. intervention in Korea cut short any public debate on the implications of NSC-68 and overshadowed the mobilization strategy.[3] Adding to the sense of national urgency, Truman's mobilization strategy was predicated on the expectation of imminent Soviet aggression by 1954—"the year of greatest danger."

The second camp, as articulated by George Kennan's 1947 "X" article in *Foreign Affairs*, viewed Soviet behavior as no different from Russian traditional foreign policy, and recommended a strategy of containment as proposed by NSC 20/4.[4] Upon assuming office, the Eisenhower administration adapted NSC 20/4 to a strategy of deterrence as articulated in NSC 149/2, which relied substantially on the superior U.S. nuclear arsenal and airpower.[5] In Eisenhower's view, the Soviet conventional threat paled in significance, compared to the potential economic and psychological damage to U.S. democratic institutions from the mobilization strategy. In an address to the nation on May 19, 1953, Eisenhower explained that the Soviet strategy against the West was to undermine liberal democracy by forcing it to pursue exorbitant military spending, which in the end would undermine the essence of capitalism and eventually cause economic collapse. And as the president often warned, "a bankrupt America . . . is a defenseless America."[6]

The president's understanding of the Soviet threat was accurate. Throughout the late 1940s and 1950s, the Cold War remained a struggle of East-West ideology, with each side vying for world leadership. The Soviets sought to exploit the devastation of World War II to attract demoralized Western European states into their camp. They also exploited colonial imperialism to weaken the West economically, create instability, gain a propaganda advantage, and rally non-Western states and peoples to the Communist banner. Accordingly, the Kremlin employed subversion of governments, obstruction of economic recovery and political stability (especially in Germany), and fomentation of civil unrest though surrogates (i.e., strikes, riots, protests, and insurgencies). While outright Soviet military aggression could not be ruled out completely, it remained unlikely. Eisenhower thus sought to ensure that the Soviets did not miscalculate by misreading U.S. resolve or perceived unreadiness.[7]

Still, NSC 149/2 remained a contentious issue in the White House. Secretary of State John Foster Dulles wanted a more aggressive strategy against the Soviet Union, proposing a rollback of the empire to Russia's traditional borders, which mirrored the NSC-68 approach. In contrast, Republican (GOP) congressmen felt that even NSC 149/2 called for higher deficit spending, which was viewed as anathema. Moreover, the GOP sentiment was tinged with isolationism under the guise of "Fortress America."[8] Even with a Republican president, garnering GOP political support for any national security policy would remain difficult. Uncertainties in the international environment also made the viability of NSC 149/2 questionable. The death of Stalin in March 1953 did not result in a thaw of East-West tensions, and Moscow rebuffed Eisenhower's April 16, 1953, "Chance for Peace" speech. The Korean War continued unabated with no apparent end. The autocratic, populist governments in Iran and Guatemala were susceptible to Soviet socialism. France and Britain were mired in the Indochina and Malaya insurgencies, respectively, which detracted from their NATO obligations and fomented anti-imperialist propaganda in the Third World.[9] The revolutionary, pan-Arab government in Egypt was intent on expelling Britain from the Suez Canal and indeed Western influence from the Middle East.[10] Indeed, the advance of the Communist bloc appeared unstoppable, and regional instability threatened the international system. Within this mélange of tensions and pressures, Eisenhower's dilemma was finding an alternate strategy to NSC 149/2, which managed these challenges without turning the nation into a garrison state.

In the meantime, Eisenhower's immediate concern was an end to the Korean War, which would bring the issue of military demobilization into the political arena. On the one hand, Eisenhower wanted to avoid a repetition of drastic demobilization—an almost time-honored American tradition—which would prevent the United States from meeting its international obligations and attending to diverse national security threats. On the other, he was equally skeptical of maintaining large conventional forces with attendant exorbitant military expenditures. Choosing the middle road, Eisenhower was determined to establish a balanced military posture all the while avoiding incessant political infighting. He decided to create consensus and teamwork by engaging senior policy leaders in a deliberative decision-making process. And a comprehensive review of national security policy would serve as the catalyst.

The Basic National Security Policy (BNSP)

To promote consensus in the development of the BNSP, Eisenhower directed in May 1953 the conduct of a six-week exercise called Solarium. Examining three alternative strategies (i.e., revised containment, a circumscribed line around the Soviet bloc, and the rollback of the Soviet empire), three study teams (referred to as Team A, B, and C, respectively) produced exceptional staff work for the president and the National Security Council (NSC) to consider. Eisenhower remarked that the team presentations to the NSC on July 16, 1953, were the best and most persuasive arguments he had ever experienced.[11]

This exercise was only the beginning though. The real work would involve iterative drafts of the proposed BNSP and iterative debates in the NSC until the administration produced a rational end product. At the end of the July 16 NSC meeting, the president shared his thoughts and imparted his guidance regarding the development of the BNSP. He assessed that there would be no winners in a world war with the Soviet Union. During the prosecution of such a war or an attempt to pursue absolute security from attack through excessive military preparations, a garrison state psychosis would develop, which in time would result in the dismantling of democratic institutions and loss of inalienable rights as the government exerted increasing control over its citizens. Even in the unlikely event that the United States emerged victorious against the Soviet Union, Eisenhower contended that the American people would have no appetite for an enduring occupation, perhaps recalling the U.S. experiences during the post–Civil War Reconstruction, the Philippines occupation from 1899 to 1940, and the occupation of the Rhineland from 1918 to 1923, not to mention the current occupations of Germany and Japan. Such occupations had required larger standing forces than the peacetime norm and did not sit well with the American public; and a potential occupation of Russia would probably require substantial occupation forces over an extended time. Hence, the best course would be to avoid a general war and adopt a strategy of deterrence. Under such a strategy, allies and forward bases would be imperative. However, to garner the necessary popular support, the administration would need to educate the American people and U.S. allies on the required measures (i.e., sufficient revenues and resources to support military readiness) as protection from the Soviet threat.[12]

The NSC Planning Board and NSC staff drew up drafts of the BNSP over a three-month period, with the resultant NSC 162/2 becoming policy on October 30, 1953. Political scientist Mena Bose and former NSC official Robert Bowie noted that NSC 162/2 was an amalgam of the best features of the three study teams. It confirmed Team A's framework of containment to resist Soviet aggression and domination of countries outside of its sphere, but it would not interfere with Soviet internal political and economic structures. While it rejected Team B's circumscribed line as a statement of U.S. policy, it did advocate the use of military force to include nuclear weapons against Soviet military aggression in Europe. Lastly, it adopted Team C's use of propaganda and covert actions to "exploit Soviet problems and complicate governance in Soviet-dominated countries."[13]

NSC 162/2 sought to protect the United States and its allies from the Soviet threat without "weakening the U.S. economy or undermining our fundamental values and institutions." The BNSP recognized Soviet "irreconcilable hostility" to the non-Communist world, the growing Soviet nuclear arsenal and capabilities to inflict severe damage on the continental United States, and the strengthening of Soviet air defenses against Western strategic airpower. While intelligence assessments considered a Soviet attack unlikely in the near future, once their nuclear arsenal and delivery capabilities developed, Soviet leaders might *miscalculate* if they thought a surprise first strike would destroy U.S. retaliatory forces. Similarly, Soviet leaders might conclude that their growing nuclear arsenal would deter U.S. intervention in the event of "Soviet peripheral aggression" (i.e., Western Europe and North East Asia), so the administration must clearly articulate to the Soviets which kinds of action would lead to general war.[14] It is clear that the underlying theme of NSC 162/2 was to prevent Soviet miscalculation of U.S. resolve. The United States regarded Western Europe and North East Asia as vital to national security. Due to Europe's wealth, industrial might, and human capital, Soviet hegemony of the continent would represent a dire global threat. Likewise, Soviet domination of Japan would expose the Pacific Rim to Soviet expansion. Thus, Soviet aggression in either region would be a casus belli.

NSC 162/2 assessed that rather than risk a general war, the Soviets would continue to rely on political warfare—division and subversion—and "exploit differences among members of the free world, neutralist attitudes, and anticolonial and nationalist sentiments in underdeveloped areas." Presciently, the report concluded that the Soviet threat would diminish in the long term "as the slackening of revolutionary zeal, the growth of vested managerial and bureaucratic interests, and popular pressures for consumption goods" took root. Correspondingly, the Soviet government might moderate its policies as Western states recovered from the war and were no longer susceptible to Soviet political warfare—and as its own systemic weaknesses created problems.[15]

As outlined in NSC 162/2, the U.S. strategic posture would rest on nuclear massive retaliation against Soviet aggression; conventional expeditionary capability to counter Soviet bloc aggression and to control strategic lines of communication; a mobilization base secure from a Soviet first strike; the "maintenance of a sound, strong and growing economy . . . over the long pull"; the maintenance of a program for rapid and effective full mobilization; and the "maintenance of morale and free institutions and the willingness of the U.S. people to support the measures necessary for national security."[16] In regards to garnering the support of the American public, Eisenhower outlined his national security goals in a national radio and television address on May 19, 1953. Similar to the themes expressed in his Inaugural Address and State of the Union message (among other speeches), Eisenhower stressed that national security policy must reflect a patient, steadfast commitment to a long-term strategy rather than reacting impulsively to every perceived threat. He warned that attempts to create complete national security would require substantial mobilization, the effects of which would create a garrison state mentality. In his judgment, a balanced military with sufficient force ceilings and alliances would provide the necessary security for an enduring defense. He concluded that his administration would remain dedicated to deterring war rather than to preparing to fight a potential war—a theme that has always resonated with Americans.[17]

Integral to this strategy was the inclusion of the economic, industrial, and military capabilities of allies.[18] The European Recovery Program (Marshall Plan) and the European Economic Community (which would become the European

Community and eventually the European Union) had accelerated European economic and industrial recovery. NATO had integrated the militaries of its member states under a unified command (a unique peacetime achievement), thereby fostering greater military burden sharing.[19] Thus, the BNSP sought to encourage greater European economic and political unity since this bolstered resistance to Soviet machinations and served to curb overdependence on the United States.

Based on solid staff work and assessments from the NSC mechanism, Eisenhower sought to adjust U.S. military forces in a manner that reflected the strategic imperatives of the BNSP. According to political scientist Samuel Huntington, the New Look embodied five essential elements: continental defense, conventional land forces, nuclear weapons, reserve forces, and strategic airpower.

In regards to continental defense, air defense (i.e., early warning radar, fighter interceptors, and air defense artillery) received greater attention, serving as "the principle counter-balance to the future strength of the Soviet strategic air force."[20] Continental defense served to protect not only the strategic forces (i.e., strategic bombers and ICBMs) but also the mobilization base. Since the administration had reduced Truman's mobilization base for reasons of the economy, in the event of a general war, mobilizing the war industry would take more time, so maintaining the continental defense at high readiness was essential.[21] Strategically, continental defense represented a sea change in U.S. defense thinking since the vast oceans no longer provided assured security from sudden enemy attacks. Now, continental defense assumed greater import and practically acted as a fourth service, competing for resources and funding.

With the end of the Korean War in July 1953 and emphasis on continental defense, a reduction in ground forces was a rational choice. The United States would avoid future entanglements in similar conflicts and would not attempt to match Soviet conventional capabilities quantitatively. The administration would exploit its advantage in naval and strategic airpower, encourage allies to build up their conventional ground forces, and create strategic depth through "tactical nuclear forces, ready reserve forces, [and] nuclear airpower."[22]

As the nuclear arsenal was a key feature of the New Look, Eisenhower made it clear that he would use nuclear weapons if he deemed it necessary and rejected plans that assumed they would never be used. Accordingly, national security strategy and defense budgets would be based on the employment of nuclear weapons should a conflict break out. While airpower remained the primary means of delivery, ground forces would employ tactical nuclear weapons as they would conventional arms against Soviet bloc forces (versus population centers). Subsequently, the United States successfully revised NATO strategy in July 1954 with the integration of tactical nuclear weapons in European defenses.[23]

Ground force reductions required a greater reliance on reserve forces. Under the National Reserve Plan (later the Reserve Forces Act of 1955), the Ready Reserve was to reach a level of 2,900,000 by 1960. Soldiers were to serve five years in the Active Forces and Ready Reserves. Alternatively, 100,000 males (17–18.5 years of age) could enlist in a six-month training program annually and serve 7.5 years in the Ready Reserves. Thus, Ready Reserve force levels rose from 578,000 in June 1953 to 913,000 in June 1956 and 1,000,000 in June 1957. Likewise, expenditures doubled to $879.9 million by FY 1957.[24]

In regards to strategic airpower, the goal was 137 air wings (126 combat wings) by June 1957 as opposed to Truman's planned goal of 143 wings. The proposed reductions included six wings of troop carrier and air transport. Due to the new emphasis on continental defense, air defense wings (interceptors armed with air-to-air missiles) increased from twenty-nine to thirty-four, the Strategic Air Command shrank from fifty-seven to fifty-four wings, and Tactical Air Command shrank from forty to thirty-eight wings. Eisenhower placed greater emphasis on airpower in fulfillment of the New Look strategy since it suggested that the United States would not confine massive retaliation solely to North America and Europe.[25] It should be stressed, however, that Eisenhower remained inscrutable regarding the decision to use nuclear weapons, whether the crisis was in Korea, Berlin, the Taiwan Straits, or Lebanon. Eisenhower's maxim was to "tell no one," not even his closest advisor, Foster Dulles, and he passed this advice on to president-elect Kennedy.[26]

Eisenhower's strategic thinking and grand strategy reflected the new realities of national security confronting the United States. For the first time in its history, the United States did not conduct a drastic demobilization—though there was pressure to do so; nor did it embark on unprecedented military force levels and expenditures—though there was heavy pressure to do this as well. Eisenhower deftly steered between both extremes, providing the nation with adequate defense based on deterrence and an era of prosperity.

The Drawdown

While the alignment of the military services rested primarily on the BNSP, Eisenhower adjusted force levels and military expenditures, based on economic and fiscal considerations on one hand and the growing Soviet nuclear arsenal on the other. Bargaining within the executive branch and between the executive and legislative branches shaped force levels and the allocation of military resources throughout Eisenhower's two terms.

The administration was keen to stabilize the military budget and keep spending below $40 billion—a goal that became elusive over time. Aside from the service chiefs bargaining for more money, the administration had to contend with the national outcry as a result of the Soviet launching of Sputnik on October 4, 1957, the claims of a missile gap, the recommendations from the Gaither Committee to strengthen the deterrence forces (at a proposed cost of $44 billion over five years), and the interventions in Lebanon and the Taiwan Straits in 1958. One silver lining was the change in congressional attitudes for greater defense spending, particularly as an economic stimulus to counter the 1959 recession.[27] Hence, the expenditures for FY 1959 rose from a proposed $37 billion to $40.1 billion, and the proposed Navy (630,000) and Marine Corps (175,000) reductions were deferred.

TABLE 8.1 Military Expenditures in Billions of Dollars[a]

	1953	1954	1955	1956
	43.6	41.2	36.5	35.8

Military Expenditures in Billions of Dollars

	1957	1958	1959	1960
	38.4	39.2	40.1	41.6

Drawdown Force Levels[b]

Services	1953	1954	1955	1956
Army	1,500,000	1,330,000	1,100,000	1,026,000
Navy	765,000	700,000	670,000	670,000
Marines	244,000	220,000	200,000	201,000
Air Force	913,000	960,000	970,000	910,000
Total	3,422,000	3,210,000	2,940,000	2,807,000

Drawdown Force Levels

Services	1957	1958	1959	1960
Army	1,000,000	900,000	861,000	861,000
Navy	675,000	645,000	645,000	645,000
Marines	200,000	190,000	190,000	190,000
Air Force	925,000	850,000	850,000	850,000
Total	2,800,000	2,585,000	2,546,000	2,546,000

a. The figures are extrapolated from the following books: Watson, *History of the Office of the Secretary of Defense*, vol. 4, 32–33, 95, 153–54; Huntington, *The Common Defense*, 70–71, 76, 93–94, 96, 111.

b. The figures are extrapolated from the following books: Eisenhower, *Mandate for Change*, 452; Huntington, *The Common Defense*, 75–76, 79; Richard M. Leighton, *History of the Office of the Secretary of Defense*, vol. 3, *Strategy, Money, and the New Look, 1953–1956*, ed. Alfred Goldberg (Washington, DC: U.S. Government Printing Office, 2001), 34, 331; Watson, *History of the Office of the Secretary of Defense*, vol. 4, 83, 142–55, 309; Russell F. Weigley, *History of the United States Army* (New York: Macmillan, 1967), 569. Ambiguities abound over exact numbers for each year due to force level proposals, approvals, and adjustments as bargaining within the administration and between the White House and Congress occurred.

From 1953 to 1956, the Army reduced its divisions from twenty to eighteen, but it retained its existing ten regimental combat teams (RCT). The loss of three divisions amounted to 52,500 personnel, so Army support, logistical, and headquarters units bore the majority of reductions (i.e., 262,500). The Marine Corps retained its three divisions and three air wings, absorbing 5,000 personnel cuts internally. The administration proposed to reduce the Marines to 193,000 (FY 1956) and 190,000 (FY 1957) but kept the ceiling at 200,000 due to congressional objections. The Navy fleet shrank from 1,126 to 1,005 ships (411 warships), but Air Force air wings rose from 114 to 131.[28]

Force reductions continued from 1957 to 1960 as subsequent BNSPs addressed the changing nature of the Communist threat and challenges. The Navy fleet stood at 901 ships in 1958 with an anticipated reduction to 864 (396 warships) in 1959. However, U.S. naval power would increase with the addition of a second nuclear-powered aircraft carrier, the first Polaris submarine with submarine-launched ballistic missiles (SLBMs), three nuclear-powered submarines, and thirteen new vessels. By 1957, Army reductions and reorganization resulted in seventeen smaller, leaner "pentomic" divisions (each with five battle groups) and nine RCTs, and reduced further to fourteen divisions by 1960. Finally, the Air Force declined to 105 wings. The Defense Department accelerated the production of the Polaris program, as well as the intermediate range ballistic missile (IRBM) and intercontinental ballistic missile (ICBM) programs.[29] Accordingly, as U.S. nuclear missile programs increased, the administration decreased the conventional military forces (notably the Army) proportionally. The decline in numbers did not necessarily translate to a decline in combat power, since older equipment (i.e., aircraft, ships, and weapon systems) were replaced with more modern or next-generation models and variants.

Under the 1955 Reserve Forces Act, soldiers were to serve three years in the reserves after active duty. However, the administration subsequently determined that "large reserve forces were not the most economical way of meeting the force requirements of mutual deterrence." Accordingly, the Defense Department announced in December 1957 its intent to reduce the size of the reserve forces and concentrate on improving the readiness of the reserves (quality versus quantity). National Guard recruits were required to serve six months of active-duty training. After another Defense Department review of the reserve forces, the administration in 1958 announced its intent to cut the National Guard by forty thousand and the Army Reserves by thirty thousand. In March 1958, the Army announced the planned elimination of six National Guard and four reserve divisions, as well as the restructuring of the remaining twenty-seven divisions into smaller, compact "pentomic" units armed with atomic weapons. However, the National Guard and Army Reserves bureaus protested against these reductions and appealed to Congress, which defeated these proposals. Hence, the National Guard and the Army Reserves remained at four hundred thousand and three hundred thousand, respectively.[30]

Maintaining American Power While Allaying Unfounded Fears

As a result of stabilized military expenditures and force reductions, Eisenhower succeeded in reducing taxes substantially in 1955 and balancing the budget by 1956. Unemployment averaged 4.9 percent during his two terms, and prosperity increased as a consequence.[31] Nevertheless, a phobia over the Soviet threat developed in national security circles. During the early years of the Eisenhower administration, fear of a Soviet first strike on the continental United States sparked assertions of a "bomber gap" in Congress, think tanks, and academia. Eisenhower assailed the bomber gap as "illusory" and based on unfounded fears, with millions of defense dollars wasted trying to fill it.[32] While the administration addressed this potential danger in NSC 162/2 and NSC 5408 (Continental Defense), critics did not believe it went far enough to safeguard the country.[33]

Regardless of the deliberative approach to grand strategy formulation, the administration was forced to defend the BNSP from critics throughout Eisenhower's two terms. Chiefs of staff of the Army General Matthew Ridgway and General Maxwell Taylor thought the cuts to the Army were excessive. Ridgway believed that the ground force reductions were not aligned with strategic objectives, security commitments, and enemy conventional forces. He contended that the BNSP relied too much on the deterrent value of the Strategic Air Command, and he felt that the economy could support higher military spending without any negative impact. In short, he reasoned that real deterrence required a sufficient number of active divisions ready to counter Communist aggression. Paradoxically, Ridgeway speculated that nuclear parity would lead the Soviet Union to aggress with conventional forces only, making a significant U.S. standing Army essential to deterrence.[34] Similarly, Taylor decried any Army force reductions below one million soldiers because such reductions limited the ability of the United States to exercise "flexible response" regardless of the size and type of aggression.[35] Eisenhower argued that Ridgway and Taylor presumed that with mutual deterrence, only conventional wars would ensue, "based upon the premise that we would never, under any kind of circumstance, provocation, or aggression, employ our nuclear strength." He felt that this was "the product of timidity . . . seeing danger behind every tree and bush." He questioned the assumption that "massive" conventional forces could respond to all forms of aggression and "quickly defeat them by conventional means. I refused to turn the United States into an armed camp."[36]

It should be recalled that the Eisenhower administration's Army force ceilings were almost double those of the Truman administration's pre–Korean War level of 593,167.[37] Paradoxically, prior to 1950, the Truman administration prepared for general war, and during the Korean War it developed an expansive mobilization base. However, by the mid-1950s, with the advent of large nuclear arsenals, fighting a general war became unthinkable (though it remained integral to planning) since it would be likely to lead to a nuclear holocaust. The administration judged that a nuclear war would be relatively short, fought by forces-in-being. Thus, a large mobilization base would be unnecessary, and the military would need to maintain high readiness with the well-trained Ready Reserve forces conducting combat operations immediately alongside the regular forces.[38]

As the Soviet Union strove for nuclear parity with the United States in the mid-1950s, consternation over a "missile gap" and the vulnerability of the civil population reached near hysteria with the Soviet launch of Sputnik on October 4, 1957.[39] However, by the time of Sputnik, the administration had already established active ballistic-missile and space-satellite programs.[40] Recognizing the Soviet nuclear ballistic missile threat to American national security early in his first term, Eisenhower directed that the NSC Science Advisory Committee establish a Technological Capabilities Panel (TCP) under MIT president James R. Killian to assess American military technology and develop countermeasures. Missile research from the Department of Defense's von Neumann Committee on intercontinental ballistic missiles (ICBMs), together with TCP recommendations, resulted in an accelerated development of ICBM nuclear warheads, which averted the development of a missile gap.[41] Eventually, these programs led to the nuclear triad, comprising ICBMs, nuclear-armed B-52 bombers, and SLBM Polaris submarines. By 1962, the United States possessed 180 ICBMs, 12 SLMB Polaris submarines, each with twelve missiles, and 630 strategic bombers stationed in the United States, Europe, and Asia. In contrast, the Soviet Union possessed only twenty ICBMs, six SLBM submarines, and two hundred long-range bombers.[42] The nuclear triad bolstered continental defense immeasurably since it made a Soviet nuclear first strike option practically impossible to implement with any degree of certainty. The U.S. alert system, the diversity, dispersal, and concealment of its nuclear platforms, and its superior technology rendered any attack on the United States an act of national suicide.

The Eisenhower administration revised the BNSP with NSC 5810/1 (May 5, 1958) as it came to terms with eventual nuclear parity.[43] The fundamental strategic environment had not changed, however. Rather than attempting to maintain a numerical nuclear superiority over the Soviets, Eisenhower opted for "sufficiency" in nuclear and conventional forces. As Air Force Secretary Donald Quarles underscored in August 1956, "The guiding standard must be not the abstract comparison of American forces with Soviet forces but rather the capability of the American forces to launch a devastating retaliation against the Soviet Union." In view of the necessity to preserve a stable economy in conjunction with the nuclear balance of terror, the administration adopted a deterrent strategy of sufficiency.[44] Secretary of Defense Neil McElroy made it clear that the United States would not compete with the Soviets in a missile arms race. In his view, the "key criterion was not the 'missile gap,' but the 'deterrent gap.'"[45] While the nuclear balance of terror, officially called "mutually assured destruction" (MAD), sparked a national sense of vulnerability bordering on panic at times (a whole cottage industry of nuclear holocaust books and films, personal bomb shelters, and civil defense shelters became a staple of American society by the 1960s), it also enhanced stability among the great powers in a bipolar world. In terms of predictability, measured actions, and deliberative diplomacy, the Cold War was the good old days.

The final BNSP—NSC 5906/1 (December 3, 1959)—reflected the administration's view that future conflicts were more likely to occur in underdeveloped countries, so the United States needed appropriate means to prevent brushfire wars from occurring or, if they did occur, to keep them from escalating. Here, economic and military assistance received greater attention. Moreover, the administration adopted a flexible response capability with U.S. and allied expeditionary forces to defeat local aggression early.[46] Differing from Taylor's Flexible Response strategy, the Eisenhower administration judged that the U.S. military-in-being, working in conjunction with allies, would prove sufficient to manage small local wars. In his book *The Uncertain Trumpet*, Taylor mischaracterized the BNSP as so wedded to Massive Retaliation that the nation could not respond to smaller contingencies. With Flexible Response, he proposed increasing military capabilities to address threats with the appropriate level of force—ranging from unconventional combat to thermonuclear war—thereby broadening the president's options. While the Eisenhower administration did not make an issue of Taylor's allegations, the fact remains that Flexible Response was a solution to a problem that did not exist . . . and one that required substantial expenditures. After all, during his presidency, Eisenhower used covert operations in Iran (1953), Guatemala (1954), and Indonesia (1958), deployed the U.S. Seventh Fleet twice in the Straits of Taiwan (1954–1955 and 1958), and conducted a joint intervention in Lebanon involving the Army, Marines, Navy, and Air Force (1958), not to mention his deft diplomacy during the Suez Crisis (1956) and the Berlin Crisis (1958). In comparison with President John F. Kennedy and his Flexible Response strategy, Eisenhower proved much more decisive and flexible, using the proper mix of the instruments of power to achieve the strategic effect he sought.

What Eisenhower continually sought to avoid was creating a large military capability because the Joint Chiefs of Staff would clamor for its use during crises, regardless of its nature. Venting in an August 20, 1956, letter to his childhood friend Swede Hazlett, Eisenhower deplored the parochialism of the service chiefs, who were quite willing to subvert the U.S. economy and strategic values in a foolhardy pursuit of complete national security.[47] While his detractors often characterized him as complacent and detached from the threats facing the United States, Eisenhower remained acutely aware of the lure of military adventurism, which could plunge the nation into fighting a war in the wrong place, against the wrong enemy, at the wrong time.

This strategic approach avoided an expensive, destabilizing arms race. U.S. military forces would remain balanced with the BNSP and the growing nuclear triad. As instilled in each BNSP, a stable and flourishing economy, strong national morale, and safeguarded democratic institutions would prove more durable than Soviet socialism.

Conclusion

In contrast to the traditional U.S. approach to military demobilization, the Eisenhower administration implemented measured force reductions, which were aligned with the BNSP. As Eisenhower assessed, the Cold War was an extended ideological conflict with a low likelihood of general war. Eisenhower did not dismiss the occurrence of a general war, but concluded that one would result from Soviet miscalculation. Accordingly, the administration's development and revision of the BNSP and the alignment of U.S. and allied armed forces sought to prevent such miscalculations.

Since the Cold War was a struggle somewhere between war and peace, the Eisenhower administration crafted a grand strategy that provided for sufficient defense while at the same time promoting robust free markets through capitalism, sustaining American morale and values, and protecting democratic institutions. In Eisenhower's view, these pillars would ensure Western perseverance over the confrontation with the Communist bloc. Deterrence—not mobilization—was the rational means to that end.

Of course, Eisenhower had to contend with the capriciousness of Congress, depending on the threat flavor of the month, as well as the hawkish nature of Secretary of State Foster Dulles and the Joint Chiefs of Staff. For the former, he held weekly meetings with congressional leaders (both formally and informally) and established the Congressional Liaison Office to coordinate policy legislation. For the latter, he used the NSC mechanism (i.e., structures, procedures, and processes) to ensure that policy proposals were well-staffed and integrated products before they came to the NSC for consideration. He encouraged debate and frank discussions in the National Security Council and listened to all viewpoints earnestly before coming to a decision. He never stonewalled dissenting views, ensuring that they got a full hearing. He always explained the reasons for his decisions, framing the core issues clearly and succinctly. In this manner, he created teamwork within the White House, though he was never able to turn the Joint Chiefs of Staff into a corporate body, free of parochialism. However, Eisenhower came as close to achieving that level of cooperation as any other president.

When he assumed office, President John F. Kennedy complained that he had inherited a multitude of problems from the Eisenhower administration. While this was true, it bears noting that all incoming administrations inherit problems. Eisenhower inherited the Korean War, a burgeoning Soviet nuclear threat, an imbalanced budget, and high defense spending. While Kennedy had Cuba, Congo, Laos, and Vietnam to contend with, he also inherited a strong economy, high employment rate, and high readiness of the armed forces. Kennedy immediately dismantled the NSC mechanism, discarded the BNSP, substantially raised military spending, and adopted the dubious notions of Flexible Response and Counterinsurgency without due scrutiny. The result was an arms race with the Soviet Union, CIA adventurism in Cuba, and entanglement in South Vietnam. None of these served to promote or protect U.S. national interests.

In hindsight, it is clear that the Eisenhower administration achieved a remarkable harmony of cooperation regarding the downsizing of the military after the Korean War. This was not only a reflection of the superb NSC mechanism he instituted in the White House but also of his exemplary leadership and executive management skills.

NOTES

1   Dwight D. Eisenhower, *At Ease: Stories I Tell to Friends* (Garden City, NY: Doubleday, 1967), 367–68.

2   Paul Nitze of the State Department's State Policy Planning Staff was the principal author of NSC-68, which viewed the Soviet Union as an imminent threat on a par

with the Third Reich. Hence, the paper recommended substantial U.S. military preparations in response. A Report to the National Security Council, "NSC 68" (Washington, DC: Government Printing Office, 1950), accessed at the website of the Truman Library at http://www.trumanlibrary.org/whistlestop/study_collections/coldwar/documents/pdf/10–1.pdf, 8 March 2012.

3 NSC-68 proposed a 300 percent increase in military spending. Samuel P. Huntington, *The Common Defense: Strategic Programs in National Politics* (New York: Columbia University, Press, 1961), 111, 113, 117.

4 NSC 20/4 reflected George Kennan's long-term Containment strategy. While Truman approved the conclusions and recommendations of NSC-68 in September 1950, it remained a contentious document. George Kennan, the chairman of the State Department's Policy Planning Board, felt that NSC-68 was an overreaction to the Soviet threat, practically recommending that the United States assume an open-ended military-industrial mobilization. Kennan left the Policy Planning Board in 1949 due to his disagreement with NSC-68. Douglas T. Stuart, *Creating the National Security State: A History of the Law That Transformed America* (Princeton, NJ: Princeton University Press, 2008), 128–30, 236–41; *George F. Kennan and the Origins of Eisenhower's New Look: An Oral History of Project Solarium*, ed. William B. Pickett, Princeton Institute for International and Regional Studies, Monograph Series 1, Princeton University, 2004, 3, 28

5 Report to the National Security Council by Executive Secretary (Lay), " NSC 149/2," 29 April 1953, accessed on the website of Department of State Office of the Historian (DOSOH), Foreign Relations of the United States (FRUS) at http://history.state.gov/historicaldocuments/frus1952–54v02p1/pg_305, 12 February 2014.

6 Dwight D. Eisenhower, *Mandate for Change: 1953–1956* (New York: Doubleday, 1963), 37, 131; Huntington, *The Common Defense*, 66.

7 See Gaddis's account of the Cold War struggle. John Lewis Gaddis, *The Cold War: A New History* (New York: Penguin, 2005). As Huntington pointed out, while President Eisenhower's foreign policy remained unchanged from President Harry S. Truman's, their national security strategies differed significantly in regards to ends, ways, and means. Huntington, *The Common Defense*, 85.

8 Robert R. Bowie, Foreign Affairs Oral History Project, Interviewed by Robert Gerald Livingston, Philipp Gassert, Richard Immerman, Paul Steege, Charles Stuart Kennedy, February 18, 2008, National Archives and Records Service, Lyndon Baines Johnson Library, accessed on the website of the Association for Diplomatic Studies and Training at http://adst.org/wp-content/uploads/2012/09/Bowie-Robert-R.2008.pdf, 11 October 2013, 15; *George F. Kennan and the Origins of Eisenhower's New Look,* 29, accessed on the website of DOSOH, FRUS at http://history.state.gov/historicaldocuments/frus1952–54v02p1/d59, 12 February 2014.

9 However, the death of Stalin actually did give China a face-saving opportunity to end the Korean War. *George F. Kennan and the Origins of Eisenhower's New Look*, 1–2.

10   See David Nichols for the rise of Gamal Abdel Nasser in Egypt and his destabiliz-
     ing policies in the Middle East. David A. Nichols, *Eisenhower 1956: The President's
     Year of Crisis, Suez and the Brink of War* (New York: Simon & Schuster, 2011).

11   Paper Prepared by the Directing Panel of Project Solarium, "Project Solarium," 1
     June 1953, accessed on the website of DOSOH, FRUS at http://history.state.gov/
     historicaldocuments/frus1952–54v02p1/d68, 19 April 2012; *Minutes of the 155th
     Meeting of the National Security Council, Thursday, July 16, 1953*, accessed on the
     website of DOSOH, FRUS at http://history.state.gov/historicaldocuments/
     frus1952–54v02p1/d78, 12 February 2014.

12   *Minutes of the 155th Meeting of the National Security Council.*

13   Robert R. Bowie and Richard H. Immerman, *Waging Peace: How Eisenhower
     Shaped an Enduring Cold War Strategy* (New York: Oxford University Press, 1998),
     144–46; Meena Bose, *Shaping and Signaling Presidential Policy: The National
     Security Decision Making of Eisenhower and Kennedy* (College Station: Texas
     A&M University Press, 1998), 34–41.

14   A Report of the National Security Council: Basic National Security Policy, "NSC
     162/2," October 30, 1953, accessed on the website of DOSOH, FRUS at http://
     history.state.gov/historicaldocuments/frus1952–54v02p1/d100, 27 February 2014,
     1–2.

15   "NSC 162/2," 3–4.

16   "NSC 162/2," 5–6.

17   Jean Edward Smith, *Eisenhower in War and Peace* (New York: Random House,
     2012), 641.

18   "NSC 162/2," 8.

19   The European Defense Community proved a disappointment though when the
     French Parliament refused to ratify a treaty in which the German and French
     militaries would operate as joint commands.

20   Huntington, *The Common Defense*, 78.

21   Huntington, *The Common Defense*, 82.

22   Huntington, *The Common Defense*, 78–79.

23   Huntington, *The Common Defense*, 79–80.

24   Huntington, *The Common Defense*, 81.

25   Huntington, *The Common Defense*, 83–84.

26   Evan Thomas, *Ike's Bluff: President Eisenhower's Secret Battle to Save the World*
     (New York: Little, Brown, 2012), 300, 321, 396–97, 408, 413.

27   Robert J. Watson, *History of the Office of the Secretary of Defense*. Vol. 4, *Into the
     Missile Age, 1956–1960*, ed. Alfred Goldberg (Washington, DC: U.S. Government
     Printing Office, 1997), 148–51.

28   Leighton, *History of the Office of the Secretary of Defense*, vol. 3, 172, 182–83;
     Huntington, *The Common Defense*, 71; Watson, *History of the Office of the
     Secretary of Defense*, vol. 4, 33–34.

29   Watson, *History of the Office of the Secretary of Defense*, vol. 4, 82–83, 143, 147.

30 Watson, *History of the Office of the Secretary of Defense*, vol. 4, 150, 152; Huntington, *The Common Defense*, 98–99.

31 "How the Presidents Stack Up," accessed from the website of the *Wall Street Journal* at http://online.wsj.com/public/resources/documents/info-presappo605-31.html, 23 February 2012; "Civilian Unemployment Rate," accessed from the website of the U.S. Department of Labor: Bureau of Labor Statistics, http://research.stlouisfed.org/fred2/data/UNRATE.txt, 23 February 2012.

32 Eisenhower, *Mandate for Change*, 454 n.8.

33 Report to the National Security Council by the National Security Council Planning Board, "NSC 5408: Continental Defense," 11 February 1954, accessed on the website of DOSOH, FRUS at http://history.state.gov/historicaldocuments/frus1952–54v02p1/d108, 22 May 2014.

34 Matthew B. Ridgeway and Harold H. Martin, *Soldier: The Memoirs of Matthew B. Ridgeway* (New York: Harper, 1956), 272–73, 288, 290–94, 319.

35 Maxwell D. Taylor, *The Uncertain Trumpet* (New York: Harper, 1960), chap. 4, passim.

36 Eisenhower, *Mandate for Change*, 453–54.

37 Weigley, *History of the United States Army*, 569.

38 Huntington, *The Common Defense*, 97–98.

39 This near hysteria coincided with the Gaither Committee study and report to the Eisenhower administration. While the original intent was to study civil defense, the committee far exceeded its mandate, looking at national defense and recommending substantial increases in military expenditures. The Eisenhower administration did accept some of the committee recommendations but rejected the call for mobilization. Accordingly, some of the committee members leaked the report to the press so as to place pressure on the administration. For a good account of the affair, see Morton H. Halperin, "The Gaither Committee," *World Politics* 13, no. 3 (April 1961): 360–84.

40 Eisenhower said the Soviet explosion of a hydrogen bomb in August 1953 first prompted him to explore the capabilities of ballistic missiles in early 1955:

> Little had been done before my inauguration. The services didn't have any money to spend on the ballistic missiles at all. So later, [Representative Carl] Curtis began to jeer about missile gaps. Yet, starting in June of '55 the effort we put on missiles, and then only a few months later starting on satellites and space program, was tremendous. It was something no one expected—it had been completely neglected.

Dwight D. Eisenhower, Dulles Oral History Interview: Princeton University, by Philip A. Crowl, 28 July 1964 (OH-14), Dwight D. Eisenhower Library, 49–50.

41 The president directed the elevation of the Science Advisory Committee into a Science and Technology Committee, located in the Executive Office and chaired by the president's scientific advisor. The president selected as the special advisor Dr. Killian, who would become a regular participant in the council. In due course, this concept grew into a national scientific agency, the National Aeronautics and

Space Administration (NASA), in the spring of 1958. Robert Cutler, *No Time for Rest* (Boston: Atlantic Monthly Press, 1965), 348–51, 352–53.

42 Graham Allison and Philip Zelikow, *Essence of Decision: Explaining the Cuban Missile Crisis*, 2nd edition (New York: Longman, January 29, 1999), Kindle e-book.

43 A Report of the National Security Council: Basic National Security Policy, "NSC 5810/1," 5 May 1958, accessed on the website of DOSOH, FRUS at http://history.state.gov/historicaldocuments/frus1958–60v03/d24, 23 September 2011.

44 Paraphrased in Huntington, *The Common Defense*, 101–2.

45 Huntington, *The Common Defense*, 103–4.

46 National Security Council Report, "NSC 5906/1," August 5, 1959, accessed on the website of DOSOH, FRUS at http://history.state.gov/historicaldocuments/frus1958–60v03/d70, 30 November 2012.

47 Eisenhower, *Mandate for Change*, 455, n.11.

9

Once Again with the High and the Mighty

"New Look" Austerity, "Flexible Response" Buildup, and the U.S. Army in Vietnam, 1954–1970

MARTIN G. CLEMIS

Since the end of World War II, drawdowns and cuts within the national defense budget in the wake of major conflicts have traditionally been met with howls of derision from critics who claim that reductions in personnel or expenditure weaken national security and undermine military prepared-ness. Whether such concern stems from party politics, handwringing by the uniformed services over diminished funding, or genuine concern for the nation's security, pushback against defense cuts have not only been inevitable in recent decades but have often been couched in terms of the purported "les-sons" of history. During the mid-1950s, then U.S. Army chief of staff General Matthew B. Ridgway and others pointed to the distressing opening of the Korean War to excoriate the Eisenhower administration's defense policy and its significant reduction in conventional ground forces. "Korea could have been won in the first two weeks if the Army had modern airborne divisions ready to go," one source argued. "But they didn't have [them] because the Army had been skimped for funds while the greater part of the defense dollar had gone to the type of weapons not used in Korea."[1] In 2012, retired Army general Robert H. Scales invoked the specter of American defeat in Southeast Asia as a means to attack the Obama administration's cuts in defense spend-ing and drawdown of U.S. combat forces. "With Dwight Eisenhower came the 'New Look' strategy that sought to reduce the Army and Marine Corps again to allow the creation of a nuclear delivery force built around the Strategic Air Command," Scales wrote. "Along came Vietnam. . . . [B]y 1970 our profes-sional Army broke apart and was replaced by a body of amateurs. The result was defeat and 58,000 dead."[2]

Conventional wisdom—often though not always buttressed with oversim-plified historical analogies–purports that defense austerity and drawdowns in standing force structure and capabilities are not only dangerous but det-rimental to the American military's ability to meet current and developing threats. Are such arguments valid, however? Does history demonstrate that reductions in defense spending and military personnel inescapably lead to a lack of military preparedness, decreased combat proficiency, and tactical failure? The answer to these questions is mixed. Some past conflicts, most notably Korea and World War II, have shown a direct correlation between peacetime military cuts and diminished combat effectiveness during the opening phases of new conflicts.

Others, however, have not. Such was the case in Vietnam. The Eisenhower administration's winnowing of Army ground forces during the 1950s, contrary to the claim made by General Scales, did not have a detrimental impact on the services' combat capabilities or effectiveness. Despite a considerable reduction in funding, numbers, and prestige during what has come to be known as the "Pentomic Era," the Army retained enough of its core competencies to be quickly rehabilitated and brought back to fighting trim by the mid-1960s. Under the defense buildup of the Kennedy and Johnson administrations, the Army rapidly regained the staffing and force structure necessary to conduct nonnuclear combat operations in support of U.S. national policy objectives in the Far East. By 1965, the year American combat troops were first introduced into South Vietnam, the Army had been refashioned into what was arguably one of the most well-trained and effective combat forces ever fielded by the United States. "All of a sudden the stick-in-the-mud dogface Army has come alive," trumpeted *Fortune Magazine* in May 1966. "It sits once again with the high and mighty: its recovered élan is the envy of the Air Force and Navy whose nuclear weapons systems and other 'fancy Dan' technology had come to overshadow the Army throughout the Eisenhower years."[3]

Eisenhower and the "New Look" Austerity

Nuclear weapons and other "fancy Dan" technologies were in fact the centerpiece of the Eisenhower administration's national defense policy. Moreover, they were the primary reason that a dramatic reduction in military personnel, particularly ground forces, was implemented at a time of sustained tension and latent conflict between communism and the West. The New Look was inspired by a number of variables, including the intractable nature and global scope of containment, the president's own desire to reign in federal spending and balance the national budget, and the availability of new and emerging military technologies that could far exceed the reach and firepower of large conventional ground armies at a much lower cost. Its animating principle, therefore, was that the best way to assure security for the United States and its allies without breaking the bank was to deter Communist "aggression" through a deft combination of economy, collective security, and, most importantly, "massive retaliatory power" in the form of strategic and tactical nuclear weapons.

New Look austerity and its emphasis on technology rather than personnel were founded on three central premises. First, the new world order forged in the furnace of World War II and shaped by the Cold War was one of protracted struggle and uneasy peace. Thanks to sustained global politico-military competition with two Communist superpowers and their proxies, the country was now required to assume a burden it had never had before during periods of relative quiescence: maintaining a sizeable defense establishment for an indefinite period of time. According to Secretary of Defense Charles Wilson, the Eisenhower administration fashioned the New Look military establishment in response to "the assumption that the communist threat to our national security is one with which we shall have to live for some time and one which will require the maintenance of effective deterrent forces for a relatively long period."[4] In December 1953, the chairman of the Joint Chiefs of Staff, Admiral Arthur W. Radford, reaffirmed that the White House and the Pentagon had designed the New Look to allow the United States to sustain an adequate level of security and military preparedness over a protracted period. The Eisenhower defense policy, he argued,

> prepares for the long pull; not a year-of crisis. It is aimed at providing a sturdy military posture which can be maintained over an extended period of uneasy peace, rather than peaking forces at greater costs for a particular period of tension. . . . The concept of the New Look is the development of an armed posture which can be supported, year in and year out, on a long-term basis; not just one year—nor two years—but for ten years or even twenty years if necessary.[5]

The second premise behind the Eisenhower defense cuts was that if a sturdy military posture was to be maintained over the "long pull," it had to be done without wrecking the American economy or retarding its future growth. The administration firmly believed that economic strength was *the* indispensable prerequisite for military strength, and this meant that Washington had to maintain effective military forces in a resourceful and economical manner—a "maximum deterrent at bearable cost" in the words of Secretary of State John Dulles—if it was to avoid overburdening the economy and undermining the social fabric and financial health of the nation. After taking office in 1953, Eisenhower repeatedly reinforced this ideal. "In providing the kind of military security that our country needs," he informed Congress, "we must keep our people free and our economy solvent. We must not endanger the very things we seek to defend. We must not create a nation mighty in arms that is lacking in liberty and bankrupt in resources. Our armed strength must continue to rise from the vigor of a free people and a prosperous economy."[6] The following year, Secretary Wilson reaffirmed this commitment to pairing a strong defense with a balanced budget. "The cost of national security will remain high for many years," he declared before the Senate Appropriations Committee.

> This cost must be bearable not only in the sense that the burden can be carried without wrecking our economy but also be within the limits of what can be supported without retarding the future growth of our economy. Over the long pull economic strength is an indispensable prerequisite for military strength. We must not fail in our efforts to achieve an ever-increasing economic strength for the free world.[7]

The New Look's third premise was that the key to a balanced budget and cost-effective security lay in the full exploitation of new and emerging technologies, most notably atomic weapons and airpower. The 1950s, Eisenhower argued, was a period of rapid technological advancement. It was vital, therefore, that the United States use technology to strengthen national defense through deterrence. "Today also witnesses one of history's times of swiftest advance in scientific achievements," Eisenhower stated. "These developments can accomplish wonders in providing a healthier and happier life for us all. But—converted to military uses—they threaten new, more devastating terrors in war. These simple, inescapable facts make imperative the maintenance of a defense organization commanding the most modern technological instruments in our arsenal of weapons."[8] According to Eisenhower, new technologies eliminated the need for large conventional ground forces because their immense striking power created "new relationships between men and materials." These new relationships, he maintained, permitted "economies in the use of men as we build forces suited to our situation in the world today."[9] Together with other programs aimed at building collective security, strengthening the reserves, and amassing strategic stockpiles, the sharp increase in utilization of advanced technologies and new weapons and delivery systems prompted both a significant reduction in personnel and a major reorganization of the Army's force structure. Eisenhower informed Congress in 1954, "As the striking power of our combat forces is progressively increased by the application of technological advances and the growth of air power, the number of military personnel is being reduced." [10]

Eisenhower substantially cut the number of military personnel during his tenure as president. The overall number of active duty personnel for all four services fell from 3.3 million in FY 1954 to 2.5 million in FY 1960.[11] Despite deep cuts in conventional capabilities and personnel, however, austerity under the Eisenhower era was relatively mild. Although yearly defense expenditures were substantially lower than the $43.6 billion spent in FY 1953, outlays for national security remained robust (averaging $39.4 billion per year). The bulk of these funds, however, went to the Air Force. Because it was the service best suited for deterrence vis-à-vis delivery of strategic atomic weapons, the Air Force was the greatest beneficiary under the New Look, averaging nearly half (47 percent) of the defense budget between 1955 and 1960. The Army, in contrast, suffered major reductions both in expenditure and in the overall number of uniformed personnel. In the years between the New Look's full implementation and Eisenhower's last year in office, the Army lost close to 40 percent of its personnel, falling from 1.4 million uniformed men and women in 1954 to 873,000 in 1960. During that same period, the Army's budget was slashed from $12.9 billion (approximately 32 percent of the overall defense budget) to $9.4 billion (roughly 23 percent of all Department of Defense outlays). For fiscal years 1955 through 1960, the Army's budget was roughly half of what the Pentagon had spent on the Air Force.[12]

The budgetary and personnel cuts imposed on the Army under Eisenhower were not the product of indiscriminate or arbitrary cutbacks in defense spending. Nor did they stem from an incapacity for strategic vision, a dangerous misreading of America's adversaries, or naiveté concerning the state of international affairs and national security threats facing the United States and its allies. Rather, the reductions resulted from the search for economy and the introduction of new doctrine and new technologies, most notably the "Pentomic" division and a small family of tactical nuclear weapons inserted into the Army's traditional repertoire. Beginning in 1956, the Army reorganized its force structure into smaller, self-contained, highly mobile divisions. Each had an organic nuclear capability and each was capable of semi-independent operations. Pentomic divisions consisted of five mobile combat groups supported by five batteries of light artillery and one battery of rockets capable of firing either high-explosive or atomic projectiles. According to the secretary of defense's semiannual report for the second half of 1956, the Army created the Pentomic division to "improve [the Army's] ability to fight atomic battles while retaining its capacity to conduct non-atomic campaigns."[13]

Some within the Army high command felt that the New Look was dangerous, despite its pursuit of new and innovative doctrine and technologies. Others asserted that the new defense policies were more than just a serious detriment to the nation's national security posture and military preparedness; they were, in their estimation, the death knell of the U.S. Army. In 1956, a then recently retired Matthew Ridgway expressed deep dissatisfaction with Eisenhower's defense cuts. According to Ridgway, the New Look's austerity measures had thrust him into the unwelcome role of the Army's executioner. "In my job as Chief of Staff, I say in all earnestness and sincerity that I felt I was being called upon to destroy, rather than to build, a fighting force on which rested the world's best hope for peace," he declared within the pages of the *Saturday Evening Post*.

> Day by day, by order of my civilian superiors, I was called upon to take actions and to advocate policies which if continued, in my judgment would eventually so weaken the United States Army that it could no longer serve as an effective instrument of national policy; it could no longer feel confident of success in battle; it could no longer fulfill its many and varied commitments around the world.[14]

In his memoirs, published that same year, Ridgway again reiterated his belief that the New Look and its emphasis on airpower and atomic weapons was folly. "We were subject again to the same dangerous delusion," he wrote, "the misty hope that air power, armed with the fission or fusion bomb, could save us in time of trouble."[15]

Kennedy, Johnson, and the "Flexible Response" Buildup

Four years after Ridgway made these statements, John F. Kennedy won the presidency using similar criticism of the New Look and the purported damage that Eisenhower's defense policy had caused to American military preparedness. In 1960, then senator Kennedy wrote that "no aspect of our defense capabilities under this Administration should be cause for greater concern than our lag in conventional weapons and ground forces."[16] Kennedy believed that deterrence against the Soviet Union vis-à-vis atomic weapons and airpower was not enough and that an overemphasis on such weapons and delivery systems was inadequate for meeting the strategic challenges of the Cold War. "In practice, our nuclear retaliatory power . . . cannot deter Communist aggression which is too limited to justify atomic war," he wrote. "It cannot protect uncommitted nations against a Communist takeover using local or guerrilla forces. It cannot be used in so-called 'brush-fire' peripheral wars. In short, it cannot prevent the communists from gradually nibbling away at the fringe of the Free World's territory and strength, until our security has been steadily eroded in piecemeal fashion."[17] In June 1960 Kennedy repeated the claim that the American military's conventional war capabilities had been severely weakened under Eisenhower and that it was vital that the Pentagon reverse course and strengthen its nonnuclear capabilities. "We must regain the ability to intervene effectively and swiftly in any limited war anywhere in the world—augmenting, modernizing, and providing increased mobility and versatility for the conventional forces and weapons of the Army and Marine Corps," he declared. "As long as those forces lack the necessary airlift and sealift capacity and versatility of firepower," he continued, "we cannot protect our commitments around the globe."[18]

Kennedy's views dovetailed with those of his top military advisor, former Army chief of staff Maxwell Taylor. Both men believed that a policy based mostly on deterrence and the threat of massive atomic retaliation was folly because it created only two strategic courses of action for the United States and its allies: atomic suicide or retreat. What America needed, they and others believed, was a defense establishment that could fight across the "entire spectrum" of warfare, from general atomic war to mid- and low-intensity conflict. "Flexible Response should contain at the outset an unqualified renunciation of reliance on the strategy of Massive Retaliation," Taylor wrote in his highly influential work *The Uncertain Trumpet*. "It should be made clear that the United States will prepare itself to respond anywhere, anytime, with weapons and forces appropriate to the situation."[19] Speaking before Congress in 1961, Secretary of the Army Elvis J. Stahr repeated this claim. "Recent events have reemphasized the need for us to be prepared to deal swiftly and effectively with Communist military adventures in any part of the world—and at any level of conflict," he declared. "To discourage such adventures, our military posture must include forces to fight all forms of war."[20] The Kennedy administration firmly believed that while a general or even atomic war between the United States and the Soviets was possible, nonnuclear limited war and military aggression on a lesser scale was far more likely. A quick survey of current events in 1961 affirmed this belief, as a myriad of small wars and insurgencies seethed throughout the developing world. By the time Kennedy took the oath of office, a number of Communist-led insurgencies were underway in Colombia, Venezuela, Laos, Vietnam, and Thailand.[21] The president and others felt it was necessary, therefore, to restructure the defense establishment so that it reflected—to paraphrase another past president—the realities of the stormy present rather than the dogmas of the quiet past.[22]

The impetus behind Flexible Response and the defense buildup under the Kennedy and Johnson administrations was to create a more balanced and flexible military establishment, one capable of "providing readily whatever degree and kind of support might be required by our national policies."[23] A plan to rejuvenate and expand American ground forces, particularly the

Army, lay at the heart of the new defense policy. In addition to reorganizing and modernizing the Army's divisional structure, the architects of Flexible Response looked to increase its nonnuclear firepower, improve its tactical mobility, and insure its ability to fight a variety of limited war contingencies on the ground. In his first State of the Union address, Kennedy informed Congress, "I am directing the Secretary of Defense to expand rapidly and substantially . . . the orientation of existing forces for the conduct of non-nuclear war, paramilitary operations, and sub-limited or unconventional wars."[24] Kennedy's first full budget proposal, submitted to Congress on January 18, 1962, reflected the desire to overturn the New Look by strengthening conventional combat forces. In addition to proposing overall defense expenditures in excess of $50 billion per year, the president recommended a spending increase of more than $3 billion per annum for general-purpose forces, most notably the Army, and $1 billion on sealift and airlift capabilities to move "combat-ready limited war forces" quickly to wherever they might be needed. He also called for substantial growth in the number of uniformed Army personnel and a proposed bump in the number of regular Army divisions from fourteen to sixteen. Significant increases in procurement for arming and supplying conventional forces were also recommended. According to Kennedy, "these forces must be equipped and provisioned so they are ready to fight a limited war for a protracted period of time anywhere in the world."[25]

By 1965 the Army buildup was virtually complete. Although President Johnson had reduced the actual military budget by $1.1 billion shortly after taking office, conventional combat units from all branches, particularly the Army, suffered little.[26] "Our forces have been made as versatile as the threats to peace are various," Johnson informed Congress on January 18, 1965.

Our Special Forces, trained for the undeclared twilight wars of today, have been expanded eightfold. Our combat-ready Army divisions have been increased by 45 percent. . . . Our tactical Air Force firepower to support these divisions in the field has increased 100 percent. This strength has been developed to support our basic military strategy—a strategy of strength and readiness, capable of countering aggression with appropriate force.[27]

In his annual report for fiscal year 1964, Secretary of Defense Robert McNamara boasted that the Army had an active duty strength of 973,000 personnel—an increase of more than 113,000 since 1961. This additional personnel allowed it to organize two new divisions and to elevate three training divisions to combat-ready status, thus raising the number of such divisions from eleven to sixteen.[28] By 1965, the Army's nondivisional force structure was also beefed up to include seven separate brigades, four regimental combat teams, and seven Special Forces groups.[29] Under the Kennedy/Johnson buildup, Army procurement and logistical readiness programs were also significantly expanded, spurring large investments in new weapons, equipment, and supplies. During this time, expenditures for equipping existing divisions rose from $1.5 billion in 1961 to $2.5 billion in fiscal years 1962 and 1963. In 1964, spending on Army procurement topped nearly $3 billion. An interim objective had also been established that year to provide the Army with "the full complement of modern weapons and equipment" for twenty-two divisions, including sixteen regular and six reserve. Among those items that were field tested and distributed to the Army during this period were the UH-1 Iroquois (Huey) and CH-47 Chinook helicopters, the M-14 rifle, the M-60 machine gun, the M79 40mm grenade launcher, the claymore antipersonnel mine, and the M-113 armored personnel carrier. Each of these, as it turned out, played a prominent role in U.S. Army combat in Vietnam.[30]

The years 1961–1965 were also a period of change in Army doctrine and training. Besides scrapping the Pentomic force structure and returning to a triangular infantry organization, the Army devoted a great deal of time and energy toward developing special warfare and airmobile capabilities. Much like the weapons and vehicles mentioned above, these new doctrines would play a central role in the war in South Vietnam. According to Secretary McNamara, the new divisional and brigade structure enacted under the Reorganization Objective Army Divisions (ROAD) concept was intended to give field forces greater firepower, mobility, and flexibility. This was to be done by facilitating "the grouping of infantry, armor, and artillery in task forces of varying composition to meet specific combat and terrain requirements."[31] The size of Army Special Forces doubled in 1962, and they were projected to be three times larger than in 1961 by June 30, 1963.[32] By the close of fiscal year 1964, more than ten thousand soldiers were assigned to seven Special Forces groups around the world.[33] New education programs for officers and enlisted men, special training for counterinsurgency operations, and advisory efforts were also accelerated at this time. In June 1965, the Army announced that it had established a separate airmobile division, the 1st Cavalry Division, as part of its sixteen-division force. Equipped with 434 aircraft (428 helicopters and six fixed-wing aircraft) that allowed up to one-third of the division's assault elements to be airlifted simultaneously, the 1st Cavalry Division was intended to improve the Army's combat effectiveness in low- and mid-intensity conflicts through high-speed vertical entry and withdrawal of combat forces on the battlefield.[34] That same year, the Army and the Air Force worked together

to develop a new concept for joint air-ground coordination to improve procedures for requesting and providing tactical air support.[35]

Army leadership lauded the Kennedy/Johnson buildup. According to Secretary of the Army Stephen Ailes in his 1965 annual report, the service had
resurrected its primary task of providing the nation with combat-ready land
forces. "Army forces," he wrote, "are in a better state of readiness today than
they have ever been in any previous peacetime period."[36] General Creighton
Abrams agreed. Speaking in front of the Preparedness Investigating Subcommittee that same year, Abrams informed the U.S. Senate that the contemporary Army was better trained and more prepared for war than any he had ever
seen. "It is my firm belief that the Army is in the best peacetime condition
in its history," he stated. "I can state unequivocally that the readiness conditions in the U.S. Army are the highest that have been attained in my 29 years
of service."[37] Although the subjectivity of such statements is obvious, later
assessments of U.S. Army preparedness and operational effectiveness confirmed these views.

The Crucible of War: U.S. Army Combat Experience in
South Vietnam

American combat forces had begun arriving in South Vietnam in March 1965.
First to come ashore was the 9th Marine Expeditionary Brigade, followed
by the U.S. Army's 173rd Airborne Brigade two months later. The 1st Brigade of the 101st Airborne Division and the 2nd Brigade of the 1st Infantry
Division arrived in July. The last to enter South Vietnam in 1965 was the 1st
Cavalry Division (Airmobile), which established itself in the rugged Central
Highlands during September and October.[38] By the end of the year, the Military Assistance Command, Vietnam (MACV) had 116,700 Army soldiers and
41,000 Marines in country.[39] Although these units were introduced incrementally, they made an impact almost immediately. Within months of their
arrival, U.S. combat forces had, in a number of limited engagements, inflicted
heavy losses on Viet Cong (VC) and North Vietnamese Army (NVA) units,
and arrested Saigon's declining strategic position. As early as August 1965 it
was evident that the infusion of American units had not only blunted the
momentum built up by the VC/NVA during the first half of the year but
had also stabilized the situation in the Republic of Vietnam (RVN). "With
the introduction and commitment of US combat forces into the RVN and
the expanded offensive ground, naval, and air operations against the VC,
some encouraging results have been obtained in halting the deterioration of
the military situation in the RVN," the Joint Chiefs of Staff (JCS) informed

Secretary McNamara on August 25, 1965. "It is imperative," the JCS continued, "that we reinforce this limited success, nurture Vietnamese morale with timely deployments and heavier air strikes, and sustain and increase the momentum which has been achieved as the initiative is gained by the United States and the RVN."[40]

The forward momentum called for by the JCS in August was in fact sustained during the fall of 1965. In September, the 101st Airborne Division conducted GIBRALTER, a large-scale search-and-destroy operation aimed at eliminating the entrenched Communist presence in Binh Dinh province, a hotbed of VC/NVA activity located along the coast in II Corps Tactical Zone (CTZ). Although the overall number of enemy KIA in the operation was modest, the mission was notable because it was the first major contact for the division as well as the first defeat inflicted on a VC main-force unit by the U.S. Army. The following month the 173rd Airborne Brigade began pushing into the "Iron Triangle," a Communist stronghold located northwest of Saigon in Binh Duong Province. Their objective was to destroy enemy forces, weaken VC/NVA control over the area, and relieve Communist pressure on Saigon. In November, the U.S. 1st Cavalry Division fought what turned out to be one of the fiercest battles of the war. SILVER BAYONET was a massive search-and-destroy operation undertaken to track down and eliminate Communist forces operating in Pleiku province, a strategically vital area located in the Central Highlands. The operation pitted elements of the U.S. 1st Cavalry against the NVA 32nd, 33rd, and 66th regiments. Famously known for two separate engagements, the "Battle of LZ X-Ray" and the "Battle of LZ Albany," the Ia Drang Valley campaign remains one of the most well-known engagements of the war due to the intense nature of the fighting and the heroic stand made by three 1st Cavalry battalions led by Lieutenant Colonel Harold G. Moore at LZ X-Ray on 14–16 November.[41] Enemy casualties for the campaign included 1,224 NVA killed. American forces, meanwhile, suffered 546 casualties, including 239 killed and 307 wounded. Despite some mishaps and a heavy reliance on overwhelming firepower, particularly artillery and air support, the Americans had performed relatively well in their first large-scale test of arms—something, as William Westmoreland later noted, that set Vietnam apart from previous American wars. "In a month of operations around Pleiku and in the Ia Drang Valley, the 1st Cavalry Division lost 300 men killed," Westmoreland wrote. "The death of even one man is lamentable, and those were serious losses," he continued,

> yet I could take comfort in the fact that in the Highlands . . . the American
> fighting man and his commanders had performed without the setbacks that

have sometimes marked the first performances in other wars. We had no Kasserine Pass as in World War II, no costly retreat by hastily committed, understrength occupation troops from Japan into a Pusan perimeter as in Korea.[42]

Despite relatively small numbers and the tenacity and combat skill demonstrated by Communist main-force units, American combat troops had prevailed on the battlefields of South Vietnam during 1965 and achieved the basic objectives laid out for the emergency phase of the war. By December, the VC/NVA war machine had been beaten back, the faltering South Vietnamese Army was back on its feet, and the impending collapse of the Saigon government had been averted.[43] Although it was evident at the time that there would be no easy victory in Vietnam, and that the road ahead was going to be long and arduous, there was, nevertheless, a feeling of guarded optimism and a growing sense of confidence in the timely arrival of American combat forces as 1965 drew to a close. "Professing to scorn the U.S. as a paper tiger, Communist China had long proclaimed Americans incapable of combat under such conditions—while prudently allowing North Viet Nam to fight its 'war of liberation,'" *Time* magazine declared in January 1966. "The Americans turned out to be tigers, all right—live ones. With courage and a cool professionalism that surprised friend and foe, U.S. troops stood fast and firm in South Viet Nam. In the waning months of 1965, they helped finally to stem the tide that had run so long with the Reds."[44]

In 1966 U.S. combat forces continued to grow in size and number, as existing Marine and Army units were augmented by the U.S. Army's 4th Infantry, 9th Infantry, and 25th Infantry Divisions and by the 11th Armored Cavalry Regiment and the 196th and 199th Infantry Brigades. By the end of the year there were fifty-nine Army and twenty-four Marine infantry and tank battalions in country, totaling close to four hundred thousand troops.[45] Although much of 1966 was spent managing the massive influx of troops and equipment, American combat units still had managed to take the war to the enemy and frustrate VC/NVA efforts to regain the initiative, as MACV continued its troop buildup and established an expanding network of bases and other military installations. One such effort was MASHER/WHITE WING, a combined operation conducted by elements from the U.S. 1st Cavalry Division and the Army of Vietnam (ARVN) 22nd Division between January 25 and March 6. The operation was a massive search-and-destroy mission launched with the purpose of driving the NVA/VC out of Binh Dinh Province. MASHER/WHITE WING inflicted terrible losses on elements of the 3rd NVA Division, generating 2,389 known enemy casualties, including 1,342 confirmed kills, and more than 600 prisoners, in a six-week engagement. American casualties were much lighter and included 228 killed and 834 wounded.[46] On September 14, elements from the 1st Infantry, 4th Infantry, and 25th Infantry Divisions, along with the 173rd Airborne Brigade, launched the largest operation of the war up to that time. Codenamed ATTLEBORO, the operation took place in Binh Duong and Tay Ninh provinces just north of Saigon. In addition to utilizing more than 20,000 U.S. and ARVN troops, the mission also, for the first time in the war, used large-scale multidivisional search-and-destroy operations to find and eliminate Communist main-force units. The total number of VC/NVA killed in action during ATTLEBORO was 2,130.[47] Throughout 1966 these large-scale operations, along with dozens more smaller engagements, mauled Communist forces as the American buildup progressed. The total number of enemy combat deaths between January and October was 48,064. American and South Vietnamese KIA, meanwhile, were much more modest, running roughly a quarter of that number.[48] By the end of the year, the number of VC/NVA killed rose to 61,631. As 1966 drew to a close, the number of American soldiers and Marines in South Vietnam had climbed to approximately 385,000.[49] With the government of South Vietnam relatively stable and most of the personnel and logistical support for the large American units in place by December, U.S. combat forces were poised to take the war to the enemy and go on the offensive in 1967.

Army historian Shelby Stanton correctly labeled 1967 "the year of the big battles." It was then that MACV, after having spent more than a year and a half building up American forces and setting the stage for large-scale efforts to sweep Communist forces from South Vietnam, had made massive, sometimes months-long, main-force operations a staple of combat in South Vietnam. In January, U.S. and ARVN units launched CEDAR FALLS, a multidivisional search-and-destroy operation conducted in III CTZ. It was the first corps-sized operation of the war and included 30,000 allied troops, including 16,000 Americans and 14,000 South Vietnamese. The objective was to locate and eliminate the headquarters for VC Military Region 4 and to clear the Iron Triangle of Communist forces. Concluded on January 26, CEDAR FALLS inflicted heavy casualties on the VC 9th Division, including 750 KIA and 280 prisoners. The following month, the U.S. 1st Cavalry and 25th Infantry Divisions, along with the ARVN 22nd Division and Republic of Korea (ROK) Capital Division, began PERSHING, a joint search-and-destroy and clearing operation that lasted more than a year. Intended to assist pacification efforts in Quang Ngai and Binh Dinh provinces, PERSHING produced more than 5,400 enemy KIA and netted 2,059 prisoners. Also in February, U.S. forces launched JUNCTION CITY in War Zone C and War Zone D, located northwest of Saigon in III CTZ. The largest operation in South Vietnam to date, the mission included four ARVN battalions and twenty-two American battalions from the U.S. 1st, 4th, and 25th Divisions as well as from the 196th Infantry Brigade, the 11th Armored Cavalry, and the 173rd Airborne Brigade. The operation was one of the largest airmobile assaults in history. The purpose of JUNCTION CITY was to locate and eliminate the headquarters of the Central Office of South Vietnam (COSVN), the command and control organization that directed and managed the insurgency in South Vietnam, and to clear Communist forces from War Zone C, a longtime Communist redoubt and infiltration route located along the Cambodian border in Tay Ninh province. The overall objective of operations was to pacify the province by driving the VC/NVA away from populated areas and out into the open where they could be destroyed more effectively with superior firepower and without incurring heavy civilian casualties. By the time it was concluded on May 14, American and South Vietnamese forces had racked up 2,728 enemy KIA.[50]

U.S. Strategy and the Utility of Force in South Vietnam: A Shield for Pacification

Large-scale search-and-destroy and sweep operations such as those mentioned above had become the hallmark of the American effort in Vietnam between 1965 and 1968. Despite their tactical success, however, these missions were often criticized and deemed inappropriate given South Vietnam's irregular war environment. Former British officer turned counterinsurgency expert Sir Robert Thompson was one such detractor of the U.S. military's "big unit war of attrition." Although he greatly admired the bravery of the American soldier and the manner in which the United States applied resources to war, Thompson found what he considered to be "an aching void" in the realms of strategy and tactics. "With regards to strategy," he lamented in 1969, "the Americans seem to have been influenced only by the very worst interpretation of Clausewitz's doctrines and by the Prussian example of Moltke, so that the sole aim of most American orthodox military commanders has always been 'the destruction of the enemy's main forces on the battlefield.'"[51] Although this critique may have contained a grain of truth—combat against Communist main forces, after all, was the primary reason American fighting units were dispatched to Southeast Asia—the overall essence of Thompson's statement was shortsighted and incomplete. This is the case because it ignored the whole complexity of MACV's mission in South Vietnam. The military strategy put in place by the United States was not—as it may have appeared to the casual observer and as many have argued—a bankrupt, one-dimensional approach based predominantly if not exclusively on attrition and the pursuit of enemy KIA. As historians Dale Andrade and Gregory Daddis have shown, Westmoreland conceived and applied a broad concept of operations that transcended simply killing the enemy and attritting his forces beyond restoration. Although the destruction of enemy units was a vital, if not the most indispensable, component within the American strategy, attrition was but one method within a larger strategic construct.[52] The strategy MACV designed and put in place for the war in Vietnam can be seen in Directive 525-4, released on September 17, 1965. According to the directive, there were three primary objectives for U.S. combat forces in South Vietnam: first, to "stem the tide" and halt the Communist offensive in the Republic of Vietnam; second, to eliminate Communist main forces and help "pacify" high-priority areas; and third, to help the Saigon government progressively restore its control over the country. "The ultimate aim," the directive read, "is to pacify the Republic of Vietnam by destroying the VC—his forces, organization, terrorists, agents, and propagandists—while at the same time reestablishing the government apparatus, strengthening RVN military forces, rebuilding the administrative machinery, and re-instituting the services of the government."[53] Four years later, these same objectives (with the exception of stanching the Communist offensive, which had been accomplished by the end of 1965) were still in place. According to the 1969 Combined Campaign Plan, the mission of allied military forces was "to defeat VC/NVA units and assist the government to extend control throughout the Republic of Vietnam."[54] As the objectives laid out in both of these plans indicate, attrition was not the strategy put in place by MACV—in fact, it was not a strategy at all. Attrition was merely a method used to advance the actual strategy the United States pursued in South Vietnam, which was to win the war by eliminating the Communist insurgency, pacifying the countryside, and helping reassert Saigon's control over its national territory.

Despite arguments to the contrary,[55] the U.S. Army was more than a cudgel in South Vietnam; it was a multipurpose instrument used to implement a number of military and nonmilitary programs and functions, including advice and support to South Vietnamese military and paramilitary forces, rural development, and civic action initiatives. Nonetheless, its strongest contribution was the ability to provide a military "shield" behind which the South Vietnamese themselves could fight a political war vis-à-vis pacification and nation building. Rural pacification, considered by many to be the key factor in winning the war in South Vietnam, was a civil-military program meant to disintegrate the Communist insurgency, reassert national sovereignty over the people and territory of South Vietnam, and build a unified, viable, and prosperous nation supported by the citizenry. A concept report generated for

Civil Operations and Revolutionary Development Support (CORDS) defined pacification as

> an integrated military and civil process to restore, consolidate, and expand government control so that nation-building can progress throughout the Republic of Vietnam. It consists of those coordinated military and civil actions to liberate the people from VC control; restore public security; initiate political, economic, and social development; extend effective RVN authority; and win the willing support of the people toward these ends.[56]

For Saigon and Washington, eliminating the Communist insurgency and establishing government authority throughout the countryside was the heart of the war in South Vietnam. These things could never come to fruition, however, without first eliminating the hostile forces that threatened to overwhelm the struggling republic with a hybrid style of warfare, one that meshed conventional military operations with guerrilla warfare, terrorism, and political agitation at the local level.

The *raison d'être* of American combat forces in South Vietnam was not to help settle the war simply by killing an intolerable and unsustainable number of VC/NVA soldiers; rather, it was to apply the armed services' traditional institutional strengths towards advancing pacification and the political struggle against communism. According to MACV, the mission of U.S. forces in 1965 was "to assist and support the [Republic of Vietnam Armed Forces] in their efforts to defeat communist subversive insurgency and to accelerate GVN control over the country."[57] This argument was repeated throughout the war. "It is worthwhile to restate our strategy," U.S. ambassador Cyrus Vance informed Congress in February 1968.

> It is to use U.S. forces primarily in search and destroy operations against VC and North Vietnamese main force units. The reasoning is that U.S. forces can be used most effectively in such actions because of their vastly superior firepower and maneuverability. . . . These search and destroy operations are designed to provide a shield behind which the pacification efforts can go forward. Absent such a shield, pacification could never get started—let alone flourish.[58]

In his final report as head of MACV, Westmoreland reiterated the argument that the fundamental purpose of U.S. combat actions was to advance pacification and nation-building efforts in South Vietnam. "Our basic objective," he wrote, "has been to establish a safe environment within which the people of South Vietnam could form a government that was independent, stable, and freely elected—one that would deserve and receive popular support." Such a government, Westmoreland argued, simply could not be created within a hostile milieu, one that was marked by persistent Communist attack and pervasive revolutionary violence. "The Viet Cong and the North Vietnamese Army occupied large parts of the country and subjected large areas to armed attacks and acts of terrorism and assassination," he declared.

> These acts were most often directed at the representatives of government in provinces, villages, and hamlets throughout the countryside, the government officials most closely associated with the people. The United States' military goal was to provide a secure environment in which the citizens could live and in which all levels of legal government could function without enemy exploitation, pressure, or violence.[59]

Ambassador William Colby, the civilian head of CORDS, supported this claim, informing the Senate Foreign Relations Committee in 1970 that pacification "operates behind the shield furnished by another aspect of our efforts in Vietnam: the military operations of the Vietnamese and allied armies. However bold, however well-conceived, however logical this program, it has been amply proven that it cannot be effective unless hostile regiments and divisions are kept away."[60]

Vance, Colby, and Westmoreland were correct; the primary mission of U.S. forces in South Vietnam was to assist the RVN by providing a secure environment in which pacification and nation building could flourish. Given the limited and strategically defensive nature of the ground war and the fact that the purpose of American intervention in Southeast Asia was to expel the Communist presence from South Vietnam and help create a viable, independent, and united South Vietnam—not to launch an all-out offensive war to crush North Vietnam or destroy its armed forces—the use of combat actions to create a defensive shield and buy time until the Saigon government and its military could mature and assume stewardship of the nation's defense was a logical and appropriate objective. The creation of safe and secure areas in South Vietnam, however, could only be achieved through the hard hand of war: aggressive, offensive combat operations that would locate and annihilate large enemy units, destroy base areas and safe havens, provide territorial security for selected areas set to undergo social and economic development, and maintain armed security once enemy forces had been removed.[61] "The military plays an indispensable role in pacification," MACV declared. "Without initial military security operations to establish the essential secure environment, the civil aspects of pacification cannot progress. Only under relatively secure conditions can progress be made in the rectification of the political, economic, and sociological imbalances which are the root causes of, and support the continuation of insurgency."[62]

The purpose of military support of pacification was to accomplish what nonmilitary means could not: eliminate Communist guerrillas and main forces and prevent their entry or reentry into populated areas. Without conventional combat operations, South Vietnam and the United States could not blunt efforts by Hanoi and the National Liberation Front (NLF) to defeat the Republic of Vietnam Armed Forces (RVNAF) or prevent the communists from disrupting the pacification program and its emphasis on rural development and socioeconomic reform. Nor could the allies, short of military action, defeat the insurgency or collapse its political administrative capabilities in rural areas. Conventional combat operations alone could shepherd pacification and the nation-building process by first destroying Communist forces within areas slated for development and then by providing sustained security after local and main-force guerrillas and regular NVA units had been expelled from populated areas. In sum, combat operations were the only means of providing the secure environment necessary for successful state building. "The role of military forces in support of pacification," MACV declared, "is to attain a requisite level of security in and around selected hamlet and village areas so that revolutionary development, civil activities, and subsequently, nation-building can proceed."[63] Sustained territorial security was the key to successful pacification and efforts to establish and maintain government authority at both the local and national level. The use of combat operations to expand and consolidate Saigon's authority, therefore, was a fundamental rather than an incidental feature of the pacification program.

The tactics and techniques used by allied main forces to support pacification were identical to those used in other operations. As noted in a 1968 MACV handbook for U.S. combatant commands, "military support of pacification is a unit mission, not a special and identifiable military maneuver. In order to accomplish this mission, units will employ standard tactics and techniques adapted as necessary to meet the requirements of terrain, enemy forces, and rules of engagement."[64] Allied forces conducted combat operations in support of pacification in two sequential stages. The first was the clearing phase. U.S./ARVN units used clearing operations to eject enemy main forces from areas set to undergo pacification and eliminate their ability to corrode government control by threatening or interfering with pacification and rural development. During this phase, allied main-force units conducted company- and battalion-sized operations to "clear" enemy forces from an area vis-à-vis sweeps, saturation patrolling, and search and destroy operations. Psychological Operations (PSYOP) and short-term civic action programs were also an integral part of these missions. Theoretically, once a core zone had been pacified and Communist forces cleared from the area, large friendly forces would hand off security duties to local territorial forces and move outward to continue offensive operations and prevent VC and NVA main forces from reentering the area.[65]

Securing operations constituted the next phase. Conducted predominantly, although not exclusively, by district- and province-level territorial units known as the Regional Forces (RF) and Popular Forces (PF), these missions had the purpose of "securing" an area that had already been cleared of enemy main forces. This was accomplished through a variety of means, including eliminating the remaining vestiges of Communist presence, developing sufficient local security forces and infrastructure to prevent a resurgence of insurgent influence, and establishing local government to implement social reform and foster community development at the village and hamlet level. Much like clearing operations, securing operations focused on maintaining area security through "aggressive offensive" combat actions, albeit at the small-unit level. Moreover, they were sustained until the insurgents' capability was reduced to "sporadic" attacks and terrorist activities. Securing operations involved mostly company- and platoon-sized activities, and they included a variety of security functions, including establishing and maintaining security outposts, conducting day and night ambushes, and fulfilling other small-unit security missions. PSYOP and civil actions programs were also stepped up during this stage.[66] Together, clearing and securing operations were designed to create the necessary safe environment so that pacification could advance.

The American combat experience in Vietnam, despite what some have argued, demonstrated that large multidivisional operations such as CEDAR FALLS and JUNCTION CITY did in fact have a place in modern counterinsurgency warfare. These missions, along with a host of others, assisted nation-building efforts by decimating Communist main-force units and by destroying VC/NVA base areas, sanctuaries, and safe havens within South Vietnam.[67] Search-and-destroy and other "big-unit" combat actions not only saved South Vietnam from imminent collapse in 1965; they also helped pave the way for pacification progress and greater government control over the countryside in the years that followed. One memo dated February 17, 1967, noted, "The build-up of Free World and Vietnamese forces has created a climate in which pacification has become a feasible objective and in which substantial progress has been made in . . . establishing the basis for deliberate forward movement in pacification."[68] The following November, Ambassador Robert W. Komer affirmed this forward movement, informing Westmoreland that the share of population living in relatively secure areas had, according to Saigon's estimates, jumped from 47 percent (7.7 million people) in mid-1965 to 72 percent (11.9 million people) by the end of September 1967. Conversely, the share of the population living in areas controlled by the Viet Cong had dropped from 22 to 14 percent during this same period. Although Komer did state that MACV estimates for the relatively secure category were more modest (67 percent) than Saigon's, these numbers still translated into an impressive gain in population security.[69]

By the end of 1969, search-and-destroy missions and other main-force combat operations had helped bring Saigon's control of population and territory to peak levels. According to a study produced by the Vietnam Special Studies Group in 1970, conventional military operations were the foundation for the unprecedented expansion of RVN control in the wake of the 1968 Tet Offensive. "Throughout late 1968 and 1969, enemy main forces were destroyed, dispersed, and forced to withdraw from populated areas of the countryside," the report read. "In most provinces studied, this change in the main-force environment was a prerequisite to the RVN control gains of late 1968 and 1969."[70] According to the 1970 Plan for Pacification and Development, the allies had significantly expanded government control and brought roughly 90 percent of the population of South Vietnam into areas that were designated "relatively secure" by the Hamlet Evaluation System (HES).[71] By December 1970, the overall population in South Vietnam living in relatively secure areas had jumped to nearly 95 percent. In the countryside, RVN control of the rural population was equally impressive, having increased more than 25 percentage points since August 1969. End-of-year estimates showed Saigon in control of more than 66 percent of rural inhabitants. "The war in South Vietnam has wound down to a point well below the levels of previous years and has entered a period of relative quiescence," the Office of the Deputy Assistant Secretary of Defense (ODASD) declared in its end-of-year report. "Pacification progress and activity has exceeded expectations, despite reduced U.S. forces and activity," the report continued. "Experienced observers returning to Vietnam after a long period out of the country unanimously agree that security conditions in the countryside are better than ever before, and that the allied main-force military campaign has achieved most of its objectives in MR's III and IV."[72] Although many of these gains were a product of the devastating losses suffered by VC units during Tet, a significant decline in Communist main-force activity beginning in 1969, and a large demographic shift from rural to urban areas, the sharp increase in RVN control was, nonetheless, made possible principally through conventional combat actions by U.S. forces.

Contemporary and historical observers have questioned allied security ratings because they were inaccurate, unreliable, and subject to inflation by officials who often manipulated the numbers to show progress. Moreover, statistics that exhibited high percentages of the population living in "relatively secure" areas failed to reflect the high levels of sustained Communist activity inside of South Vietnam despite unprecedented levels of government control over the countryside. HES was an admittedly imperfect instrument that simply could not capture the war in its entirety or measure its intangibles—the social and political intricacies that defined the conflict at the local level. Yet despite its flaws and in spite of the fact that security ratings did not reflect the political realities of South Vietnam, the program did provide a reasonably accurate picture of the degree of government or Communist control over population and territory. What HES did provide were useful insights into national security trends; and after March 1965, the trend was clear: pacification had made substantial progress thanks to the main-force war and the "shield" provided by American combat forces. Conventional military operations and the lavish use of firepower and mobility were an indispensable corollary to pacification. In fact, the success of U.S. arms against the VC/NVA was the foundation upon which the large pacification gains of 1968–1969 were made. In addition to quantitative analysis provided by HES, there is a large body of qualitative evidence, particularly monthly province reports, military region overviews, and studies conducted by the Pacification Studies Group, that identify the direct correlation between U.S. combat operations and improved pacification conditions. In 1970 Robert Komer declared,

> Without the regular ARVN and Americans pushing back the enemy's conventional units and in effect acting as a shield for the pacifiers, the enemy's big units would have come in and messed up pacification before it could even get off the ground. In sum, you cannot talk about winning in Vietnam post 1964 by pacification alone without the big unit effort.[73]

Komer was not alone in this sentiment. In September 1968 Abrams, then head of MACV, informed the White House National Security Council, "Where we are in Vietnam is due to the application of raw power. That is why the enemy is where he is, why pacification has moved. . . . When you turn off the power you have got an entirely new ball game."[74] The following year Abrams again made this argument. "The accelerated pacification program, which we feel is progressing quite favorably," he declared, "is made possible largely by friendly military initiative which keeps the enemy from concentrating his forces against our pacification program."[75] Abrams's predecessor agreed. "At the time we entered, the government held only a few enclaves," Westmoreland informed the House of Representatives Committee on Appropriations in February 1970.

> It took a great deal of effort, sweat and blood to expand the enclaves to the point that the countryside opened up. In the process of that, we have had to grind down the guerrilla force, which has been done. Pacification has been extended bringing more people and area under government control. The indigenous enemy in the south has been reduced. The enemy now has been required to take refuge in remote areas of South Vietnam, in Cambodia, in Laos, and in the DMZ area.[76]

Conclusion

The U.S. Army performance was unparalleled in its history, when evaluated by its performance during tactical engagements with VC/NVA forces, and in its ability to apply mobility and firepower to advance pacification and extend government control over the countryside. New Look austerity did little to undermine the operational proficiency and combat effectiveness of the U.S. Army, which in a relatively short span of years was able to quickly rebuild itself and hone its combat skills to a fine point under the Kennedy/Johnson defense buildup. The argument Robert Scales posited before Congress—that Eisenhower's defense cuts and massive reduction in ground forces destroyed the Army as an institution and produced American defeat in Vietnam—is not supported by historical evidence. Eisenhower's policies had absolutely nothing to do with the failure of U.S. political objectives in Southeast Asia. Nor did they play a role in the institutional malaise or spiritual decay of the Army during the latter stages of the war. In short, the New Look and its austerity measures had no bearing on the operational aptitude or combat proficiency of the U.S. Army sent to Vietnam. One cannot dispute the detrimental impact defense cuts had on the Army's overall numbers and prestige during the 1950s. These setbacks, however, were quickly overcome by the mid-1960s thanks to the Kennedy and Johnson administration's reemphasis on conventional war capabilities.

The American combat experience in South Vietnam proved that the Kennedy/Johnson buildup had indeed built a highly capable and effective conventional ground force. Despite the war's failed outcome and in spite of the convergence of a number of social, political, and institutional factors that undermined the mission, esprit de corps, and institutional vitality of the U.S. Army, the service demonstrated high levels of operational skill and combat proficiency in South Vietnam.[77] The Army—contrary to what a number of scholars and other individuals have argued over the years—did not help lose the war by dogmatically adhering to an ill-suited conventional-war doctrine that willfully ignored counterinsurgency and the political dimension of the war.[78] In fact, it was the service's ability to incorporate conventional combat operations and the application of firepower and mobility into a larger strategic construct—one that included pacification and nation-building activities—that staved off defeat in 1965. These operations helped Saigon achieve peak levels of political and military control over the country in the years that followed, and assured the survival of South Vietnam for a decade after direct U.S. intervention. In 1980, former South Vietnamese general Cao Van Vien testified to this fact. "The multitudinous intervention of U.S. forces in South Vietnam since 1965," he wrote, "was a timely move that pulled our country away from the brink of disaster. . . . This intervention had helped South Vietnam reverse its checkmate position and made it possible for the free republic to survive for another ten years."[79]

Historians have also acknowledged a high level of combat proficiency among U.S. combat forces in Vietnam, including a number of scholars who have generally been critical of the American war in Southeast Asia. George C. Herring has argued that while the overall impact of U.S. ground operations during the first two years of American intervention is hard to assess, the combat performance of American troops is not. "American troops fought well, despite the miserable conditions under which the war was waged," Herring wrote. "In those instances when main units were actually engaged," he continued, "the Americans usually prevailed, and there was no place in South Vietnam where the enemy enjoyed security from American firepower. It was clear by 1967 that the infusion of American forces had staved off what had appeared to be certain defeat in 1965."[80] William Duiker, a historian of Vietnamese communism, agreed. "In fairness, it should be pointed out that the U.S. strategy, however wasteful of U.S. resources and however damaging to the civilian population, did pose enormous problems for the insurgent leadership and seriously set back the course of the revolution in the south," Duiker wrote. "Aggressive search-and-destroy missions," he maintained, "disrupted enemy operations and gradually drove them from base areas in the mountains while depriving them of provisions and recruits in the highly populated lowlands."[81] According to Eric M. Bergarud, "the armed forces sent to Vietnam were by far the best ever sent to war by the United States."[82]

A number of former military officers have also given the Army high marks in combat proficiency. Westmoreland's former intelligence chief, Philip B. Davidson, is one. "While the strategy of attrition had not hurt Hanoi enough to cause them to cease their aggression," he wrote, "it did achieve positive results. It seized and held the tactical initiative in South Vietnam; it disrupted enemy activities; it forced the enemy to resort to constant movement to avoid destruction; and it drove the major enemy units away from the population centers."[83] Others were less equivocal. "On the battlefield itself, the Army was unbeatable. In engagement after engagement the forces of the Viet Cong and of the North Vietnamese Army were thrown back with terrible losses," former U.S. Army colonel Harry G. Summers trumpeted in 1982.[84] Summers made a similar proclamation three years later. An analysis of combat actions in Vietnam, he argued, "makes clear that 'any good soldier' could, *and did*, 'handle guerrillas,' and American Army and Marine infantrymen handled this enemy the same way they had always handled the enemy—not by any new and esoteric techniques of guerrilla war but by the age-old infantry method of closing with the enemy and destroying him by fire and maneuver."[85] Former Army officer turned military historian Adrian Lewis perhaps said it best. "The United States Army deployed to Vietnam," he declared, "was the best trained, best equipped army of any deployed to war in the twentieth century."[86]

The U.S. Army's operational proficiency and combat effectiveness in South Vietnam was exceptional and must be judged on its prescribed role and its performance within that role—not on the overall failure of the United States to achieve foreign policy objectives in Vietnam. No one can deny that Washington ultimately failed to achieve its political and grand strategic aims in Southeast Asia. Nor can they repudiate the fact that the Army, as an institution, progressively disintegrated as the war ground on under a host of debilitating and systemic problems (many of which were self-inflicted), including low morale, widespread breakdowns in troop discipline, instances of brutality and atrocity, drug abuse, crime, and racial unrest. These unfortunate trends, along with the collapse of the South Vietnamese military and the fall of Saigon in April 1975, however, did not result from poor American combat skills or lack of military preparedness rooted in defense austerity. They were, instead, the product of a confluence of larger and more powerful forces—social, political, and military—many of which were far beyond the Army's ability to influence or control.

Examining the American military experience in Vietnam within the historical context of the Eisenhower drawdown and Kennedy/Johnson buildup generates two broad conclusions. First, defense drawdowns and cuts in the defense budget and force structure can and have been reversed within a relatively short period time. Although Vietnam has been shown to be the historical exception rather than the rule in this matter, America's combat record in Southeast Asia demonstrates that the Army has been able to quickly rehabilitate itself when called upon and when given the resources it needs to address current and emerging national security threats. As we have seen, Matthew B. Ridgway's protests that the U.S. Army under the New Look had been weakened to the point that it could no longer serve as an effective instrument of American policy were grossly inflated. Within several years after Eisenhower had left office, the malaise of the Pentomic Era had dissipated and the U.S. Army was once again a confident, first-rate fighting force. The Army demonstrated its combat capabilities repeatedly on the battlefields of South Vietnam, as it time and again decimated Viet Cong guerrillas and NVA regulars in combat. This success provided a main-force shield behind which pacification and nation-building activities advanced.

Second, possession of the best-trained, best-equipped, most combat effective, and most operationally competent Army does not guarantee success on the strategic or grand strategic levels. Despite the fact that the U.S. Army sent to Vietnam in 1965 was one of the finest ground forces ever sent to war, the United States failed to achieve its political objectives in Southeast Asia. The U.S. military may have won every battle in Vietnam, as Harry Summers once boasted to a former North Vietnamese officer, but this fact (as Summers's counterpart shot back) was "irrelevant" given the war's outcome. In short, America had lost the war in Vietnam despite a high level of combat effectiveness and tactical victory. The failure of American policy in Southeast Asia despite the superiority of its armed forces, therefore, raises a number of important historical questions concerning the limitations of American military power, the sagacity of Cold War foreign intervention and the exportation of democracy vis-à-vis armed force, the strength and reliability of our allies, the wisdom and competency of past policymakers, and the strategies, methods, and actions of Hanoi and the National Liberation Front. For it is in these areas, and not in the realm of defense cuts and the U.S. Army drawdown of the 1950s that historians need to look for answers concerning American defeat in Vietnam.

NOTES

1 "General Ridgway Helping Bring Second Look at 'New Look,'" *Washington Post Times Herald*, August 2, 1954.

2 Robert H. Scales, "Repeating a Mistake by Downsizing the Army Again," *Washington Post*, January 5, 2012.

3 Charles J. V. Murphy, "A New Multi-Purpose U.S. Army," *Fortune Magazine* 73 (May 1966): 123.

4 Department of Defense, *Semiannual Report of the Secretary of Defense, January 1 to June 30, 1956* (Washington, DC: Government Printing Office, 1957), p. 59.

5 "Text of an Address by Admiral Radford on the Defense Plan of the Nation," *New York Times*, December 15, 1953.

6 "Text of Eisenhower's Defense Reorganization Proposal and His Message," *New York Times*, May 1, 1953.

7 "New Look in U.S. Defense Policy," *Manchester Guardian*, March 16, 1954.

8 "Text of Eisenhower's Defense Reorganization Proposal."

9 "Text of President Eisenhower's Message to Congress on the State of the Union," *New York Times*, January 8, 1954.

10 "Text of President Eisenhower's Budget Message to Congress for the Fiscal Year 1955," *New York Times*, January 22, 1954.

11 Department of Defense, *Semiannual Report of the Secretary of Defense, January 31 to June 30, 1954* (Washington, DC: Government Printing Office, 1955), p. 3; Department of Defense, *Annual Report of the Secretary of Defense, July 1, 1959, to June 30, 1960* (Washington, DC: Government Printing Office, 1961), p. 4.

12 *Annual Report of the Secretary of Defense, July 1, 1959, to June 30, 1960*, p. 34.

13 Department of Defense, *Semiannual Report of the Secretary of Defense, July 1 to December 31, 1956* (Washington, DC: Government Printing Office, 1957), p. 2.

14 Matthew B. Ridgway, "My Battles in War and Peace, Part I: Conflict in the Pentagon," *Saturday Evening Post*, January 21, 1956, p. 46.

15 Matthew B. Ridgway, *Soldier: The Memoirs of Matthew B. Ridgway* (New York: Harper, 1956), p. 273.

16 John F. Kennedy, *The Strategy of Peace* (New York: Harper & Row, 1960), p. 183.

17 Ibid., p. 184.

18 "Text of Kennedy's Speech to Senate Advocating New Approach on Foreign Policy," *New York Times*, June 15, 1960.

19 Maxwell D. Taylor, *The Uncertain Trumpet* (New York: Harper, 1959), p. 146.

20 House of Representatives, *Military Posture Briefings*, Hearings before the Committee on Armed Services, 87th Congress, First Session, 1961, pp. 643–44.

21 Douglas S. Blaufarb, *The Counterinsurgency Era: U.S. Doctrine and Performance, 1950 to Present* (New York: Free Press, 1977), pp. 52–55, 169.

22 In December 1862, Abraham Lincoln wrote a letter to Congress in an effort to persuade legislators to support his plan for compensated emancipation. In it, Lincoln wrote, "The dogmas of the quiet past, are inadequate to the stormy present. The occasion is piled high with difficulty, and we must rise—with the occasion. As our case is new, so we must think anew, and act anew." Roy P. Basler, ed., *Abraham Lincoln: His Speeches and Writings* (New York: Da Capo, 2001), p. 688.

23 Department of Defense, *Annual Report for Fiscal Year 1962* (Washington, DC: Government Printing Office, 1963), p. 3.

24 "Transcript of Kennedy Address to Congress on U.S. Role in Struggle for Freedom," *New York Times*, May 26, 1961.

25 "Text of the President's Message and Budget Analysis," *New York Times*, January 19, 1962.

26 Robert E. Thompson, "Johnson Lauds Defense, Asks Slash in Budget," *Los Angeles Times*, January 22, 1964.

27 "Text of President's Message to Congress on Defense," *Washington Post*, January 19, 1965.

28 Department of Defense, *Annual Report for Fiscal Year 1964* (Washington, DC: Government Printing Office, 1965), p. 16.

29 Department of Defense, *Annual Report for Fiscal Year 1965* (Washington, DC: Government Printing Office, 1966), p. 21.

30 *Annual Report for Fiscal Year 1964*, pp. 16–17.

31 Ibid., p. 16.

32 *Annual Report for Fiscal Year 1962*, p. 18.

33 *Annual Report for Fiscal Year 1964*, p. 17.

34 *Annual Report for Fiscal Year 1965*, pp. 134–36.

35 Ibid., p. 134.

36 Ibid., p .115.

37 United States Senate, *U.S. Army Readiness*, Hearings before the Preparedness Investigating Subcommittee of the Committee on Armed Services, 89th Congress, First Session, May 18, 21; June 2, 3, and 30, 1965, pp. 95–96.

38 For a full list of units and their dates of service in Vietnam, see: Shelby L. Stanton, *Vietnam Order of Battle* (Washington, DC: U.S. News Books, 1981).

39 Shelby L. Stanton, *The Rise and Fall of an American Army: U.S. Ground Forces in Vietnam, 1965–1973* (Novato, CA: Presidio Press, 1985), p. 65.

40 Memo to the Secretary of Defense: Future Operations and Force Deployments with Respect to the War in Vietnam, 10 November 1965, Folder 08, Box 03, Larry Berman Collection (Presidential Archives Research), Vietnam Center and Archive, Texas Tech University (hereafter TTUVA).

41 David Burns Sigler, *Vietnam Battle Chronology: U.S. Army and Marine Corps Combat Operations, 1965–1973* (Jefferson, NC: McFarland, 1992), p. 8.

42 William C. Westmoreland, *A Soldier Reports* (New York: Doubleday, 1976), pp. 157–58.

43 John M. Carland, *Stemming the Tide: May 1965 to October 1966* (Washington, DC: U.S. Army Center of Military History, 2000), p. 355.

44 "The Guardians at the Gate," *Time*, January 7, 1966.

45 Stanton, *Rise and Fall of an American Army*, pp. 65–66.

46 Sigler, *Vietnam Battle Chronology*, p. 12; Stanton, *Vietnam Order of Battle*, p. 9.

47 Sigler, *Vietnam Battle Chronology*, pp. 25–26.

48 Carland, *Stemming the Tide*, p. 365.

49 Sigler, *Vietnam Battle Chronology*, p. 31.

50 Ibid., pp. 33, 36–39; Stanton, *Vietnam Order of Battle*, p. 10.

51 Robert Thompson, *No Exit from Vietnam* (New York: McKay, 1969), p. 129.

52 See: Dale Andrade, "Westmoreland Was Right: Learning the Wrong Lessons from the Vietnam War," *Small Wars & Insurgencies* 19 (June 2008): 145–81; and Gregory

A. Daddis, *Westmoreland's War: Reassessing American Strategy in Vietnam* (New York: Oxford University Press, 2014).

53 MACV, Memo, "Tactics and Techniques for Employment of U.S. Forces in the Republic of Vietnam," 17 September 1965, pp. 2–3, Folder 03, Box 03, Larry Berman Collection, TTUVA.

54 RVNAF Joint General Staff & MACV, *1969 Combined Campaign Plan*, 23 October 1968, p. 5, RG 472 / A1 120 / Box 2 / Folder: Combined Campaign Plan/1969 (Part 1 of 2), National Archives and Records Administration, College Park, MD (NARA II).

55 See note 78.

56 Civil Operations and Rural Development Support (hereafter CORDS), Report, "Revolutionary Development Concept—Record of MACV Part 1," no date, p. 1, Folder 0804, Box 0029, Vietnam Archive Collection, TTUVA.

57 Military History Branch, Headquarters, United States Military Assistance Command, Vietnam, *1965 Command History*, p. 161.

58 Memo to President Lyndon B. Johnson from W. W. Rostow: Cy Vance's Response to Senator Edward Kennedy, 01 February 1968, Folder 16, Box 09, Larry Berman Collection (Presidential Archives Research), TTUVA.

59 Admiral Ulysses S. Grant Sharp, CINCPAC, and General William C. Westmoreland, COMUSMACV, *Report on the War in Vietnam (as of June 30, 1968)* (Washington, DC: Government Printing Office, 1968), p. 6.

60 Senate Committee on Foreign Relations, *Vietnam Policy and Prospects, 1970: Civil Operations and Rural Development Support Program*, Hearings before the Senate Committee on Foreign Relations, 91st Congress, Second Session, February 17, 18, 19, and 20, and March 3, 4, 17, and 19, 1970, p. 4.

61 Republic of Vietnam Central Pacification and Development Council, *1969 Pacification and Development Plan*, "Annex I: Military Support 1969 Pacification and Development Plan," p. 1, USAMHI.

62 MACV, *Handbook for Military Support of Pacification*, February 1968, p. 1, Folder 08, Box 04, Douglas Pike Collection: Unit 11—Monographs, TTUVA.

63 MACV, *Guide for Province and District Advisors*, 01 February 1968, p. 2.3, Folder 32, Box 01, Robert M. Hall Collection, TTUVA.

64 MACV, *Handbook for Military Support of Pacification*, p. 43, TTUVA.

65 Ibid.

66 Ibid.; CORDS, "Revolutionary Development Concept," pp. 2–3, TTUVA.

67 Bernard W. Rogers, *Cedar Falls–Junction City: A Turning Point* (Washington, DC: Government Printing Office, 1974, 1989), p. v.

68 Memo: Pacification and Nation-Building in Vietnam—Present Status, Current Trends and Prospects, 17 February 1967, Folder 05, Box 06, Larry Berman Collection (Presidential Archives Research), TTUVA.

69 Memo, Komer to Westmoreland, November 11, 1967. DepCORDS files, U.S. Army Center of Military History, Washington, DC.

70 Vietnam Special Studies Group, The Situation in the Countryside, 13 May1970, p. 13 / RG 472 / A1 462 / Box 17 / Folder: 1601–04A Situation in the Countryside / Draft / #39 / 1970, NARA II.

71 The Hamlet Evaluation System (HES) was a computer-assisted reporting system used to assess the pacification program. It was designed to evaluate the security and development of nearly every hamlet in South Vietnam by examining military activity and the level of social, political, and economic development in regions where there was a government presence. Source: Central Pacification and Development Council, *1970 Pacification and Development Plan*, 1, USAMHI.

72 Southeast Asia (SEA) Analysis Report November/December 1970, p. 1, RG 472 / A1 472 / Box 6 / Folder: Southeast Asia Analysis Reports Mar 1970–Dec 1970, NARA II.

73 Robert W. Komer, *Organization and Management of the "New Model" Pacification Program, 1966–1969* (Santa Monica, CA: RAND Corporation, 1970), p. 90.

74 "Minutes, National Security Council Meeting," September 12, 1969, Department of State Office of the Historian, *Foreign Relations of the United States (FRUS). Volume 6, January 1969–July 1970* (Washington, DC: United States Government Printing Office, 2006), Document No. 120, p. 400.

75 Quoted in Graham A. Cosmas, *MACV: The Joint Command in the Years of Withdrawal, 1968–1973* (Washington, DC: Center of Military History, 1984), p. 245.

76 House Committee on Appropriations, *Department of Defense Appropriations for 1971*, 91st Cong., 2nd sess., 1970, p. 95.

77 The factors that contributed to the Army's spiritual malaise and institutional dysfunction after 1968 included the war's unpopularity, civil and cultural unrest in the United States, ambiguous political and military objectives, a strategically defensive war policy, the conflict's irregular nature, and a defective personnel policy that involved self-defeating terms of enlistment as well as a poorly designed individual rotation system.

78 The argument that firepower-intensive methods, including search-and-destroy operations and attrition, were not only inappropriate but counterproductive within the context of irregular war in South Vietnam has been told so often that it has assumed the guise of conventional wisdom. Among the more well-known works that make this claim are: Robert Thompson, *No Exit from Vietnam* (New York: McKay, 1969); Guenter Lewy, *America in Vietnam* (New York: Oxford University Press, 1978); Andrew F. Krepievich, *The Army and Vietnam* (Baltimore, MD: Johns Hopkins University Press, 1986); Larry E. Cable, *Conflict of Myths: The Development of American Counterinsurgency Doctrine and the Vietnam War* (New York: New York University Press, 1986); Donald W. Hamilton, *The Art of Insurgency: American Military Policy and the Failure of Strategy in Southeast Asia* (Westport, CT: Praeger, 1998).

79 Cao Van Vien and Dong Van Khuyen, *Reflections on the Vietnam War* (Washington, DC: U.S. Army Center of Military History, 1980), p. 49.

80 George C. Herring, *America's Longest War: The United States and Vietnam, 1950–1975* (New York: Wiley, 1979), p. 153.

81 William J. Duiker, *Sacred War: Nationalism and Revolution in a Divided Vietnam* (New York: McGraw-Hill, 1995), p. 206.

82 Eric M. Bergerud, *The Dynamics of Defeat: The Vietnam War in Hau Nghia Province* (Boulder, CO: Westview, 1991), p. 87.

83 Phillip B. Davidson, *Vietnam at War: The History, 1946–1975* (New York: Oxford University Press, 1988), p. 407.

84 Harry G. Summers, *On Strategy: A Critical Analysis of the Vietnam War* (New York: Ballantine, 1982), p. 1.

85 Harry G. Summers, foreword in Stanton, *The Rise and Fall of an American Army*, p. xii.

86 Adrian R. Lewis, *The American Culture of War: The History of U.S. Military Force from World War II to Operation Iraqi Freedom* (New York: Routledge, 2007), p. 264.

PART IV

Searching for a New Paradigm

10

Post-Vietnam Drawdown

The Myth of the Abrams Doctrine

CONRAD C. CRANE

In 1986, Colonel Harry Summers wrote in an article describing the reorientation of the Army drawing down after Vietnam that chief of staff of the Army General Creighton Abrams sought to deliberately create "an interrelated structure that could not be committed to sustained combat without mobilizing the reserves."[1] During the 1970s, the Army shifted many of its combat-support and combat-service-support capabilities to the reserve component (RC), a force structure maintained through the post–Desert Storm drawdown as well. Summers, who was a young major working for Abrams at the time of the reorganization, said it aimed to "correct one of the major deficiencies of the American involvement in the Vietnam War—the commitment of the Army to sustained combat without the explicit support of the American people as expressed by their representatives in Congress."[2] His interpretation became the standard understanding for the primary intent of the "Abrams doctrine" that has shaped the U.S. Army force structure ever since. That view became so entrenched that a study conducted by the Reserve Component Employment Study Group for the Defense Department in 1999 to analyze the advisability of putting more combat-support and combat-service-support capabilities back into the active component (AC) recommended against giving the AC the capacity to conduct contingencies independent of the RC because doing so would eliminate the Army's "political check and balance" preventing the executive branch from committing troops without a debate in Congress on mobilization.[3]

Such an interpretation seems a questionable usurping of the president's constitutional prerogatives. If that was the actual intent of the "Abrams Doctrine," then it also failed miserably to limit innumerable Army deployments in the 1990s and beyond. However, the actual historical record shows that the Army's reorientation of the reserve component started many years before Abrams became chief of staff of the Army, so it was not really his initiative. In addition, his further adjustments to the force structure were more a product of his astute assessment about what he could maintain for the active component of an Army dealing with the new "Total Force" policy, fiscal realities connected to a significant drawdown, perceived mission requirements, and the completion of the shift to an all-volunteer armed force.

By 1969, it was clear to American military leaders that their post-Vietnam force structure would be reduced in size. Because mistrusted reserve forces had not been called up for the war and instead active forces had been expanded through the draft, there was a lot of redundancy between active and reserve components, especially in the Army. This duplication could most easily, and most cheaply, be fixed by reducing active forces. However, Vietnam had also delayed modernization programs for the major combat units of the active component, so shifting support capabilities to the reserves also made sense to save money to facilitate that process. In addition, President Nixon had campaigned with promises to end the draft, and his election portended its demise. Army chief of staff General William Westmoreland had already begun to focus more on reserve capabilities and responsibilities when, in August 1970, Secretary of Defense Melvin Laird issued a memorandum to the services directing them to consider reserve components the primary augmentation for emergencies instead of the draft, as part of the "Total Force" necessary to meet security needs. In 1973, as the draft was phasing out, Secretary of Defense James Schlesinger formally "codified" the concept as the "Total Force Policy which integrates the Active, Reserve, and Guard forces into a homogenous whole."[4]

In the meantime, General Westmoreland continued to pursue other reduction initiatives. He assigned two of the most important to the assistant vice chief of staff of the Army, General William DePuy. The first was the WHEELS Study, which slashed one hundred thousand wheeled vehicles from the Army inventory. Though reduction plans cut total service strength in half, that was only a 22 percent cut in equipment, but it still elicited howls of protest from those "whose ox was gored." The second was called STEADFAST, and involved the reorganization of the unwieldy Continental Army Command. Eventually the school system and Combat Developments Command were also drawn into the mix, resulting in the creation of TRADOC and FORSCOM in 1973.[5]

A common theme in Army drawdowns has been an assault on headquarters staffs. During 2013, Major General Jeffrey Snow of the Department of the Army G-3/5/7 asked the U.S. Army Heritage and Education Center's Historical Services Division to provide some historical examples of successful headquarters reductions. Analysis showed that all such programs were successful in peacetime, but they also were all failures when conflicts began and capabilities had to be recreated. This pattern continued after Vietnam. When General Creighton Abrams became chief of staff in June 1972, he ordered the implementation of the STEADFAST recommendations and went after other headquarters as well. His goal was to decentralize and streamline Army command and control structures. He reorganized Army Material Command while setting up Health Services Command and the Military Personnel Center (MILPERCEN). He also targeted seven overseas commands. His proposal to eliminate U.S. Army Pacific Command (USARPAC) (and eventually commander in chief Pacific Command [CINCPAC] as well), motivated from his experience in Vietnam working with those headquarters, ran into great resistance from the Joint Staff. He eventually did disband USARPAC, and U.S. Army Southern Command as well, though eventually those headquarters had to be reconstituted, since the requirements and missions performed by the Army Service Component Commands did not go away.[6] Those Army headquarters were responsible for many essential support missions for all services as well as some degree of command and control of all ground forces in the theater.

Abrams encountered similar problems trying to reduce his own Department of the Army staff. He believed it was much too big, and cuts there were necessary first in order to lessen the number of people in other headquarters who might be opposed to other aspects of his reorganization. One subordinate speculated that Abrams would have cut his staff in half immediately and then half again later on if he could have.[7] For example, there were between five hundred and six hundred people in the office of the deputy chief of staff for operations (DCSOPS). As a first step before attacking any other reorganization, the new chief of staff wanted that figure reduced to a rather arbitrary 395. As one of his key subordinates recounted later, "The squeals that came out of DCSOPS were fantastic."[8] Yet that staff section was soon brought down to a strength closer to 350, without losing any apparent capability. But that proved a hard level to maintain, especially after DCSOPS absorbed new responsibilities from other consolidations, and within a couple of years, that staff section was back over 650 personnel.[9]

Abrams's drawdown plans would never have been accepted without his astute interpersonal skills, abetted by his reputation as one of the last real American heroes. He had led Patton's spearhead that relieved Bastogne during the Battle of the Bulge, served as a corps chief of staff in Korea, and managed Vietnamization while heading the Military Assistance Command. He was admired and respected, even by those who disagreed with him. But he also took great pains to cultivate relationships and determine how to deal with each decision maker individually. Abrams worked closely with Major

General Francis Greenlief, the chief of the National Guard Bureau, to make sure that the desires of that key component in the reorganization were heard and met.[10] Once Abrams had the new headquarters structure resulting from STEADFAST determined, he did not trust getting it approved by his staff officers or through a large briefing to key decision makers. Instead, he had his staff create a dozen "yellow boards" that he could "shuffle like cards" illustrating what he wanted to do, and he then personally briefed the secretary of the Army and the secretary of defense to get their approval. He followed that with similar personal briefings to the chairpersons and senior minority representatives on the "big four" congressional committees. All of this was completed before he had been in office two months.[11]

But his most masterful performance involved crafting and obtaining the force level for the sixteen-division active force that he so coveted. Neither that number, nor the 785,000 total personnel for the active force, were the result of any sophisticated analysis. The chief of staff sat around with his key subordinates and discussed the strength issue, and they believed those figures were the most reasonable that they could get "in the environment in which we were operating."[12] The next step, and the key one, was to get support for that "judgment call" from Secretary of Defense James Schlesinger. Secretary of the Army Howard "Bo" Calloway went along to introduce the subject, but he let his service chief do all the talking. Abrams was most concerned with end strength, believing he could fashion the structure he wanted within those parameters, but he did not discuss specific numbers at any time during the briefing. Secretary Calloway later stated that the chief of staff's briefing left the secretaries "in a complete state of euphoria." Abrams "never mentioned 785,000, never mentioned the number of divisions he wanted. He crossed the Delaware with Washington, he fought the Civil War, he fought every other war our country's ever had, and when he got all through, Secretary Schlesinger said, 'You're going to get them.'"[13]

With the 785,000 end strength established for the active component, Abrams then told his staff to figure out how to structure the sixteen divisions that he believed were necessary to provide a reasonable chance of meeting strategic requirements without resorting to nuclear weapons.[14] That was quite a shock to his subordinates, considering that Army plans up to that point had contemplated getting a bit over thirteen divisions out of an end strength above eight hundred thousand. Staff planners were forced by necessity to continue the emphasis on transferring combat support and combat-service-support organizations to the reserve component, especially those at corps level and higher. There is no documentation to support Summers's claim that Abrams also had a dominant vision to ensure that no president could ever again fight another Vietnam without mobilization. No Army leader ever mentioned that rationale in any congressional testimony. In fact, Secretary of Defense Schlesinger considered the Army chief of staff the epitome of the "good servant" who always deferred to civilian control of the military and would not purposefully try to circumvent it. However, General John Vessey, who had to conduct many briefings in Washington to explain the "round out concepts" Abrams's staff was developing, stated that the chief of staff definitely intended that effect "with malice aforethought," and they often discussed it between themselves. Other gifted subordinates like Summers also realized the limitations the new structure could place on the executive branch, though they were careful not to trumpet that publicly until a decade later.[15]

Lewis Sorley, in his book *Thunderbolt: General Creighton Abrams and the Army of His Times*, is convinced that Abrams intended to limit presidential power, despite the lack of documentary evidence or mention in contemporary interviews in the Abrams Papers at USAHEC (U.S. Army Heritage and Education Center). If Sorley is indeed correct, than the implications for American civil-military relations are problematic, since it seems clear that the secretary of defense was not aware of that intent. Interpretations that the true motivation for the new force structure was purposefully concealed from civilian leaders or that the justification was only created after the fact to preserve current personnel policies are both troubling. However, it is much more probable that General Abrams was not primarily motivated by the desire to establish that sort of check and balance on military deployments. He and some subordinates might have seen that result as a positive collateral spinoff from the new personnel policies, but it was not a primary reason for them. Harry Summers's influential book *On Strategy: The Vietnam War in Context*, a mishmash of Clausewitzian and Jominian analysis of U.S. involvement in Southeast Asia, distorted American military views of that war for many decades with many negative repercussions.[16] His portrayal of the Abrams doctrine and its motivations has been even more widely accepted, and may have done even more damage to our proper understanding of that war and its outcomes. By the mid-1990s, with the promulgation of the so-called Weinberger and Powell doctrines, many critics of civil-military relations perceived a military "clinging to orthodoxy" that expressed "blanket opposition to missions that fail to conform to their own preferences and priorities," especially those involving peacekeeping operations or irregular warfare. Abrams's perceived creation of the mobilization "check and balance" on the president's ability to deploy military force has been interpreted as the beginning of that trend.[17]

While historians might have some disagreement about the actual intent of the restructuring of the Army after Vietnam, there is more consensus about its actual impact. Not only did presidents continue to deploy the Army on smaller-scale contingencies (SSCs) without congressional approval: those operations often had significant requirements for the same combat-support (CS) and combat-service-support (CSS) capabilities that had been reduced or shifted. And as Heritage Foundation defense analyst James Carafano has pointed out, the new policy did not translate into better reserve component readiness, as such units continued to suffer from serious preparedness problems.[18]

Operations in the 1990s highlighted a number of organizational deficiencies. SSCs strain force structure in a number of special ways. Traditional counts of units deployed in the theater underestimate the total personnel involved in the operation. The number of CS/CSS personnel supporting the mission in Somalia outnumbered soldiers actually serving in the theater by up to four times or more. Cross-leveling of personnel to fill units to wartime strength or for unique requirements can have a considerable ripple effect on readiness. The ten companies of military police that deployed to Somalia required augmentation from sixty-two different units.[19] SSCs are particularly hard on certain active-duty "high-demand/low-density" units in the quartermaster and transportation branches, such as general supply companies and water purification units. Somalia required all of the Army's active air movement control teams and three quarters of the active petroleum supply companies.[20] The Army was forced to increase its supply of active and reserve Civil Affairs personnel to meet shortages revealed by 1990s deployments.[21] Extending the Bosnia mission beyond the six months initially projected highlighted additional inadequacies in the total available number of a variety of other CS/CSS units that are distributed between active and reserve components.[22]

Excessive deployments for SSCs had some negative effect on retention of active soldiers, but had even more significant impact on reserve and National Guard units not accustomed to such use. Considerable portions of the Army's CS and CSS units were in the reserve component as the new millennium opened, including 66 percent of the CS and 72 percent of the CSS in echelons above division units that are often so critical for stabilization phase tasks in SSCs.[23] Whatever Creighton Abrams's motivation to move so much of the Army's CS/CSS structure out of the active component, he could not have foreseen the future course or tempo of service missions. In fiscal year 1986, reserve components contributed nine hundred thousand man-days of service; by fiscal year 1999 that figure had skyrocketed to 12.5 million man-days. Increased deployments also required more training time and caused more problems with concerned civilian employers. Additionally, using reserve forces for peacekeeping missions significantly raised Army costs for personnel, transportation, and training, while heightening awareness of key military occupational specialty shortages in some reserve organizations.[24]

The pace of deployments changed the traditional part-time nature of reserve duty. By the time soldiers from the 49th Division returned from Bosnia, some of them had served more than 380 days of active duty within two years. Twenty-six reportedly filed labor complaints before deploying to keep from losing their civilian jobs.[25] There has been plenty of media coverage about the problems faced by guardsmen and reservists sent overseas on unexpectedly long or repetitive deployments, and the situation is especially acute for those high-demand/low-density CS/CSS units mentioned above.[26]

SSC requirements also had significant potential impact on the Army's ability to fulfill its strategic requirement to fight two major theater wars (MTWs) simultaneously. The Congressional Budget Office noted that the service's rather ad hoc approach to forming task forces for peace operations due to AC/RC imbalances would significantly detract from its ability to garner enough forces for two MTWs.[27] U.S. European Command had to develop a Balkan Disengagement Plan to redeploy its units to other major contingencies that might arise.[28] Analyses of the Army's ability to conduct two nearly simultaneous MTWs revealed many force shortfalls for that particular scenario. The Army National Guard (ARNG) Division Redesign Study recommended the conversion of up to twelve ARNG combat brigades into CS/CSS units to help make up for a shortfall of 124,800 personnel in those specialties identified by Total Army Analysis 2003 as essential to carry out the national military strategy. The Army designated initial units for conversion, but the whole process, which was derailed by requirements for the global war on terrorism, did not adequately address all the shortcomings mentioned in SSC after-action reports.[29]

There are many examples of those. As Operation UPHOLD DEMOCRACY in Haiti dragged on, Army roles and missions expanded throughout the restoration efforts.[30] Other governmental agencies were slow to arrive or build up resources, so the military picked up the slack. Generally, the other departments had not done the detailed planning that the Department of Defense had, and often wanted more support than DoD expected to provide.[31] A typical example was when the ambassador to Haiti asked for military advisers to help set up new government ministries until efforts from the U.S. Agency for International Development and the State Department could be established. The result was a ministerial advisor team from the 358th Civil Affairs (CA) Brigade, "the first large scale implementation of a civil administration effort since World War II."[32] The scope and pace of the missions of CA, a branch whose units are mostly in the reserve component, increased so rapidly that they threatened to spin out of control, and raised fears that such actions would only heighten Haitian expectations that U.S. forces could fix all the nation's problems, and thus set the people up for great disappointment later.[33]

These expanded missions caused many other problems. Engineer planning, equipment, and personnel were inadequate for their required civil affairs and reconstruction projects. Soldiers had to develop new policies and procedures to set up internal security and expend funds. This often required "working around" Title 10, U.S. Code, restrictions. There were not enough military police, so other soldiers assumed expanded roles in maintaining law and order, including staffing and operating detention facilities and developing new crowd control techniques. Items like latrines and police uniforms were in short supply. Neither personnel were available to establish proper liaison with the myriad civilian organizations working in the country, nor doctrine to inform decisions. As in previous SSCs, intelligence assets were severely taxed, and the force in Haiti had to rely heavily on theater and national intelligence assets to make up for deficiencies.[34]

As the nature of the stability operations and support operations in the Balkans evolved, so did the requirements of the peacekeeping force. The mission demanded fewer combat troops and more engineers, military police, and civil affairs personnel. Intelligence requirements changed and expanded. After-action reports highlighted many shortfalls in force structure and peacekeeping policies, many of them common to previous SSCs. Army lawyers again proved adept at "thinking outside traditional fiscal rules and applications" to support operational requirements.[35] The roles of scarce military policemen expanded to include performing as maneuver battalion task forces and working with international law enforcement agencies.[36] There were problems with shortages and recall procedures for RC engineer, military intelligence, and civil affairs augmentation.[37] The massive engineering requirements for Operations JOINT ENDEAVOR and JOINT GUARD especially highlighted branch deficiencies with command and control, construction unit allocations, and bridging.[38] A split-based logistics system trying to meet requirements both in the Balkans and back in the Central Region of Europe required considerable augmentation and still strained CS/CSS assets considerably.[39] Liaison officers were in great demand, not just as Joint Commission observers with the Entity Armed Forces but also to coordinate with the myriad non-governmental organizations and other agencies.[40] There were shortages of linguists throughout the theater, which especially exacerbated problems with intelligence. Military intelligence doctrine was completely inadequate for supporting peace operations, and understaffed intelligence units had to adapt as best they could for the complex "multi-service, multi-agency, and multi-national" situation further complicated by a host of treaty requirements.[41]

Contrary to the argument for the "Abrams Doctrine" first made by Harry Summers, there is no documentary evidence that in the drawdown after Vietnam, General Creighton Abrams purposefully intended to create an Army structured to force the president to obtain congressional approval to deploy it. If he actually did have that goal, as some claim, then he failed miserably. Not only did later presidents freely send soldiers into SSCs around the world, but the perception that the Army had actively tried to prevent such deployments provided ammunition for many critics of civil-military relations. There is plenty of evidence that Abrams wanted to preserve active component divisions, and his staff continued ongoing programs to shift CS/CSS assets to the reserve component to successfully achieve that short-term objective. There was an ironic long-term cost, however. For when the Army of the 1990s was deployed to those SSCs that the Abrams Doctrine was supposedly designed to avoid, the force found itself deficient in those very CS/CSS elements that had been cut or shifted, but were found to be essential to stability and peacekeeping operations.

General Creighton Abrams faced the common dilemma of all Army chiefs of staff after wars: how to shape the force in the face of an inevitable drawdown. His solution provided the structure he thought the future would require, and he proved surprisingly successful in getting the force that he desired. It operated magnificently in Operation DESERT STORM, but after another drawdown eliminated many of those division flags he had tried so hard to save, the AC/RC imbalance resulting from his "doctrine" would cause increasing strains for soldiers in the SSCs that some claim it was designed to avert. While this case reveals the deft way in which Abrams was able to execute his vision for Army force structure, it also illustrates the difficulty of accurately predicting what the future missions of the service will be.

NOTES

1 Colonel Harry G. Summers Jr., "The Army after Vietnam," in Kenneth J. Hagan and William B. Roberts, eds., *Against All Enemies* (Westport, CT: Greenwood, 1986), 363.

2 Ibid.

3 Reserve Component Employment Study Group, *Reserve Component Employment 2005 Study Report* (Washington, DC: DoD, 1999), 1, 12–13, Annex E. By that time the concept of the "Abrams Doctrine" was firmly ensconced in policy documents throughout the government.

4 Richard B. Crossland and James T. Currie, *Twice the Citizen: A History of the United States Army Reserve, 1908–1983* (Washington, DC: Office of the Chief, Army Reserve, 1984), 212–15; Leslie Lewis, C. Robert Roll, and John D. Mayer, *Assessing the Structure and Mix of Future Active and Reserve Forces: Assessment of Policies and Practices for Implementing the Total Force Policy* (Santa Monica, CA: RAND, 1992), 1.

5 Romie L. Brownlee and William J. Mullen III, *Changing an Army: An Oral History of General William E. DePuy, USA Retired* (Washington, DC: USGPO, 1988), 174–79.

6 Interview of LTG Donald Cowles by LTC Albin G. Wheeler and LTC Ronald E. Craven, pp. 49–51; and Interview of GEN James G. Kalergis by LTC Tom Lightner, pp. 18, 28–29, both in "The General Creighton Abrams Story" files, Papers of Creighton Abrams, U.S. Army Heritage and Education Center, Carlisle Barracks, PA.

7 Kalergis, 28.

8 Cowles, 40.

9 Ibid., 40–41.

10 Kalergis, 25.

11 Ibid., 30–31.

12 Cowles, 41.

13 Ibid., 41–42.

14 Divisions were considered the key organizational building block for determining Army capabilities. Those two-star commands also had a major influence on how many general officer billets the service received.

15 Lewis Sorley, *Thunderbolt: General Creighton Abrams and the Army of His Times* (New York: Simon & Schuster, 1992), 350–68.

16 The traditional American approach to war, inspired by the military theorist Henri Jomini, has been an engineering one based on applying universal tenets epitomized by the Principles of War. On the surface, Summers's book seems to be based upon the more complex theories of Carl von Clausewitz, who emphasizes the role of politics, chance, and genius in war. In reality, Summers tries to take Clausewitz and shoehorn his dictums into Jominian principles.

17 Sorley, 35–68. Conrad C. Crane, *Avoiding Vietnam: The U.S. Army's Response to Defeat in Southeast Asia* (Carlisle Barracks, PA: Strategic Studies Institute, 2002), 6–16; A. J. Bacevich, "The Use of Force," *Wilson Quarterly* 19 (Winter 1995): 56.

18 James Jay Carafano, "The Army Reserves and the Abrams Doctrine: Unfulfilled Promise, Uncertain Future," *Heritage Lectures No. 869*, Heritage Foundation, April 18, 2005, http://www.heritage.org/research/lecture/the-army-reserves-and-the-abrams-doctrine-unfulfilled-promise-uncertain-future.

19 Stephen J. Hosmer, et al., *Bettering the Balance: Large Wars and Small Contingencies*, RAND Arroyo Center, 1997, p. 2, available on the RAND website at http://www.rand.org/publications/IP/IP167/.

20 Congressional Budget Office, *Making Peace While Staying Ready for War: The Challenges of U.S. Military Participation in Peace Operations* (Washington, DC: Congressional Budget Office, December 1999), chapter 3, p. 5.

21 U.S. Government Accounting Office, *Contingency Operations: Providing Critical Capabilities Poses Challenges*, GAO/NSIAD-00-164 (Washington, DC: U.S. Government Accounting Office, July 2000), p. 5.

22 U.S. Government Accounting Office, *Bosnia: Military Services Providing Needed Capabilities but a Few Challenges Emerging*, GAO/NSIAD-98-160 (Washington, DC: U.S. Government Accounting Office, April 1998), pp. 7–9. These units include Broadcast Public Affairs Detachments, Replacement Battalion Headquarters, Rear Tactical Operations Centers, Target Acquisition Detachments, Movement Control Battalion Headquarters, Centralized Movement Control Teams, Air Terminal Movement Control Teams, Public Affairs Detachments, Engineering Fire Fighter Detachments, Military History Detachments, and Medical Distribution Units.

23 U.S. Army Program Analysis and Evaluation Directorate, *America's Army . . . into the 21st Century* (Washington, DC: HQDA, 1997), p. 9.

24 Reserve Forces Policy Board, *Reserve Component Programs* (Washington, DC: Office of the Secretary of Defense, March 2000), xxvii; U.S. Government Accounting Office, *Force Structure: Army Is Integrating Active and Reserve Combat Forces, but Challenges Remain*, GAO/NSIAD-00-162 (Washington, DC: U.S. Government Accounting Office, July 2000).

25 David T. Fautua, "Army Citizen-Soldiers: Active, Guard, and Reserve Leaders Remain Silent about Overuse of Reserve Components," *Armed Forces Journal International*, September 2000, pp. 72–74.

26 Steven Lee Myers, "Military Reserves Are Falling Short in Finding Recruits," *New York Times*, August 28, 2000, p. 1; Marsha Low, "Military Reserves Fall Short," *Detroit Free Press*, September 11, 2000; Myers, "Fallout in Texas from Bosnia Duty," *New York Times*, September 15, 2000; David Foster, "More Missions for Part-Time Soldiers Strain Lives at Home," *Boston Globe*, September 23, 2000, p. 4; Deborah Martinez, "Reserve Ranks Dwindle as Number of Deployments Increases," *Corpus Christi Caller-Times*, September 24, 2000; "U.S. Leans Too Heavily on Guard, Reserves," *Austin American-Statesman*, October 11, 2000, 10.

27 *Making Peace While Staying Ready for War*, summary, p. 7.

28 "Pentagon Crafts 'Balkan Disengagement Plan' in Event of Major War," *Inside the Pentagon*, September 7, 2000, p. 1.

29 Major General William A. Navas Jr., *Army National Guard Fiscal Year 1999 Posture Statement* (Arlington, VA: ANG Office of Policy and Communication, 1999), pp. 7–8; Army National Guard Bureau, "Army National Guard Division Redesign Study Phase I Update," briefing (Washington, DC: Army National Guard Bureau, October 13, 1999).

30 This expansion of missions is evident from the Operation UPHOLD DEMOCRACY Logistics Support Operations briefing from CINCUSACOM

CD-ROM, *Operation UPHOLD DEMOCRACY: U.S. Forces in Haiti*, U.S. Atlantic Command, 1997. Copy in U.S. Army War College Library, Carlisle, PA.

31 Joint Universal Lessons Learned System entry 10829–67459, USACOM CD-ROM, *Operation UPHOLD DEMOCRACY: U.S. Forces in Haiti*. Copy in U.S. Army War College Library, Carlisle, PA. Civilian agencies did not have the staff structure, standard procedures, or training to conduct such planning.

32 Memorandum, from 358th Civil Affairs Brigade to Commanding General, U.S. Army Civil Affairs and Psychological Operations Command, SUBJECT: After Action Report, USACOM Operation Uphold/Maintain Democracy, May 26, 1995, p. 3, USACOM CD-ROM, *Operation UPHOLD DEMOCRACY: U.S. Forces in Haiti*. Copy in U.S. Army War College Library, Carlisle, PA.

33 Joint Universal Lessons Learned System entry 11566–55234, USACOM CD-ROM, *Operation UPHOLD DEMOCRACY: U.S. Forces in Haiti*. Copy in U.S. Army War College Library, Carlisle, PA.

34 Joint Universal Lessons Learned System entries 00676–58398, 00969–70100, 01040–06216, 02656–20553, 10355–63106, 10447–74360, 10758–27517, 11558–362234, 11640–05029, 11640–61460, 50257–20594, 50258–39326, 92638–89373, USACOM CD-ROM, *Operation UPHOLD DEMOCRACY: U.S. Forces in Haiti*. Copy in U.S. Army War College Library, Carlisle, PA.

35 Headquarters, U.S. Army Europe, *After Action Report: Operation Joint Guard*, November 1998, pp. 9–26. U.S. Army Heritage and Education Center, Carlisle, PA.

36 Ibid., pp. 9–36.

37 *After Action Report: Operation Joint Guard*, pp. 4–5, 5–18. Problems were so acute that the AAR asked for both the reserves and the National Guard to realign their units and specialties for peacekeeping missions.

38 Colonel David A. Kingston, *Towards a More Relevant Engineer Command* (Carlisle Barracks, PA: USAWC, 2000); Headquarters, U.S. Army Europe, *Operation Joint Endeavor: After Action Report*, May 1997, pp. 206, 210, U.S. Army Heritage and Education Center, Carlisle, PA.

39 *Operation Joint Endeavor*, pp. 130–31.

40 Center for Army Lessons Learned, *Joint Military Commissions: Lessons Learned from Operation Joint Endeavor* (Fort Leavenworth, KS, May 1996).

41 *Operation Joint Endeavor*, pp. 78–94; Lieutenant Colonel Melissa E. Patrick, *Intelligence in Support Operations: The Story of Task Force Eagle and Operation Joint Endeavor* (Carlisle Barracks, PA: USAWC, 2000).

11

The "Good" Drawdown

The Post-Vietnam Alignment of Resources

ANTULIO J. ECHEVARRIA II

Vietnam is over and I don't have to make the obvious point that
the world conditions have changed. We no longer enjoy any advantages, conventional or integrated.
—General Donn Starry, 1980[1]

It may seem contradictory to refer to any drawdown of U.S. military forces
as "good," particularly if it took place while they were attempting to deter
a much larger opposing force. Yet, that was ultimately the case for the U.S.
Army during the period of downsizing that followed the Vietnam War.
The units that deployed to Desert Shield/Desert Storm in 1990/1991, fifteen
years after the end of the Vietnam War, were among the best the Army has
ever fielded. They were transformed into effective fighting units, it is commonly said, due to the hard work of senior officers and noncommissioned
officers who dedicated themselves to "fixing" the Army's shortcomings in
recruitment, training, doctrine, and equipment.[2] That story is generally true.
However, it is also true that the Army rebounded from its low point in the
years just after Vietnam because it returned to a clearly defined and critical
mission, namely, deterrence, and its leaders openly and repeatedly renewed
their commitment to accomplishing that mission. Without deterrence, the
Army's personnel, training, and equipment programs would have lacked the
coherence necessary to complete its rebirth.

What the example of the post-Vietnam downsizing shows, as do other case
studies in this volume more or less, is that a successful drawdown depends
not only on how well the Army manages those things over which it has direct control, such as its training and doctrine, but also on how it influences
those things over which it exercises only indirect control, such as its primary
national security mission. It is widely believed the Army does not have the
power to choose its missions, but that is only partially correct because it is not
obliged to assume a passive role in the way its missions are defined. Certainly,

it cannot opt to carry out only specific kinds of missions, but it can shape its missions, and it can shape policymakers' expectations about any mission. The Army has control over how seriously it takes any mission it receives, and it can influence how earnestly U.S. policymakers take such missions as well. The Army chose to focus predominantly on deterrence and warfighting after Vietnam, and it was able to convince American political leaders of the need to give priority to those missions, which resulted in greater fiscal support from Congress and increased trust on behalf of the public. Unfortunately, the Army maintained its focus on deterrence and warfighting too narrowly and for too long, well after it had demonstrated an obvious and unparalleled expertise in those missions, at the expense of those operations—such as large-scale counterinsurgencies—that were not truly warfighting, but were far more than "lesser includeds."

The Army's post-Vietnam drawdown might have been one of the good ones, but it did not start out that way. The first six years, from 1973 to 1979, were extremely painful ones, characterized by pay compression, declining enlistment rates, high attrition, low morale, and egregious "mis-norming." In 1973, more than fifteen thousand soldiers had tested positive for drug use; by 1979, more than twenty-two thousand soldiers were officially enrolled in drug and alcohol rehabilitation programs.[3] In 1979, basic military pay was such that one-third of service members in the ranks of E-4 and below qualified for food stamps. As regards "mis-norming," the U.S. military "thought it was accepting 5 percent of its personnel from those with AFQT IV [Armed Forces Qualification Test], when in fact during 1977–79 over one-quarter of all active recruits with no prior service were AFQT IV."[4] Even President Richard M. Nixon, who had earlier championed the transition to a volunteer Army, was moved to refer to it as a failure. "I considered the end of the draft in 1973 to be one of the major achievements of my administration," he wrote. "Now seven years later, I have reluctantly concluded that we should reintroduce the draft . . . the volunteer army has failed to produce enough of the quality personnel we need."[5] His words amounted to a clear indictment of a six-year-long experiment, and, perhaps unremarkably, they met with little disagreement from the Army's senior leadership. In fact, in 1980, Army chief of staff General Edward C. Meyer openly referred to the all-volunteer force as a "Hollow Army," though the metaphor was also used in a number of contexts by other officers, and for reasons having little to do with Meyer's.[6] For his part, Meyer considered the Army's forward forces in Europe, Korea, and Panama to be at full strength; however, tactical forces within the United States (aside from the 82nd Airborne Division) were "some 17,000 under strength" with numerous companies and platoons "zeroed out."[7] The Army's official historical summary for fiscal year 1979 affirms that of the ten divisions stationed state-side, only four were capable of deploying overseas in an emergency.[8]

The Army's numbers had dropped precipitously, from a conscript force of 1.3 million to an all-volunteer force of approximately 780,000 personnel. That equated to a reduction of nearly 40 percent of its personnel strength. Fortunately, the next decade was one of rebirth for the Army—materially, morally, and intellectually. The Army's recruiting slogan, "Be All You Can Be," seemed to speak not only to the young men and women it wished to attract at the time but also to the self-image it desired to project. The 1980s saw better pay; more realistic and rigorous training, reflected in part by the establishment of the National Training Center (NTC); and higher standards both for the trainers, in this case the Opposing Forces or OPFOR, and those units benefiting from the training. The institution of the after-action review, or AAR, was also instrumental.

The Army of the 1980s was able to focus on critical warfighting missions, especially deterrence of the Warsaw Pact in Europe and of North Korea in Asia. Its elite units, such as the Rangers, the 82nd Airborne Division, and the 101st Airborne Air-Assault Division, stood ready to handle the so-called lesser includeds. Its overall force structure of eighteen active duty divisions (thirteen heavy, eleven light) and eight reserve divisions was robust, especially by contemporary metrics.[9] It was a balanced force of heavy, light, and specialty units, all of which also addressed the major combat functions essential to the modern, integrated battle—which necessitated the "close interaction between all air and ground capabilities" so as to win not only the "close fight" but also the "deep battle" against the enemy's follow-on echelons.[10] Moreover, the Total Force Concept, initiated by Secretary of Defense Melvin Laird, helped increase (at least on paper) the personnel available for deployment without the costly burden of maintaining a large standing Army. Along similar lines, the "Roundout" brigade concept was designed to plus-up (or round out) a two-brigade active Army division with a National Guard maneuver brigade to form a three-brigade division.

These policies became controversial in the way they were executed, however, and inspired calls for reform.[11] Military professionals of any era would probably argue that attracting quality personnel is more important than adding new weapons and equipment. However, the Army's programs to upgrade its primary weapon systems, the "Big 5," meant its rebirth was to be taken seriously. The new systems were the Abrams Main Battle Tank, the Bradley Infantry Fighting Vehicle, the Patriot Missile System, the Blackhawk Helicopter, and the Apache Attack Helicopter.[12] These would be outnumbered by the Soviet "Big 7" (T-72 Tank, BMP Amphibious Assault Vehicle, ZSU-23/4 Anti-Aircraft Weapon, MI-24 Hind-D Helicopter, M-1973 152MM SP Gun, M-1974

122MM SP Gun, SA-3 Gecko Surface-to-Air Weapon), but were considered more than a match qualitatively.[13] Although these programs were not without their growing pains, the U.S. Department of Defense's investment in them paralleled its investment in attracting and developing quality personnel.

The Army also had significant tactical and operational challenges to address in order to prepare itself for its deterrence mission. The first of these concerned how to restore mobility to the battlefield. As the 1973 Arab-Israeli conflict demonstrated, the "lethality" of the battlefield had increased tremendously with the greater range and accuracy of modern weapons. Egyptian antitank weapons, especially wire-guided missiles, and anti-aircraft missiles, surprised the Israelis by inflicting heavier losses than anticipated.[14] The war demonstrated the effectiveness of Soviet weapons, as well as the need for new tactics and other countermeasures. This newfound lethality was aptly expressed in the motto, "If it can be seen, it can be hit; if it can be hit, it can be killed." Its implications for the Army, indeed for any armed force, was that attrition-style strategies would rule the day. That was not a situation NATO forces could accept. The Warsaw Pact outnumbered NATO by a ratio ranging from 1.2:1 to 2.4:1, depending on mobilization and deployment timetables, one's assessments of the varying caliber of the military and paramilitary formations involved, and the decade in which the assessments occurred.[15]

The period of the 1970s, for instance, was characterized as one of "pessimism" by Western defense analysts due to the low morale and lack of readiness of U.S. forces, which constituted roughly 35–40 percent of NATO strength.[16] In contrast, as the invasion of Afghanistan (1979–1989) began to sap Soviet combat power during the 1980s, the military balance in Europe inclined more in NATO's favor. Furthermore, Soviet doctrine reportedly urged using every possible combat-multiplier, including chemical, biological, and nuclear weapons. Depending upon how such weapons were used, and where the Warsaw Pact's main effort was weighted, their effects might create gaps in NATO's defenses, especially if they were launched into rear areas and against densely populated urban centers. The harm inflicted on noncombatants and civilian infrastructure would have been catastrophic, and would surely have impaired NATO's ability to shift forces to counter the Soviet main effort. If attacked with such weapons of mass destruction, NATO might well have responded in kind, but the result along the front lines might still have favored the attacker. "Fight Outnumbered and Win" thus became NATO's and the U.S. military's motto. The U.S. Army's "Big 5," in fact, were designed in part to fight and win against superior odds and in "dirty" environments.

The strategic situation in Western Europe gave rise to two schools of thought within the U.S. military in general, and the Army in particular. These were known broadly as the "maneuverist" and "attritionist" schools, and their debates raged fiercely across the pages of U.S. military journals. One expert referred to the back-and-forth between these schools as "the longest, most intoxicating and creative professional debate which ever occurred in the history of American military thought."[17] It is not clear how "intoxicating" they were to those outside these schools of thought; however, the debates themselves were at once evidence of the growth, or regrowth, of operational expertise within the U.S. Army—which drew precepts from the study of not only Wehrmacht and modern Israeli Defense Force doctrines but also numerous classical theorists—as well as proof of how far it had yet to go. The opposing schools at times misrepresented each other in the enthusiasm with which they argued their positions; in the process, they also distorted both the meaning of attrition and the nature of maneuver. The debates were also a by-product of the U.S. military's transition from a doctrine of "Active Defense" (1976) to that of "AirLand Battle" (1982).[18] The former was linked, unfairly, to the attritionist school, while the latter was related, inaccurately, to the maneuverist school.

AirLand Battle was about much more than maneuver and, in fact, represented a novel synthesis of modern and classical theories of war fused together within a practical, conceptually sound, yet complex framework. The basic concept was easy enough to grasp: to engage the multi-echeloned formations of the Warsaw Pact simultaneously, though through different systems, and to synchronize strikes throughout the depth of the battlefield with a focus on disrupting, if not destroying, the enemy's main effort. Not only was it based on out-maneuvering the enemy in multiple dimensions—physical, psychological, electromagnetic, and so on—but also it relied on accurate and timely attrition of key targets, such as command centers. It was not only the right answer for the U.S. Army, given its numerical inferiority; it was also the best answer for NATO. The key principles of AirLand Battle were concrete and familiar enough for other Western militaries to internalize, and it suited the larger military strategy of deterrence. However, it is highly unlikely that a conscript force could have mastered its four famous tenets—agility, initiative, depth, and synchronization—well enough to manage them against a numerically superior foe on a highly fluid and lethal battlefield. It is also worth noting that it took the Army six years to arrive at AirLand Battle after having instituted Active Defense. By then, the Cold War was already in its final decade, albeit few defense analysts, if any, realized as much. The point is that even with the ever-present threat of war, the Army still required considerable time to develop, test, and train its operational doctrine.

The U.S. Army also embraced the concept of an operational level of war at this time, the idea of which was to facilitate the difficult task of converting political (or strategic) aims into actionable military objectives, and to ensure that tactical actions were executed according to a larger scheme, or campaign, which in turn ultimately met the goals of strategy.[19] It also served a secondary, but crucial function in that it enabled the "plugging in" of various multinational contingents, each of which came in sundry sizes and operated under different tactical doctrines, command authorities, and logistical systems. The operational level of war, generally associated with corps-level headquarters, thus provided NATO with a common command framework, and associated procedures and protocols, capable of coordinating a broad range of military operations.

Nonetheless, instituting the operational level of war was not without controversy. Two key issues were at the center of this controversy. The first was whether the operational level of war gave military commanders too much authority, and at the same time shielded them from political guidance or "influence." The second issue was that the operational level of war and "operational art" came to take center stage in professional military education, at the expense of the study of military strategy. This result, as some have argued, may have created a generation (or more) of officers well schooled in conducting military operations, but less skilled in crafting strategies.[20] The Army was also very visible in what some scholars have referred to as the Clausewitzian "Renaissance," which included the study of the nature of war, its fundamental principles, and the roles of friction and chance, as well as strategic and operational concepts such as center of gravity.[21] The 1986 edition of Field Manual 100-5 declared that the "essence of operational art" was "the identification of the enemy's operational center of gravity and the concentration of superior combat power against that point to achieve decisive success."[22] The center-of-gravity concept, and similar terms, were far from easy to pin down and gave rise to endless debates, many of which remain unresolved. Nevertheless, they offer evidence of the rebirth of professional interest within the Army, and its tolerance for dissenting opinions.

In some ways, the operational level of war allowed for the "restoration" of conventional conflict, at least in staff colleges and war colleges, and map studies and training maneuvers in Western Europe, such as the annual "Reforger" exercise (Return of Forces to Germany). This restoration would prove instrumental to the Army's rebirth, for it was the service responsible for large-scale operations and sustainability. The threat of nuclear escalation had made conventional war seem obsolete. Clearly, no modern state could afford to risk a general conflict on the scale of the Second World War. Consequently, armed conflict seemed to have become a matter of so-called small wars—except within the context of large-scale deterrence missions in which war could be fought again and again as a series of "what if" scenarios, and as an exercise for commanders and staff officers to practice their skills. Even if a large-scale land war was something to be deterred, rather than fought, one still needed a well-equipped and well-trained Army for it.

By the early 1990s, a "new" body of doctrine was under development; it was officially referred to, somewhat unfortunately, as "military operations other than war," or MOOTW.[23] This doctrine covered missions ranging from show of force to humanitarian assistance. The phrase was unfortunate because it implied that such operations were outside war and, by extension, less important than war; hence, the term "lesser-includeds." As the campaigns in Iraq and Afghanistan would later show, some counterinsurgency operations, even when conducted against an enemy relatively small in number, were something more than a lesser included. The Army conducted some half-dozen so-called lesser includeds during this period: El Salvador (1979–1991), Colombia (1978–2011), the aborted rescue operation in Iran (1980), Grenada (1983), Panama (1989), and Somalia (1992–1994), though this one was technically just outside the timeline under examination here. The interventions in El Salvador and Colombia have been described as "wins" by defense pundits.[24] The U.S. intervention in El Salvador (fifty-five advisors, $6 billion) did not actually bring about victory for the Salvadoran armed forces, but it prevented their defeat at the hands of Marxist insurgents. Similarly, U.S. assistance to Colombia (eight hundred soldiers, six hundred contractors, $7 billion) since 2000 coincided with the success of President Alvaro Uribe's new strategy, which reduced the size and influence of the FARC (Revolutionary Armed Forces of Colombia).

The post-Vietnam era also saw Army officers make increasing references to "come as you are wars," or what some analysts later called "no notice, no plan" operations. The operation in Grenada (October 1983) was one such war for which no real contingency plan existed.[25] From October 25 to November 2, 1983, a joint force of Army rangers, Navy seals, Marines, and paratroopers conducted a series of airborne and amphibious assaults to rescue nearly seven hundred U.S. and other civilians.[26] The operation took place with little prior planning and coordination, and incomplete combat intelligence; however, these shortfalls only underscored the importance of operational science—the analysis of the mission, the gathering of intelligence, the development and selection of courses of action.[27]

In contrast, planning for Operation Just Cause (December 1989) began some twenty-two months before the actual commitment of troops. Combat intelligence was much more detailed, though far from perfect, and the forces scheduled to participate were able to rehearse their roles some weeks beforehand.[28] In a joint operation that lasted eleven days, a U.S. force comprised of twenty-eight thousand troops (Army rangers, airborne troops, light infantry, Navy seals, and Marines) overcame approximately fifteen thousand Panamanian Defense Forces and captured dictator Manuel Noriega.[29] In many ways, Just Cause benefited from the after-action reviews conducted for previous operations, such as Desert One in Iran and the intervention in Grenada. By comparison, the after-action analyses of U.S. operations in Somalia were extensive, despite the relatively small size of the forces involved.[30] One reason for this attention was the high casualties—nineteen killed and ninety-one wounded—most of which came from the Joint Special Operations Task Force Ranger's battle in the middle of Mogadishu on the night of October 3–4, 1993.[31] The task force had the mission of capturing Somali warlord Mohamed Farah Aideed, who was disrupting the humanitarian assistance operations within the city and its surroundings. The task force's casualties were considered avoidable—had the armor and other support requested for the quick reaction force been provided. However, U.S. Defense Secretary Les Aspin, who stepped down in the aftermath of the failed operation, had denied the request.[32]

One might summarize these half-dozen operations, albeit crudely, as four "wins" and two "losses." Such a perspective would in turn suggest that the theory of "lesser includeds" was about right; indeed, such an outlook may well have misled the Army and the analysts within the Defense Department into believing that the Army's situation was healthier than it actually was. Ironically, the U.S. Army had a well-developed body of doctrine concerning guerrilla warfare and insurgencies that had emerged during the Korean conflict. Examples include FM 31–20 Operations against Guerilla Forces (February 1951); FM 31–21 Organization and Conduct of Guerilla Warfare (October 1951; updated 1955 and 1958); and FM 31–15 Operations against Airborne Attack, Guerilla Action, and Infiltration (January 1953). In addition, articles began to appear more frequently in professional journals regarding guerilla warfare and how to counter it. This doctrine was revised and updated during the Vietnam conflict, though the U.S. Special Forces assumed the lead for these missions. The new publications included FM 31–15 Irregular Forces (May 1961); FM 31–16 Counterguerilla Operations (February 1963; updated March 1967); FM 31–22 U.S. Army Counterinsurgency Forces (November 1963); FM 31–73 Advisor Handbook for Counterinsurgencies (April 1965); and Advisor Handbook for Stability Operations (October 1967).[33] One might debate the effectiveness of some of the methods or techniques outlined in this body of doctrine.[34] However, an initial base of knowledge clearly did exist—going back to 1860—concerning how to deal with guerrilla warfare and insurgencies.[35] The larger problem for the U.S. Army, then, was its failure "to remember" and to access its own institutional knowledge.

Conclusions and Recommendations

The post-Vietnam drawdown was one of the "good" ones, but it came at a price. Initially, it unfolded much too quickly with the rapid transition to an all-volunteer force, and the imposed changes were too radical. After the first six years, the Army managed to transform into a better-quality (though less than perfect) fighting force. This transformation was occasioned by the introduction of state-of-the-art weaponry (the Big 5), along with new doctrine, and a revolution in training. The deterrence mission in Europe and Korea was central to the Army's rebirth; it gave the Army a *raison d'etre* that justified its force structure, and it provided a "floor," an end strength the Army could not fall below without jeopardizing deterrence. It could also do some of the so-called lesser includeds, but these would fall primarily to the Army's elite and specialty units.

It was also a healthy period, generally, for the Army in terms of developing and augmenting its professional knowledge. It discovered the operational level of war and developed an elegant maneuver doctrine that proved itself in Desert Storm. However, this discovery was a double-edged sword. On the one hand, it boosted the sense of professionalism within the Army by carving out an area of study with which professionals could concern themselves. On the other hand, it also narrowed their focus to the study of operations at the expense of military strategy and what one might call the lower end of the spectrum of operations. Army officers also generally studied three types of warfare—conventional, unconventional (including counterinsurgency and military operations other than war), and nuclear war—though not to the same degree or with the same intensity. Nonetheless, there was no holistic concept of war to put these into perspective.

Regrettably, the Army and U.S. citizens paid the price in Iraq and Afghanistan for its decision to concentrate overwhelmingly on deterrence and warfighting. With the collapse of the Berlin Wall and the dissolution of the Warsaw Pact, the bulk of the Army's conventional deterrence mission evaporated. The deterrence mission in Korea remained, of course; but South West Asia (Iraq) posed only a modest, on-and-off-again threat. In short, the strategic situation reversed itself and deterrence became the "lesser included" mission; instead, operations other than war have become the lion's share of what contemporary armed forces are asked to do. The Army's focus on deterrence and warfighting left it ill prepared to conduct the more difficult of those operations, counterinsurgencies, except with respect to elite and specialty units. As a result, the Army after 9/11 had to adapt on the fly, which many units did well but without the benefit of prior training or doctrine, to a situation in Iraq that by the mid-2000s was spiraling out of control. This adaptation was hardly the "revolution" some have claimed. Counterinsurgency concepts and doctrine had long been part of the Army's professional knowledge. However, they were buried deep in its institutional memory and needed to be rediscovered. Hence, it is more accurate to see this adaptation as a "renaissance" since the basic techniques had to be rediscovered, republished, and taught anew.

The Vietnam case suggests the following observations for the Army going forward. First, how well the Army manages its drawdown depends less on its ability to assess its past operational performance, though that is important, and more on its ability to prepare itself for its next mission. The two are not always related. The Army has direct control over its own postwar assessment; it can conduct as extensive an after-action review of its own performance as it desires.[36] In so doing, it should keep in mind the nature of the missions it conducted in Iraq and Afghanistan; these missions do not necessarily have clear-cut outcomes. The Army should acknowledge this fact and incorporate it into its after-action reviews and professional education efforts without allowing it to become an "excuse" or a justification for dismissing such missions as aberrations, as it did after Vietnam. Rather, it should find ways to deal with this ambiguity more effectively—as in helping political leaders manage their expectations—while also not allowing the "strategic communications" campaigns of other armies, some of which claim longstanding expertise in such missions, to create false impressions.

Perhaps the most critical factor in a healthy drawdown is the nature of the Army's "next" mission, and its willingness to put that mission at the center of its personnel, training, and equipment programs. That was true after Vietnam, and will probably prove true in the decades ahead. The Army can and should influence the expectations of the country's political leadership; it has done so rather effectively in the past, particularly during the era before the Vietnam War.[37] If the Army concentrates only on internal issues, such as its personnel policies or training programs, it will probably forfeit its ability to manage a drawdown over the long term. Instead, it should also devote energy to addressing external issues, such as the military implications of the changing strategic environment. Obviously, the Army does not have direct control over its "next" mission. However, it can raise awareness of the kinds of missions the strategic environment might require, such as greater deterrence posture in Eastern Europe, and how the Army's capabilities make it well suited for such missions. It can and should, in other words, proactively shape policymakers' perceptions and help frame defense debates. However, if it portrays that environment as too complex, too ambiguous, too uncertain, and too volatile, it may well paint itself into a proverbial corner from which it cannot persuade decision makers that it is capable of handling the situation. The Army should shape the discussion toward missions rather than conditions.

To be sure, good fortune in the form of a presidential administration under Ronald Reagan, which sought to strengthen America's defense posture, helped validate the Army's focus on deterrence. That focus culminated in the victory of Desert Storm and enabled the Army to put the ghost of Vietnam behind it. As President George Bush declared in March 1991, "the specter of Vietnam has been buried forever in the desert sands of the Arabian Peninsula."[38] That specter was not entirely exorcised, however. The lack of progress in Operation Iraqi Freedom between 2004 and 2007 led some critics to wonder whether Iraq was becoming another "quagmire" like Vietnam, costing a great deal in blood and treasure but delivering little in return.[39] Moreover, contemporary debates over the efficacy of counterinsurgency doctrine hinge on whether the Army repeated the mistakes of Vietnam by transitioning to counterinsurgency techniques too late or by failing to carry them through properly.[40] Thus, the ghost of Vietnam still lingers. Nevertheless, the years ahead may see that ghost displaced by the more recent specter of Iraq; avoiding "another Iraq" may become just as important to policymakers as avoiding "another Vietnam" was previously. In other words, the Army can almost certainly count on having another opportunity to remake itself.

NOTES

1   Donn A. Starry, "Army of the Future," U.S. Army Material Development and Readiness Command Executive Seminar, Feb. 14, 1980, in Lewis Sorely, ed., *Press On! Selected Works of Don A. Starry*, vol. 2 (Leavenworth, KS: Combat Studies Institute, 2009), 669.

2   James Kitfield, *Prodigal Soldiers: How the Generation of Officers Born of Vietnam Revolutionized the American Style of War* (Washington, DC: Brassey's, 1995); for a more critical analysis, see Suzanne C. Nielsen, *An Army Transformed: The U.S. Army's Post-Vietnam Recovery and the Dynamics of Change in Military Organizations*, Letort Papers, Carlisle Barracks, 2010.

3   Compare: *Department of the Army Historical Summary: FY 1973* (Washington, DC: Center for Military History, U.S. Army, 1975), 91; and *Department of the Army Historical Summary: FY 1979* (Washington, DC: Center of Military History, U.S. Army, 1982), 75.

4   Gary R. Nelson, "The Supply and Quality of First-Term Enlistees under the All-Volunteer Force," in William Bowman, et al., eds., *The All-Volunteer Force after a Decade* (Washington, DC: Brassey's, 1986), 31–32; and David S. C. Chu and

John P. White, "Ensuring Quality People in Defense," in Ashton B. Carter and John P. White, eds., *Keeping the Edge: Managing Defense for the Future* (Cambridge, MA: Harvard University Belfer Center, 2000), 203–34.

5 Richard Nixon, *The Real War* (New York: Simon & Schuster, 1980), 201; see also Bernard F. Rostker, *I Want You! The Evolution of the All-Volunteer Force* (Santa Monica, CA: RAND, 2006), 363; and Leonard Wong, Thomas A. Kolditz, Raymond A. Millen, and Terrence M. Potter, *Why They Fight: Combat Motivation in the Iraq War*, Carlisle Barracks: Strategic Studies Institute, 2003, p. 24.

6 Frank L. Jones, *A "Hollow Army" Reappraised: President Carter, Defense Budgets, and the Politics of Military Readiness*, Letort Papers Series, Carlisle Barracks, Strategic Studies Institute, 2012, pp. 42–43.

7 House Armed Services Committee, Investigations Subcommittee, *National Defense Funding Levels for Fiscal Year 1981*, 96th Cong., 2nd sess., May 29, 1980, p. 18; cited from Jones, *"Hollow Army" Reappraised*, 10.

8 *Department of the Army Historical Summary: FY 1979* (Washington, DC: U.S. Army Center of Military History, 1982), chp. 2, p. 5.

9 *Army Historical Summary: FY 1979*, 6.

10 John L. Romjue, "The Evolution of the Airland Battle Concept," *Air University Review* (May–June 1984): 1–13, www.airpower.maxwell.af.mil/airchronicles/aureview/1984/may-jun/romjue.html.

11 James Carafano, "Total Force Policy and the Abrams Doctrine: Unfulfilled Promise, Uncertain Future," Heritage Foundation, February 2005, https://www.fpri.org/articles/2005/02/total-force-policy-and-abrams-doctrine-unfulfilled-promise-uncertain-future.

12 John L. Moore, ed., *U.S. Defense Policy: Weapons, Strategy, and Commitments*, 2nd ed. (Washington, DC: Congressional Quarterly, 1980), 13–14.

13 William J. Lewis, *The Warsaw Pact: Arms, Doctrine, and Strategy* (New York; McGraw Hill, 1983).

14 William E. DePuy, "Implications of the Middle East War on U.S. Army Tactics, Doctrine, and Systems," n.d., in Richard Swain, ed., *Selected Papers of General William E. DePuy*, vol. 1 (Leavenworth, KS: Combat Studies Institute, 1985), 75–111.

15 Compare: International Institute for Strategic Studies, *The Military Balance, 1977–78* (London: IISS, 1977), and International Institute for Strategic Studies, *The Military Balance, 1985–86* (London: IISS, 1985).

16 Congressional Budget Office of the Congress of the United States, *Assessing the NATO/Warsaw Pact Military Balance* (Washington, DC: Government Printing Office, December 1977), xv.

17 Shimon Naveh, *In Pursuit of Military Excellence: The Evolution of Operational Theory* (London: Frank Cass, 1997), 263.

18 Department of the Army, *FM 100-5 Operations*, August 20, 1982 (Washington, DC: GPO, 1982), 2-1, 2-2; see also Swain, "Filling the Void: The Operational Art and the U.S. Army," in B. J. C. McKercher and Michael Hennessy, eds., *The Operational Art: Developments in the Theories of War* (Westport, CT: Praeger,

1996), 159; and Allan English, "The Operational Art," in *The Operational Art: Canadian Perspectives, Context, and Concepts*, Allan English, Daniel Gosselin, Howard Coombs, and Laurence M. Hickey, eds. (Kingston, Ontario: Canadian Defence Academy, 2005), 16.

19 See the discussion in Antulio J. Echevarria II, "American Operational Art, 1917–2008," in John Andreas Olsen and Martin van Creveld, eds., *The Evolution of Operational Art from Napoleon to the Present* (Oxford: Oxford University Press, 2011), 137–39.

20 Justin Kelley and Michael Brennan, *Alien: How Operational Art Devoured Strategy*, Carlisle Barracks, Strategic Studies Institute, 2009.

21 On the Clausewitzian renaissance, see Christopher Bassford, *Clausewitz in English: The Reception of Clausewitz in Britain and America, 1815–1945* (Oxford: Oxford University Press, 1994), 202–5; Lloyd Matthews, *Winning the War by Winning the Peace: Strategy for Conflict and Post-Conflict in the 21st Century* (Carlisle Barracks, PA: Strategic Studies Institute, 2004).

22 English, "Operational Art," 16.

23 Joint Publication, *JP 3–07. Joint Doctrine for Military Operations Other Than War* (Washington, DC: GPO, 1995); see also the analysis of Thomas L. McNaugher, "The Army and Operations Other Than War: Expanding Professional Jurisdiction," in *The Future of the Army Profession*, Lloyd J. Matthews, ed. (Boston: McGraw-Hill, 2002), 155–78.

24 This discussion of these interventions is drawn from Antulio J. Echevarria II, *Reconsidering the American Way of War: US Military Practice from the Revolution to Afghanistan* (Washington, DC: Georgetown University Press, 2014); see also Stephen Watts, Caroline Baxter, Molly Dunigan, Christopher Rizzi, *The Uses and Limits of Small-Scale Military Interventions* (Santa Monica, CA: RAND, 2012).

25 Jonathan M. House, "Operation Urgent Fury—Grenada, 1983," in *The United States Army in Joint Operations, 1950–1983* (Washington, DC: Center of Military History, 1992).

26 U.S. Dept. of Defense, *Grenada: October 25 to November 2, 1983* (Washington, DC: GPO, 1983).

27 Daniel P. Bolger, *Americans at War, 1975–1986: An Era of Violent Peace* (Novato, CA: Presidio, 1988), 276–80, describes the process.

28 Rep. Les Aspin, Chairman, House Armed Services Committee, "Operation Just Cause: Lessons and Warnings in the Future Use of Military Force," Washington, DC: House Armed Services Committee Report, January 12, 1990.

29 *Operation Just Cause: The Incursion into Panama* (Washington, DC: Center of Military History, 2004), 44; casualties were 23 KIA, 322 WIA (U.S.); 314 KIA, 124 WIA, and 5,300 EPWs (PDF); estimates of civilian casualties range from two hundred to several thousand.

30 *United States Forces, Somalia after Action Report* (Washington, DC: GPO, 1995, repr. 2004); Kenneth Allard, *Somalia Operations: Lessons Learned* (Washington, DC: National Defense University, 1995).

31 Richard W. Stewart, "Historical Overview: The United States Army in Somalia, 1992–1994," in *Somalia after Action Report*, 13.

32 Many lessons from the operations in Somalia applied to peacekeeping and peace enforcement missions in general. The first of these was that military forces were not the best tools for peacekeeping operations, but were usually the only ones available. Second, unity of effort in such operations is a luxury, not a norm. While coordinating the efforts of allies and coalition partners is difficult as a rule, peacekeeping operations involve a number of players for whom even the appearance of cooperation with the military is anathema. Third, open and continuous communications with the public are essential, whereas, in conventional operations, it is usually best to conceal one's intentions from the public as long as possible. Fourth, a clear exit strategy connected to the mandate is critical, as peacekeeping operations can evolve into open-ended nation-building exercises, which can prove extremely costly, and for which few allies or coalition partners will sign on. Finally, in peacekeeping operations, legitimacy, restraint, and perseverance were considered important enough to enshrine as principles. Stewart, "Historical Overview," 13; Allard, *Somalia Operations*, 4–7, and chapter 2.

33 Echevarria, "American Operational Art," 152.

34 For such a discussion, see Andrew Krepenevich Jr., *The Army and Vietnam* (Baltimore, MD: Johns Hopkins University Press, 1986).

35 Andrew J. Birtle, *U.S. Army Counterinsurgency Operations Doctrine, 1860–1941* (Washington, DC: U.S. Army Center of Military History, 1998).

36 The U.S. Army actually commissioned few studies of Vietnam that were not considered cursory or superficial. However, individual Army officers and defense scholars conducted independent assessments that were unflinchingly critical. Compare Lloyd Matthews and Dale E. Brown, eds., *Assessing the Vietnam War: A Collection from the Journal of the U.S. Army War College* (Washington, DC: Brassey's, 1987); Lawrence E. Grinter and Peter M. Dunn, eds., *The American War in Vietnam* (Westport, CT: Greenwood, 1987).

37 Thomas Crosbie, "The US Army's Domestic Strategy, 1945–1965," *Parameters* 44, no. 4 (Winter 2014–2015): 105–18.

38 Cited from David Fitzgerald, *Learning to Forget: U.S. Army Counterinsurgency Doctrine and Practice from Vietnam to Iraq* (Stanford, CA: Stanford University Press, 2013), 87.

39 Jeffrey Record, *Beating Goliath: Why Insurgencies Win* (Washington, DC: Potomac, 2009).

40 "Debate on Counterinsurgency: Gentile vs Nagl," *Small Wars Journal*, May 1, 2013, http://smallwarsjournal.com/blog/debate-on-counterinsurgency-gentile-vs-nagl; Celeste Ward Gventer, "Counterinsurgency: A Debate Far from Over," *Foreign Policy*, June 15, 2012; http://foreignpolicy.com/2012/06/15/counterinsurgency-a-debate-far-from-over/.

12

Preaching after the Devil's Death

U.S. Post-Cold War Drawdown

RICHARD A. LACQUEMENT JR.

Introduction

The post–Cold War drawdown of the U.S. armed forces between the fall of the Berlin Wall in 1989 and the terrorist attacks of September 11, 2001, is a fascinating story that provides rich material for analyzing Americans' understanding of their nation's place on the world stage and the appropriate role for their armed forces. Embedded in a broad sweep of historical experiences and habits, this particular drawdown casts light on the evolution of the United States' international aspirations and the potential contributions of its armed forces.

There are two main questions that frame a drawdown in response to a major change in the international context. First, how much of the United States' resources (budget, population, etc.) should be allocated to defense? Second, what posture, in terms of force structure and doctrine, should the U.S. armed forces adopt to serve society's security interests? The post–Cold War drawdown bore little resemblance to earlier patterns of mobilization for war and demobilization for peace. Rather, it was characterized by retention of a substantial standing force. The most salient aspect of the post–Cold War era is that the United States opted for continued and even increased international engagement and leadership. The more benign international environment for the United States primarily accounts for the downward pressure on the magnitude of resources for defense, while the significance of remaining national security threats and opportunities generally account for the modest magnitude of the resource drawdown. In contrast, the tremendous continuity in the posture of the U.S. armed forces (force structure and doctrine) is more puzzling given the changing character of security threats and opportunities. Analyzing the dynamics of the 1989–2001 drawdown is valuable today since U.S. global leadership—indeed primacy—continues to frame U.S. national security imperatives and provides the associated rationale for the U.S. armed forces' capabilities.[1]

Historical Context

For most of U.S. history the pattern for the armed forces was to maintain a very small, standing, peacetime military establishment that would be increased in time of war to meet the needs of the immediate crisis. Forces mobilized for war would be largely demobilized as soon as the war was over. This "feast or famine" pattern[2] accorded well with societal norms in which Americans perceived wars as aberrations, large standing armed forces as inherently dangerous to the republic (as threats to liberty, democracy, and peace), and resources devoted to the armed forces as unproductive and a drain on the national economy.[3] This pattern held true from the Revolution through the immediate aftermath of World War II.[4]

By 1950, the emergence of the Soviet Union as a clear and present danger first brought a halt to the post–World War II demobilization and then, after the start of the Korean War in 1950, led to a partial remobilization. The U.S. government assessed the USSR as a global competitor of unacceptable and incompatible ideology and ambitions. U.S. policy coalesced as an effort to defeat global communism and its state sponsors, particularly the Soviet Union.[5] The strategy chosen to attain this goal was containment. With emphasis on military means, containment led the United States to maintain a force of considerable size outside a period of declared war. For the United States, most leaders and the public conceived of the Cold War as a global conflict in which the United States led the free world. During the Cold War, particularly after the beginning of the Korean War in 1950, the United States settled into its new leadership role with a commensurately more robust standing military establishment.

The Cold War and the subsequent era of continued U.S. leadership altered the dynamics of earlier force reduction patterns and American society's views of national security. Nonetheless, the basic societal tensions remain about the line between war and peace, the danger of standing armed forces, and the negative economic impact of defense spending. The collapse of the Soviet enemy that had induced the creation of a considerable military establishment could have logically led to demobilization. It did not. After the end of the Cold War the United States assumed a position of dominance and hegemony across the globe unmatched by any power in history.[6] The U.S. decision to maintain its position of leadership in the world was an important and little-debated element of tremendous consequence to shaping the future size, form, and function of the U.S. armed forces.

Although the United States recognized the need for a stronger military establishment to complement its increased role in the world, the desire to find the greatest economies continued to carry forward some of the effects of feast or famine evident in the era prior to World War II. In the wake of World War II and some of the major military engagements in the midst of the Cold War (Korea, Vietnam), the United States sought to balance its investment in armed forces against more desirable uses of national resources for economic and other societal endeavors.[7]

In the wake of wars, the professional military establishment of the United States worked mightily to strengthen its grasp of expert knowledge derived from experience in the recent war and to anticipate applicability for future conflicts. That is, the armed forces sought to learn from their recent experiences and use that learning for the future. This has resulted in the creation of various narratives for the future at the core of the debates between military and civilian leaders about the appropriate size and structure of the armed forces. There have been intense debates among military leaders, civilian leaders (both executive and legislative), and the broader public about the missions, size, and shape of the U.S. armed forces. The debates induce civilian-military negotiation over the armed forces' professional expertise and jurisdictions of practice, the needs of American society, and the various theories of war and national security. These topics provide an invitation to struggle between executive departments such as the Department of State and the Department of Defense (a 1947 aggregation of the military services that subsumed the previously independent Department of War and Department of the Navy), among the military services themselves, within the communities of the individual services (such as the branches and functional communities),[8] and between active and reserve components. Assessments of competing values are rarely resolvable by objective measures. The inefficiencies and inability to render fixed and enduring answers subject the questions of defense and military force creation to the subjective realm of politics. Interdepartmental, interservice, and intraservice rivalry, much bemoaned, is an endemic feature of the American national security decision-making process. It is yet another manifestation of the American predilection for divided and shared powers that prevent the unchecked accretion of power to the state. The "masks of war"[9] that define interservice rivalry are, in this light, a significant and valuable component of American governing habits. The marketplace of ideas and theories of effectiveness for national defense is a flourishing one . . . but one that can create frustration for those (the military) who must pitch their wares as well as those (civilians in the executive branch, legislature, and public as a whole) who must sort through the complexities of the arguments that only they hold the power to resolve.

The 1989–2001 Drawdown Summary

The sections that follow summarize the 1989–2001 drawdown. The sections summarize debates and decisions about the magnitude of resources allocated to defense as well as about how the armed forces should be postured (in terms of force structure and doctrine) to support U.S. interests and aspirations in the new national security context.

The "mellowing"[10] of the USSR began with Gorbachev's ascendance in 1985. The culmination of the Cold War was marked decisively by the collapse and dissolution of the Soviet Union in 1991. The United States lost the enemy that had largely defined its force structure and doctrine since the Korean War.

In 2001 the United States entered a new era of war in response to the 9/11 attacks and the threat of terrorist groups with a global reach.[11] Although the end of the Cold War and the beginning of the Global War on Terrorism make useful bookends for exploring the post–Cold War drawdown, the period itself was not particularly peaceful. The 1990–1991 Persian Gulf War (Operation Desert Storm/Shield) and subsequent operations for the containment of Iraq (Provide Comfort, Northern Watch, Southern Watch, Desert Fox), Somalia (Provide Hope), Haiti, Bosnia, and Kosovo all entailed the use or the threatened use of coercive force by the United States' armed forces.

From 1989 to 1999, the United States implemented a gradual drawdown of its armed forces while seeking to clarify the purposes the force should serve and the structure such forces should assume to meet future contingencies.[12] By 2001 the U.S. armed forces had reduced in size by about one-third, while remaining structured and oriented very similarly to the way they had been for the anticipated conventional conflict with the Soviet Union. This occurred despite calls for major restructuring to respond to a high-tech revolution in military affairs (most evident from combat operations during the 1991 Gulf War) and despite participation in many complex, smaller-scale contingencies awkwardly referred to as Military Operations Other Than War, or "MOOTW" (e.g., Panama, Iraq containment, Somalia, Haiti, Bosnia, and Kosovo). In sum, despite changes in the security context, U.S. armed forces underwent a reduction without any significant restructuring.

The Resulting Post–Cold War Force: Reduction without Restructuring

There are many indicators that highlight the resulting contours of the post–Cold War drawdown. Although there are some examples of restructuring, the vast majority of evidence reflects continuity with the Cold War. In many instances the evidence supports the overarching one-third resource reduction shared proportionally across the force. Key metrics of the drawdown that reflected more continuity than change include service sizes, budget share, key service elements (divisions in the Army and Marine Corps, carrier battle groups in the Navy, fighter and bomber wings in the Air Force), and service vision and doctrine. From 1989 to 2001, the personnel in the U.S. armed forces went from approximately 2.1 million to 1.4 million active forces, a 33 percent decrease.

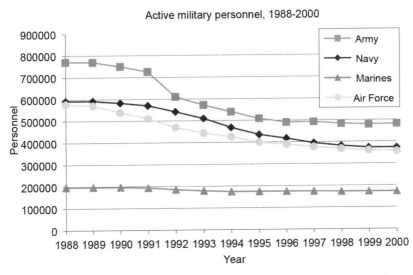

Figure 12.1: Active Military Personnel Strength by Service. *Source*: Lacquement, *Shaping American Military Capabilities after the Cold War*, 44.

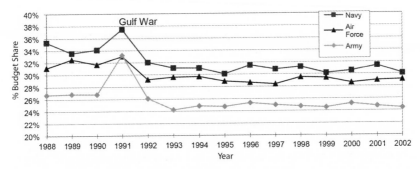

Figure 12.2: Defense Budget Authority Share by Service. *Note*: This is similar to a chart in Lacquement, *Shaping American Military Capabilities after the Cold War*, 50; however, this chart runs through 2002 whereas the one in the book ends with 1997.

TABLE 12.1: Force Structure—Change and Continuity

CHANGE		CONTINUITY
Restructure	Reduction	
• Special Operations forces • Airlift and sealift • Reserves • Nuclear forces • Defense procurement • Army IBCTs	• Conventional forces • Personnel • Production	• Service roles and missions • Shape of the armed forces (by service and key service elements) • Selection of future weapons • Shape of the defense budget —By service —By appropriations category
Ambiguous: Strategic Doctrine and Vision		

Some restructuring across major defense programs was reflected in disproportionately higher cuts to some programs (nuclear forces, defense procurement) and relative increases in budget share to others (special operations forces, airlift, and sealift). There were also some organizational structure changes (e.g., aerial expeditionary forces [AEF] in the Air Force, the development of interim brigade combat teams [IBCT] in the Army, and, later, Army concepts to favor focus on brigade combat teams as the main unit of combat power [see figure 12.1]).[13] Nonetheless, the dominant character of the drawdown was proportionately shared reductions with little change to basic force structure and doctrine (see table 12.1).

Overall Defense Context

Subsequent U.S. military performance raises questions about how well the United States dealt with the uncertainty of the post–Cold War era. Without the clarity of a particular foe, the period raised questions about the appropriate choices for the maintenance and development of armed forces for an uncertain future. Questions at the time challenged assumptions that existing forces and techniques for their employment (military ways and means) were still adequate for the policy aims (ends) of the new era.[14] Subsequent operations in Afghanistan and Iraq after 2001 suggest that U.S. armed forces, while extremely capable in some areas (such as conventional, tactical combat), were not adequately prepared to contribute to the full range of operational requirements commensurate with U.S. policy objectives. Additionally, although the armed forces demonstrated a commendable "first battle" readiness, they had great difficulty attaining success in meeting overarching war aims.

Drawdown Debates and Decisions

The end of the Cold War represented a major change in the international security context for the United States. With the collapse of the Soviet Union and its alliance system, the security threats to the United States were significantly reduced. Within the United States, one of the political consequences of the more benign international environment was a pivot in emphasis towards domestic political issues.

East-West tensions had dramatically eased with the ascendance of Mikhail Gorbachev to leadership in the Soviet Union.[15] Gorbachev led Soviet withdrawal from Afghanistan, reduced the size of Soviet conventional armed forces, and relaxed control over subordinate countries in the Warsaw Pact. The lifting of the "iron curtain" was most dramatically and electrifyingly marked by the opening of the Berlin Wall in November 1989. Less than a year later the Soviets had acceded to German reunification.

When the Soviet Union collapsed, the most salient, existential threat to the United States abated. The United States' interest in world order and stability remained. Until the collapse of the Soviet Union, much of the justification for U.S. force structure and doctrine centered on thwarting Soviet aggression against the United States, its allies, and other non-Communist states. The United States' primary focus was on strategic defense. Containment of the Soviet Union centered on preventing its inroads into new areas. Most regional and internal conflicts in which the United States intervened (directly or indirectly) throughout the Cold War era—Greece, Philippines, China, Korea, Cuba, Vietnam, El Salvador, Afghanistan—were mainly intended to stop Communist expansion beyond the boundaries settled at the end of World War II (and defined primarily by the limit of advance of the Red Army). After the Cold War, the dominant justification for the U.S. military shifted to emphasis on a combination of residual commitments to regional stability (in particular with respect to Korea and Iraq), defense of the democratic "zone of peace,"[16] and a more active role in advancing U.S. aspirations for the expansion of democracy and market economies.[17]

American policy aims always have a layer of universal aspiration for the promulgation of liberal government, economics, and social values.[18] After the Cold War, the tremendous disparity in American power relative to any other country offered the potential for a more active approach to the promulgation of such values. A long-standing assumption by many Americans is that the spread of such values would manifest in both economic and security gains. In short, the promulgation of U.S. values had both a normative and a material benefit. The world would be a better, safer place, and American prosperity would increase. President George H. W. Bush's hope for a "New World Order"[19] and the subsequent statement by President Bill Clinton of America's "National Security Strategy of Engagement and Enlargement"[20] were clear signals of the active role the United States would assume in world affairs.[21] President Clinton's national security strategy noted that "[a] framework of democratic enlargement . . . increases our security by protecting, consolidating and enlarging the community of free market democracies."[22]

Domestically, after the end of the Cold War, the consideration of the order of magnitude of defense resources was framed by a general expectation of a peace dividend. Democratic members of Congress, who were in the majority, were particularly vocal in advocating for significantly reduced investment in defense to permit greater investment in other social needs.

In the United States, inflation and hefty defense spending in the early 1980s had put the U.S. budget deeply into the red. The sustained cost of the Carter/Reagan defense buildup (1979–1985) seemed decidedly less justified as the Soviet Union began to take on a more benign aspect. Comforted in the positive accomplishments of the defense buildup—a useful investment for more than just immediate threats, to be sure—and no longer confronted with a bellicose Soviet foe, the downward trend in defense spending began in 1985.[23]

The debate in the United States included little challenge to the idea of U.S. leadership or primacy. Nor was there any significant opposition to the idea that the end of the Cold War must yield some economic savings (that is, a "peace dividend"). Rather, with respect to defense, the issues most contested were about the magnitude of resources for defense overall, as well as attention to the circumstance for the use of such forces—that is, how far to draw down forces and how to restructure the remaining forces on the basis of immediate and anticipated requirements.

Overall, the public and its leaders in both the executive and legislative branches weighed in heavily on issues regarding the use of the armed forces and on the relative significance accorded to national security within the federal budget. The military and its leaders received great latitude to decide how the reductions would be undertaken, particularly with respect to the concepts of force structure and doctrine. The most important actor in the process was the president. As the dominant power in the American political system, particularly with respect to agenda setting, the president has the first and most powerful voice on the use of the armed forces to support U.S. national security policy.[24] Congress holds the power of the purse, but is a much more diffuse body of individuals and constituencies that are harder to combine into directed action. Building congressional coalitions around defense issues is difficult outside of immediate conflicts. This also helps to explain the tendency towards feast or famine in earlier eras (a reflection of general agreement about the relative importance of defense compared to other national priorities at a given moment) and the power of inertia in the absence of crisis.

The president and Congress represent civilian control of the military and were the dominant forces in deciding the overarching questions of the U.S. role in the world, the circumstances for the use of American armed forces, and the overall order of magnitude of resources dedicated to national defense. However, senior military officers were the ones who articulated how the U.S. armed forces would support national security strategy. In that regard, the shape of the U.S. armed forces' post–Cold War drawdown was most powerfully influenced by the vision and efforts of military leaders, the most influential among whom was General Colin Powell.

General Powell was the chairman of the Joint Chiefs of Staff from October 1989 to October 1993. His vision for the drawdown, the Base Force concept, set the overall trajectory and, in hindsight, accounted for the overwhelming majority of the magnitude of the drawdown.[25] As national security advisor for President Reagan (1987–1989), Powell witnessed the early stages of Soviet reform and opening that would lead to the end of the Cold War and the eventual collapse of the Soviet Union. More so than many others around him, Powell sensed that the changes in the USSR were profound and enduring. Powell, who was the commander of U.S. Forces Command in 1989, advocated for military leaders to give greater attention to how to get ahead of drawdown pressures he felt were sure to come as the public and their civilian leaders responded to lessening international tensions.

In May 1989, at Carlisle Barracks, Powell addressed a symposium that included many other four-stars and pressed the issue of what the Army would need to do to respond to the end of the Cold War. Noting the changes by the Soviet Union, he asserted that the "Bear is benign."[26] He suggested that Army leaders might have to consider a question about their future in the absence of the Soviet enemy similar to an old saw that asked, "What will all the preachers do when the Devil is dead?"[27] Powell pressed the point that the armed forces were entering a new drawdown period and must work to avoid the hollowing of the force that had been a common feature in previous drawdowns.

In October 1989 Powell became the chairman of the Joint Chiefs of Staff (CJCS). The Goldwater-Nichols Department of Defense Reorganization Act of 1986, which had become law under his predecessor, Admiral William Crowe, contained many important changes to strengthen coordination and integration of the U.S. armed forces. A key element of the act was the increased power it gave to the CJCS as the "[p]rincipal military advisor to the President, the National Security Council, and the Secretary of Defense."[28]

Powell took full advantage of the chairman's new powers and made it clear to the service chiefs that he would lead, and not just rely on their consensus, in presenting his advice to the secretary of defense and the president.

Powell laid out his vision for what he termed the Base Force to the service chiefs soon after becoming chairman. Two important elements of the Base Force proposal were the shift of strategy away from containment of the Soviet Union to preparation for two major regional contingencies (MRC) and the judgment that a 25 percent reduction in forces and budgets was the floor, or base, sufficient to support the strategy.[29] Powell led development of the proposal, attained the acquiescence of the service chiefs, and presented it to the secretary of defense and, ultimately, the president for approval.

Secretary of Defense Dick Cheney was representative of many civilian national security stalwarts in the first Bush administration who remained suspicious of the Soviet Union and who were concerned about the possible reversal of the changes Gorbachev had instigated. Hardened Cold Warriors like Cheney worried about the opaque nature of the Soviet Union and its potential to quickly resume a more confrontational approach towards the United States and the free world. The fall of the Berlin Wall in November 1989 was a tangible effect of relaxed Soviet control over its European satellites that made any such reversal very difficult.

In the months following the fall of the Berlin Wall, Powell overcame resistance to the Base Force concept, first within the Office of the Secretary of Defense (OSD), including the secretary of defense, and then among the service chiefs, particularly the Army chief of staff, General Carl Vuono, and the Marine Corps commandant, General Alfred Gray. With Cheney's approval, Powell briefed the concept to the president and gained his approval in June 1990.[30]

Although there was considerable logic to the proposed reductions engendered in the Base Force, Powell, Cheney, the service chiefs, and others were worried about the difficulty they would face in stopping momentum down a possibly slippery slope. Democratic leaders in Congress did indeed seek steeper reductions to defense spending but were also mindful of being painted as "soft on defense" and possibly vulnerable to Republicans on national security issues.[31] Walking the line between party priorities for domestic issues that would benefit from a substantial peace dividend and the need to maintain a measured, respectable stance on national security framed much of the Democratic approach towards the end of the Cold War and the drawdown of the U.S. armed forces. Georgia senator Sam Nunn (chairman of the Senate Armed Services Committee) and Wisconsin representative Les Aspin (chairman of the House Armed Services Committee) led Democratic challenges to the Bush administration in the effort to shape the drawdown.

There were basically two major approaches that were at the center of the debate. The Bush administration's approach, articulated in the Base Force concept, included a 25 percent reduction of forces and the shift of basic strategy from global containment of the Soviet Union to the maintenance of capabilities to respond to two major regional contingencies. The Democrats in Congress pressed for a more fundamental reassessment of the purpose and structure of American armed forces that would also permit much greater budget savings. Efforts to revisit basic roles and missions of the services to attain greater efficiencies received strong attention from Senator Nunn.[32] Representative Aspin argued that the entire force should be reviewed and reformed from "the bottom up."[33] In general, the Democratic leaders accepted the 25 percent budget reduction as a good start, but not enough to reflect the changed international landscape. A key difference was that whereas both approaches engendered reductions to the armed forces, the Base Force did not include any significant moves towards restructuring of the armed forces, whereas Democratic alternatives did.[34]

By 1992, Powell and the Bush administration had been successful in holding out against more dramatic defense budget reductions as well as against commensurate pressures for reshaping the armed forces. Although not successful in attaining any major restructuring changes, the Democrats could claim credit for pressing the case for a peace dividend while articulating a responsible approach to national security. Attaining savings while maintaining a sufficiently strong stance on national security helped inoculate the Democrats against vulnerability on defense issues in the 1992 presidential election.

With the end of the Cold War and the recent blows of an economic recession, Democratic candidate Bill Clinton was able to focus the 1992 campaign on domestic issues (summed up neatly by one of his campaign advisers in the statement that "[i]t's the economy, stupid") to defeat Bush.[35]

In 1993 leadership of both the legislature and the executive branch gave President Clinton and his Democratic allies the opportunity to implement the changes they had proposed. With Les Aspin as secretary of defense, initiating the Bottom Up Review became a reality.[36] However, the ability to promulgate preferred defense changes faced four obstacles. First, General Powell remained the chairman of the Joint Chiefs of Staff. In many regards, his instincts for the temper of the country and the appropriate way to reconcile his (and other military leaders') preferred approach to drawdown had done much to meet the most powerful pressures for adjusting to the end of the Cold War. Second, there were important remaining security challenges that confronted a United States that fashioned itself as the leader of this new world (dis)order, including the legacy of the 1990–1991 Persian Gulf War (such as substantial residual security efforts to contain Iraq); violence in the Balkans as Yugoslavia sundered; humanitarian disaster in Somalia; continued fighting in Central America; and the survival of Communist regimes in China, Cuba, North Korea, and Vietnam. Third, President Clinton himself, whether or not he meant to do so so dramatically, immediately shifted the focus of defense issues away from the drawdown and onto the issue of homosexuality in the armed forces. In his first days in office, President Clinton reiterated his intention, declared during his presidential campaign, to end the restriction on the service of gay people in the armed forces.[37] The proposal triggered significant resistance, including from many military leaders, most prominently the CJCS, General Colin Powell, and the service chiefs.[38] The six-month effort to reconcile strong views on both sides of the issue ultimately led to the "Don't ask, Don't tell" policy compromise. The gays-in-the-military issue had put the president and the Democrats on the defensive with respect to the armed forces and served as a major distraction from other issues.[39] Lastly, Les Aspin had a difficult time getting out of the blocks as secretary of defense, including difficulty moving his review ideas forward. The Bottom Up Review (BUR) process started with many of the concepts he had championed from the House of Representatives.[40] In the Department of Defense, however, substantial changes fell by the wayside. For example, the use of smaller-scale contingencies as a force-sizing component was removed as the services defended the existing force-sizing framework, albeit with some concession to pressures for reduction centered on the idea that the two major regional contingencies need not be fully resourced for simultaneous execution. Rather, the idea that one contingency would receive priority initially provided some shift in assets between the two contingencies in a manner that maintained the two-war framework but with a smaller force. The military's defense of the Base Force and the two-major-regional-conventional-war framework for drawdown remained. In the end, the Bottom Up Review led to further budget reductions of almost 7 percent (and commensurate force reductions to most major programs),[41] with no significant restructuring of the armed forces.

What proved to be the main contours of the post–Cold War drawdown had been set and can be summed up as a one-third reduction in the defense budget as measured from the peak of 1985. Of course, the drawdown did not occur all at once. The reductions associated with the BUR, when tacked on to those previously promulgated as part of the Base Force, envisioned the completion of the reductions by 1999.[42]

The Report on the Bottom Up Review was issued in October 1993.[43] The events in Somalia that same month seem to have put an end to any significant discussions of further drawdown. With the "End of History"[44] proving more elusive than many might have hoped a few years earlier, with the president and Congress more concerned with domestic issues in the United States, and with the military establishment now firmly focused on readiness of remaining forces to address the new strategic framework (two major regional contingencies, later major theater wars), the post–Cold War drawdown was solidly set.

With the completion of the Bottom Up Review, some voices of dissatisfaction remained, but there was little power behind them. In the Pentagon, Secretary Aspin's declining influence and effectiveness bottomed out in the wake of the October 1993 "Blackhawk down" incident in Somalia.[45] Placed at the center of the storm, Aspin came under pressure from the president and others in the administration to resign. Aspin tried to convince the president to keep him on, but in the end succumbed. Disheartened and physically worn, Aspin submitted his resignation, readily accepted by the president, on December 15, 1993, after less than a year in office.[46]

To some of the more demanding critics, mainly from the left side of the aisle, the Bottom Up Review was a disappointment. The expression of dissatisfaction came mainly in the form of congressional requirements for new studies and reports to be rendered to Congress. In Congress, Senator Nunn and the new House Armed Services Committee chairman, Representative Ron Dellums, led others to press defense leaders (civilian and military) for greater attention to the potential efficiencies available through reconsideration of roles and missions and for continued review of the strategy the armed forces would support.

The first of these major requirements was for an independent Commission on Roles and Missions (CORM). Including the now former Secretary of Defense Les Aspin, the CORM may have signaled dissatisfaction but did little to deliver any major reforms. Among its recommendations, however, was for Congress to require the executive to conduct another study. This time the requirement would be for a major review of defense at the beginning of each presidential term, that is, quadrennially.[47] Congress accepted the recommendation and added it as a requirement in the next national defense legislation. The law mandated the first of the Quadrennial Defense Reviews (QDR) for 1997.[48] Neither the CORM nor the first QDR (1997) moved the needle much at all. In both cases, the studies that Congress hoped might induce significant changes did little to convince military leadership to alter their preferred conceptions of future forces and the manner in which those forces should be employed.

It seems clear that by early 1994 the policy guidance for the post–Cold War drawdown was largely in place and the window of opportunity for major change had closed.[49] The United States had been active in various military interventions around the globe, most prominently in Somalia, the Balkans, Iraq, and Haiti, as well as a robust, continued forward presence in Europe, Japan, and Korea. The public clamor for a peace dividend had largely subsided. The American economy was strong, and the federal budget was running a surplus.[50] With respect to the shape of the U.S. armed forces, military leaders and their staffs were largely comfortable with positions they had staked out on force structure and doctrine.

The end to the drawdown in overall budget terms can be dated to 1999. President Clinton signaled the change in his 1999 State of the Union address.[51] President Clinton's FY 2000 budget submission proposed the first increase to defense spending, in real terms, since 1985. In 2000, both major party presidential candidates, Texas governor George W. Bush and Vice President Al Gore, promised increases to defense spending. In fact, Gore promised higher defense budget spending than Bush. Among the distinctions the Bush campaign promulgated was a declaration that it would not call upon the military to do nation building and that he would do more to transform the armed forces for high-tech challenges of the future.[52]

Bush ultimately prevailed in the presidential contest. When Bush assumed the presidency he had a powerful lineup of seasoned national security professionals at the top of the administration, including two former secretaries of defense and a former chairman of the Joint Chiefs of Staff. Former Secretary of Defense Dick Cheney was vice president, and former Secretary of Defense Donald Rumsfeld resumed the post he had held in the Ford presidential administration. Retired general and former CJCS Colin Powell joined the administration as secretary of state.

In the early months of the administration, Rumsfeld took the lead in shaping the second Quadrennial Defense Review (2001). The early stages of the effort suggested there might be major, transformative changes that would shift emphasis from conventional forces, particularly ground forces, toward more high-tech capabilities associated with the so-called Revolution in Military Affairs (RMA). By September 2001, however, Rumsfeld was preparing to announce a report that would reflect very little change to the status quo. When the report did come out on September 30, 2001, it was not a particularly transformative document. In force structure and doctrine, some of the more dramatic changes that had been suggested in the early months of the new administration had largely disappeared.[53]

More importantly, the terrorist attacks of September 11, 2001, changed the fundamental context for American national security. The United States entered a time of war that would last more than a decade and from which it has yet to fully emerge.

Assessment: Looking Back and Looking Forward

There are several measures by which the post–Cold War drawdown may be assessed. But one measure—effectiveness in attaining policy aims—stands above the others. The U.S. armed forces are organized, trained, and equipped to serve the national security interests of American society. The United States survives and thrives today while yet another major peer competitor met its demise. The end of the Cold War and the collapse of the Soviet Union represented a major success for which the armed forces of the United States deserve part of the credit. Many also argue that U.S. success was a function not just of military prowess and power but also of restraint in not letting the pursuit of military power undermine broader economic well-being—something that has been the bane of great powers throughout history.[54]

In the wake of the Cold War, the maintenance of that force-in-being provided (and still provides) a powerful deterrence to any other state or group of states that might seek to threaten the territory or interests of the United States through force. The tremendous capabilities of the U.S. armed forces across every major domain of warfare provide an important hedge against the most dangerous security threats, including the truly existential threats of nuclear-armed competitors.

Nevertheless, there are many other circumstances for the use of armed forces in the service of important or vital security interests. For several of the events in which the United States has employed armed forces to serve various policy aims, the results have not been as successful as policymakers or military leaders would have hoped. The most obvious examples include the indisputably unsatisfactory results of military operations, at least so far, in both Afghanistan and Iraq.

How should we measure the effectiveness of the post–Cold War military drawdown? The armed forces had a mixed record of performance in the two major post-9/11 conflicts (Afghanistan and Iraq) that can be at least in part attributed to shortcomings in the analysis and preparation of the armed forces that took place in the midst of the post–Cold War drawdown.

Ready forces did well in first battles in Afghanistan and Iraq but proved less capable in supporting larger policy aims that defined the wars.[55] This continued a trend begun in Vietnam where the U.S. Army won the first battles, for a change, but did not succeed at achieving national objectives. "You fight as you train" is a common refrain in military circles, and indeed the U.S. armed forces delivered strong performances in its first battles after the drawdown. But one of the more profound lessons of military history is that winning battles is not the same as winning wars.[56] Time and time again, the ultimate outcomes of war have gone against the winners of first battles. Ultimately, few would argue with the idea that winning the first battle and winning the war is the preferred combination. But winning battles without successfully connecting such prowess to political success can only be judged a failure.

As with the Cold War itself, a major measure of effectiveness includes what *didn't* happen. That is, there has been no war among great powers and there has not been any serious threat of great power war. However, this suggests another challenge. Effectiveness in deterring great power war may induce opponents to seek other ways and means to pursue their objectives. Hence, first battles in subsequent wars, like Afghanistan and Iraq, were, as usual, not definitive, and the U.S. armed forces were confronted with the age-old strategic dilemma of dealing with determined foes seeking whatever means might still remain to serve their policy aims. At core is the Clausewitzian insight that "war is thus an act of force to compel our enemy to do our will,"[57] achieved through interaction with an enemy that seeks to achieve *its* will. Success in achieving the most costly policy aims (particularly as the cost is perceived by an opponent) requires that the compelled enemy no longer has the ways, means, or hope to pursue its will.

The shallowness of the post–Cold War drawdown and the equivocation in recent years about "turning the page" on a period of war[58] while U.S. armed forces remain active in combat operations in Afghanistan and other places makes the pre–World War II pattern of feast and famine decidedly quaint, if not archaic.[59] As the 2015 National Security Strategy makes clear, the United States still pursues world leadership and continues to see its active engagement as indispensable to global stability.[60] This well-established conception of U.S. security and prosperity as being intimately entwined with the rest of the world entails an important continuing role for U.S. military power that goes well beyond battle or even war. Buildups and drawdowns will probably continue to reflect the general order of magnitude of societal security needs relative to times of crisis or emergency, most dramatically with respect to war. Nevertheless, there is a baseline of military capabilities required to prevent violence that threatens the United States' most prized values and interests and to help shape the environment in which those values and interests thrive. Mastery of the many ways in which armed forces underpin broad national security interests requires consideration of their utility that should not be limited to readiness for first battles. While such preparedness is necessary to prevent any opponent from overthrowing the United States by force, it is hardly sufficient for supporting the United States' leadership role in accomplishing more than mere defense.

Conclusion: Summary and Assessment

The consensus about resourcing for defense in the wake of the Cold War supported maintaining a strong U.S. leadership role in the world, and, commensurately, a large military establishment to support such leadership. This conceptual continuity, maybe even simple inertia, was the dominant impetus that accounts for the limited scope of the drawdown in overall budgetary and personnel terms. With respect to the question of how to posture the armed forces for the future (force structure and doctrine), the limited changes to the force structure and vision for the armed forces was overwhelmingly a matter of civilian deference to strong military preferences. Chairman of the Joint Chiefs of Staff Powell set the parameters for the U.S. armed forces' post–Cold War drawdown. If the international security context looked more benign, there were nonetheless still major features that militated against a rapid and deep drawdown.

Retaining large standing armed forces made considerable sense as an important component of leadership in the world. U.S. leaders attended closely to the provision of the common goods for the international community—with the common good of international security prominent among them. The foundation of security backed by the United States set the context for far-reaching economic prosperity, international stability, strengthened diplomatic networks reinforced by international organizations, maturing norms of international law, and dramatic expansions of civil liberties across international society. In the wake of the Cold War, the United States provided defense and security as a common good on behalf of an even larger community.[61]

The U.S. armed forces were valuable instruments of power for United States efforts to protect the global commons, deter the rise of peer competitors, and address remaining security threats in Korea, Southwest Asia, Central America, and Africa. Though the order of magnitude of the threat to the United States may have dramatically declined, the activities of the United States armed forces in the decade after the end of the Cold War actually increased. That is, the armed forces became more operationally engaged. The U.S. armed forces were much more actively involved in operations in the decade after the Cold War than throughout the Cold War.[62] Additionally, the overall strength and health of the U.S. economy made the diversion of resources from defense to other parts of the U.S. economy less compelling.[63]

Demobilization of the U.S. armed forces might fit the historical logic of American habits if the Cold War's conclusion is seen as a World War III that was, thankfully, resolved short of cataclysmic violence. But the Cold War faded to a conclusion without a distinct break between war and peace.

As the Soviet Union collapsed, the United States continued to maintain an active role for its armed forces around the world. The 1991 Persian Gulf War with Iraq marked a crescendo of U.S. military action in the Middle East with origins beyond the Cold War. On the Korean peninsula, the demise of the Soviet Union did not resolve the still-unfinished war begun in 1950. In the Balkans, Somalia, and El Salvador, conflicts that may have been embedded in earlier Cold War dynamics took turns that commanded continued United States attention, including the use of armed forces. The end of superpower competition and the threat of catastrophic global conflict justified a reduction in the resource commitments to defense. But remaining security challenges— old and emerging—and the many opportunities that global leadership offered combined to increase American military activity and to moderate any historical propensity towards military demobilization that may have remained. In fact, even in comparison to other post–World War II era drawdowns, the post–Cold War drawdown was modest. Measured by the amount of time from beginning to end of the drawdown, the post–Cold War drawdown was a less precipitous drawdown than those that occurred after World War II, Korea, or Vietnam.[64]

The United States reduced its armed forces by one-third. The U.S. armed forces retained structure and doctrine for conventional war with an adversary envisioned to be much the same as the Soviet Union and its armed forces. Major restructuring of the armed forces to better account for the high technology potential of the Revolution in Military Affairs and the immediate requirements of stability operations and irregular challenges were considered but not implemented. The drawdown delivered a significant peace dividend from the end of the Cold War. In light of subsequent performance, however, it is difficult to argue that the armed forces adequately restructured to anticipate the range of security challenges to come.

NOTES

This chapter draws on analysis and research that resulted in an earlier book: Richard Lacquement, *Shaping American Military Capabilities after the Cold War* (Westport CT: Praeger, 2003). This chapter summarizes the major events of the post–Cold War drawdown as well as adding insights from more recent scholarship.

1 For example, see the most recent National Security Strategy, Barak Obama, February 2015, https://www.whitehouse.gov/sites/default/files/docs/2015_national_security_strategy.pdf (accessed March 2016).

2 In times of war, very few constraints existed on the magnitude of the means commanded for national defense, and the armed forces experienced a feast of

resources. But in time of peace the armed forces went through a famine of military resources. Warner R. Schilling, "The Politics of National Defense: Fiscal 1950," in *Strategy, Politics, and Defense Budgets*, ed. Warner R. Schilling, Paul Y. Hammond, and Glenn H. Snyder (New York: Columbia University Press, 1962), 7–9.

3 See Samuel P. Huntington, *The Soldier and the State: The Theory and Politics of Civil-Military Relations* (Cambridge, MA: Belknap Press of Harvard University, 1957), particularly regarding the "policy of extirpation," 155–57. Also see Jason Warren, "Insights from the Army's Drawdowns," *Parameters* 44, no. 2 (Summer 2014): 5–9.

4 The United States mobilized massively for World War II. After Japan's surrender in 1945 the United States pursued rapid efforts to demobilize and had largely done so by 1949, with remaining forces engaged in the continued occupations of Germany and Japan.

5 Paul Nitze, "United States Objectives and Programs for National Security," NSC-68, Report to the President through the National Security Council, 14 April 1950, reprinted in *Naval War College Review* (May–June 1975): 51–108; George Kennan ("X"), "The Sources of Soviet Conduct," *Foreign Affairs* 25, no. 3 (July 1947): 582. In both documents, the demise of the Soviet Union, or at least a radical change to Soviet character, was the end sought.

6 In earlier eras the Roman Empire around the Mediterranean basin and the Chinese Empire in East Asia form probably the closest parallels within their respective regions to the dominance the United States exercised globally in the twentieth and twenty-first centuries. Great Britain certainly exerted tremendous influence across the globe in the eighteenth, nineteenth, and twentieth centuries but faced peer or near-peer competitors in most regions that attenuated its global influence. That is, France, Russia, Spain, Japan, and the United States, among others, contested British influence within their regions.

7 See Millen chapter, this volume.

8 Examples of various branches and communities within the services include Army and Marine Corps branches such as infantry, armor, artillery, military intelligence, aviation, and engineers; Navy communities such as line (e.g., surface warfare, submarine warfare, special warfare) and staff (e.g., supply, medical); and Air Force communities such as operations, logistics, and support.

9 Carl H. Builder, *The Masks of War: American Military Styles in Strategy and Analysis*, a RAND Corporation Research Study (Baltimore, MD: Johns Hopkins University Press, 1989); Brian McAllister Linn, *The Echo of Battle: The Army's Way of War* (Cambridge, MA: Harvard University Press, 2007).

10 In George Kennan's words, the United States, through containment, should "promote tendencies which must eventually find their outlet in either the break-up or the gradual mellowing of Soviet power." Kennan, "Sources of Soviet Conduct," https://www.foreignaffairs.com/articles/russian-federation/1947-07-01/sources-soviet-conduct (accessed 17 March 2016).

11 Bush speech to a joint session of Congress and the nation, 20 September 2001, http://teachingamericanhistory.org/library/document/address-to-a-joint-session-of-congress/ (accessed 14 March 2016).

12 U.S. defense budget reductions actually began in 1985, driven primarily by an assessment from the Democrat-led Congress that the Carter/Reagan buildup (begun in 1979) had gone far enough.

13 Lacquement, *Shaping American Military Capabilities after the Cold War*, 34.

14 Strategy is defined as, "The alignment of ends, ways, and means—informed by risk—to attain goals." U.S. Army War College definition from Strategy Education Conference, September 2014. See John C. Valledor, "Strategy Education across the Professional Military Education Enterprise," Strategic Studies Institute, May 2015, http://www.strategicstudiesinstitute.army.mil/index.cfm/articles/Strategy-Education/2015/05/18#end24 (accessed 14 March 2016).

15 Mikhail Gorbachev became secretary general of the Communist Party of the Soviet Union in 1985.

16 Richard Cheney, *Defense Strategy for the 1990s: The Regional Defense Strategy* (Washington, DC: Department of Defense, January 1993), 1.

17 President William Clinton, *National Security Strategy of Engagement and Enlargement*, July 1994, http://nssarchive.us/NSSR/1994.pdf (accessed 14 March 2016).

18 Richard Immerman, *Empire for Liberty* (Princeton, NJ: Princeton University Press, 2010).

19 For example see, George H. W. Bush, "Address before a Joint Session of the Congress on the Persian Gulf Crisis and the Federal Budget Deficit," 11 September 1990, http://www.presidency.ucsb.edu/ws/?pid=18820 (accessed 14 March 2016).

20 Clinton, *National Security Strategy*, 1994.

21 See also, George W. Bush, "The Freedom Agenda," http://georgewbush-whitehouse.archives.gov/infocus/freedomagenda/.

22 Clinton, *National Security Strategy*, 1994, 5.

23 See Office of Management and Budget, *Budget of the United States*, Historical tables. http://www.whitehouse.gov/omb/budget/Historicals.

24 Richard Neustadt, *Presidential Power and the Modern Presidents* (New York: Free Press, 1991).

25 For a detailed description of the Base Force, see Lacquement, *Shaping American Military Capabilities after the Cold War*, chapter "The Base Force (1990)," 65–78. Other useful general treatments include Lorna Jaffe, *The Development of the Base Force, 1989–1992* (Washington, DC: Office of the Chairman of the Joint Chiefs of Staff, July 1993); and Colin Powell's memoir, *My American Journey*, especially chapter 17, "When You've Lost Your Best Enemy," 435–58.

26 Jaffe, *Development of the Base Force*, 12.

27 Colin Powell, "National Security Challenges in the 1990s: The Future Just Ain't What It Used to Be," *Army* 39, no. 7 (July 1989): 12–14.

28 Goldwater-Nichols Department of Defense Reorganization Act of 1986 (PL 99–433), U.S. Code, Title 10, Subtitle A, Part I, Chapter 5, 151. Joint Chiefs of Staff: Composition; Functions (b) (1). Previously, the chairman had been required to convey the consensus of the collective body of the chiefs. With Goldwater-Nichols, the CJCS would now have the power to provide his judgment to the president regardless of the collective views of the service chiefs. For more detailed discussion of the act, see James Locher, *Victory on the Potomac: The Goldwater-Nichols Act Unifies the Pentagon* (College Station: Texas A&M University Press, 2002).

29 Jaffe, *Development of the Base Force*, 21.

30 Jaffe, *Development of the Base Force*, 35.

31 Particularly in the aftermath of the Vietnam War, Democrats had been subjected to strong attacks from Republican opponents as being weak on defense issues. In contrast, the Republicans positioned themselves as strong on defense and more willing to stand up to the Soviet Union and other national security threats.

32 Sam Nunn (U.S. senator), "The Defense Department Must Thoroughly Overhaul the Services' Roles and Missions," *Vital Speeches* 20 (1 August 1992): 717–24.

33 Les Aspin (U.S. representative), "An Approach to Sizing American Conventional Forces for the Post-Soviet Era: Four Illustrative Options," unpublished paper, House Armed Services Committee, 25 February 1992.

34 For a summary analysis of the Senator Nunn speeches in March and April 1990, see Jaffe, *Development of the Base Force*, 28–30. For the speeches themselves, see Sam Nunn, *Nunn 1990: A New Military Strategy* (Washington DC: Center for Strategic and International Studies, 1990).

35 One of the indicators of the shift from foreign to domestic focus was the nature of the field for the 1992 presidential election. It was remarkable to many how little benefit George H. W. Bush derived from his foreign policy successes, particularly the end of the Cold War and success against Iraq in the 1990–1991 Persian Gulf War. One indicator of the assumed strength of President Bush was the choice by prominent Democrats to remain on the sidelines of the 1992 election since Bush's reelection seemed like a foregone conclusion in late 1991/early 1992.

36 For a detailed description of the Bottom Up Review (BUR), see Lacquement, *Shaping American Military Capabilities after the Cold War*, chapter 5, "The Bottom Up Review," 79–98. Other useful general reference for the Bottom Up Review include the report itself, Les Aspin, *Report on the Bottom Up Review*, October 1993, http://oai.dtic.mil/oai/oai?verb=getRecord&metadataPrefix=html&identifier=ADA359953 (accessed 14 March 2016).

37 Bill Clinton, *My Life* (New York: Vintage, 2004), 450, 483–86.

38 General Carl Mundy (Marines), General Gordon Sullivan (Army), General Merrill McPeak (Air Force), and Admiral Frank Kelso (Navy). President Clinton notes the opposition of the chairman and all of the service chiefs but singles out Mundy as the most adamant in his opposition. Clinton, *My Life*, 483.

39 Aspin Papers, University of Wisconsin, Madison (temporarily available at the Mudd Manuscript Library, Princeton University, in 1997 per the author's files), particularly boxes 2, 3, 4 and 10, containing files from Aspin's time as Secretary of Defense.

40 Aspin, "An Approach to Sizing American Conventional Forces for the Post-Soviet Era: Four Illustrative Options," 25 February 1992.

41 *Report on the Bottom Up Review*, 107. Change in proposed budget authority, cumulative, FY 1995 to FY 1999, from a baseline of $1.325 trillion to $1.234 trillion (93.1 percent of baseline that represents a reduction of 6.9 percent).

42 *Report on the Bottom Up Review*, 28.

43 *Report of the Bottom Up Review*, front cover. The results of the review were presented in September 1993 at a press conference by Secretary of Defense Les Aspin and Chairman of the Joint Chiefs of Staff General Powell; see http://www.c-span.org/video/?49768-1/defense-department-review (accessed 17 March 2016). The printed report was published in October 1993.

44 Francis Fukuyama, *The End of History and the Last Man* (New York: Free Press, 1992).

45 Raids in Somalia in October 1993 that led to the deaths of eighteen rangers and the capture of one American aviator.

46 For a note in preparation for his conversation with President Clinton to try to avert resignation, see Aspin Papers, box #10, Secretary of Defense historical files, handwritten note annotated for meeting on 14 December 1993 with President Clinton. Aspin's handwritten note outlines his case to remain Secretary of Defense. Aspin's letter of resignation and President Clinton's acceptance of his resignation are dated 15 December 1993. For copies of both documents, see http://www.presidency.ucsb.edu/ws/?pid=46243 (accessed 17 March 2016). In a sad ending to a remarkable life of public service, Aspin died 21 May 1995, just before the release of the CORM report.

47 Commission on Roles and Missions (CORM), 4–9, http://edocs.nps.edu/dodpubs/topic/general/ADA295228.pdf (accessed 15 March 2016).

48 Requirement for quadrennial security review passed by Congress as part of the Military Force Structure Review Act, of the National Defense Authorization Act for Fiscal Year 1997. William S. Cohen, *Report of the Quadrennial Defense Review* (Washington, DC: Department of Defense, May 1997), 1.

49 John Kingdon, *Agendas, Alternatives, and Public Policies*, 2nd edition (Boston: Little, Brown, 1995).

50 The Clinton administration oversaw budget surpluses for four years starting in 1998. These were the first budget surpluses since 1969. See Office of Management and Budget data online. Table 1.1—Summary of Receipts, Outlays, and Surpluses or Deficits (–): 1789–2020, http://www.whitehouse.gov/omb/budget/Historicals.

51 President Bill Clinton, "State of the Union Address," 20 January 1999. Address accessible at http://clinton4.nara.gov/WH/New/html/19990119-2656.html.

52 George W. Bush, "A Period of Consequences," speech given at the Citadel, South Carolina, 23 September 1999, http://www3.citadel.edu/pao/addresses/pres_bush. html (accessed 15 March 2016); and Stuart A. Ibberson, "Candidates Offer Differing Views on Future of Military," *Journal of Aerospace and Defense Industry News*, 3 November 2000. Also see the party platforms: Democratic Party Platforms: "Democratic Party Platform of 2000," 14 August 2000, online by Gerhard Peters and John T. Woolley, *The American Presidency Project*, http:// www.presidency.ucsb.edu/ws/?pid=29612; and Republican Party Platforms: "Republican Party Platform of 2000," 31 July 2000, online by Gerhard Peters and John T. Woolley, *The American Presidency Project*, http://www.presidency.ucsb. edu/ws/?pid=25849.

53 For a more detailed description of the 2001 QDR, see Lacquement, *Shaping American Military Capabilities after the Cold War*, chapter 8, 127–38.

54 Paul Kennedy, *The Rise and Fall of the Great Powers: Economic Change and Military Conflict from 1500 to 2000* (New York: Random House, 1987) and William McNeill, *The Pursuit of Power: Technology, Armed Force, and Society since A.D. 1000* (Chicago: University of Chicago Press, 1982).

55 Winning first battles was a major theme in many circles during the post–Cold War drawdown. The most prominent articulation of the argument for better readiness at the onset of war was Charles Heller and William Stofft, eds., *America's First Battles, 1776–1965* (Lawrence: University of Kansas Press, 1986). The chapter on the Korean War and the failure of the initial American units to halt North Korean forces provides the more detailed explanation behind the rallying cry of "No more Task Force Smiths."

56 Antulio J. Echevarria II, *Toward an American Way of War* (Carlisle, PA: Strategic Studies Institute, March 2004).

57 Carl von Clausewitz, *On War* (Princeton, NJ: Princeton University Press, 1976), 75.

58 Barack Obama (President), Remarks by the President on the Defense Strategic Review, 5 January 2012 (in conjunction with publication of defense planning guidance: "Sustaining U.S. Global Leadership: Priorities for 21st Century Defense"), http://archive.defense.gov/news/Defense_Strategic_Guidance.pdf (accessed 15 March 2016).

59 Rosa Brooks, "There's No Such Thing as Peacetime," *Foreign Policy*, 13 March 2015, http://foreignpolicy.com/2015/03/13/ theres-no-such-thing-as-peacetime-forever-war-terror-civil-liberties/.

60 Obama, National Security Strategy (supra note 1).

61 Expanding on the foundation built in support of allies and other partners in the midst of Cold War efforts to contain the Soviet Union.

62 The U.S. armed forces were involved in more interventions in the twelve years between 1989 and 2001 (eighty-two instances) than in the forty-five years of the Cold War (forty-seven instances). See Richard Grimmett, *Instances of Use of the*

United States Armed Forces Abroad, 1798–2009 (Washington, DC: Congressional Research Service, 27 January 2010).

63 For most of the 1990s, the U.S. economy was very healthy. A recession at the end of the Bush administration gave way to a robust recovery that continued for the rest of the decade. One of the manifestations of economic strength was budget surpluses achieved by 1998 and sustained through 2001.

64 Length of various drawdowns: post–World War II: 1945–1949, five years; post-Korea: 1952–1955, four years; Vietnam: 1968(71)–1975, five years; post–Cold War 1985(90)–1998, nine years.

EPILOGUE

KEVIN W. FARRELL

Most readers are familiar with George Santayana's now-famous quotation, "Those who do not remember the past are condemned to repeat it." Many are also undoubtedly acquainted with the phrase, attributed in different forms to individuals ranging from Karl Marx to Otto von Bismarck, to the effect that "[h]istory repeats itself anyway." Perhaps, however, the most fitting quotation that relates to this superb collection of chapters addressing American military drawdowns is one attributed to none other than Sir Winston Churchill: "The only thing we have learned from history is that we don't learn from history." If current leaders reversed the trend Churchill bemoaned, they would ensure a better-funded American military apparatus between wars and, failing that, a relatively modest outlay in the education of military officers that this volume makes clear is a sure investment.

Even though the American wars in Afghanistan and Iraq (and surrounding regions) linger on to various degrees at the time of this writing, on July 9, 2015, the U.S. Army announced publicly a reduction of at least 40,000 troops from its active rolls, dropping active component end-strength from 490,000 to 450,000.[1] The announcement came with the implication that additional cuts are possible. Once again, political and fiscal realities have trumped the strategic challenges faced by the United States. Over the course of this book, its authors have approached the topic of drawdowns from a variety of angles. While their conclusions do not all coincide, one thing seems clear: the drawdown experience in American history has never flowed smoothly or satisfactorily. The benefit of hindsight has indicted each effort. Contemporary assurances while the drawdowns were ongoing, and optimism about the future, always combined with political expediency to overwhelm the strategic thinkers who warned of the dangers to come—mostly without effect. The only partial exception might be found in the period of the 1960s prior to the Vietnam War that led to the creation of a highly competent, professional, and conscription-based ground force. Ironically, this superb force ultimately was ground into ineffectiveness during the lengthy and unhappy American experience in Vietnam.

As the authors have amply demonstrated, the "liberty paradox" is older than the republic itself, and the tension between skepticism and fear of a large standing Army and the need for a force adequate to meet the defense requirements of the nation continues to inform American defense policy, and in particular the size and shape of its Army. Despite many missteps in a saga centuries old, the consistent bright spot seems to be the recognition of the importance of educating the officer corps to be intellectually prepared to meet the challenges of an uncertain future.

The various "peace dividends," including the most recent one that followed the end of the Cold War, all proved to be illusory. Despite conscious efforts by the thirty-second U.S. Army Chief of Staff, General Gordon Sullivan, who during his tenure from 1991 to 1995 campaigned vigorously to prevent another "Task Force Smith"—a reference as our authors make clear to the ill-prepared U.S. Army fighting in Korea in 1950—the results were poor. A struggle to find a coherent strategy in the wake of the Cold War led to a U.S. Army poorly prepared to defeat insurgencies in Afghanistan, Iraq, and other regions, despite unprecedented expenditures on ground forces. Churchill's famous reference to the Battle of Britain has been turned on its head, and it could indeed be said of the recent efforts: "Never has so much been spent on so few who struggled so hard to achieve so little." Before the "smoke clears" in the wake of yet another lengthy conflict, we have already begun a new drawdown. What remains to be seen is whether the retrospection that occurred following past American wars, which led to attempts at reform, will even be possible in the current climate.

There can be no denying that the strategic position of the United States, especially in the Middle East and southwest Asia, but also around the world, has been reduced in the wake of the lengthy campaigns in Afghanistan and Iraq. As the senior leaders—political and military—enact another reduction to the U.S. Army, there has been scant attention paid to the unsatisfactory outcome of the extraordinary effort in both regions. The quest for an adequate "COIN" (Counterinsurgency) Strategy that emphasized the inherent superiority of light infantry and special operations forces combined with technological solutions dominated this approach. As this book makes clear through its numerous historical examples, something entirely different is required to solve such complex problems.

As far back as the Great Narragansett War, when Indian "insurgents" adopted flintlock muskets, thinking enemies have consistently adopted techniques, tactics, and technology used by the greater power to level the playing field. It is therefore vital that the officer corps of the United States Army is intellectually agile and able to adapt to war's ever-changing character. The great irony of the current situation is that as ground forces shrink in size, while technological advantage remains the military's greatest strength, the ethos of the

U.S. Army has increasingly geared toward underequipped dismounted light infantry forces. Instead of leadership placing a premium on its technological advantage and collective training, it subverts this qualitative advantage, emphasizing instead physical fitness and "toughness." Although it is essential for any ground force to be physically fit and mentally tough, these attributes alone are insufficient to maintain a qualitative advantage over adversaries who possess an almost limitless advantage in terms of abundant and inexpensive manpower. Military operations of the twentieth and early twenty-first century have demonstrated conclusively that the agility and ingenuity of a combined arms force has proven to be the most difficult to master and the most effective on the battlefield. Nonetheless, this is precisely the force that suffers disproportionately as the ground forces in general, and the U.S. Army in particular, experience significant reductions.

Although it is perhaps counterintuitive, the power and relevance of mounted forces on the battlefield continue to make them the most versatile force available. The development of excellent Union cavalry, which operated both mounted and dismounted by the U.S. Civil War's end, demonstrated this historical flexibility. Mounted forces are increasingly presented as anachronistic even though leaders in these organizations have to process "modern" multiple tasks simultaneously and reconcile the strategic and tactical on a regular basis. Unfortunately, mechanized forces are often referred to as "heavy" and costly, while critics overlook their inherent firepower and protection. In the postwar rush to reduce martial structure, and hence costs, mounted forces are often the first the nation reduces. More important, as demonstrated by the current study, is the fact that the leaders who succeed in these organizations are uniquely suited to deal simultaneously with complex problems on multiple levels.

Despite the plethora of various "academies" and "silver bullet" courses taught by self-proclaimed experts of counterinsurgency, the military efforts in Iraq and Afghanistan always suffered from the disconnect between large headquarters—best epitomized by "the Green Zone" in Baghdad—in secure areas with comfortable living conditions and geographically dispersed combat arms battalions attempting to impose order and control. While bloated multinational commands produced massive PowerPoint presentations that attempted to link the political and military challenges, while always demonstrating "progress" in the campaign, frontline soldiers in combat battalions strove to achieve the impossible task of implementing tactical solutions to an ambiguous, if not outright illusory, strategic framework. There was an inherent tension between providing multinational partners with meaningful staff billets to promote alliances, and inefficiencies associated with different national standards for performance. U.S. officers considered less worthy candidates for command also often staffed higher American headquarters. In the theaters of both Iraq and Afghanistan there was an enduring tension, with higher headquarters attempting to depict a strategic framework strangely detached from the reality of the situation on the ground, while combat battalions deployed throughout the area of operations struggled to implement an incomprehensible strategic framework in a chaotic and dangerous environment. Tactical leaders—those at the battalion and company level—consistently demonstrated an ability to develop ingenious approaches to the reality they faced on the ground dealing with insurgents in an inhospitable and confusing environment. Their "strategic" leaders, on the other hand, operated in a radically different realm dominated by PowerPoint presentations and metrics that purported to show consistent progress. This added to the universal perception of bloated headquarters, which has always translated into cuts in postwar eras. The government in the post–U.S. Civil War era dealt with perceived bloat by eliminating all headquarters above regiment. This proved barely sustainable for the final frontier push against Native Americans, while wholly and embarrassingly inadequate in the Spanish-American War, leading to the development of the U.S. Army War College and other reforms to shore up higher-level Army management.

This is not an argument against headquarters, but for better-led and -staffed headquarters with educated and motivated officers who are in touch with the actual combat situation. History shows that for every buildup after a Task Force Smith there is a concomitant increase in headquarters' numbers and size, necessary to command and control, supply, and plan for these forces. Thus, headquarters are necessary to fight and win, but like any other formation, these elements need to have educated officers with proper training and experience.

The optimism that runs through much of this book, despite the often-disappointing outcomes, indicates that the only hope for a successful outcome to the seemingly inevitable drawdown will be the need for more than the usual warnings against the danger of cutting the force too deeply. Instead, as this volume makes clear, with the fundamental American attitude towards its Army unlikely to change, investment in the one area that has proved to be its consistent strength offers the only viable salve: robust education of its officer corps. Not only has this esteemed group of historians explored the fascinating and complex relationship between the United States and its Army, but it has also served a contemporary purpose of helping guide a difficult process in a dangerous and complex world. Let us hope that military and political leaders prove Churchill's prognostication wrong, and take heed of the insights related here.

NOTE

1 *Army Times*, July 9, 2015.

ABOUT THE CONTRIBUTORS

Scott Bertinetti, Colonel, U.S. Army, is a faculty instructor in the Department of Military Strategy, Planning, and Operations at the U.S. Army War College, Carlisle Barracks, Pennsylvania, where he also serves as the Director, Strategic and Operations Planning.

Ashley Bissonnette is Senior Researcher at the Mashantucket Pequot Museum & Research Center, as well as a Visiting Assistant Professor of Public Health at Eastern Connecticut State University.

John A. Bonin is Professor, Concepts and Doctrine, for the U.S. Army War College at Carlisle Barracks and is a retired Army colonel with over thirty years of service. He has served as the War College's military doctrine advisor since April 2003, and since 2011, as an Academic Full Professor. He has twice been selected as the General of the Army George G. Marshall Chair of Military Studies at the War College and is the lead author of Joint Publication 3-31, *Command and Control of Joint Land Operations*, as well as author of *Unified and Joint Land Operations: Doctrine for Landpower*, published for the Land Warfare Papers, August 2014.

Martin G. Clemis was awarded a U.S. Army's Center for Military History Dissertation Grant for the 2012–2013 academic year, and received the U.S. Army Heritage Center Foundation's Robert L. Ruth and Robert C. Ruth Fellowship in 2010, as well as the John Votaw Endowed Research Fellowship in 2011.

Conrad C. Crane is Chief of Historical Services for the Army Heritage and Education Center and previously served as the Director of the U.S. Army Military History Institute. Crane was the General Douglas MacArthur Chair of Research with the Strategic Studies Institute at the U.S. Army War College, and has held the General Hoyt S. Vandenberg Chair of Aerospace Studies. His twenty-six-year military career concluded with a nine-year tour as Professor of History at the U.S. Military Academy at West Point. Crane has authored and edited several books on the Civil War, World War I, World War II, Korea, and Vietnam, and has written and lectured widely on the issues of airpower and landpower. He was the lead author for the groundbreaking Army-USMC counterinsurgency manual, FM 3-24 (December 2006). For that effort, *Newsweek* named him one of the people to watch in 2007. In November 2008, he was named the international Archivist of the Year by the Scone Foundation.

Antulio J. Echevarria II became the editor of the *US Army War College Quarterly: Parameters* in February 2013. Prior to that, he was the Director of Research for the U.S. Army War College. Echevarria is the author of *Reconsidering the American Way of War, Clausewitz and Contemporary War, Imagining Future War,* and *After Clausewitz.*

Kevin W. Farrell, Colonel, U.S. Army, retired after over thirty years of commissioned service. His most recent book is *The Military and the Monarchy: The Case and Career of the Duke of Cambridge in an Age of Reform.* He was the senior military advisor to the Brad Pitt Hollywood film *Fury,* released in 2014. He is currently a Managing Partner and Consulting Historian for Battlefield Leadership, LLC.

Edward A. Gutiérrez is a lecturer at Northeastern University and the consulting historian for the state of Connecticut's *Remembering World War One* project. He is the author of *Doughboys on the Great War: How American Soldiers Viewed Their Military Service.*

Richard A. Lacquement Jr., Colonel, U.S. Army (retired), is the Dean of the School of Strategic Landpower, U.S. Army War College. He is the author of *Shaping American Military Capabilities after the Cold War.*

Michael E. Lynch, a retired U.S. Army officer, is a research historian at the U.S. Army Heritage and Education Center and an Assistant Professor at the U.S. Army War College. His previous publications include "'Not Due to Vicious Habits': Local Black Veterans' Struggle for Civil War Pensions," in *Black History of Shippensburg, Pennsylvania, 1860–1936.*

Peter Mansoor, Colonel, U.S. Army (retired), is the General Raymond E. Mason Jr. Chair of Military History at the Ohio State University. He assumed his current position in 2008 after a twenty-six-year career in the U.S. Army that included two combat tours, which culminated in his service as executive officer to General David Petraeus in Iraq. He is the author of *The GI Offensive in Europe: The Triumph of American Infantry Divisions, 1941–1945, Baghdad at Sunrise: A Brigade Commander's War in Iraq*, and *Surge: My Journey with General David Petraeus and the Remaking of the Iraq War*.

Michael R. Matheny, Colonel, U.S. Army (retired), with thirty years of active military service, is a Professor of Military Strategy and Operations at the U.S. Army War College. He is the author of *Carrying the War to the Enemy*.

Kevin McBride is Director of Research at the Mashantucket Pequot Museum & Research Center, as well as Associate Professor of Anthropology at the University of Connecticut. McBride is Project Director of the "Battlefields of the Pequot War" project (a long-term initiative begun in 2007) and the "Battlefields of King Philip's War" project with the Mashantucket Pequot Museum & Research Center—the National Park Service American Battlefield Protection Program supports both projects.

Raymond Millen is a retired Army officer who served from 2001 to 2008 as the Director of European Security Affairs at the Strategic Studies Institute, Carlisle Barracks. He is currently the Professor of Security Sector Reform at the Peacekeeping and Stability Operations Institute, Carlisle Barracks. Millen has authored the books *Command Legacy: A Tactical Primer for Junior Leaders* and *Burden of Command*, as well as numerous articles and monographs on NATO, counterinsurgency, Afghanistan, and Security Sector Reform issues.

Michael S. Neiberg is the Henry L. Stimson Chair of History in the Department of National Security and Strategy at the U.S. Army War College. He is the author of *Dance of the Furies: Europe and the Outbreak of World War I, The Blood of Free Men*, and *Potsdam: The End of World War II and the Remaking of Europe*.

Jason W. Warren, Major, U.S. Army, is an Assistant Professor at the U.S. Army War College and has served in the same position in the History Department at West Point. He is the author of *Connecticut Unscathed: Victory in the Great Narragansett War, 1675–1676*.

Samuel Watson is Professor of History at the United States Military Academy, where he has taught American and military history since 1999. Watson is the author of *Jackson's Sword* and *Peacekeepers and Conquerors*, which together won the Society for Military History's Distinguished Book Award. He is also an editor for *The West Point History of the Civil War* and *The West Point History of the American Revolutionary War*, and a volume editor for *The West Point History of Warfare*.

INDEX

Letters *f* or *t* following a page number indicate a *figure* or *table*.